The Book of Baseball Literacy

Nearly 700 People, Places, Events, Teams, Stats, Stories, and More— Everything You Need to Know in One Massive Book

3rd Edition

David H. Martinez

For my sweet children, Sophie and Tyler

Someday I hope you enjoy baseball as much as I do.

CONTENTS

INTRODUCTION

When I was writing the first edition of this book, the baseball strike of 1994–1995 was in full swing, and many observers were predicting the death of baseball. But within just a few years, baseball became as popular as ever. Any fans who gave up on the sport were replaced by new fans who discovered or rediscovered the joys of the game.

When I was writing the *second* edition of the book, the steroid scandal was just taking off, and we would all soon be speculating about who was shooting up and how much it helped them. Again, many people believed baseball was on the verge of falling apart. Yet even in the darkest days of the scandal, attendance continue to grow, and baseball remains as popular as ever.

If nothing else, these ups and downs prove that baseball is resilient. It can withstand strikes, scandals, and world wars, and come out the other side with new generations of fans who simply don't care about the off-field stuff. You just love baseball.

This third edition is aimed at you. I've completely updated it to cover all the momentous people and events of the past few years, and I've edited and added to the rest of the book as well.

In this book, you'll find the entire relevant history of baseball, laid out in small chunks. You want to learn about Honus Wagner and John "Pop" Lloyd? Turn to Chapter 1. Charlie Comiskey and Marvin Miller? Chapter 2. AstroTurf and the Baker Bowl? Chapter 5. You want an explanation of sabermetrics? Turn to Chapter 7. You want the titles of some of the greatest baseball books ever written? They're in Chapter 6. Wonder what happened in 1904 to cancel the World Series? Chapter 3. What were the Negro leagues all about? Chapter 4. The origin of baseball rubbing mud? Chapter 8. In short, this book has all the people, places, events, records, statistics, folklore, literature, and other minutiae that all baseball fans should know about and care about.

Careful readers will notice a few surprising inclusions. Amos Rusie, for example. He played a hundred years ago, and he doesn't hold any significant records. Why does the modern fan care about him? Read his entry to find out. And Sol White, Martin Dihigo, Turkey Stearnes. . . never heard of them? They played before white baseball decided to admit people of color. After being shunted aside and forgotten by most of mainstream society, they won't be forgotten here.

Of course, this book contains all the greats of the game: Ruth, Gehrig, and Williams. Mays, Mantle, and DiMaggio. Grove, Koufax, and Mathewson. Rickey, MacPhail, and Landis. Smith, Scully, and Angell. But you won't find, for example, every member of the Hall of Fame. Why? Because my purpose was to identify the people who really made a mark on the game, the people without whom a responsible history could not be written. So you're not going to find Joe Medwick, Chick Hafey, Lloyd Waner, and many other putative Hall of Famers. But you will find some significant non–Hall of Famers, such as Roger Maris and Dick Allen.

I didn't want to simply give you the same old facts and stories you've heard a million times. So throughout the book, you're going to find a lot of opinions—fully supported by the evidence, of course—and some wonderful anecdotes that you probably haven't heard. On the other hand, because I didn't want to cheat you out of baseball's classic lore, I've tried to strike a good balance between old and new.

I've devoted the lion's share of the book to the people who have made baseball great. Chapter 1 has players and managers, Chapter 2 has everybody else who has influenced the game: executives, broadcasters, writers, commissioners, umpires, and a few other surprises. In each entry, my aim is to focus on why that person is important to the game and its history through his accomplishments on or off the field.

The remainder of the book—Chapters 3 through 8—covers all the other parts of the game; the chapter titles give more detail. Again, in my choices, I was aiming for significance. Chapter 3 was perhaps the toughest. What are the most significant events in baseball history? A hundred different people will give you a thousand different answers. But between Chapter 3 and the rest of the book, I think I've covered just about everything significant. Some events have affected baseball so greatly that their stories are told in more than one entry. The Black Sox scandal, for example, has earned space in Chapters 1, 2, 3, and 6. Everything is cross-referenced.

In Chapter 4, you can find brief histories of all the current major league teams, and a few defunct teams too. There's also information the different major leagues as well as a few minor leagues, the Negro leagues, and other groups that aren't easy to classify, such as the Hall of Fame's Veterans Committee

Many current major league ballparks are profiled in Chapter 5. And because no history is complete without a mention of some old classics, I've also included the grand cathedrals of baseball such as the Polo Grounds and Ebbets Field.

Chapter 6 is a catchall covering the lore of the game. You'll find great book titles, games, sayings, poems, songs, eras, baseball-related companies, nicknames, famous stories, and other fun stuff. This chapter includes everything from *Bull Durham* to the "Bloody Sock" to the Rawlings Company.

Chapter 7 is where you're going to find all the statistics fans have come to expect from a baseball book. For beginners as well as veterans, I've provided explanations of what some stats measure and signify. There are also histories of all the major awards and introductions to advanced statistical measurements.

In Chapter 8, you'll find a sampling of important baseball rules and game terminology, as well as discussions of business-related facts. Not every baseball term is included; that would take its own book (such as *The New Dickson Baseball Dictionary*). The words and phrases I've chosen should give you a broader understanding of the game, not explain it entirely. Some terms are obvious, such as *double play, strike zone*, and *base on balls*. Others, such as *waivers, National Agreement*, and *reserve clause*, aren't. In most cases, I've tried to illustrate the meaning of each term with anecdotes, examples, and word origins.

Throughout the book, you'll see lots of words and phrases in SMALL CAPS, which means probably what you think it means: that the word or phrase appears as an entry elsewhere in the book. This cross-referencing lets you enjoy the book however you want. You can read it cover to cover, or you can follow a thread wherever it takes you.

You probably want to get into the meat of the book now, and I don't want to stop you.

1
PLAYERS AND MANAGERS

Henry Aaron
"Hammerin' Hank"
Outfielder, 1954–76

Aaron was a slugging outfielder who could do pretty much anything on the field. He impressed not with highlight-reel play, as his contemporary WILLIE MAYS did, but rather with relentless consistency. Aaron himself admitted it: "If I had to pay to go see somebody play for one game," he once said, "I wouldn't pay to see Hank Aaron. I wasn't flashy. I didn't hustle after fly balls that were 20 rows back in the seats. But if I had to pay to see someone play a three-game series, I'd rather see myself." Aaron won only a single MVP Award during his career, yet he was among baseball's top players from 1955 to 1974 and appeared in 21 straight All-Star Games. He never hit 50 home runs in a season, but he certainly would have if he had played his peak years in a hitter's park like Atlanta-Fulton County Stadium rather than a pitcher's park like Milwaukee County Stadium.

Aaron still holds numerous important baseball records, including career total bases (6,856) and runs batted in (2,297). Of course, the one record for which he is most known—career home runs (*see* 755), which he owned after breaking BABE RUTH'S career mark on April 8, 1974 (*see* 1974: AARON PASSES THE BABE)—fell to BARRY BONDS in 2007. Because of the taint of steroids, many people believe Aaron is still the legitimate record-holder.

Jim Abbott
Pitcher, 1989–99

Abbott never played minor league ball after starring at the University of Michigan and on the U.S. Olympic baseball team. When he hit the majors, he took just three years to develop into an 18-game winner, and in 1993 he pitched a no-hitter—all despite having been born with only one hand. Teams regularly tested Abbott's ability to field grounders, but it never bothered him. In one fluid motion, he would transfer glove and ball to his partial right arm, take the ball out of the glove, and calmly toss to first it in time to get the runner. (In high school, an opposing team bunted eight straight times against him, and Abbott retired seven of eight.) He never let other teams ruin his concentration, and he is an inspiration to millions.

Grover Cleveland Alexander
"Old Pete"
Pitcher, 1911–30

Alexander is one of the least-remembered great players in baseball history. His stats are astounding: 373 career victories (tied for third all time) and three 30-win and nine 20-win seasons (including one at age 40). What makes his numbers even more amazing was that he had his best seasons playing for the Phillies in the National League's most hitter-friendly ballpark, the BAKER BOWL. And that during the second half of his career, he was both alcoholic and epileptic.

Greatness came early to Alexander. In 1911, he led the league in wins, complete games, shutouts, and innings pitched—the best season a rookie pitcher ever had. He was traded to the Cubs in 1917, then entered the military in 1918 as one of the biggest baseball stars to fight in that war. He saw significant action on the front and returned from World War I partially deaf, epileptic, and alcoholic. Even so, he remained a great pitcher for the Cubs. In 1926, he was traded to the Cardinals, where he finally contributed to a World Series–winning team. The pinnacle of his career came when he struck out Tony Lazzeri of the Yankees with the bases loaded in Game 7 of the 1926 Series, preserving the Cardinals' lead and St. Louis's first championship.

He fell on hard times after retirement, as drinking and poverty got the best of him. His induction to the Hall of Fame in 1939 gave him some comfort, but it wasn't enough. Over the last 10 years of his life, he suffered through a heart attack, a serious injury caused by an epileptic seizure, and cancer. He died in 1950, two years before Ronald Reagan played him in *The Winning Team* and made Alexander the only major league player named after one U.S. president and portrayed on film by another.

Dick Allen
Infielder, 1963–77
Allen burst onto the scene as a rookie in 1964 and led the league in runs and triples while smacking 29 homers with the Phillies. Eight years later he won the MVP Award as a first baseman with the White Sox. In between, he made several All-Star teams and walloped mammoth home runs that, in one case, actually cleared the roof of the ballpark—inspiring Willie Stargell to say, "Now I know why they boo Ritchie all the time. When he hits a home run, there's no souvenir."

At his peak, Allen was one of baseball's most feared hitters—and one of its most fiercely independent personalities. As an African-American, he experienced brutal racism first-hand, both in the majors as Philadelphia's first black superstar and while playing in the minors in Little Rock, Arkansas, where he was that city's first black minor league player. Those experiences no doubt contributed to his attitudes and actions. And his innate individualism also created plenty of problems for him.

The view among some historians is that he was a disruptive influence in the clubhouse who, in BILL JAMES'S words, "kept his teams from winning." Allen did fight with at least one teammate. He hated to practice and usually arrived at the park later than everybody else. He ran afoul of the law. In early September 1974, he abruptly walked out on the team, even as he led the American League in homers and slugging percentage. There is some controversy about why he left the team—James wrote that he retired to force a trade, and *Total Baseball* wrote that he left to tend to his horses. But both his manager and general manager told historian Craig Wright that nagging injuries were responsible. Allen did mount a comeback the following season but he wasn't the same.

Many teammates loved him; pitcher Jim Kaat, who played with Allen in Chicago, nicknamed him "Mose" because Allen could carry the team like Moses into the promised land. And some of Allen's managers heaped almost nothing but praise on him. "He was the greatest player I ever managed," Chuck Tanner told Wright. Red Schoendienst said, "He did a real fine job for me." Gene Mauch said, "He was irreplaceable as a player."

Allen has long been the subject of a Hall of Fame debate. The induction of Jim Rice in 2010 seems to have made the case that Allen belongs, too, because Allen was a better player than Rice and possesses similar career numbers. But all the peripheral stuff—the controversies, the retirement, the perceived attitude problems—and the length of his career have conspired to keep him out. And in 2014, Veterans Committee voters rejected Allen yet again. By his talent alone, Allen should have been a shoo-in, but in baseball, as in life, talent isn't always enough.

Walter Alston
"Smokey"
Manager, 1954–76
A virtual unknown at his hiring in 1954—he possessed just one at bat of major league playing experience—Alston nevertheless became one of baseball's most respected managers. For 23 years, Alston skippered the Brooklyn and Los Angeles Dodgers, all with one-year contracts. He was thrown into the baseball fire in 1954, asked to manage a Brooklyn team that had just won the pennant. He replaced the popular Charlie Dressen because Dressen asked for a multi-year contract. Alston, with no major league managerial experience, made no such demand. He then clashed with the team's biggest star, JACKIE ROBINSON; suffered through injuries to key players; and finished a disappointing second. But the next season, with Robinson still publicly questioning Alston's skills, he managed the club to Brooklyn's only World Series title. Including his nearly two decades in Los Angeles, Alston's teams captured seven pennants and four World Series, and he holds the record with seven All-Star Game victories as a manager.

Sparky Anderson
Manager, 1970–98
Manager of the Cincinnati Reds' "BIG RED MACHINE" of the 1970s and the Detroit Tigers from 1979 to 1998, Anderson won seven division titles and was the first man to win a World Series in each league. In Cincinnati, Anderson was known as "Captain Hook," owing to his penchant for changing pitchers quickly. In fact, his early teams led the league in saves five times. But when he got to Detroit, his teams usually finished in the middle or the bottom of the league in saves.

Anderson ranks sixth on the all-time list of managerial wins (and will probably stay in that position for many years to come), and he was named to the Hall of Fame immediately after retirement—a retirement that almost came sooner than expected, when the Tigers placed him on an indefinite leave of absence because of Anderson's refusal to manage Detroit's prospective "replacement" team during the strike in 1995. Luckily, cooler heads prevailed, and Anderson returned to the club until his official retirement three years later.

Cap Anson
"Pop"
Infielder, 1871–97
Manager, 1879–98
One of the biggest stars of the 19th century, Anson was an excellent first baseman and a pioneer in the use of such strategies as platooning, the hit-and-run, and pitching rotations. He won five pennants as manager of the Chicago White Stockings (the team that became the Cubs), and he owned practically every batting record when he retired. When you include players from the 19th century, Anson still ranks as the Cubs' all-time leader in runs scored, hits, doubles, and RBIs (and is second in games played, at bats, and triples).

But Anson also has a dark claim to fame: He helped ease the institution of baseball's color line when, on at least two occasions, he threatened to forfeit exhibition games against teams with African-American players. (The players in question are also in this book: MOSES FLEETWOOD WALKER and GEORGE STOVEY.) Certainly, Anson wasn't the only baseball official to encourage the adoption and continuation of the color line; it was truly a vast conspiracy among managers, team owners, and league officials. But as the game's biggest star, Anson was an early leader of the segregation movement that lasted until 1945, when BRANCH RICKEY decided to change the world.

Luis Aparicio
"Little Louie"
Shortstop, 1956–73
The greatest fielding shortstop in American League history, Aparicio still holds league marks for lifetime games, assists, putouts, and total chances. The 1956 Rookie of the Year won nine straight stolen base titles and nine GOLD GLOVE awards on the way to Hall of Fame induction in 1984. Owing to his stolen base skills, Aparicio batted

leadoff throughout most of his career, even though his on-base percentages were typically well below the league average. As a result, he never scored 100 runs in a season—the benchmark for a good leadoff batter. Still, his combination of speed and fielding skill made him the OZZIE SMITH of his generation.

Jeff Bagwell
First baseman, 1991–2005

When the Boston Red Sox decided they needed a left-handed reliever during the heated 1990 pennant race, they settled on a 37-year-old journeyman named Larry Andersen, who was then pitching for the Houston Astros. *Sure, you can have Andersen,* the Astros told the Red Sox; *all it will cost is your young infield prospect Jeff Bagwell.* Andersen pitched well in 15 games that season for the Sox, who won the division. All Bagwell did was win the Rookie of the Year in 1991 and become one of the best players in baseball. It's probably the most lopsided trade in Sox history since the BABE RUTH deal back in 1919 (*see* 1919: THE SOX SELL THE BABE).

Bagwell possessed a keen batting eye, great power, amazing durability for most of his career, excellent speed (stealing as many as 31 bases in a season), quality fielding skills (one GOLD GLOVE), and perhaps the quickest bat in the majors. Even more incredible about his career is that he won the 1994 MVP Award and put up great numbers despite playing most of his home games in a terrible ballpark for hitters, the ASTRODOME. By the time he moved into hitter-friendly Enron Park (now Minute Maid Park), his peak was over. Sure, he had several excellent seasons but he never quite reached the MARK MCGWIRE slugger level (50+ home runs) that I thought he would.

He always struck me as a clear first-ballot Hall of Famer. But since becoming eligible in 2010, he has fallen well short of the 75 percent needed for enshrinement. He's a casualty of the whisper campaigns tarring many modern-day sluggers as steroid users, even without any actual evidence. Enter "Jeff Bagwell steroids" into Google and you'll get tens of thousands of results. I wouldn't be surprised if it comes out that he used performance-enhancing drugs. But I'm not prepared to eliminate from Hall of Fame consideration everybody who played in the 1990s, and I'm also not interested in trying to sort out the clean and dirty players based purely on speculation. Bagwell has a strong case, and mere rumors shouldn't keep him from the honor he deserves.

Frank Baker
"Home Run"
Third baseman, 1908–22

Baker earned his nickname after smacking home runs in consecutive games of the 1911 World Series, one off Rube Marquard and the other off CHRISTY MATHEWSON—an amazing feat at the time. Baker won four home run titles and two RBI championships to establish himself as a top slugger of the DEAD BALL ERA. After retiring from baseball, one of his claims to fame is that he discovered JIMMIE FOXX while managing a minor league team in Maryland.

It has become commonplace to ridicule Baker's nickname because his league-leading home run totals were "only" 9, 10, 11, and 12. To do so, however, is to miss the point of baseball's evolutionary patterns and to misunderstand baseball statistics. Baker's slugging percentages were consistently above the norm, and he played on some of the best teams of his age (including the 1911–1914 A's teams that boasted the famed "$100,000 INFIELD"). If he played now, he would probably still be among the best sluggers, probably hitting 25–40 homers every year and playing a key defensive position. His selection to the Hall of Fame is well deserved.

Ernie Banks
Infielder, 1953–71

Playing his entire career for the lowly Cubs, Banks nevertheless won back-to-back MVP Awards in 1958–59, the first player to do so in National League history. Active in the time of MANTLE, MAYS, and AARON, Banks hit more home runs from 1955 to 1960 than any player in either league. He was a solid fielder and won two GOLD GLOVES at shortstop, but he moved to first base in the middle of his career after suffering a knee injury and, in fact, played more games at first than at short.

With his trademark expression "Let's play two today!"—which he first uttered in 1969—he epitomized the type of player who is sorely missed today, a man who plays every game with a smile on his face and a spring in his step. Long after retirement, he explained his attitude to a reporter for Salon.com: "When the other guy's getting tired, I want to be able to say, 'Come on, let's do some more.' It's a kind of philosophy of my own life, to create the energy enough to keep on going." It served him well as a player and as a successful businessman.

Cool Papa Bell
Outfielder, Negro leagues, 1922–46
One of the greatest of the NEGRO LEAGUE players, Bell was nick-named for his ability to remain calm under pressure. He was an excellent hitter with blinding speed and top-notch defensive skills, on a par with MAYS, DIMAGGIO, and SPEAKER. In a 1935 exhibition game against major leaguers at Yankee Stadium, Bell scored from second on a sacrifice fly. SATCHEL PAIGE, who played with him, maintained that Bell was so fast he once switched off a lamp and was in bed before the light went out. Unlike most baseball mythology, this story may actually be true; Bell admitted, however, that the switch was faulty.

A few years after the color line was broken, BILL VEECK offered Bell a chance to play for the St. Louis Browns, but the 48-year-old Bell declined. He was inducted into the Hall of Fame in 1974, after the Hall finally agreed to induct a number of Negro league stars.

Johnny Bench
Catcher, 1967–83
Bench came up the big leagues late in the 1967 season with as much hype as any first-year player ever had, whereupon he correctly predicted that he would win the 1968 Rookie of the Year Award. He quickly became the top catcher of his time—possibly any time—and won two MVP Awards while playing with Cincinnati's "BIG RED MACHINE" teams that won four pennants.

As a hitter, Bench was one of the top sluggers in baseball for several years, leading the league twice in home runs and three times in RBIs. As a fielder, he won 10 consecutive GOLD GLOVES, possessed the most-feared throwing arm in baseball history, and is now the standard to which all catchers are compared. When Bench was still in the minor leagues, he met the great TED WILLIAMS, who autographed a baseball for Bench that read, "To Johnny Bench, a sure Hall of Famer." Williams's prediction came true when the Hall of Fame elected Bench in 1989.

Moe Berg
Catcher, 1923–39
The subject of the immortal phrase "GOOD FIELD, NO HIT," Berg was a well-liked but seldom-used third-string catcher for most of his

career. But his real contribution to the world came off the field, as he was perhaps baseball's most fascinating character. For starters, he was certainly the most erudite player of his time, a Phi Beta Kappa from Princeton who claimed to speak several languages (although, the saying went, he couldn't hit in any of them) and earned a law degree from Columbia during off seasons.

When he wasn't dazzling academia with diamond stories, he could be found pursuing another hobby: working as a spy for the U.S. Office of Strategic Services (OSS), the forerunner of the CIA. Nicholas Dawidoff's book *The Catcher Was a Spy* points out that Berg's spy career was about as successful as his major league career. For one thing, Berg insisted on looking the part of a Hollywood spy, right down to the gray fedora and OSS-issue watch. He once accidentally dropped his pistol onto the lap of the person sitting next to him on a train. His big mission during World War II was to determine whether the Germans were building an atomic bomb. Luckily, they weren't, for Berg bungled his assignment anyway.

Following his spy career, Berg led a nomadic life, sponging off friends and relatives but enjoying himself wherever he went. Berg's own memoirs would have been entertaining even if not a hundred percent true. Unfortunately, he died before he could write them; he once supposedly fired a potential co-author when the writer confused him with Moe from "The Three Stooges."

Yogi Berra
Catcher, 1946–65
Manager, 1964, 1972–75, 1984–85

One of the greatest catchers of all time—and one of the most amusing—Berra is as renowned for his numerous World Series records as for the malapropisms, mixed metaphors, and mangled musings he has uttered, known as YOGI-ISMS. But it is as a catcher that he should be remembered.

In his 2004 book *Brushbacks and Knockdowns*, author Allen Barra called Berra "the greatest team sports player of the 20th century," and it's hard to dispute the claim. Berra won three MVP Awards, but he had at least five other seasons that were equal to the MVP years. Flawless defensively with excellent power, Berra was the anchor of the most dominant dynasty in baseball history as his Yankees captured 14 pennants in Berra's 19-year career. Due to the dominance, Berra played in more World Series games (75) than anyone—a record that will surely stand forever. After his career, Berra embarked on a successful career of managing, coaching, and celebritydom that included two pennants and countless commercials.

Craig Biggio
Catcher/second baseman/outfielder, 1988–2007

Author BILL JAMES once called Craig Biggio the "most underrated player in baseball history," and it's hard to argue. How often do you hear Biggio's name mentioned during discussions of the greatest players of the 1990s? Rarely. He finished high in MVP voting only twice—fourth in 1997, fifth in 1998. Yet by most statistical measures, he deserved much greater recognition throughout his career.

For one thing, Biggio rarely got hurt. During his prime years of 1993 to 1999—including strike-shortened 1994—he averaged 151 games, 116 runs scored, 40 doubles, 17 home runs, 76 walks, and 19 hit-by-pitch for a .303 batting average, .397 on-base percentage, and .473 slugging percentage. And it all came while playing in a bad park for hitters and a difficult defensive position. Speaking of defense, Biggio was an incredible athlete who took on three of the toughest positions on the diamond. He came up as a catcher, then moved to second base (where he spent his best years), then, at 37, moved to center field. Did he win? He sure did. As a member of Houston's "Killer B's" club, he joined JEFF BAGWELL, Lance Berkman, Derek Bell, and Carlos Beltran to help his club to the post-season six different times.

In June 2007, he smacked his 3,000th career hit, all but guaranteeing his eventual Hall of Fame induction, which occurred in 2015. Fans in Houston, where he played his entire career, loved his hustle and appreciated his skill for almost two decades. It's time for the rest of baseball to appreciate Craig Biggio as one of the five or ten greatest second basemen of all time—and as one of the half-dozen best players of his era.

Wade Boggs
Third baseman, 1982–99

He didn't have much power or speed, yet at his peak, Boggs was one of baseball's most valuable players (even though MVP voters never actually gave him their award). He was a hitting machine, cranking out seven consecutive 200-hit seasons and smacking double after double off the GREEN MONSTER at Fenway. He played third base well enough to win two GOLD GLOVES, and he was named to 12 All-Star teams. How did he do it? Unusually strong plate discipline—he absolutely refused to swing at a bad pitch—and superstition. His pre-game meal consisted of chicken every day. He would wake up, practice, run sprints, and more at the same time and with the same routine each day. Whatever it was, it certainly worked for him.

Boggs hung on at the end of his career with Tampa Bay, long enough to notch his 3,000th hit and guarantee his selection to Cooperstown. It was overkill, because the Hall of Fame would have accepted him either way. He was inducted in his first year of eligibility in 2005.

Barry Bonds
Outfielder, 1986–2008

Knowing what we know now about Bonds and performance-enhancing drugs, I propose we divide his career into two eras: pre-steroids (1986–1998) and post-steroids (1999–2008). Let's talk first about the pre-steroids Bonds, because in many ways, he was the perfect baseball player, the heir to WILLIE MAYS (Barry's godfather) in terms of consistency and all-around ability. You want power? 30-45 homers per year. Speed? 20-40 steals. Batting eye? 100-150 walks per year plus on-base percentages well about .400. Fielding? Eight GOLD GLOVES. Respect? Three MVP Awards and four other top-five finishes. He was clearly the best player of the 1990s and he might have ultimately been recognized as the best left fielder of all time, ahead of TED WILLIAMS, STAN MUSIAL, and RICKEY HENDERSON.

But now let's talk about the post-steroids Bonds. According to the meticulously researched book *Game of Shadows*, released in 2006, Bonds began taking steroids and other performance-enhancing drugs in earnest following the 1998 season. After an injury-marred 1999—possibly caused by steroid overuse—Bonds put together a string of dominance over five consecutive seasons unmatched in baseball history, even by BABE RUTH. He posted slugging percentages ranging between .688 and .863, home run totals between 45 and 73, on-base percentages between .440 and .609, and walk totals between 117 and 232. These are video game numbers. And they came when opposing pitchers and managers were so scared of pitching to Bonds that he would get only 1 or 2 decent pitches per game. This dominance won him four more MVP Awards. During that time, he blew past the 500,

600, and 700 home run marks, then surpassed HANK AARON'S lifetime record of 755 and ended at 762. (*See* 73, 755, 762.)

According to *Game of Shadows*, however, Bonds did most of it while working out obsessively with a team of personal trainers and taking a complicated cocktail of steroids, human-growth hormone, and other supplements that were not tested for or officially banned by baseball until 2002. He also lied about it to the public and possibly to a grand jury investigating one of his suppliers; he was tried in court and convicted on charges of obstruction of justice in 2011. (The conviction was eventually overturned in 2015.)

Did Bonds cheat? Technically, maybe not, because the substances he used were not strictly banned by baseball, and he did not fail a drug test. Morally and practically, that's up to you to decide.

What can baseball do about his records? Nothing. The numbers will—and should—stand. We can't wipe them off the books, as some people have proposed, because where would you stop? Would you have to take away the Giants' 2002 pennant? We could put an "asterisk" next to them, but we don't know who else was juicing, so it wouldn't be fair to single out Bonds. No, I think we as fans will simply have to realize that the 1990s and early 2000s were the "steroid era" (sportswriter JOE POSNANSKI has dubbed it the "Selig Era") and decide for ourselves how to deal with it. If you choose to believe that Bonds's behavior constitutes cheating and his records shouldn't count, that's fine. But everything did happen—he did hit 73 home runs, he did draw 232 walks, the Giants did win the pennant— and nothing can change that.

As for the Hall of Fame... that's a stickier issue. So far (as of January 2015), the members of the BBWAA who vote on Hall induction have voted no on Bonds and the other greats who've been named as PED users (ROGER CLEMENS, RAFAEL PALMEIRO, MARK MCGWIRE, Sammy Sosa, and others). My take is this: Every era of baseball history has had its players and managers who sought every possible edge to win, even if it meant breaking the rules or breaking the law. Beginning in the 1960s, players including the greats of the game openly ingested amphetamines to improve their attention and focus. The 1951 Giants, led by Hall of Famer LEO DUROCHER, used a telescope and a buzzer to steal opponents' signs. The 1890s Orioles, including Hall of Famer JOHN MCGRAW, regularly cheated on the field to win games. Hall of Famers GAYLORD PERRY and WHITEY FORD threw illegal spitballs. The list goes on. In the 1990s and early 2000s, players used PEDs for that same edge, and the baseball establishment—along with the baseball media—looked the other way. In fact, the BBWAA even awarded multiple MVPs and Cy Youngs to Bonds and Clemens during this period. Now that same group of voters is actively keeping Bonds and Clemens and the others out of the Hall of Fame. Bonds and Clemens are two of the greatest players in the history of the game. They rewrote record books. They dominated the game. And they belong in the Hall of Fame.

Jim Bouton
Pitcher, 1962–70, 1978

Though he won 21 and 18 games in consecutive seasons with the Yankees, Bouton is best known as an iconoclastic troublemaker who was, in fact, way ahead of his time. In contrast to most players of his era (or any era), Bouton was a literate man who actually read books and believed that he was entitled to be treated with dignity and respect by the team that employed him. While still pitching in the majors, Bouton angered the baseball community with his tell-all book *BALL FOUR*, the book that forever changed the public perception of professional athletes.

For a long time, major league baseball shamed itself by not inviting Bouton to old-timer's games, but in the late 1990s, the Yankees finally relented. Baseball needs guys like Bouton.

Roger Bresnahan
Outfielder/catcher, 1897–15
Manager, 1909–1912, 1915

A member of the Hall of Fame, Bresnahan is most known for having popularized shin guards and chest protectors for catchers—which were soundly jeered and criticized until everybody in the league adopted them. Some publications credit Bresnahan for actually *inventing* those tools. In fact, other players in other leagues had been using them for several years before Bresnahan starting wearing them on a regular basis in the major leagues.

George Brett
Infielder, 1973–93

A member of the 3,000-hit club, Brett is the only player to win batting titles in three different decades. In his best season, 1980, Brett flirted with the .400 mark for much of the year before finishing at an astounding .390. The lifelong Kansas City Royal led the team to seven division titles, two pennants, and the franchise's only World Series victory in 1985. He also starred, notoriously, in one of baseball's oddest chapters, the Pine Tar Incident (*see* 1983: THE PINE TAR INCIDENT), when he came unhinged after hitting a game-winning home run and none other than BILLY MARTIN accused him of cheating.

Brett retired following the 1993 season when he determined that his play was not up to his high standards, even though he was still a fine player. In the view of many baseball historians (including this one), Brett ranks behind only MIKE SCHMIDT and perhaps Eddie Mathews and ALEX RODRIGUEZ among the greatest third basemen of all time. He's now a member of the Hall of Fame and an executive with his old club.

Roy Campanella
"Campy"
Catcher, 1937–57 (including Negro leagues)

The great catcher for the Brooklyn Dodgers let his powerful bat and unsurpassed fielding skills take his teams to five pennants and one World Series championship. "Campy" was known for his cheerful demeanor and once said, "You have to be a man to play professional baseball, but you have to have a lot of little boy in you, too." But that disposition didn't keep him from dominating opposing pitchers on the way to three MVP Awards. In fact, had it not been for the COLOR LINE—which stalled the beginning of Campanella's career in the major leagues—and for the tragic auto accident that paralyzed him in 1958, there might be no doubt as to who was the greatest catcher of all time: not BENCH or BERRA or COCHRANE; it might have been Campanella.

Jose Canseco
Outfielder, 1985–2004

Canseco has made almost as many headlines for what he has done off the field as for what did at the plate. He busted onto the scene in

1986 to smack 33 homers and win the Rookie of the Year Award. In 1988, he captured MVP honors while becoming the first player in history to hit 40 homers and steal 40 bases. He helped his A's to three straight pennants from 1988 to 1990, and he was as feared by pitchers as any batter in the game. Meanwhile, off the field, he had a number of run-ins with the law for speeding and possessing a weapon, and his squabbles with his wife made news when she crashed her car into his. He even made the tabloids after being seen coming out of Madonna's New York City apartment.

After being traded to the Rangers in 1992, his career took a turn for the worse. Never known for stellar fielding, he starred in highlight films around the world when a fly ball bounced off his head and over the fence for a home run. A season later, he convinced his manager to let him pitch a game in relief. The experiment became a horrendous failure when he blew out his arm so badly it required surgery. He returned to slug home runs for several teams, and his career came to a close in 2001.

Yet still, he refused to fade away. In 2005, his best-selling book, *Juiced*, detailed his alleged role as the Johnny Appleseed of steroid use in baseball. It turned out that he'd been using since almost the beginning of his career, and he accused several former teammates of shooting up with him. In the book, he actually defended the use of steroids. The other players denied the accusations, of course, but when one of the accused, RAFAEL PALMEIRO, actually failed a drug test in mid-2005, his claims received a boost of credibility (which led to a followup book called *Vindicated*).

For a few exciting moments, Canseco was just about the best baseball player on the planet. But his lasting contribution to the game will be that he shined a powerful light on the biggest scandal in modern baseball history.

Steve Carlton
"Lefty"
Pitcher, 1965–88
The top left-handed pitcher of the post-KOUFAX era and winner of a then-record four Cy Young Awards, Carlton famously won 27 games in 1972 for a Phillies team that won only 59 total games. Throughout his career, Carlton didn't speak to reporters but let his pitching talk for him: 329 career victories, 4,136 career strikeouts—including

4,020 in the NL, a league record. His best pitch was a wicked slider—probably the greatest slider in baseball history—that would start out as a strike but break down and in for righties, down and away for lefties, safely out of the zone, just as the batter would start to swing. When batters stopped swinging, his career was finished. The Hall of Fame was happy to take him in 1993.

Ray Chapman
Shortstop, 1912–20

A popular star for the Indians, Chapman was in the midst of a career that may have taken him to the Hall of Fame when he was accidentally beaned in the skull and killed by a fastball from Carl Mays. It was not just the only on-field death in major league history; the tragedy also changed baseball forever. *See* 1920: TRAGEDY ON THE DIAMOND.

Oscar Charleston
Outfielder, Negro leagues, 1915–1950

Generally regarded as the greatest NEGRO LEAGUE ballplayer of all time, Charleston was a strong hitter, great fielder, and legendary baserunner who would today be remembered with COBB, RUTH, DIMAGGIO, MANTLE, and MAYS if he had been white or born fifty years later. Instead, his wonderful accomplishments were largely ignored by fans and the media. In exhibition games against white major leaguers, research shows Charleston batted .318 with 11 homers in 195 at bats, including one off WALTER JOHNSON to give SMOKEY JOE WILLIAMS a 1–0 victory. "Charleston could hit that ball a mile," said DIZZY DEAN. "When he came up, we just threw and hoped like hell he wouldn't get hold of one and send it out of the park." Charleston played a shallow center field, able to cut off singles that might otherwise drop in front of him but also able to outrun any drive over his head.

After his peak years ended, Charleston played a major role in integrating the major leagues by encouraging BRANCH RICKEY to sign ROY CAMPANELLA. Charleston died in 1954, 22 years before the baseball Hall of Fame got around to honoring him.

Hal Chase
"Prince Hal"
First baseman, 1905–19

A fascinating, charismatic figure, Chase was universally regarded as the best defensive first baseman of his era—and perhaps of all time. He was also universally regarded as a crook. Throughout his career, his managers accused him of purposely trying to lose games, and he was brought up on charges before the National League president in 1918. Though he was acquitted on that charge due to lack of evidence, he was suspended by his own team a year later for the same reason. According to most accounts of the 1919 BLACK SOX SCANDAL, Chase helped connect the players to the gamblers, and he made a fortune betting against the Sox.

Every now and then, you may read ill-informed baseball fans and writers claiming that Chase was one of the greatest first basemen of all time. They're wrong. Let's put aside the allegations of throwing ballgames for a moment—charges that followed Chase wherever he went but were never technically proven. If we look only at the statistics, it's hard to see why people might believe he was that great. We're talking about a .291 career hitter with no power and an absurdly poor on-base percentage. He never drove in or scored 100 runs, and he only led the league in three categories: home runs (Federal League) in 1915 and hits and batting average (National League) in 1916. As far as fielding, he never led the league in fielding average, which, of course, is not the only measure of fielding excellence but is a pretty good one. On the other hand, he did lead the league in errors five times.

You could argue that Chase's skills transcended statistics. But the way to measure such a claim is through pennant victories. How many pennants did Chase's alleged talents win for his teams? Zero. Certainly you could make a pretty good all-star team of players who never won a pennant, such as ERNIE BANKS, Rod Carew, Ferguson Jenkins, Ralph Kiner, and others. But Chase wasn't as good as any of those guys, and when you're discussing the true greats, you have to take into account the entire record. The bottom line is, did he help his teams win? There is little evidence that he ever did anything but help his own wallet.

Eddie Cicotte
"Knuckles"
Pitcher, 1905, 1908–20

Cicotte (which is pronounced SEE-cot) has two claims to fame. First, he was the first knuckleball pitcher to achieve success in the major leagues, hence his nickname "Knuckles." He also threw a pitch he called a "shine ball," in which he would take a dirty ball and rub it against his uniform to "shine" one side of it. In fact, the shining was purely to fool the hitter; Cicotte would usually just throw the knuckler. For the first decade of his career, he was just an average starter. But from 1917 through 1920, he was one of the best in the game, averaging over 22 wins per year during that time. His best season came in 1919, when he went 29 and 7 with a 1.82 ERA for the pennant-winning Sox.

Which leads us to Cicotte's other claim to fame, or rather, claim to infamy: Cicotte accepted money from gamblers to throw two games of the 1919 World Series. It was his confession that blew the 1919 BLACK SOX SCANDAL wide open, and he was subsequently kicked out of baseball with seven other members of the team. Cicotte said he took the money from the gamblers to provide for his family what legitimate means of money-earning could not. Later in life, he became philosophical about the scandal. "I've tried to make up for it by living as clean a life as I could," he told a reporter. "I'm proud of the way I've lived, and I think my family is, too."

One famous story about Cicotte is probably not true. According to the legend, Cicotte had a clause in his contract calling for a $10,000 bonus if he won 30 games in 1919. He was benched for two weeks—from September 5 until September 19—possibly on orders from the penurious Sox owner CHARLES COMISKEY, and he finished the season with just 29 victories, thus losing the bonus. This is supposedly one of the motivations for Cicotte's decision to throw the series. This story has been repeated endlessly in baseball literature, including by me in previous books. However, there is one major problem with the story: Cicotte's own confession indicates he had been approached about the fix and he had agreed to it in August or early September, much sooner than the benching. If his inaction for those two weeks was ordered by the owner to avoid a bonus, it doesn't seem to have affected the timeline of events of the scandal. Knowing how much of a tightwad Comiskey was, I highly doubt he would offer a $10,000 bonus—which was much more than Cicotte's season salary—to anyone. It's also possible that the alleged bonus was for 1917.

This is just one of many inconsistencies surrounding the scandal. In fact, Cicotte's story (and the entire Black Sox story) is much too complicated for me to do it justice. You should read *EIGHT MEN OUT* by Eliot Asinof, which was published in 1963, as well as *Burying the Black Sox* by Gene Carney, which was published in 2007 and uses information not available to Asinof.

Roger Clemens
"The Rocket"
Pitcher, 1984–2007
Clemens dominated hitters for more than 20 years and achieved levels of greatness nearly unsurpassed in baseball history. He shares the record for strikeouts in a nine-inning game—20, tied with Kerry Wood and RANDY JOHNSON (but Clemens achieved the feat twice)—and he once notched a 1.93 ERA in FENWAY PARK and a 1.87 ERA at Houston's Minute Maid Park, both amazing totals for such great hitters' parks.

But did he do it cleanly? That is the question.

From 1986 through 1992, Clemens was as good as they come as he averaged 19 wins and 239 strikeouts while capturing his first three Cy Young Awards. Then after injuries seemed to have stopped him, he resurrected his career and won Cy Young Awards in 1997 and 1998, giving himself a then-record five awards. When he finally won a World Series in 1999 with the Yankees, he achieved the one remaining goal in his great career. But still he wasn't finished. He won another Cy Young Award in 2001 for the Yankees and continued to win in the post-season. After his contract ran out in 2003, he "retired" from the Yankees, only to come back with his hometown Houston Astros, where—you guessed it—he won another Cy Young Award, this one at the age of 41, running his career total to 7. He continued to pitch and dominate in 2005, defying his age. Then after that season, he "retired" again—only to come back mid-way through the 2006 season in Houston and pitching for half of the 2007 season back in New York to middling success.

But as with all stars in the last decade of the 20th century, Clemens' success is tainted by performance-enhancing drugs (PEDs). He was named in the MITCHELL REPORT and accused by both his alleged dealer and by his (former) friend Andy Pettitte of using steroids and human-growth hormone. Clemens denied the allegations, and though he was charged with lying to Congress, he was acquitted of perjury charges in 2012.

Let's ignore the PEDs for a minute and look at another aspect of Clemens's career. A strong case can be made that not only was Clemens the greatest pitcher of his generation—a no-brainer—but also that he was the greatest pitcher of all time. Here's some of the evidence to back that up:

He posted career totals that are almost unmatched in baseball history: 354 wins (9th on the all-time list), 4,672 strikeouts (3rd), .658 winning percentage (3rd among pitchers with 300 wins). He led the league in ERA seven times, despite pitching most of his career in hitter's parks.

Beyond the numbers, most people would agree that athletic prowess as a whole has improved over the past century. Many old-timers claim that ballplayers today are inferior to those in the past, but I scoff at that notion. In sports that are measured objectively—track and field, swimming, and so on—athletic ability has improved dramatically. For example, the seventh-place finisher in the 100-meter dash at the 2012 Olympics would have easily won the gold medal as recently as 1984. Are we to believe that baseball players are exempt from this evolutionary trend? If you buy into this argument, it stands to reason that the greatest players of the modern era are, on the whole, greater than those of previous eras.

Before you disagree too vehemently, please know that I believe this argument can be taken too literally. Every generation produces athletes who would dominate at any time. The most accomplished players of recent times—ALBERT PUJOLS and BARRY BONDS—aren't necessarily the greatest player of all time. And WILLIE MAYS would be just as great today as he was in the 50s and 60s. Same with BABE RUTH and HONUS WAGNER and TED WILLIAMS and so on.

Back to Roger Clemens. Is he the greatest of all time? Without taking steroids into account and based on his numbers and the overall level of competition he faced, I think so. But I wouldn't argue too much if you presented a plausible alternate theory. The top pitchers are just too close in skill and achievement to make such a statement with absolute certainty.

The other question is: Does Clemens belong in the Hall of Fame? The BBWAA says no, but I say yes. Read my entry on Barry Bonds for more about that.

Roberto Clemente
Outfielder, 1955–72

Possessor of perhaps the best outfield arm of all time, Clemente also excelled at the plate, lashing line drives in droves on the way to four batting titles, 13 seasons over .300, and exactly 3,000 career hits. He won an MVP Award and helped his Pittsburgh Pirates to two World Series victories. Fans who saw him play can tell stories about the amazing things Clemente could do in the outfield, like throw out a runner at home from the warning track on one bounce, or gun a runner at third on the fly from the right-field corner. He was that good and that memorable.

During his career, he fought to help Latin ballplayers gain acceptance into the major league fraternity, but his dedication and valor didn't end on the field: His death on New Year's Eve 1972 occurred while he was aboard a mercy mission carrying supplies to earthquake-ravaged Nicaragua.

One story from 1971 illustrates the way Clemente played the game—and lived his life. He was 37 years old and worn down by 17 seasons of bold and sometimes reckless outfield play. But on that day, he proved to 14,933 baseball fans at the Houston Astrodome what his teammates and his family already knew: that he was the kind of player who would run into a brick wall to help his team.

It happened on August 27, as his Pittsburgh Pirates were coasting to their second straight division title. They played the first game of a three-game series in Houston and led 7-3 in the eighth inning. A right-handed hitter caught a pitch off the end of the bat and sent the ball high into the air, curling toward the right-field foul line, where a brick wall separated the field from the fans. Clemente was playing the hitter to pull the ball, in right-center, giving him a long run to make the out. He began to sprint madly. When the ball reached its peak and began its descent, Clemente seemed too far from it to make the catch. A regular human being would have slowed down at that point and let the ball drop; no point risking a nasty confrontation with that brick wall. The ball would have been foul anyway. But such was not Clemente's style.

He kept running after it, and the ball kept twisting toward the stands. Fans in the first dozen or so rows stood up to catch the souvenir, assuming that it would bounce on the hard turf and into the seats. Then they saw Clemente sprinting toward them, and they must have thought about that brick wall, and they must have realized that he wasn't going to stop in time. Clemente himself certainly didn't. He just kept running and running, his eyes fixed on the ball, his mind focused on one single effort: making the catch for out number three. He reached out and, two steps in front of the wall, made the catch. Then he braced himself for the impact. Smack! The wall didn't give an inch. Clemente did. The force knocked him to the ground, but he never let go of the ball. He got up slowly and tossed the ball back toward the infield. The game went on.

Later in the clubhouse, a reporter asked him why he had taken the risk; why did he go after such a meaningless out? Clemente looked confused. He didn't understand the question. The reporter explained: He could have hurt himself—was the catch really worth it? Why didn't Clemente let the ball drop? Clemente paused. Then he answered simply, "I wanted to catch the ball." And the reporters understood. Anybody who knew Clemente knew that there was only one way for him to do anything—the right way. The score of the game, the position of brick walls, the risk of injury—none of that made a difference. You dedicate yourself to something, you accept the responsibility, and you go all out. Always.

Ty Cobb
"The Georgia Peach"
Outfielder, 1905–28
Manager, 1921–26

Up until BABE RUTH came along, Cobb was clearly the greatest player in American League history; only HONUS WAGNER had him beat for the overall title. With the wood in his hands, Cobb had no superiors—or even equals. He captured 11 batting titles (if you count the disputed 1910 BATTING RACE), posted three seasons over .400, and rapped out almost 4,200 hits. Playing in a time when home runs were rare, Cobb led the league in slugging percentage eight times and won a TRIPLE CROWN. He was also a terror on the base paths, stealing bases and otherwise creating tremendous havoc. He held the single-season record for stolen bases until Maury Wills broke it in 1962 and the mark for career steals until Lou Brock surpassed him in the 1970s. Though not a great fielder, Cobb was fast enough to catch up to most of his mistakes and competitive enough to work hard. The one honor that eluded him was a World Series victory; his Tigers captured three pennants early in Cobb's career but couldn't win the big one.

The big blot on Cobb's legend is that he was probably the meanest man who ever played major league baseball—a racist bully who would kick, spit, spike, punch, or shoot anything that got in his way. He once tore into the stands during a game to beat up a heckler, not even stopping when he discovered that the man had no arms or legs. And it wasn't the murder of his father by his mother when Ty was 18 that put the demons into his soul; as Cobb himself would have said, he was an SOB before that and an even bigger SOB afterwards. After baseball, he led the life of a bitter old man, estranged from his ex-wives and children. Lucky for him he invested his money wisely, so he was able to retire a wealthy man. But at his death in 1962, he had kept few friends in baseball, and only three former players showed up at the funeral.

Mickey Cochrane
Catcher, 1925–37
Manager, 1934–38
The greatest catcher of his era, Cochrane won two MVPs and played on five pennant-winners with the Athletics and Tigers—player-managing two of them. He could hit like few other catchers, batting over .320 seven times with good power and excellent strike zone judgment. Remarkably consistent, he appeared in 120 to 135 games for 10 straight seasons, but his career came to an end after being beaned in the head on a pitch from Bump Hadley of the Yankees in 1937. The pitch nearly killed him: he remained unconscious and near death for 10 days before he finally pulled through. (Yet it was still nearly a decade before teams started using batting helmets.) Although Cochrane is largely forgotten except among real baseball fans, his legacy lived on in New York: MICKEY MANTLE'S father named his son after Cochrane.

Eddie Collins
"Cocky"
Second baseman, 1906–30
Manager, 1924–26

A superb fielder, baserunner, and hitter, as well as a player-manager for a few years, Collins is unquestionably one of the two or three greatest second basemen of all time. He was a model of consistency throughout his career, batting around .340, scoring 100 runs, stealing 50 bases, and playing flawless defense year in and year out. A member of the Athletics' famed "$100,000 INFIELD," Collins later went to Chicago and played with the 1919 BLACK SOX team that threw the World Series. Collins, however, was part of the educated clique of players—he had attended Columbia University—and the gamblers never even thought to approach him. It also didn't hurt that his relatively generous contract with Philadelphia was honored by the White Sox after he came over in a trade.

He finished his career with 3,312 hits and a career average of .333 in addition to six pennants. He went on to become the general manager of the Boston Red Sox, where he helped sign both TED WILLIAMS and Bobby Doerr. But he couldn't bring a championship to Boston as he did to Philadelphia.

Bobby Cox
Manager, 1978–2010

The most successful manager of his generation, Cox is best known for winning 14 consecutive division titles with the Atlanta Braves, a record that will surely stand forever. In addition, his teams won five pennants and he captured four Manager of the Year Awards. Yet with all that success, he was able to win only a single World Series title.

Was there something about his teams or his managerial style that caused them to wilt in October? I doubt it. His teams were strong and deep, built on pitching without overlooking hitting and defense. He managed several future Hall of Famers—including GREG MADDUX, Tom Glavine, John Smoltz, and Chipper Jones—during the primes of their careers, but he was equally committed to rejuvenating his team with young stars as the veterans faded away. He was fiery on the field, as evidenced by his record 158 ejections (surpassing JOHN McGRAW). Yet he seemed to enjoy himself, too.

The only explanation for why his teams didn't win more championships is that it's just a historical quirk: He managed most of his career in the modern Wild Card era, when just getting to the World Series is more difficult than in previous eras because of the extra round of playoff games. And when his teams did make it to the World Series, they kept it close almost every time. They lost in 1991 on a seventh-game, extra-inning nail-biter by a score of 1-0 (*see* 1991: MORRIS COMES UP REAL BIG). In 1992, they lost the sixth and final game 4-3 in 11 innings. In 1996, they lost again in six games, including the last two by one run. Only in 1999 were Cox's Braves ever blown out of a World Series. With a little more luck, Cox could have won two World Series, maybe three. But it didn't work out that way, and you can't hold Cox responsible. He's one of the greats, and he was elected to the Hall of Fame in 2014.

Candy Cummings
Pitcher, 1872-1877
A member of the Hall of Fame not for his stellar career (only six major league seasons), but because he claimed to have invented the curveball. Candy (which was 19th-century slang for "best") said he was "inspired" by watching a clamshell curve in the air when thrown. He claimed he threw his first curveball in an amateur baseball game in 1867. However, several of Cummings's contemporaries—such as HARRY WRIGHT and HENRY CHADWICK—maintained that curves had been around since the 1850s. But for some reason, the Hall of Fame's voters chose to believe Candy's story.

Rod Dedeaux
College baseball coach
Perhaps the most accomplished coach in college baseball history, Dedeaux headed the University of Southern California's baseball program from 1958 until 1978, during which he captured 10 national championships. Dedeaux played for the Brooklyn Dodgers in 1935 after graduating from USC years earlier. While coaching at his alma mater, he recruited a number of future major league stars, including TOM SEAVER, Dave Kingman, Fred Lynn, Ron Fairly, and Don Buford.

Dizzy Dean
Pitcher, 1930–41, 1947

The SANDY KOUFAX of his time, Dean was one of the two or three best pitchers in baseball for four years until a line drive broke his toe during the 1937 All-Star Game. He played with St. Louis's infamous "GAS HOUSE GANG" where he became the game's most colorful character. He once boasted that he and his brother, Paul, whose nickname was "Daffy," would win 45 games in a season. When they won 49, Dizzy defended his bravado by noting, "It ain't braggin' if you can do it."

After his playing days ended, Dean enjoyed a long career as a broadcaster, where he was able to get away with expressions like "He slud into third" and "The runners return to their respectable bases." (In that respect, he is the model for every other poorly educated jock to make his way onto television or radio where he's given free rein to adapt the rules of English grammar and usage.) My favorite Dean story is the one about him getting hit with a thrown ball while sliding into second; the newspaper headline the next day supposedly read, "X-Ray of Dean's Head Shows Nothing."

Martin Dihigo
"El Maestro"
Infielder/outfielder/pitcher, Negro leagues, 1923–45

Cuban-born Dihigo was a master of versatility. Men who saw him play, from CUMBERLAND POSEY to BUCK LEONARD to Johnny Mize, hailed Dihigo as the one of the greatest all-around players in history. He hit from both sides of the plate for both average and power. He pitched with great skill. He stole bases. He had perhaps the best outfield arm of his time, yet he could play any position. He managed for many years. He also played almost anywhere organized baseball existed: the United States, Cuba, Mexico, Puerto Rico, Venezuela, you name it. The Hall of Fame in the U.S. isn't the only Hall to honor Dihigo; he is also a member of the Cuban and Mexican Baseball Halls of Fame.

Joe DiMaggio
"The Yankee Clipper"
Outfielder, 1936–51

A nearly flawless ballplayer, DiMaggio won three MVP Awards, played in 10 World Series during 13 major league seasons, was immortalized in a Simon and Garfunkel song, and received almost every other accolade a player could get. It is barely an overstatement to say that he towered over the American League nearly every year he played, leading the league at various times in homers, RBIs, batting average, and slugging percentage. But he's best known for the 56-game hitting streak (*see* 56) that transfixed the nation in 1941.

DiMaggio led a near-storybook life: The son of poor Italian immigrants, he made it big in New York City, where his famous hitting streak captured the heart of America; after his career ended, he married the nation's most famous movie star, Marilyn Monroe, and when that ended painfully, it was said (by musician Oscar Levant) that "it just proves a man can't be a success at two national pastimes." When he passed away in 1999, the entire sports world mourned.

And then the book came out. Richard Ben Cramer's biography *DiMaggio: The Hero's Life* was published not long after his death and was the first book to describe DiMaggio as unschooled, uncaring, egocentric, and fiercely protective of his image above all else. It's an exquisitely written and painstakingly researched book, probably the best-written baseball biography I've ever read. But it's not for everyone. If you like your baseball heroes sanitized for your protection, skip it. If you want the real story, read it.

Larry Doby
Outfielder, 1942–59, including Negro leagues

Signed by Indians owner BILL VEECK soon after JACKIE ROBINSON broke baseball's COLOR BARRIER, Doby integrated the American League on July 5, 1947. Unlike Robinson, Doby jumped straight from the NEGRO LEAGUES to the majors without the benefit of seasoning in the white minor leagues. Still, Doby took only a year to become one of the top players in the league—a slugging center fielder with excellent strike zone judgment and great fielding skills, basically a mid-century version of Dale Murphy or Carlos Beltran. He led the league in homers twice, RBIs and runs once each, and played on seven All-Star teams and two pennant winners. For a long time, he never received much support for the Hall of Fame, and it's hard to understand why. His career totals in the majors aren't that impressive—253 homers, 970 RBIs, .283 batting average—but he deserves some credit for the extra burden placed on him as one of baseball's sometimes forgotten pioneers. The VETERANS COMMITTEE could have done the right thing by selecting him for the shrine in 1997, the fiftieth anniversary of the breaking of the color line, but instead they waited a year and selected him in 1998.

Don Drysdale
Pitcher, 1956–69

When Dodgers manager WALTER ALSTON once ordered Drysdale to intentionally walk a batter, Drysdale instead responded by hitting the batter with his first pitch. "Saved three pitches" was Drysdale's logic—an attitude that typified his pitching style and explains why he is the leader in hit batsmen among post-war pitchers. From his six-foot, five-inch frame, he whipped the ball toward the plate sidearm, frightening most right-handed hitters (except HANK AARON, who slugged 17 homers off Drysdale during his career, the most against any single pitcher). Drysdale won a Cy Young Award in 1962, tossed a then-record 58-2/3 consecutive scoreless innings in 1968, captured three strikeout crowns, and, joining SANDY KOUFAX in a lethal one-two punch, helped his teams to four World Series appearances. Following his career, Drysdale worked for many years as a broadcaster who delighted in downgrading the modern ballplayer: "If the game gets any more namby-pamby," he once said, "they'll be hitting off a tee."

Leo Durocher
"The Lip"
Shortstop, 1925, 1928–41, 1943, 1945
Manager, 1939–73

A scrappy shortstop with St. Louis's "GAS HOUSE GANG," among other teams, before embarking on a five-decade career as manager, Durocher is best known for asserting that "nice guys finish last." In fact, as he notes in his excellent autobiography, called NICE GUYS FINISH LAST, when he spoke those words, he was referring to a specific group of nice guys—the New York Giants of the mid-1940s—not to nice guys as a whole. Durocher, on the other hand, prided himself on being unpleasant and even downright mean while on the field, and his career can be charitably described as controversial. At any given point in his career, he could have been found feuding with owners, players, other managers, and league offices—enough to warrant a one-year suspension in 1947. But he was worth the controversy: his 2,008 managerial victories for the Dodgers, Giants, Cubs, and Astros rank him high on the all-time list. After years of being snubbed, Durocher was finally named to the Hall of Fame in

1994, two years *after* his death—another example of wonderful timing by the VETERANS COMMITTEE.

Dennis Eckersley
"Eck"
Pitcher, 1975–98

When he retired, Eck was universally acknowledged as the greatest relief pitcher of all time. But it was an unlikely career path. From 1975 through 1986, he worked as a quality starting pitcher, posting double-digit win totals nine times with the Indians, Red Sox, and Cubs. Then, in 1987, when his career seemed finished as a starter, he was traded to the Oakland A's, which turned out to be the best move of his life. He quickly became baseball's premier closer, converting 45 saves in his first full year out of the bullpen. Over the next half-decade, Eckersley redefined relief pitching with his live fastball and pinpoint control. In 1989, he allowed just 32 hits and 3 walks in 57 innings. In 1990, at the age of 36, he was even better: 73 innings, 41 hits allowed, 4 walks, 0.61 ERA, 48 saves. Two years later, he captured the Cy Young and MVP Awards while posting 51 saves and a 1.91 ERA as the A's won their fourth division title in five seasons. Eckersley was selected to the Hall of Fame in 2004, his first year of eligibility—only the third relief specialist so honored at the time.

Today, fans and broadcasters frequently use the term "walk-off," as in "Pujols hit a walk-off homer in the bottom of the ninth to win the game for the Cardinals." Eckersley invented that term, possibly not long after he surrendered Kirk Gibson's game-winning home run in the first game of the 1988 World Series, one of the greatest walk-offs in history (*see* 1988: GIBSON BLASTS THE ECK).

Buck Ewing
Catcher, 1880–97

Though the statistics don't seem to bear this out, Ewing is often called the greatest player of the 19th century. He played just about every position on the field and also managed for several years, but he was best known as a catcher, where he was the first player to throw from the crouch and one of the first to use a big mitt. Although you can be unimpressed with the stats—a .303 career average with little power—you can't discount the fact that CONNIE MACK and many others called him the greatest catcher they ever saw, and he was the biggest star in the game before HONUS WAGNER. When the Hall of

Fame was still in its infancy, Ewing was chosen for the honor in 1939, well ahead of such other eligible greats as Ed Delahanty, ROGERS HORNSBY, KING KELLY, and many others.

Bob Feller
"Rapid Robert"
Pitcher, 1936–56

The greatest strikeout pitcher of his era, Feller was a star by the age of 17, when he struck out 15 batters in his first major league start and tied the major league record with 17 Ks a few weeks later. His big weapon was a fastball that was clocked at close to 100 mph. How did they measure it in those days before radar guns? At least two ways. One was by using special Army ordinance equipment, which measured him at 98.6 mph (and which you can see on YouTube). And the other, much more interesting way, was to put a guy on a motorcycle about 100 feet behind him and have him accelerate to 80 mph or so; Feller would throw the pitch just after the bike rode by him, and they would see which made it to the plate first. Feller won.

The problem with Feller and his fastball is that he wasn't always able to control it, and he totaled 100-plus walks in nine different seasons. However, in spite of the walks, Feller led the league in victories six times. Had it not been for World War II, which robbed Feller of four peak seasons, he would have finished with over 320 victories and 3,400 strikeouts. As it was, he totaled an impressive 266 wins and 2,581 Ks—all with the Indians—in a Hall of Fame career.

Rollie Fingers
Relief pitcher, 1968–85

The best closer of his era, Fingers was equally known for his trademark handlebar mustache as for his career total of 341 saves, which was tops on the all-time list until 1993. Unlike many modern-day relievers, Fingers had a remarkably long career as an effective player, and he pitched at a time when closers often came into the game in the 7th inning, not just in the 9th—so he would throw 120-130 inning per season, not the 75 or 80 that today's closers throw. In the early 1970s, he helped his A's to five straight division titles and three straight World Series victories by averaging 9 wins and 20 saves per year. Two trades later, he won the 1981 MVP and Cy Young Awards with a 6–3 record, a league-leading 28 saves, and a 1.04 ERA. At the end of his career, the only team that offered him a contract was Cincinnati, which at the time was owned by Marge Schott and had a team policy forbidding facial hair. Rather than shave off his trademark, Fingers retired. In fact, his exact words to the Reds GM were, reportedly, "Well, you tell Marge Schott to shave her Saint Bernard, and I'll shave my mustache."

Curt Flood
Outfielder, 1956–71
Flood is the All-Star outfielder who sued baseball to end the RESERVE CLAUSE and achieve FREE AGENCY. For fourteen seasons in St. Louis, he had starred as a good-hitting, great-fielding center fielder for three pennant winners. But he was traded before the 1969 season to Philadelphia, and the shock of being traded suddenly and remorselessly—after he had established a successful photography business in St. Louis—proved too much for him to take. Choosing to sacrifice his career and his $90,000 salary to achieve better treatment for players, Flood took his case all the way to the Supreme Court. Although he lost a mind-boggling decision (*see* 1972: LABOR UNREST AND FLOOD V. KUHN), his defiance helped usher in the free agency era. Every athlete in every major sport today owes Flood a huge debt.

Whitey Ford
"The Chairman of the Board"
Pitcher, 1950–67
The New York Yankees' star left-hander holds almost every World Series pitching record, including career victories (10), losses (8), games (22) innings pitched (146), and strikeouts (94). The winningest pitcher in Yankee history, Ford captured one Cy Young Award and retired with a record of 236-106 for a .690 winning percentage, the highest among 20th-century pitchers with long careers. Ford succeeded not with overpowering stuff but with guile. He knew how to mix his pitches and keep hitters off balance. He also admitted to doctoring the baseball, bragging that he could cut the baseball in more ways than any other pitcher. But he never got caught. "No, I never threw a spitball," he once said with tongue in cheek. "Except when I had to get someone out really bad." Ford and teammate MICKEY MANTLE were inseparable during their days with the Yankees, so it was only fitting that they were inducted into the Hall of Fame together in 1974.

Rube Foster
Pitcher/outfielder/manager/executive, Negro leagues, 1898–26

Part JOHN MCGRAW, part CHRISTY MATHEWSON, part BAN JOHNSON, part P. T. Barnum, Foster himself was a true original. He earned his nickname when he out-pitched major league star RUBE WADDELL in a 1904 exhibition game. Often player-managing, he led his teams to a crop of pennants in various NEGRO LEAGUES. One club won 110 out of 120 games, another 123 of 129. Throughout his career, he acted as player and promoter, manager and executive. He formed the Negro National League in 1920 and ruled as Ban Johnson did the American League—with strength and vision. To maintain competitive balance, he shifted players from team to team, and he loaned money to failing franchises to keep them afloat. Ultimately, however, the stress was too much: In 1926, he succumbed to mental illness and died four years later in an institution. The Hall of Fame recognized him in 1981.

Jimmie Foxx
"Double X," "The Beast"
First baseman, 1925–45

In an era of exceptional hitters, this A's and Red Sox star outclassed almost everybody. He was the first American Leaguer to challenge BABE RUTH'S record of 60 homers, finishing with 58 in 1932—and he might have broken the record if he hadn't injured his wrist in a household accident with several weeks remaining in the season. He was also the first player to capture three MVP Awards. Additionally, he won a TRIPLE CROWN and led his teams to three pennants. A huge, broad-shouldered man who possessed muscles atop muscles, Foxx was a nimble first baseman who could also fill in at third base (135 career games), catcher (109), and even on the mound (10). Among the all-time greats, Foxx ranks behind only LOU GEHRIG and perhaps ALBERT PUJOLS among the greatest first basemen of all time.

After his career, like many great athletes of his day, he struggled to find and keep a good job after discovering that life as a baseball player doesn't really prepare you for much. Foxx also battled alcoholism. But one job he did seem to enjoy was managing the Fort Wayne Daisies of the ALL-AMERICA GIRLS PROFESSIONAL BASEBALL LEAGUE. Wait—what? Yes, the Tom Hanks character from the movie "A League of Their Own" is based very loosely on Jimmie Foxx.

Eddie Gaedel
Pinch hitter, 1951

A 65-pound, three-foot-seven-inch midget, Gaedel made headlines when he was sent by St. Louis Browns owner BILL VEECK to bat during a game as one of the most memorable publicity stunts in baseball history. It happened on August 19, 1951, against the Tigers. Detroit pitcher Bob Cain tossed four pitches but none could penetrate Gaedel's one-and-a-half-inch strike zone, and Gaedel—wearing jersey number 1/8—walked. He had wanted to swing at a pitch, but Veeck ordered him not to; he even joked that he would be on the roof with a high-power rifle, ready to shoot if Gaedel looked as if he was going to swing. The day after the stunt, Veeck received a telegram from AL president Will Harridge condemning the action, but Veeck's purpose had already been achieved, and Gaedel's 15 minutes of fame assured.

Lou Gehrig
"The Iron Horse"
First baseman, 1923–39

The greatest first baseman of all time, Gehrig was a quiet, humble man who let Yankee teammates BABE RUTH and JOE DIMAGGIO garner most of the headlines and the big salaries. "It's a pretty big shadow," Gehrig once said, referring to Ruth. "It gives me lots of room to spread myself."

Gehrig grew up in relative poverty in New York City, a child of German immigrants who wanted nothing more than that their son graduate from college with a good career ahead of him. He spent two years at Columbia on a football scholarship, but when his father needed an emergency operation, Gehrig signed with the Yankees to pay the medical bills. He typically batted fourth in the Yankees' lineup, behind Ruth and, later, DiMaggio, so he got plenty of chances to drive in runs, and he took full advantage. During his career, he averaged 147 RBIs per season—more than just about anybody gets in one season today—with a high of 184, still the American League record. And his teams appeared in seven World Series. Gehrig combined tremendous power, clutch hitting, and great strike zone judgment with unprecedented durability: he never missed a game beginning in 1925 and lasting for 2,130 games until a fatal disease (amyotrophic lateral sclerosis, a disease now known as LOU GEHRIG'S DISEASE) forced him out of the lineup on May 2, 1939. Gehrig succumbed to the disease two years later. *See* 2,130; 1939: THE LUCKIEST MAN SPEAKS.

Bob Gibson
"Hoot"
Pitcher, 1959–75

About Gibson, teammate TIM MCCARVER once said that he "always pitches when the other team doesn't score any runs." Such was certainly the case in 1968 when Gibson, an accomplished power pitcher for the St. Louis Cardinals, fashioned an ERA of 1.12 with 22 victories in what has been called the greatest season by a pitcher in history (*see* 1968: THE YEAR OF THE PITCHER). The five-time 20-game winner was dominant in other years as well, winning two Cy Young Awards. Great performances in the 1967 and 1968 World Series—including a Series-record 17 strikeouts in one game—firmed his reputation as one of the most intimidating hurlers of all time. His Hall of Fame induction in 1981 merely made it official. Today, as the debate rages over whether athletes should act as role models, Gibson's comment from 1970 has gained new meaning: "Too many people think an athlete's life can be an open book," he said. "You're supposed to be an example. Why do I have to be an example for your kid? *You* be an example for your kid."

Josh Gibson
Catcher, Negro leagues, 1930–46

Almost everyone who saw him play—including fellow Hall of Famer WALTER JOHNSON—believed that Josh Gibson was the greatest catcher of all time. Gibson was a slugger who could hit a ball farther than anyone and could throw out speedy baserunners from his knees. For part of his career, he teamed with the flamboyant SATCHEL PAIGE to form the what might be the greatest battery of all time. Gibson was just 33 years old, already a 16-year veteran, when the Dodgers broke the color barrier with JACKIE ROBINSON, and Gibson was reportedly bitter that he had been passed over. It was rumored that Gibson's struggles with alcohol kept BRANCH RICKEY from selecting him, because Rickey wanted a model citizen as much as he wanted a great ballplayer. Certainly BILL VEECK or another forward-thinking owner would have signed Gibson after 1947, but a brain hemorrhage took his life that year. The Hall of Fame recognized him in 1972.

Dwight Gooden
"Doc," "Doctor K"
Pitcher, 1984–2000

A sad case of talent wasted, Gooden started his career with more than a bang—it was a nuclear explosion. His debut season in 1984, which won him the Rookie of the Year trophy, was one of the best first years ever by a pitcher, and it came before Gooden was even old enough to drink. The next year, he won a Cy Young Award with an even more dominant season. He followed that up in 1986 with a 17-6 season that helped his Mets win the World Series. His record for the first three years of his career: 58 wins, just 19 losses, 744 strikeouts. But in 1987, it began to fall apart. That year, he missed a month of the season while being treated for cocaine addiction. Two years later, an arm injury felled him. For the next four years, he posted progressively worse records, and in 1994, he received a one-year suspension for failing a drug test. Although he came back to regain a modicum of effectiveness, and he even pitched an improbable no-hitter, his career was effectively over in 1993. There will be no Hall of Fame for Gooden—which comes as a surprise to all of us who watched him dominate the game for those few joyous years.

Goose Gossage
Pitcher, 1972–94

A devastatingly effective relief pitcher, Gossage helped redefine the role of closer with his menacing stare, goofy mustache, and 100-mph fastball. He saved games through pure intimidation, daring hitters to stand in the box against him. Few ever felt comfortable. With relief specialization a recent phenomenon in baseball, it was interesting to watch how Gossage was treated by Hall of Fame voters. He totaled 310 saves with nine teams, and at his peak, he was the best in the game; his 1981 strike-shortened season—0.77 ERA, 20 saves in 32 games—is one of the top 10 seasons ever posted by a reliever. Hall of Fame voters made him wait until his ninth try before selecting him in 2008.

Pete Gray
Outfielder, 1945

Having lost his right arm at the age of six, Gray nevertheless worked to become an exceptional minor league outfielder—batting .333 with only six errors in 1944—before joining the defending AL champion St. Louis Browns in 1945. Gray's promotion to the majors symbolizes the dearth of baseball talent in America while most able-bodied men were fighting World War II. Although his story is inspiring, it doesn't have a happy ending: Gray batted just .218 in 234 at bats and never appeared in a major league uniform after that season.

Hank Greenberg
"Hammerin' Hank," "The Hebrew Hammer"
First baseman, 1930–47
One of the dominant hitters in an era of great ones, Greenberg's star shone brightly in almost all of the nine seasons he was a regular. Playing against the likes of RUTH, GEHRIG, DiMAGGIO, FOXX, and WILLIAMS, Greenberg somehow found a way to lead the league at various times in home runs (four times), RBIs (four times), runs (once), doubles (twice), and walks (twice), helping his teams win four pennants while himself capturing two MVP Awards. He made his name with the Detroit Tigers, but at the end of his career he spent one season with the lowly Pittsburgh Pirates, who thought enough of Greenberg to make him baseball's first $100,000-per-year player.

Aside from being an awesome offensive force, Greenberg is best known for two things. One, he was the first established major league player to enlist in the Army after Pearl Harbor. He had been drafted in late 1940 and served until December 5, 1941, when he was released when the law changed to exempt men over the age of 28. But after the Japanese attack, Greenberg re-enlisted, became an officer, and served for 45 months—the longest tenure of any major leaguer during the war.

Greenberg's second major claim to fame is that he was the first Jewish superstar in baseball, possibly in all of American sports. As such, he was the idol of millions of Jewish sports fans, but he was also subjected to all sorts of anti-Semitic taunts from opposing fans and bench jockeys, which he generally ignored but not always: he once challenged the entire Yankees team to fight when the taunts got too vicious. He famously sat out a game on Yom Kippur in the heat of the 1934 pennant race, an action that has been celebrated among American Jews as much as SANDY KOUFAX'S similar decision in 1965. Greenberg's last season with the Pirates coincided with JACKIE ROBINSON'S rookie year, and because Greenberg had some idea for what Robinson would face as a fellow pioneer, the two became friends, and Robinson credited Greenberg for helping ease the way for his success.

Ken Griffey, Jr.
"Junior"
Outfielder, 1989–2010

Griffey joined the American League with much fanfare in 1989: a 19-year-old kid with loads of talent, called the second coming of WILLIE MAYS and other hyperbole. For his first four seasons, Junior dazzled fans with spectacular catches, deep home runs, and youthful exuberance. But his stats—25 home runs per year and a .515 slugging percentage—didn't seem to show his true potential. Then, in 1993, he notched a 45-home run campaign that quieted any skeptics. In strike-shortened 1994, he elevated his game further by smacking 40 home runs in just 433 at bats—and he followed that up with even better years, including a couple of 56-homer campaigns.

In 2000, the year before he was to become a free agent, he forced the Seattle Mariners to trade him to Cincinnati for basically a few journeyman ballplayers, a trade that threatened to go down as the most lopsided in history. Yet when the Mariners went on to win 116 games in 2001 while Griffey struggled through several injury-plagued seasons, it was the Mariners who had the last laugh.

Until the injuries, Griffey was on a pace to break Hank Aaron's career record of 755 home runs. He did finish with an astounding 630—good for fifth all time—and now ranks among the top five or six center fielders of all time, probably just behind Mays, COBB, MANTLE, and DIMAGGIO. And because he has never been implicated as a steroid user, his fame and admiration has only grown since his retirement.

Lefty Grove
Pitcher, 1925–33

A surly man renowned for his hatred of losing, Grove fed off that demeanor to fashion a pitching career that some have called the greatest of all time. Known for his fastball, Grove got his professional start with the minor league Baltimore Orioles, where BABE RUTH also began. During Grove's five seasons there, the team captured five International League pennants. The New York Giants offered $75,000 for Grove, but Orioles owner Jack Dunn held out for $100,000, which is what the Philadelphia Athletics ended up paying. It was the wisest move of A's manager/owner CONNIE MACK'S career. Pitching in the hitting-rich 1920s and 1930s, Grove led the league in ERA a record nine times, in winning percentage five times, and in strikeouts for each of his first seven seasons. Plus he won 20 games eight times and pitched in three World Series. He finished with a career record of 300–141 for a .680 winning percentage—the highest among 300-game winners.

He shares the American League record with 16 straight victories; after he lost potential win number 17 by a score of 1–0 on a misjudged fly ball, Grove showed his temper by tearing up the locker room, his uniform, and anything else he got his hands on.

Amazingly, Grove suffered only two injuries during his career, one a sore arm in 1934 and the other a mysterious ailment that stumped doctors in 1938: Grove told author Donald Honig that doctors couldn't find a pulse in his pitching arm. Somehow, he still led the league in ERA.

Ned Hanlon
Infielder/outfielder, 1880–92
Manager, 1889–1907
Possibly the most influential baseball manager you've never heard of, Hanlon led the famed BALTIMORE ORIOLES of the 1890s to three pennants by employing "inside baseball" tactics such as the hit and run, squeeze, sacrifice, and others. (The Orioles didn't *invent* those tactics, but they were the most successful at using them.) These strategies dominated baseball for the next quarter century, partly because of their success but mostly because four of the players Hanlon managed became the most celebrated managers of their time: Miller Huggins, JOHN MCGRAW, Hughie Jennings, and Wilbert Robinson. Combined, Hanlon's protégés won a total of 21 pennants between 1900 and 1930, and each was eventually elected to the Hall of Fame. Hanlon was the last of the bunch to be elected, finally making it in 1996.

Rickey Henderson
Outfielder, 1979–2003
Henderson combined power, speed, strike zone judgment, and high-average hitting like no player in history, easily earning him the title of greatest leadoff hitter in baseball history. In his prime during the 1980s, he could steal 80 to 100 bases, smack 10 to 20 homers, score 100+ runs, and draw enough walks to give him an on-base percentage

over .400. He's one of the few lead-off hitters to win an MVP Award, and he holds career records for both runs and steals.

He was a great player, a first-ballot Hall of Famer who probably deserves even more accolades than he gets. But he was almost equally famous for me-first escapades such as playing cards in the clubhouse while his Mets teammates lost in extra innings during the playoffs, and holding out in spring training for a bigger salary. So how do we factor in that extra stuff in our evaluation of him as a player? In the case of an unparalleled talent like Henderson, we don't. Sure, he made good copy for sportswriters, and he created a few headaches for management. But his antics never seemed to distract his teams from winning. And win they did. He played in the post-season eight times and won two World Series. Even with the baggage, you'd be crazy not to want Henderson on your team.

Keith Hernandez
First baseman, 1974–91

The best-fielding first baseman of his time—perhaps of all time— Hernandez played his best years with the Cardinals and Mets, winning the 1979 MVP (shared with Willie Stargell) and starring for two World Series champs. He captured a position-record 11 GOLD GLOVES and holds the all-time National League record for career assists by a first baseman. Despite his accomplishments, Hernandez has fallen well short of election to the Hall of Fame. Voters seem to have forgotten his contributions to the game, which came not through gaudy stats but through quiet excellence. His credentials are slightly different from a similarly excellent player like Orlando Cepeda or Tony Perez. What sets Hernandez apart from them is that Hernandez has a true claim to fame: possibly the greatest defensive first-baseman of all time. Players who can legitimately lay claim to an honor like that (Bill Mazeroski comes to mind) deserve special consideration by the Hall. Not to mention the fact that, as Jerry Seinfeld so artfully put it, Hernandez "played in Game 6!" (*See* 1986: WORLD SERIES GAME 6, METS VS. RED SOX.)

Rogers Hornsby
"Rajah"
Second baseman, 1915–37
Manager, 1925–37, 52-53

The best-hitting second baseman of all time, Hornsby averaged over .400 for a five-year period, slugged 20-plus homers seven times, won two TRIPLE CROWNS, and led the league in a multitude of categories throughout the 1920s (his *BASEBALL ENCYCLOPEDIA* entry is half boldface). For his career, he batted .358, second highest of all time, and has earned the title of baseball's greatest right-handed hitter (a title that FRANK THOMAS almost usurped and that ALBERT PUJOLS is challenging as of this writing). Of Hornsby's fielding, praise is harder to come by. TY COBB once wrote, "Hornsby couldn't catch a pop fly, much less go in the outfield after them, [and] could not come in on a slow hit…" (Cobb, however, was known to hold a grudge and may have stretched the truth.)

Yet for such a great ballplayer, Hornsby sure had trouble keeping a job. He alienated teammates and management wherever he played. He was traded five times, once after the 1926 season, during which he had player-managed the Cardinals to a World Series victory, then again a year later, after he'd led the league in runs, walks, slugging, and on-base percentage—and then again a year after that. Which begs the question: If he was so great, why did team after team decide they didn't want him anymore? And why did most of those teams *improve* after trading him?

Unfortunately, that's a question that can't be satisfactorily answered. Hornsby was a selfish, moody man—but so were Cobb and TED WILLIAMS and BABE RUTH (and Michael Jordan, for that matter). Great athletes usually are; selfishness is usually tied directly to their drive to become great. Yet Hornsby, as great as he was with the bat, somehow couldn't transcend his personality and make management feel like his team was better with him on it. Maybe management was wrong to trade him. Or maybe they got some great offers (Frankie Frisch was one of the players the Cardinals got in return for Hornsby, but the Giants and Cubs didn't get Hall of Famers when they traded him). If you look just at the numbers, Hornsby is the greatest second baseman of all time. But when you consider the entire record, you have to come to a different conclusion.

Carl Hubbell
"The Meal Ticket," "King Carl"
Pitcher, 1928–43

The top National League left-hander of his time, Hubbell earned his nicknames with a trademark screwball that carried the Giants to three pennants. He actually threw two different screwballs: a sidearm pitch that dropped down and away from right-handed batters and a faster, overhand throw that broke more sharply. In fact, his left arm was permanently damaged by all the screwballs. The Cardinals' Pepper Martin said "his left hand turns the wrong way" and called him a freak. "No wonder he's such a good pitcher," Martin added. And the great writer Jim Murray wrote that his left arm "looks as if he put it on in the dark."

Still, it was no doubt worth it for Hubbell. His accomplishments are many: a streak of 46-1/3 consecutive scoreless innings, five 20-win seasons, and three ERA championships. But his most famous feat came in the 1934 All-Star game, when he struck out five future Hall of Famers in a row—BABE RUTH, LOU GEHRIG, JIMMIE FOXX, Al Simmons, and Joe Cronin.

Catfish Hunter
Pitcher, 1965–79

A Hall of Famer with 224 career victories and five 20-win seasons, Hunter helped lead his A's to three World Series titles in the early 1970s. He earned his nickname not because of any real love of fishing but because A's owner CHARLES FINLEY, perennially seeking publicity, wanted his prodigy to have a country nickname. Hunter and Finley had a strained relationship during the player's tenure with the club. But when Finley reneged on Hunter's 1974 contract by failing to pay $50,000 to an insurance annuity, the Players Association filed a grievance on behalf of Hunter asserting that as a result of the violation, Hunter should be released from his contract with the A's. An independent arbitrator agreed, and Hunter became baseball's first FREE AGENT. He signed a multimillion-dollar contract with the Yankees and helped them to three pennants before retiring in 1979.

Monte Irvin
Outfielder, 1938–56 including the Negro leagues

An excellent outfielder who played eight seasons in the white major leagues with the Giants, Irvin is in the Hall of Fame more for his 11 years in the NEGRO LEAGUES, where he was one of its best players. When BRANCH RICKEY was deciding whom to select as the man to break baseball's color line, most people believed Irvin would be the choice. COOL PAPA BELL said, "Monte was our best young ballplayer at the time. He could do everything. He could hit that long ball, he had a great arm, he could field, he could run." But Rickey picked JACKIE ROBINSON, and Irvin had to wait an extra two years before getting his chance in the majors.

Joe Jackson
"Shoeless Joe"
Outfielder, 1908–20

A top player of his time, Jackson was one of the eight players thrown out of baseball following the 1919 BLACK SOX SCANDAL. He averaged .356 for his career, third best of all time, but that's because he was kicked out before his career could enter a normal "decline" phase.

The subject of numerous books, including W. P. Kinsella's excellent novel *Shoeless Joe* (upon which the film *FIELD OF DREAMS* is based), Jackson was an illiterate South Carolina mill worker who earned his nickname when he played a minor league game barefoot. In the majors, he batted .400 once and slugged over .500 six times in an era when home runs were hard to come by—all with one of baseball's sweetest swings, so sweet that BABE RUTH was said to have copied it.

Despite the taint of the Black Sox scandal, Jackson made a good life for himself after baseball, learning to read, raising a family, and becoming a successful businessman. "I have read now and then that I am one of the most tragic figures in baseball," he said a few years before his death. "Well, maybe that's the way some people look at it, but I don't quite see it that way myself." He never fought his suspension because he said he had enjoyed a good career, accomplished many things, and "there wasn't much left for me in the big leagues." And he still deserves a place among the greats, even if it's just in the record books and not the Hall of Fame.

That brings up the question: Should he be enshrined? In one of his harsher moments, the great author BILL JAMES once wrote, "My own opinion is that the people who want to put Joe Jackson in the Hall of Fame are baseball's answer to those women who show up at murder trials wanting to marry the cute murderer." James wrote those words before none other than TED WILLIAMS came out in favor of putting

Jackson in the Hall (not that James would ever back down from his statement). But Ted Williams doesn't make the rules for the Hall of Fame. Whether or not Jackson played his best (he did hit .375 during the Series), he took money from gamblers, and he knew about the attempt to throw the Series. He deserved to be banished from the game in 1920 and nothing has changed that should get him reinstated now. Forgive him? Sure. But I think the Hall is better off without him.

Reggie Jackson
"Mr. October"
Outfielder, 1967–87
One of the greatest World Series performers ever—hence the nickname—Jackson was a 14-time All-Star who smacked 563 home runs, led his teams to the postseason 11 times, and, on the other side of the coin, struck out a record 2,597 times. The controversial Jackson, who was as loved and hated as any player in history, was fond of making grandiose claims such as, "The only reason I don't like playing in the World Series is I can't watch myself play." (About Jackson, teammate Darold Knowles once said, "There's not enough mustard in the world to cover that hot dog.") There was no question he could talk a good game, but it's equally evident that he delivered. Between 1970 and 1983, no American League team *without* Jackson in the lineup won the World Series, while Jackson's teams—the 1972–74 A's and 1977–78 Yankees—captured five championships. Additionally, he was one of baseball's first high-priced free agents, who before the 1977 season turned down a higher salary from Montreal to play for the Yankees because, Jackson said, "If I play in New York, they'll name a candy bar after me." Which, of course, they did.

Derek Jeter
Shortstop, 1995–2014
Jeter was so good and became a star so young that he finished his career as one of the five greatest shortstops of all time. He was a key member of the great Yankee dynasties from the mid 1990s to the 2000s, loved by fans, respected by teammates, and appreciated by even the opposition. With his clutch hitting and generally positive attitude, he was the kind of player even curmudgeonly old-timers can praise with clichés like "He plays the game the right way."

Jeter is unquestionably one of the greatest hitters ever at his position, hitting for a high average with medium power and a good batting eye. As a fielder, he won five GOLD GLOVE awards, but did he deserve any of them? That is the question of the decade—the question that has vexed the SABERMETRIC community for years. Every advanced fielding metric that has been developed since the 1990s has shown that not only was Jeter never an elite shortstop, he was not even an *average* shortstop. The statistics seem to show that even in his prime, he couldn't go into the hole, and he couldn't make long throws. One researcher, Michael Humphreys, said, "Basically, he's OK at easy plays and terrible on all others; in other words, all the plays that matter."

Yet those are fightin' words for Jeter fans. For them, no amount of statistical evidence could persuade them that Jeter was not an excellent fielder. "I don't trust fielding stats; you have to watch him play every day," they would say. And maybe they're right. After all, the Yankees won all those pennants with him at short. He couldn't possibly be that bad, could he?

Ultimately, if you believe in advanced fielding stats, you have to believe that Derek Jeter is a subpar fielder. If you believe fielding skill can't be adequately measured statistically, then you can believe anything you want about Jeter. It's a matter of faith.

Tommy John
Pitcher, 1963–1989

John was a solid, if unspectacular, pitcher for the Indians, White Sox, and Dodgers who, in 1974, blew out his elbow, and then proceeded to change baseball. That year, the lefty was cruising along with a 13-3 record, on track for the best season of his career at age 31. Then he permanently damaged the ulnar collateral ligament in his pitching arm and hit the disabled list. In the past, such an injury would have meant premature retirement. But John had the good fortune of being close to a true pioneer in orthopedic surgery, Dr. Frank Jobe. Jobe's radical idea was to replace the damaged ligament with a healthy ligament from John's other arm. It was a risky surgery, and Jobe laid odds on John's recovery to pitch in the majors again at 1 in 100. Rehabilitation was grueling and took a full 18 months, but it was all worth it when John returned to the majors in 1976 literally better than ever. He went just 10-10 that year, but in 1977, at the age of 34, he won 20 games for the first time ever and finished second in Cy Young

Award balloting. He followed that season with win totals of 17, 21, and 22. He continued pitching until the age of 46 and finished his career with 288 victories.

Today, Tommy John surgery, as it's known, occurs frequently enough that the recovery rate is about 85 to 90 percent and rehabilitation requires only about a year for pitchers and six months for position players. In fact, many pitchers discover they can throw harder than they could before the surgery (most likely as a result of all the strength training during the rehabilitation period, not as a result of the new elbow ligament). It is an understatement to say that Tommy John surgery has saved the careers of countless pitchers, making baseball today a better game.

Randy Johnson
"The Big Unit"
Pitcher, 1989–2009

Six-feet, ten inches tall, Johnson used his long left arm to whip the ball toward home plate at 100 mph, scaring left-handed hitters so much that only a handful even dared to stand in against him. Right-handers fared little better. It took him a few years to master his control, but once he figured it all out, he posted a run of seasons as great as any pitcher in history. He won at least 17 games 10 times; led the league in strikeouts nine times, including a momentous 372 in 2001; won five Cy Young Awards and finished second three times and third another time; led the league in strikeouts five times; and carried the Arizona Diamondbacks to the 2001 World Series title with clutch pitching performances, including saving Game 7 a day after pitching seven innings in Game 6. Because his first big season didn't come until he was 27 years old and injuries robbed him of several prime seasons, I thought he had no chance to reach 300 victories. But he persevered until age 45 and finished with 303 victories and 4,875 strikeouts. He was elected to the Hall of Fame on his first try in 2015.

Intimidation is an overused term in professional sports, but it's completely appropriate when discussing Randy Johnson pitching against left-handed hitters (they batted just .199 against him with a .294 slugging percentage). One of the great All-Star game moments came in the 1993 contest, when left-handed John Kruk stood in against Johnson. It was Johnson's second All-Star appearance, but because interleague play hadn't happened yet, almost no National Leaguer had ever faced him. And poor Kruk was the first lefty to do the honors.

Johnson's first pitch flew three feet over Kruk's head, and it became immediately clear that Kruk wanted no more to do with Randy Johnson. The next pitch was a fastball right over the plate, and Kruk bailed out of the box as he took it for strike one. He shook his head and laughed, knowing he was overmatched. The next two pitches were over the outside part of the plate, but by the time Kruk swung, he was halfway up the first base line. It was the easiest strikeout of Johnson's career.

Walter Johnson
"The Big Train"
Pitcher, 1907–27
Manager, 1929–35

A contender for the title of greatest pitcher of all time, Johnson recorded 417 victories with 12 seasons of 20-plus victories, five ERA titles, 12 strikeout crowns, and a record 110 shutouts—among many outstanding achievements. He possessed the best fastball of his time as well as magnificent control, and he was among the biggest stars in the game almost every year he pitched. He finished his career with 3,508 career strikeouts, considered an unbreakable record until the 1980s.

Saddled with mediocre-to-poor teams most of his 21-year career, the Washington Senators ace had to wait 17 years before he was able to showcase his enormous talents in the World Series. But he made the most of his opportunity, winning the final game of the 1924 Series against the Giants with a clutch four-inning relief performance just two days after pitching a complete game.

A consummate gentleman, Johnson never questioned an umpire's authority and hated to throw inside pitches for fear of injuring opposing hitters—a character "flaw" that TY COBB, among others, exploited to great success by crowding the plate. Such knowledge makes Johnson's statistics even more impressive.

Willie Keeler
"Wee Willie"
Outfielder, 1892–09

The five-foot, four-and-a-half-inch, 140-pound Keeler is most famous for having described his batting style with the immortal words, "I HIT 'EM WHERE THEY AIN'T"—a philosophy that he put to good use. With 2,962 career hits for the Dodgers, Orioles, Giants, and Yankees, Keeler compiled a .345 career average, including a high of .424, won two batting titles, and shares the National League record with a 44-game hitting streak in 1897. A skilled bunter, Keeler played most of his career when fouls were not counted as strikes, so he could remain at bat bunting foul balls until he got one in; the rule was changed in 1901 partly in an effort to negate his success.

Mike Kelly
"King"
Outfielder/catcher, 1878–93
Manager, 1887–91

A stylish star who would wear an ascot and silk hat to the ballpark, Kelly was perhaps the most popular player of his day. He was also a great player, although his statistics, while impressive, do not seem to reflect his skills. He played all nine positions and helped revolutionize catching by becoming one of the first to use finger signals to call pitches. He stole as many as 84 bases in one season as the inventor of the hook slide, led his teams to six pennants, and was purchased by a rival team in 1887 for a record $10,000—$5,000 of which went to Kelly himself for the use of his photograph for team promotions. A song about him, "Slide, Kelly, Slide," became a major pop hit. He toured with a Vaudeville troupe. And he may have been the inspiration for "CASEY AT THE BAT." He lived fast and died young, succumbing to pneumonia at the height of his popularity at age 37.

Sandy Koufax
Pitcher, 1955–66

The most dominant pitcher of his era, Koufax began his career as an erratic fastballer with control problems and compiled a record of 36-40 during his first six years with the Dodgers. But before the 1961 season, on the advice of coaches, Koufax changed his pitching motion, and the rest is history: five consecutive ERA titles; three 20-win seasons; four strikeout crowns, including a league-record 382; three Cy Young Awards and one MVP; four no-hitters, including a perfect game; six All-Star appearances; three pennants; and two World Series championships. In fact, his run from 1961–66 is hailed as the greatest period of dominance ever by a pitcher (although RANDY JOHNSON'S 1997–2002 and PEDRO MARTINEZ'S 1997–2003 are other serious contenders for that title)

Following his stupendous 1966 season, which cemented his reputation among the baseball gods, the 31-year-old Koufax did the unthinkable: He retired from the game, blaming chronic arthritis caused partly by a 1964 injury. The Hall of Fame welcomed him on the first ballot in 1972 as its youngest-ever inductee. If Koufax had played 30 years later, his career would not have ended so prematurely. He would have been protected and kept on a strict pitch count; he would have undergone surgery and taken a year off to recover. He would win 16 to 19 games a year instead of 22 to 28, but he would have pitched until age 40. In short, he would have been Pedro Martinez.

Napoleon Lajoie
"Larry"
Second baseman, 1896–1914
Manager, 1905–09
Nap Lajoie was probably the American League's most popular player during his career—popular enough that his Cleveland team was actually known as the "Naps" in his honor for several years. He was also one of its best overall performers. He could hit, hit for power, field, and throw; the only thing he lacked was speed. Lajoie also set a 20th-century record for batting average with a .426 mark in the American League's inaugural 1901 campaign.

Lajoie began his career with the Philadelphia Phillies in 1897 and four years later, despite legal threats, jumped over to the AL's Athletics, becoming one of the focal points of the 1901 AMERICAN LEAGUE WAR. In fact, the National League took the case all the way to the Pennsylvania Supreme Court, which prohibited Lajoie from playing with the Athletics. But AL President Ban Johnson was a step ahead of the NL: He simply transferred Lajoie to Cleveland beginning with the 1902 season, where Lajoie would play until 1914. There, he won two batting titles and led the league at various times in hits, doubles, RBIs, and slugging percentage. The final totals: 3,242 hits, 1,599 RBIs, a .338 average, and a 1937 Hall of Fame induction.

Charlie Lau
Coach
Widely proclaimed as baseball's foremost hitting guru until his death in 1984, Lau's theories have influenced a generation of players. Lau himself played 11 seasons as a catcher for six teams, only once appearing in more than 100 games and never batting .300 for a full season.

But he was a hard-working student of the game who developed his successful theories through countless hours of analyzing the best hitters. Lau emphasized a balanced stance, an aggressive forward motion, and a slight downswing on the ball. TED WILLIAMS and others who disagree with Lau's theories have argued that they rob a player of his power—and indeed, none of Lau's direct disciples ever hit 40 homers. But it's hard to argue with a batting theory that strongly influenced GEORGE BRETT, WADE BOGGS, and Hal McRae, who among them led the league dozens of times in various offensive categories.

Buck Leonard
First baseman, Negro leagues, 1933–50
A 1972 Hall of Fame inductee, Leonard was one of the NEGRO LEAGUES' most feared sluggers, teaming with JOSH GIBSON on the HOMESTEAD GRAYS to form a 1-2 punch equal to the Ruth-Gehrig tandem that then existed in that "other" league. Leonard played an intelligent first base but was known better for his high-average power hitting, earning him the moniker "The Black LOU GEHRIG." By the mid-1940s, Leonard was one of the league's most popular players, and he was probably its third-highest-paid player, earning $1,000 per month during the season—just below Gibson and SATCHEL PAIGE. According to some sources, Leonard was offered a major league contract by BILL VEECK'S St. Louis Browns when he was 45 years old, but he turned it down, fearing that he would embarrass himself. I really wish he had taken the offer and joined the league as a pinch hitter or fill-in first baseman.

Pop Lloyd
Shortstop, Negro leagues, 1905–31
Lloyd was called "the Black Wagner" while active, and HONUS WAGNER said he felt honored to have been compared to him. Lloyd was probably the NEGRO LEAGUES' most popular player during his career, a slugging shortstop known—like Wagner—for scooping up infield dirt and rocks when fielding grounders. Active until the age of 58— hence the nickname "Pop"—Lloyd missed by 40 years the chance to play in the white major leagues. But he was philosophical about his playing career: "I do not consider that I was born at the wrong time," he said in 1949, two years after JACKIE ROBINSON'S major league debut. "I felt it was the right time, for I had a chance to prove the ability of our race in this sport, and because many of us did our very best to uphold the traditions of the game and of the world of sport,

we have given the Negro a greater opportunity now to be accepted into the major leagues with other Americans." Lloyd died in 1965, seven years before the Hall of Fame dedicated part of its shrine to Negro league stars and 12 years before he was selected for the honor.

Greg Maddux
Pitcher, 1986–2008

One of the best pitchers of his generation—and any generation—Maddux dominated not through an overpowering fastball or a devastating curveball. He dominated with unmatched intelligence, pinpoint control, and a huge repertoire of different pitches. BARRY BONDS, who is one of the few players who had consistent success against him, once said that Maddux possessed 17 different fastballs, each thrown with a different combination of speed, rotation, and arm motion. He probably had eight different curveballs and six different change-ups and… you get the picture. That variety—plus his mastery of every pitch plus his knowledge of opposing hitters—is how he was able to win at 15 games per year for 17 straight seasons—an all-time record—with excellent winning percentages and amazing ERAs. His best season was probably 1995 when he was 19-2 with a 1.63 ERA. Watching him pitch was like watching an artist at work.

Most impressive of all, Maddux not only played during the steroid era, he also played home games in hitter's parks during his prime years, which makes his four Cy Young Awards and all-around dominance all the more impressive.

Mickey Mantle
"The Mick"
Outfielder, 1951–68

Undoubtedly the greatest switch-hitter of all time, a case can be made that, at his peak, Mantle was also the greatest center fielder of all time, with apologies to MAYS, DiMAGGIO, and COBB. Among that group, only Cobb was faster, and only Mays was a better fielder. None had more power, none judged the strike zone better, and none played on more pennant winners. During his 18-year career, Mantle won three MVP Awards, slugged 536 homers, won the 1956 TRIPLE CROWN, and led his Yankees to 12 World Series.

Ah, but the injuries. Mantle's countless ailments cost him thousands of at bats and, conservatively, 100 home runs. Compounding the injuries was his refusal to care for his body—an attitude that probably stemmed from his knowledge that Hodgkin's Disease had taken the lives of nearly every male member of his family by middle age, and Mantle believed he would never live past 40.

Following his premature retirement at the age of 36, Mantle became haunted by the idea that he could have been better: a better player on the field and a better father to his children. The stress he put on himself led to alcoholism, and in 1994, the 62-year-old Mantle checked into the Betty Ford Clinic, resolving to overcome his disease and to exorcise the ghosts inside him. Only weeks after finishing his treatment, tragedy struck: His 36-year-old son died of a heart attack after earlier battling Hodgkin's and a drug addiction. Then in 1995, Mantle was diagnosed with cancer and underwent liver transplant surgery. But the cancer had spread too quickly, and the disease took Mantle's life. When he passed away, the entire nation mourned the loss.

Firpo Marberry
Pitcher, 1923–36

Every baseball innovation has a grandfather, and when it comes to modern relief pitching, Marberry is it. Before Marberry, teams' bullpens were generally filled with failed starters or regular rotation members in between starts. But beginning in his second year in the bigs, Marberry was mostly assigned to the bullpen and summoned into close games in the late innings. That year, 1924, Marberry pitched in 50 games, finished 31 of them, and notched 15 saves, leading the league in all three totals (albeit retroactively, because no one at the time tracked such things). He also helped the Washington Senators win their first World Series.

It took about a decade, but other teams eventually began adopting the idea of the relief ace. The first teams to go all in with closers were pennant winners: the Yankees with Johnny Murphy and Joe Page, the Dodgers with Hugh Casey, and the Phillies with Jim Konstanty (who even won the 1950 MVP Award). By the 1950s, most teams had closers getting 10-20 saves per year, and the numbers kept growing. Now, it's unthinkable not to have a closer.

Since the 1990s, closers have been called in almost exclusively to protect leads in the ninth inning. Is that the optimal use of their talents? A lot of researchers say no, but who knows? What we need now is some innovation in the use of relief aces. Bring him in with the score tied or your team down a run. Let him pitch 2-3 innings every few days instead of 1 inning every day. Just try something new and see what happens. That's what Senators manager Bucky Harris did with Firpo Marberry in 1924, and it worked out great. It's time for some new thinking.

Roger Maris
Outfielder, 1957–68

Maris will forever be remembered for a single feat: smashing 61 homers in 1961 to break BABE RUTH'S single-season record (*see* 61; 1961 SEASON). Of course, that record was shattered in 1998 by MARK MCGWIRE, but Maris's story remains important. Unlike the joy and excitement that ensued when McGwire broke the record, Maris faced a far more hostile environment as he attacked Ruth's record. In fact, the pressure placed on Maris during that momentous year by the fans, the media, teammates, opposing players, and the league office helped extinguish the light of a player who was turning into one of baseball's brightest stars. In 1960, the Yankee right fielder had captured the MVP Award with a wonderful season. After 1961, however, he wouldn't top 33 homers or 100 RBIs—although he was still in his 20s. Even so, at his peak, he was a complete ballplayer, with good defensive skills to go along with his dead-pull hitting.

For many years, Maris was the subject of a Hall of Fame debate. Some argued that the most famous record in baseball, plus his general excellence as a player, should have been enough to put him in the Hall. Others argued that the Hall should reward greatness over the course of an entire career, not just over one or two seasons. Hall of Fame voters always took the latter view. In earlier writings, even I predicted that eventually the Hall would enshrine him, simply because I wrongly believed Maris would hold his record forever. Although I couldn't have predicted McGwire's great season, it is now obvious that my belief in the infallibility of the record was more than a little naïve.

Still, Maris's chances for induction have actually received a boost in recent years due to the revelations about steroid use among modern players. At the height of the steroid scandal, some activists—newspaper columnists, politicians looking to score points—lobbied to have all recent home run records stricken from the books, putting Maris back on top of the list. They claim that only Maris's record is "clean." I think that's a ridiculous suggestion built on hysteria and hyperbole, but I can easily envision a future in which the call for clean records results in induction for Maris.

Billy Martin
Infielder, 1950–61
Manager, 1969, 1971–83, 1985, 1988
A scrappy but truly average infielder during his playing days, Martin made his name on the basis of two things: his managing skills and his temper. Growing up in Berkeley, California, Martin fought early and often. And throughout his career as both a player and manager, Martin seemed to keep finding himself in situations where that training came in handy. "Lots of people look up to Billy Martin," said JIM BOUTON. "That's because he just knocked him down."

It was his hotheadedness that got him hired and fired as manager nearly a dozen times—including five times with GEORGE STEIN-BRENNER'S Yankees. Martin's self-destructive behavior finally caught up with him in 1989 when his truck skidded off the road and crashed, killing himself and injuring a friend. Both Martin and his friend were drunk at the time, and the friend was supposedly in better shape to drive. Martin wasn't wearing his seatbelt.

Occasionally there is talk of inducting Martin into the Hall of Fame. I don't think he belongs. While he was a resourceful manager who won four division titles and two pennants, he was not an all-time great. His career won-loss totals don't measure up to the real Hall of Fame managers, such as DUROCHER, ALSTON, MCCARTHY, or MCGRAW. Factor in Martin's boorish behavior off the field and the fact that he couldn't keep a job—does that spell Hall of Fame? It doesn't to me.

Pedro Martinez
Pitcher, 1992–2009
"I am a pitcher because I like the challenge of being responsible for the game, of being in charge of the action. If the shortstop makes an error, I am responsible. I let the batter hit the ball," Pedro Martinez once said, explaining the attitude that propelled him to the top of baseball.

Winner of three Cy Young Awards, Martinez had possibly the greatest combination of power (a 97-mph fastball) and control of any pitcher ever, and he ranks first all-time among modern pitchers in his ratio of strikeouts to walks. During his historic 1999 season, Martinez rarely allowed hitters to touch anything. While leading his Red Sox to the wild card title, he won 23 games (vs. just 4 losses), posted a 2.07 ERA (in FENWAY PARK, no less), and struck out 313 hitters to set a major league record with 13.2 Ks per nine innings (since surpassed by RANDY JOHNSON). He followed that up with another Cy Young Award in 2000. In all, he finished in the top five in Cy Young balloting seven times.

After the age of 30, injuries limited him to just six or seven innings per start, or around 100 pitches (a fact not fully appreciated by his manager Grady Little in that notorious 2003 AMERICAN LEAGUE CHAMPIONSHIP GAME against the Yankees). But for those 100 pitches, he was about as good as anyone.

He finished his career with 219 victories against 100 losses for an astounding .687 winning percentage, second highest (behind WHITEY FORD) among modern pitchers with at least 200 wins. And the Hall of Fame elected him on the first ballot in 2015.

Christy Mathewson
"Big Six," "Matty"
Pitcher, 1900–16
Manager, 1916–18

Mathewson was perhaps the most admired baseball hero of his time, a college-educated, clean-cut gentleman in an era dominated by scrappy, uneducated athletes. And the New York Giants star could pitch a little, too: 12 seasons of 20-plus victories, including four of 30 wins or more; five ERA crowns; five strikeout titles; four pennants; and 373 career victories to place third on the all-time list. Famous for a "fadeaway" pitch, now called a screwball, Mathewson was also the master of control and intelligent pitching, once going 68 consecutive innings without issuing a walk. His greatest performance on the mound came during the 1905 World Series, when Matty tossed three shutouts against the Athletics in six days.

Off the field, Matty demonstrated his integrity and courage as one of the only famous names to stand up to gamblers. During the crooked 1919 World Series (*see* 1919: THE BLACK SOX SCANDAL), he and columnist Hugh Fullerton worked together to identify suspicious plays. Earlier, as Reds manager, he had suspended HAL CHASE for "indifferent play" and suspected him of taking bribes. Few other major leaguers had the guts to make such accusations.

In 1936, Mathewson was chosen as one of the first five players to enter the Hall of Fame—an honor shared with BABE RUTH, WALTER JOHNSON, TY COBB, and HONUS WAGNER. Alas, Mathewson was the only member of the "Immortal Five" not in attendance at the induction. He had died in 1925 of tuberculosis possibly stemming from exposure to poison gas in World War I during a training exercise.

Willie Mays
"The Say-Hey Kid"
Outfielder, 1948–73 including the Negro leagues
Mays's legend transcends baseball. First the numbers: 660 career homers, now fourth on the all-time list; two MVP Awards; two seasons of 50-plus homers; 10 seasons of 100-plus RBIs; 20 All-Star Game appearances—the list could go on forever. He could steal bases, leading the league four times. And he could field: His 440-foot, back-to-home-plate catch in dead center field in the 1954 World Series is one of baseball's most famous moments (*see* 1954: THE CATCH)—and Mays always said it wasn't even his best grab.

He played his first professional years in the NEGRO LEAGUES just as major league integration began to take hold. In 1951, he came to the Giants and immediately went into a horrible slump. But after receiving a vote of confidence from manager LEO DUROCHER, Mays began to hit; his first homer came off of the best left-hander in baseball at the time, WARREN SPAHN. (Later, Spahn would joke, "I'll never forgive myself. We might have gotten rid of Willie forever if I'd only struck him out.")

Following his Rookie of the Year campaign, Mays lost two years to the Korean War, seasons he wished he could have back at his retirement because he came within only 55 of breaking BABE RUTH'S career home run record. He returned from service in 1954 to slug 41 homers, win the batting title, and capture MVP honors while helping his Giants to the championship.

For the rest of his career, baseball fans stood in awe of his fantastic play—enough so that many fans and writers have called Mays the greatest player in the history of the game. I lean toward Babe Ruth for that honor, but I can understand their point. As a player, Mays could literally do it all. As a cultural icon, he was nearly the equal of Ruth, for he seemed to represent all that was good in America. With his joyous enthusiasm and always-smiling face, he seemed to embody a passion for life that all Americans could aspire to. And, like JACKIE ROBINSON'S, Mays's acceptance as a national hero certainly helped the civil rights movement. When JOE DiMAGGIO died in 1999, Mays became the unofficial holder of the title "greatest living ballplayer"—a title he truly deserves.

Joe McCarthy
"Marse Joe"
Manager, 1926–50
A Hall of Fame manager with baseball's all-time highest winning percentage (.614), McCarthy skippered three teams during his 24-year career. He first managed the Cubs, where he won the 1929 pennant, then moved to the Yankees, where he achieved his greatest success: eight pennants and seven World Series titles in 15 years. He finished his career with the Red Sox, where he came close but couldn't win a pennant from 1948 to 1950.

Despite his success, McCarthy had his detractors, who called him a "push-button manager." After all, how hard is it to win games when you have the likes of RUTH, GEHRIG, and DiMAGGIO in your lineup? In modern terms, he's a little like JOE TORRE, who won all those pennants thanks to a lineup filled with star players and an owner who wasn't afraid to buy new stars when necessary. And when McCarthy actually had to do some real managing with the Red Sox, he came up short year after year. With guys like McCarthy, Torre, and even STENGEL, the greatness of a manager is a chicken-and-egg thing: are they great managers because their teams are great, or are their teams great because they're great managers? I don't think we can ever truly answer that question.

Tim McCarver
Catcher, 1959–80
Broadcaster
McCarver is best known for two things. First, he was STEVE CARLTON'S personal catcher during their times with St. Louis and Philadelphia; in fact, it was joked that when they died, they would be buried 60 feet, six inches apart. When his playing career ended,

McCarver went into broadcasting, and it is there that he has achieved his greatest fame. As the lead color commentator for Fox Sports, he is probably the most recognizable baseball broadcaster working today. He has won three Emmys, was awarded the Ford C. Frick Award by the Hall of Fame, and regularly covers the biggest games in baseball: World Series, playoffs, All-Star Game. Criticism of McCarver is almost as rampant as praise for his work. Among the knocks: that he overanalyzes, that he states the obvious, that he tries to be clever when he should just try to be clear. But he is a keen observer of the action on the field, and he has a great memory.

He also once made the most famously prescient observation in modern broadcasting history: It was the bottom of the ninth of Game 7 of the 2001 World Series between New York and Arizona. Yankee relief ace MARIANO RIVERA was on the mound having just allowed the tying run, and now was just trying to send it to extra innings. With the bases loaded and one out, the Yankees had to play the infield in as Rivera faced left-hander Luis Gonzalez. McCarver observed that Rivera's cut fastball often results in bloop hits that go just past shortstop. The next pitch was a cut fastball. Gonzalez swung and blooped a hit that went just past shortstop. If the Yankees had been playing regular depth, DEREK JETER might have caught it. Instead, the ball landed safely and the Diamondbacks won the game and the Series. I know McCarver made many observations every game that don't pan out. But this one was on the game's biggest stage, and he deserves credit for it.

Willie McCovey
"Stretch"
First baseman, 1959–80
Baseball history is dotted with men who earned the admiration and respect of fans, teammates, and opposing players not just for their stellar work on the field but also for their quiet grace and dignity off it. HONUS WAGNER, STAN MUSIAL, and LOU GEHRIG are members of this fraternity. So is Willie McCovey. Beginning and concluding his 22-year career in San Francisco, McCovey remains the most popular player in San Francisco Giants history. Every year, the Giants honor one player who exemplifies sportsmanship and service to the community with the "Willie Mac Award." And when the Giants opened their new ballpark in 2000, the stretch of the Bay on the other side of the right field fence was renamed McCovey Cove. Of course, it was McCovey's play on the field that carried him to the

Hall of Fame: 521 career home runs, an NL-record 18 grand slams, three home run titles, the 1959 Rookie of the Year award, and the 1969 MVP Award.

Joe McGinnity
"Iron Man"
Pitcher, 1899–1908

Famous for pitching both ends of doubleheaders—including three twin-bill victories in one month—McGinnity's nickname originally stemmed from his work in an iron foundry but perfectly applied to his pitching abilities. In addition to the doubleheaders and two 30-win seasons, the 1946 Hall of Famer compiled a superficially amazing 246 victories during just 10 seasons in the majors, mostly with the Giants.

The reason he is included in this book is that he is a good example of how much pitching has changed since the turn of the last century. McGinnity played in an era when pitchers could conserve their energy against some batters because the threat of the home run was virtually nonexistent. He and his contemporaries could therefore rack up 350-plus innings and 30-plus victories in the same way today's pitchers throw 250 innings with 20 victories. In their own context, McGinnity's stats are really no better than those of Ferguson Jenkins or CATFISH HUNTER, whose numbers don't seem as impressive on the surface.

Mark McGwire
"Big Mac"
First baseman, 1986–2001

At retirement, McGwire went down in history as the greatest slugger of all time. A few years earlier, however, nobody would have thought so. Back in 1995, when I wrote the first edition of *The Book of Baseball Literacy*, the biggest oversight I made was failing to include McGwire. Yet the reason was simple: It looked like injuries had derailed what had been a very promising career.

In his first full season, with the Oakland A's, McGwire slammed 49 home runs, a rookie record, to win the 1987 Rookie of the Year Award. His next few seasons were inconsistent, but he hit rock-bottom in 1990 when he batted .201 with just 22 homers in 154 games. He bounced back in 1992 by smacking 42 home runs and leading the league in slugging percentage. But then the back injuries came and nearly ended his career. He played 27 games in 1993, 47 in 1994, and 104 in 1995. Still, the power was evident: He slugged 57 homers in those 178 games. But it wasn't at all clear that McGwire could stay healthy long enough to fulfill his promise.

In 1996, however, McGwire got healthy, and he embarked on the most amazing run for a slugger since BABE RUTH (though surpassed by BARRY BONDS from 2000-2004). That year, McGwire slammed 52 homers in just 130 games. The next season, he raised that total to 58, despite being traded from the A's to the Cardinals in mid-season. And in 1998, he put together a season for the ages (*see* 1998: THE SEASON THAT SAVED BASEBALL). He and Sammy Sosa staged a summer-long assault on ROGER MARIS'S single-season home run record. Sosa finished with 66, but McGwire posted an even more stunning total: 70. The next season, McGwire came back with an almost equally stunning total of 65. All this despite being pitched around relentlessly: He was walked 162 times in 1998 and 133 times in 1999.

Yet it has all been tainted. During his 1998 chase, a reporter found in his locker a bottle of a dietary supplement called Androstenedione, which was banned by the Olympics and many other sports leagues, but not baseball. Andro is a steroid "precursor," and in 2004, its sale was even banned completely in the United States. Its presence in McGwire's locker led to speculation that his power surge was fueled by steroids, but it was only in the wake of the BALCO scandal and JOSE CANSECO'S book that people really took a hard look at McGwire's exploits. McGwire didn't help himself when, during his Congressional testimony in 2005, he refused to discuss whether he took steroids at all in his life. "I'm not here to talk about the past," he said infamously.

In 2010, when returned to the Cardinals as batting coach, McGwire finally came clean and admitted taking steroids during his career. He apologized for it, but claimed that he injected only to recover from injuries, not to improve his batting stroke. Most observers didn't believe him, and he seemed to get no credit for making the admission and apology at all. And so what once appeared to be a smooth sail into the Hall of Fame now looks impossible. He received only 23.5 percent of the vote in his first year of eligibility in 2007 and hasn't improved on it since. It's hard to see a path to Cooperstown for

McGwire, despite the impressive statistics and the impact he had on the game.

John McGraw
"Muggsy," "Little Napoleon"
Third baseman, 1891–1906
Manager, 1901–32

Feisty, combative, scrappy—three words often used to describe McGraw. During his playing days as third baseman of the rough-and-tumble Baltimore Orioles, McGraw was known for a good batting eye and a fierce desire to win that included such actions as tripping baserunners, spiking fielders, and baiting umpires—and his punching hand was always at the ready. But it was as a manager that McGraw achieved baseball immortality. During his 30 years at the helm, McGraw's New York Giants captured 10 pennants and three World Series.

Hailed as a managerial genius by contemporaries and historians, McGraw helped mold the careers of a dozen Hall of Famers, including CHRISTY MATHEWSON, CARL HUBBELL, and MEL OTT. What was the key to his success? His coach Arlie Latham summed up his strength better than anyone else ever did: "McGraw eats gunpowder every morning for breakfast and washes it down with warm blood." If you screwed up, McGraw made you pay. If you played well, he loved you and was fiercely loyal. If you weren't cutting it, he released you (then maybe hired you as a coach). If you were on the other team, he disliked you. If you were in the other league, he loathed you. And his players were expected to feel the same way or incur his wrath. The word "legendary" gets overused, but it was practically invented for John McGraw.

Denny McLain
Pitcher, 1963–72

McLain is the answer to the trivia question, Who was the last pitcher to win 30 games in one season? Actually, McLain had a much more interesting life than his statistics can possibly show. He won back-to-back Cy Young Awards (in 1968 for his 31-6 season and the following year in a tie with Mike Cuellar) and led his Tigers to the 1968 World Series. But his career took a fast downward spiral after that. First, he was suspended from the league for bookmaking and consorting with gamblers. Then he got caught illegally carrying a gun—another suspension. And he dumped buckets of ice water on sportswriters to earn yet another suspension. Such activities, of course, affected his playing ability—and just three years after being on top of the baseball world, not even 30 years old, he was out of the game.

But his troubles didn't stop there: He went bankrupt. He suffered a mild heart attack. He was caught smuggling cocaine. Finally, in 1984, he was convicted of a number of charges, including racketeering and extortion, and was sent to jail. The conviction was overturned on a technicality after McLain had spent 29 months in prison, but he later pleaded guilty to the charges and received probation in addition to the time served. In today's debate over whether athletes are role models, McLain serves as a strong argument for "no."

Dave McNally
Pitcher, 1962–75

While CATFISH HUNTER was baseball's first actual free agent, McNally and ANDY MESSERSMITH were the two men who actually pioneered the system for FREE AGENCY in use today. McNally was one of the top pitchers in baseball for several years, a four-time 20-game winner with the Orioles. But in 1975, unhappy with the Montreal Expos' contract offer after an off-season trade, McNally began playing without a signed contract; the club renewed his previous year's contract automatically, as clubs believed they could do at the time. By the middle of the year, an injured wrist began to bother him, and he decided to retire.

Knowing McNally's contract situation, MARVIN MILLER of the MAJOR LEAGUE BASEBALL PLAYERS ASSOCIATION (MLBPA) asked him to help in their test case against baseball's reserve clause; Messersmith, for different reasons, also volunteered to be part of the test. The MLBPA believed that not having signed the contract made the two men free agents at the end of the year. In a stunning decision, arbitrator Peter Seitz agreed with the MLBPA and granted Messersmith and McNally the right to negotiate with any club. Although Messersmith was the focal point of the case, McNally's role should not be forgotten: The Expos offered him a 1976 contract for over $100,000—in effect trying to buy him off to avoid the grievance against baseball—but the 33-year-old McNally remained firm. He turned down a lucrative offer in order to help future ballplayers.

Andy Messersmith
Pitcher, 1968–78

Messersmith was one of baseball's top pitchers for several years in the early 1970s, earning as much as $90,000 per year. Before the 1974 season, he'd been traded from the Angels to the Dodgers, where he enjoyed his most productive season. So in 1975, he asked Dodgers owner WALTER O'MALLEY to include a no-trade clause in his contract. O'Malley refused and renewed the contract without Messersmith's signature, as clubs were allowed to do because of the RESERVE CLAUSE written into every player's contract.

Messersmith, along with DAVE MCNALLY, played the entire season without signing the contract—an action that the MAJOR LEAGUE BASEBALL PLAYERS ASSOCIATION (MLBPA) believed would automatically make the two players FREE AGENTS at the end of the season. The owners contested the assumption, and the case went to arbitration, where arbitrator Peter Seitz ruled in favor of the players in a momentous decision. Although McNally chose to retire, Messersmith signed a multiyear contract with the Atlanta Braves worth $1 million but failed to live up to the big money. Traded twice again, he returned to the Dodgers, a shadow of his former self.

Ironically, as former MLBPA president MARVIN MILLER points out in his excellent memoir, *A Whole Different Ballgame*, O'Malley fought to keep Messersmith a Dodger forever by binding him to the reserve system; what Messersmith wanted was a no-trade clause that *would have kept him* a Dodger forever. Instead, O'Malley's stubbornness accelerated the free agency era.

Minnie Minoso
Infielder/outfielder, 1946–64, 1976, 1980, including the Negro leagues

Back in the 1990s, the commissioner's office halted what it considered a travesty: the White Sox's plan to suit up Minnie Minoso for a game to continue his streak of playing a game in every decade since the 1940s. The Sox had pulled the stunt twice before, in 1976—when the 53-year-old Minoso became the oldest player ever to get a hit in the major leagues—and again in 1980. These antics unfortunately altered the image of a man who, when young and healthy, was one of baseball's most exciting players.

Though he didn't play in the majors full-time until age 28 because of baseball's COLOR LINE, Minoso stayed around long enough to lead the league at various times in hits, stolen bases, doubles, and triples while tallying 1,963 hits and a career average of .298—mostly with the White Sox. In the current debate over players who are worthy of the Hall of Fame but not in it, Minoso's name often arises. Does he belong? Look at it this way: Minoso didn't have a full-time major league job until he was 28. Give him back six of those years and he probably ends up with close to 3,000 hits, at least 1,000 more RBIs, and a higher batting average—definitely Hall of Fame material. It was the color of his skin that kept Minoso from enjoying a more productive career. It shouldn't keep him out of the Hall of Fame, too.

Joe Morgan
"Little Joe"
Second baseman, 1963–84
"Little Joe" stood just five-feet-seven, but among baseball's best second baseman, no one ever stood taller. The winner of back-to-back MVPs in 1975 and 1976, Morgan excelled in every facet of the game and, in many ways, was the perfect ballplayer. At the plate, he hit for a medium-high average with a great batting eye and good power— enough that he was the all-time leading home run hitter among second basemen until Ryne Sandberg (then Jeff Kent) broke the record. On the base paths, Morgan combined speed with brains to compile 689 career steals at an 81 percent success rate. And in the field, he won five GOLD GLOVES. He ignited Cincinnati's "BIG RED MACHINE" to two World Series victories during his MVP years, refusing to be overshadowed by illustrious teammates PETE ROSE and JOHNNY BENCH. But his winning didn't end with the Reds. He joined the Astros in 1980 and helped them win the division title. Two years later, he nearly took the Giants to the playoffs, instead settling for knocking the Dodgers out of the division race with a home run on the last day of the season. The following year, he moved to Philadelphia, where he helped aging "Wheeze Kids" win the NL pennant. Detect a pattern here? Morgan was a winner, and he's the guy I would pick if I could choose anyone in history to be my second baseman.

Thurman Munson
Catcher, 1969–79
Grouchy and proud, enigmatic and immensely talented, Munson continued the New York Yankees string of superstar catchers—Bill

Dickey, YOGI BERRA, Elston Howard, and Munson—who among them won five MVPs and numerous pennants. Munson could hit for power and average and he could even run a little. Behind the plate, he had no superiors. He was, in fact, in the midst of a Hall of Fame-caliber career when tragedy struck. On August 2, 1979, the 32-year-old Munson was flying his private jet home to be with his family, as he often did, when he lost control and crashed. His death cast a pall over YANKEE STADIUM, where Munson had endeared himself with the fans through his consistently gritty performances. In this era of pampered superstars, it's unlikely that the likes of Munson will be seen again.

Stan Musial
"Stan the Man"
First baseman/outfielder, 1941–63

They love Stan Musial so much in St. Louis that they built a statue of him to stand guard in front of BUSCH STADIUM. Such is a fitting tribute to a man who was a rock of consistency throughout his 22-year career. Durable and strong, he never missed more than 20 games in a season nor batted below .300 until he was 38 years old—a full 17 years straight. He led the league 46 times in various major offensive categories, won three MVPs, helped his teams to four pennants, and appeared in 24 All-Star games—where he holds career records for All-Star home runs (6), extra-base hits (8), and total bases (40). At his retirement in 1963, he held almost every National League career batting record, including hits (3,630), runs (1,949), doubles (725), and RBIs (1,951).

A fan favorite wherever he went, Musial earned his nickname in Brooklyn, where fans would grimly say, "There's that man again" whenever Musial stood at the plate in his trademark "peek-a-boo" batting stance that looked as if he were peering around a corner.

For his career, Musial rarely struck out, showed excellent power, never got hurt, and played every inning, every at bat as if it were the seventh game of the World Series. Musial was, in fact, a near-flawless ballplayer who earned the respect of everyone from opposing players to reporters to rival fans, and he belongs in a select group of superstar players—along with the likes of WAGNER, MATHEWSON, JOHNSON, and GEHRIG—who were universally beloved for their sportsmanship and excellence.

Phil Niekro
Pitcher, 1964–87

Niekro didn't become a regular starter until the age of 28, but he still was able to win 318 games and lose 274. The key to his success was the Niekro knuckleball, which he perfected while toiling for the lowly Atlanta Braves. By employing a pitch that puts little strain on the arm, Niekro was the National League's preeminent workhorse throughout the 1970s, leading the league in innings pitched and complete games four times each. He also led the league in victories twice and in losses a record four straight times—including a serendipitous season when he led in both wins (21) and losses (20). He remained an effective pitcher until the age of 48—121 of his victories and 103 of his losses came after he turned 40. Combined with his brother Joe, who knuckled his way to a 22-year career of his own, the Niekro brothers totaled 539 career victories, 10 wins more than Jim and GAYLORD PERRY for the all-time lead among major league siblings.

Joe Nuxhall
Pitcher, 1944, 1952–66

When the World War II draft took most able-bodied men, major league baseball was forced to make do with what was left. Fifteen-year-old Joe Nuxhall was too young for war, but not too young, according to the Cincinnati Reds, to pitch in the majors. In his only appearance of 1944, the nervous Nuxhall faced nine batters, getting two outs, surrendering two hits, and walking five. He then went to the minors and resurfaced in 1952 to start his real career as a productive if unspectacular hurler, finishing his career with a 135–117 record over 16 seasons. The funny thing is, the Reds originally asked Nuxhall's father to try out for the club, but Joe, who accompanied his father by chance, impressed the Reds more.

When the club signed him, he was believed to be the youngest-ever major leaguer; later research unearthed a 14-year-old named Fred Chapman who pitched for Philadelphia's American Association club in 1887.

Sadaharu Oh
Outfielder, Japanese leagues, 1959–77

With 868 career homers, Oh qualifies as the world's all-time home run champion. When he first came up with the Yomiuri Giants, however, his greatness was hardly evident. Formerly a pitcher, Oh batted just .161 as a rookie. But when he began studying martial arts, he learned how to attain total control over his physical and spiritual self. Baseball success soon followed, and the stats are amazing: nine MVP Awards, 15 home run titles, five batting championships, back-to-back Triple Crowns, and nine "Golden Glove" awards for fielding excellence. Possessing a distinctive, exaggerated leg kick that reminded observers of a dog doing business at a hydrant, Oh smashed his 868 dingers in just 9,250 at bats—a better percentage than HENRY AARON or BABE RUTH. But during a famous 1974 home run hitting contest, Aaron bested Oh 10–9 before 50,000 fans in Tokyo.

How would Oh have done in the U.S.? Impossible to know. But Clete Boyer, who had a 20-plus-year career as a player and coach in the majors, saw Oh at his peak and said he had the strength of Aaron and the eyesight of TED WILLIAMS.

Buck O'Neil
First baseman, Negro leagues, 1937–55

An excellent performer in the NEGRO LEAGUES, O'Neil became the first black coach in major league baseball when he joined the Cubs for the 1962 season. Most of his contributions to the game, however, have come off the field. He spent several years as the head of the NEGRO LEAGUE HALL OF FAME and was a tireless ombudsman for the sport as a whole. We all got to know him pretty well in KEN BURNS'S *BASEBALL* documentary; out of all the experts Burns featured, O'Neil was the most eloquent, most sincere, most engaging of all.

In 2006, a special Hall of Fame committee inducted a number of Negro league veterans and executives—but, inexplicably, not O'Neil. This was a travesty. O'Neil did more to further the cause of Negro league baseball than anyone in recent times. And unlike most of the new inductees, he was alive and could have actually enjoyed the honor. They similarly chose not to induct MINNIE MINOSO, again without explanation. There was no excuse for these oversights, and those committee voters should be ashamed of themselves. When O'Neil passed away in 2007, the oversight became even more egregious—and shameful.

Mel Ott
Outfielder, 1926–47

Ott joined the New York Giants at the age of 17 because manager JOHN MCGRAW didn't want to send him down to the minors for fear that a coach might ruin him. McGraw made the right choice, as Ott became a regular at age 19 and smashed 42 homers at 20, the youngest ever to reach the 40-homer plateau. The 5-foot-9, 170-pounder generated his power from a high leg kick that helped him capture six National League home run crowns during his 22-year career. He became adept at jerking the ball into the short right-field porch at New York's Polo Grounds, so two-thirds of his 511 career homers came at home. But whether home or away, Ott was one of the most feared hitters in the league, drawing at least 80 walks 16 different seasons. He also played a flawless right field and was talented enough to log substantial time at third base when the Giants needed it. He led his teams to three pennants, appeared in 12 All-Star games, and became one of the most popular players in Giants' history. Less successful as a manager, Ott was the subject of LEO DUROCHER'S famous edict that "nice guys finish last"—also the title of Durocher's autobiography. Ott was elected to the Hall of Fame in 1951.

Satchel Paige
Pitcher, 1926–53, 1965, including Negro leagues

The most famous player in NEGRO LEAGUE history, Paige was its preeminent showman in addition to perhaps its best pitcher. Locked out of major league ball due to the COLOR LINE until he was well past his prime, he pitched against white players often enough during winter barnstorming trips that DIZZY DEAN, JOE DIMAGGIO, and Charlie Gehringer, among others, called Paige the best pitcher they ever saw. For much of his career, he was the biggest gate attraction in the league. Huge crowds would gather to watch whether he fulfilled his promise to strike out the side on nine pitches, and he usually came through. His salaries were good—probably as high as $40,000 per year—though not as good as they would have been in the major leagues.

When Cleveland owner BILL VEECK finally brought Paige to the majors in 1948, the pitcher was 42 years old, the oldest rookie in major league history. Still, he could fill the seats. His first three starts drew over 200,000 fans to set night-game attendance records in Cleveland and Chicago. His major league stats seem undistinguished—28–31, 3.29 ERA—until you remember his age, which Veeck tried to say was higher than it was. To generate publicity, Veeck claimed his "team of detectives" had determined Paige was born in 1899 when in fact Paige always knew he was born in 1906.

In another publicity stunt, the Kansas City Athletics hired Paige to pitch a game in 1965; the 59-year-old tossed three shutout innings, allowing only one hit. By the time he was finished, Paige estimated that he and his overpowering fastball (known variously as his "bee ball," "trouble ball," and "Long Tom") had seen action in more than 2,500 games, winning 2,000 of them, against Negro league and semipro teams; other estimates include 100 no-hitters, 22 strikeouts in one game, and as many as 153 games pitched in one calendar year. Take those estimates with an appropriately sized grain of salt.

Aside from his dominance on the mound, Paige's unique brand of wit and charm has entered American folklore. In his much-quoted "How to Stay Young," Paige offered these suggestions: "Avoid fried meats, which angry up the blood. Keep the juices flowing by jangling around gently as you move. Don't look back; something might be gaining on you." But Paige was no clown. When the Hall of Fame decided to honor a number of stars with a special wing for Negro leaguers in 1972, Paige observed, "The only change is that baseball has turned Paige from a second-class citizen to a second-class immortal." Paige's criticism encouraged the Hall of Fame instead to put the Negro leaguers in the same wing as everybody else—a decision that, in retrospect, seems like a no-brainer.

Paige's life story is uniquely American, and any fan would benefit from a reading of his autobiography, *Maybe I'll Pitch Forever*, or one of his several biographies.

Rafael Palmeiro
First baseman, 1986–2005

Cuban-born Palmeiro quietly put together a Hall of Fame-caliber career, featuring more than 3,000 hits and over 500 home runs. Then he threw it all away when he tested positive for steroids in 2005—casting doubt on all his achievements. Making matters worse was that he had vehemently denied drug use during Congressional testimony earlier that very year. Palmeiro served his 10-game suspension while offering a difficult-to-fathom defense: he had unwittingly injected the steroids while believing they were simply vitamin B12 shots given to him by teammate Miguel Tejada. I don't know what's worse: telling a story that strains credulity, or selling out a teammate.

Will the Hall of Fame ever select him? Highly doubtful. Despite his impressive statistics, Palmeiro never finished high in MVP voting and never seemed to break through as a true star. In another era, those facts wouldn't have been held against him because his career numbers are so impressive. However, in the steroid era, he barely stands out above the crowd.

Gaylord Perry
Pitcher, 1962–83

Perry won 314 games and was the first pitcher to capture Cy Young Awards in both leagues, but he will always be remembered for the illegal pitch he did or did not throw: the spitball. Actually, the question of whether he threw the spitter has long been answered; he even titled his autobiography *Me and the Spitter*. Throughout his career, which began with San Francisco in 1962 and ended seven teams and 22 years later, opposing managers, batters, and umpires repeatedly tried to catch him with incriminating evidence—Vaseline, K-Y Jelly, a nail file—and found nothing... until August 23, 1982, when umpires finally caught him in the act and ejected Perry for throwing an illegal pitch. But as Perry himself would admit, it was the *threat* of the spitball that scared hitters, not the pitch itself. He threw it perhaps once or twice a game, perhaps not at all. He didn't make his living off it. So those who might claim that Perry cheated his way to five 20-win seasons and 3,534 strikeouts are wrong. Hall of Fame voters never doubted his credentials, electing him in 1991.

Mike Piazza
Catcher, 1992–2007

The greatest hitting catcher of all time, period. MICKEY COCHRANE, Bill Dickey, JOHNNY BENCH, and ROY CAMPANELLA each put together a few seasons that match up well with Piazza's statistics, but Piazza has them beat when it comes to consistency. Unlike just about every other great-hitting catcher, Piazza did not have a bad season until he reached his mid-30s. During his prime, he hit between 30 and 40 homers every year, with 90 to 120 RBIs, a batting average over .330, and an on-base percentage around .400. In his career, he hit 396 home runs as a catcher (427 total), the most in history. And he did the damage in two of the toughest parks for hitters in the National League (Dodger Stadium and Shea Stadium).

As a Dodger, he won the 1993 Rookie of the Year Award and should have won the 1997 MVP Award when he banged out 201 hits, slammed 40 homers, drove in 124 runs, and batted an amazing .362. Sent to the Mets during the tumultuous 1998 season in which he was traded twice within one week, Piazza insisted on playing catcher even though his teams wanted to shift him to first base to save him from injury. He finally did spend some time at first in 2004, but by then age and fatigue had already taken its toll and his batting stroke was fading. He finished his career as a DH. Piazza's defensive skills were never considered above average, so he won't be considered as the *greatest* catcher of all time. But with the wood in his hands, he had no equals.

Is he headed for the Hall of Fame? By the numbers, he deserves induction. But there's a whisper campaign about him as a possible PED user. Jeff Pearlman's biography of ROGER CLEMENS, *The Rocket that Fell to Earth*, quotes two players claiming Piazza used drugs and "everyone knew it." Yet Piazza was not named in the MITCHELL REPORT and he never failed a drug test. I guess it's just a fact of modern life that nearly every muscular hitter from the 1990s is going to be suspected as a PED user even despite a lack of evidence.

Wally Pipp
First baseman, 1913–28
It was poor Wally Pipp who, as a member of the New York Yankees in June 1925, asked for the day off ostensibly because of a headache but probably because he just wanted to go the racetrack. Manager Miller Huggins took the opportunity to take a look at a young slugger just recruited out of Columbia University named LOU GEHRIG. The rest, of course, is history: Gehrig would set a major league record by playing 2,130 consecutive games (*see* 2,130); Pipp would be traded the next season. Certainly Pipp's life and career encompassed more than that fateful summer day. He had been a slick-fielding, good-hitting first baseman for a dozen years, leading the league in homers twice and triples once. Nevertheless, his name lives in infamy. Even today, fans and players warn of the "Wally Pipp syndrome" when a player removes himself from the lineup due to illness and a young phenom takes his place.

Kirby Puckett
Outfielder, 1984–95

Kirby Puckett was a rare breed: a player who played every day, every inning with a smile on his face and a spring in his step. He truly loved the game and played like it. Built like a fireplug—standing 5'8" and weighing over 200 pounds—he was a high-average, line-drive hitter who led the league in hits four times and RBIs and batting average once each. He also played on two championship teams, the 1987 and 1991 Twins. In the latter World Series, Puckett's leadoff homer in the bottom of the 11th won Game 6 to send the Series to Game 7, which the Twins captured in 10 innings (*see* 1991: MORRIS COMES UP REAL BIG). An eye illness cut short his career, but he put up good enough numbers and made enough friends throughout baseball that he was voted into the Hall of Fame on the first ballot in 2001.

After the Hall of Fame induction, however, Puckett's veneer of respectability wore off. He was tried and acquitted on assault charges, and he was revealed as an adulterer. When he died suddenly in 2006, most fans preferred to remember his on-field exuberance instead of his off-field behavior.

Albert Pujols
"The Great Pujols," "Prince Albert"
Infielder/outfielder, 2001–present

Pujols burst onto the scene in 2001 with an unreal rookie season of 37 home runs, 130 RBIs, a .329 average, .403 on-base percentage, and .610 slugging percentage—at the tender age of 21. He showed no sophomore slump, or junior slump, or senior slump, or even post-graduate slump as he finished in the top three in MVP voting each of the next four years, finally winning it when BARRY BONDS got hurt in 2005. He has since won two more awards (as of 2014). In fact, he came up so young and excelled so quickly that he'll rewrite the record books if he can stay healthy. There's already a good case to be made that he's the greatest right-handed hitter of all time. And signing a huge free-agent contract with the Angels prior to the 2012 season hasn't changed a thing, even though he's suffered through some injuries and has not quite approached the heights he achieved in his 20s (very few players ever have).

My favorite Pujols moment came in the 2005 NL Championship Series against Houston. With the Cardinals on the brink of elimination, down by two runs in the ninth inning of Game 5, Pujols came to the plate against the dominating closer Brad Lidge. There were two outs and two on. The first pitch came in low and Pujols swung feebly, misjudging Lidge's slider. On the next pitch, Lidge threw a fastball, and Pujols connected. He uncoiled his long swing and sent the ball deep into the upper deck. I think it may have hit the back wall of Minute Maid Park, near the concession stands, well over 450 feet from the plate. The whole stadium stood in awe of his moon shot. Watching at home, two thousand miles away, I stood up, too.

Charles Radbourn
"Ol' Hoss"
Pitcher, 1880–91
Radbourn played part of his career in an era when pitchers threw underhand from 50 feet away and a team's pitching staff usually consisted of two or three men. These facts should go a long way toward explaining why Radbourn's 1884 season is so amazing: a 59–12 record (some record books credit him with 60 wins), 678 innings, and 441 strikeouts—all major league records that will never be broken. That season, his Providence Grays won the National League pennant and faced the American Association's New York Metropolitans in the first postseason championship to be known as a "World's Series" (*see* 1884: THE FIRST WORLD SERIES, TECHNICALLY) "Hoss," who earned his nickname not because he was built like a horse but because he had the stamina of one (at least for that one season), lasted in baseball just 11 years, putting together only three really good seasons, so his 309–195 record is deceiving. Still, Hall of Fame electors honored Radbourn in 1939 among one of the first groups of inductees, more than 40 years after his death.

Manny Ramirez
Outfielder, 1994–2011
He was a poor fielder, he had a poor attitude, and he just didn't seem to care about anything except one thing: hitting. But oh, was he a master at that. With tons of power, a high average, and a great batting eye, he was the kind of hitter you'd want if you were creating one from scratch. But was he the kind of teammate you'd want? Would you want to put up with the me-first attitude, the seeming indifference to everything around him? I would. After all, in spite of his antics, Ramirez was a winner. He appeared in the postseason 11 times and won four pennants with two different teams (Cleveland and Bos-

ton). He couldn't have been that much of a clubhouse distraction if his teams were so successful.

With 555 career home runs, Ramirez would have been a shoo-in for the Hall of Fame but for two teensy, weensy things: failed drug tests in 2009 and 2011, which cast doubt over his entire career. The first time, when he was with the Dodgers, he got caught using a female fertility drug, which is often used by drug cheats in combination with anabolic steroids, and was suspended for 50 games. After the second failed test, which would have earned him a 100-game suspension, Ramirez decided to retire.* His skills were basically gone anyway, so it was just a doubly ignominious way to end one of the most fascinating careers of recent times.

*He made brief attempts at a comeback with the A's in 2012 and the Rangers in 2013, but never made it to the majors. I think we've seen the last of him.

Pete Reiser
"Pistol Pete"
Outfielder, 1940–52

The HERB SCORE of hitters, Reiser had a lasting effect on baseball despite an abbreviated career. In 1941, his first full season, he led the league in batting average, slugging percentage, doubles, triples, and runs scored while playing a mean center field. His Dodgers won the pennant for the first time in over 20 years, and Reiser finished second in MVP voting. The 22-year-old's promise seemed boundless. Then came the injuries. Reiser played the outfield with such abandon that walls didn't seem to matter. In 1942, he slammed into the Ebbets Field fence with such force that he had to be taken off the field on a stretcher. He did the same in 1947. He weathered broken bones, beanings, and dislocations and came back for more. But the injuries took their toll, and Reiser's stats reflect his deteriorating physical condition. When he retired in 1952, his true legacy was beginning to appear: outfield warning tracks and padded fences.

Cal Ripken, Jr.
"Iron Man"
Shortstop/third base, 1981–2001

A career-long Oriole, Ripken revolutionized the shortstop position. Before Ripken, shortstops were generally lithe, light-hitting fielding specialists in the mold of OZZIE SMITH and LUIS APARICIO. In fact, Ripken came to the big leagues as a third baseman. But his manager, EARL WEAVER, had a hole at shortstop and believed that Ripken could fill it in spite of Ripken's size: six-four, 215 pounds. Nevertheless, he proved himself to be a superb fielder who excelled because he knew how best to position himself against opposing hitters and he had an incredibly strong arm. Ripken also served as the model for today's shortstops who are expected to deliver at the plate as well as in the field. He hit over 400 home runs in his career, 345 as a shortstop, which was the career record for home runs by a shortstop when he retired. (ALEX RODRIGUEZ hit just one fewer homer as a shortstop before moving to third base, so he could easily break Ripken's mark if he changes position again.)

Ripken captured a Rookie of the Year Award and two MVPs, played on a World Series champion his second season, and was elected to the All-Star Game almost every year of his career. But what drove him to true superstardom was his quest for the all-time record for consecutive games played, which was held by LOU GEHRIG until Ripken broke it in September 1995—though not without controversy. Even a cursory examination of his statistics showed that Ripken's offensive numbers declined as the streak grew longer, and many in baseball and the media called for him to take a rest. But as the total grew higher, it was too late for that. The streak became bigger than Ripken himself, and to give up when he was so close would have been ridiculous. And in any case, even at his worst, Ripken was better than 90 percent of the shortstops around. The streak finally ended in 1998 at 2,632 (*see* 2,632), when he took himself out of the lineup for the Orioles' final home game. He moved back to third base in 1997, and he went on the disabled list for the first time ever in 1999. His effectiveness as a player declined quickly after that, but not his popularity among fans or the respect of his peers. He retired in 2001 and was elected almost unanimously to the Hall of Fame in 2007.

Mariano Rivera
"Big Mo"
Pitcher, 1996–2013

Without question the greatest closer of all time. Why? No other closer ever reached a peak so high for so long. In 15-plus seasons, he never had a bad year, unless you count 2007, when he posted a 3.14 ERA. The secret to his success is no secret at all: his cut fastball, which rode in on left-handers and away from right-handers. In addition, he rarely walked anyone, and he struck out almost a batter per inning. He was great in the regular season and even greater in the postseason. And because he was a Yankee, there was a ton of postseason action, where he delivered a lower ERA, fewer baserunners per inning, and an even better strikeout to walk ratio than the regular season. He went through an entire postseason without allowing a run five separate times in his career. And the Panama native did it all with class and quiet dignity. He was a Yankee even Yankee-haters couldn't bring themselves to hate. Although a freak injury ended his 2012 season abruptly, he came back for one final year in 2013, baffling hitters with his old stuff as if he were a 25-year-old again. Then he retired for good.

Brooks Robinson
"Hoover"
Third baseman, 1955–77
Considered the greatest fielder among third basemen of all time, "Hoover" (like the vacuum cleaner) won a record 16 straight GOLD GLOVES and set career records for assists, putouts, double plays, and fielding average. He played in 15 consecutive All-Star games and led his Orioles to five division titles and four pennants. At the plate, he possessed medium-range power, usually slugging 20 to 25 homers a year, with batting averages around .270. He won an MVP in 1965 when he led the league in RBIs and smashed 28 homers in addition to playing stellar defense at the hot corner. His play during the 1970 World Series cemented his reputation as an all-time great when he made a number of spectacular catches and throws to nail disbelieving Cincinnati hitters. He's the most popular player in Baltimore history, where it's heresy to claim that there was ever a better third baseman than Brooks. He's certainly in the top five.

Frank Robinson
Outfielder, 1956–76
Manager, 1975–77, 1981–84, 1988–91, 2002–06
Robinson became major league baseball's first black manager when he took over the Cleveland Indians in 1975, and he went on to manage the Giants, Orioles, and Expos/Nationals. In addition, he has worked in the commissioner's office. Somehow, though, his stature off the field has overshadowed his greatness on it, for one rarely hears stories about what a great player he was. And he was a great one. The first man to win MVPs in each league, Robinson slugged 30 or more

homers 11 times, played in 11 All-Star games, and led his teams to five pennants. After the 1965 season, the Reds considered Robinson "an old 30" and traded him to the Orioles. Bad move: Robinson tore up the American League to win the TRIPLE CROWN with a .316 BA–49 HR–122 RBI season and led Baltimore to its first-ever World Series victory. He finished his career with 586 home runs, fourth on the all-time list at his retirement.

Jackie Robinson
Infielder, 1945–56, including Negro leagues

Jackie Robinson was a true American hero who had a greater impact on baseball—and on society—than any other baseball player in history. The story of his signing to play in the majors has become part of American folklore. In 1945, when Dodgers general manager BRANCH RICKEY went looking for the "right kind of man" to break major league baseball's 60-year-old COLOR BARRIER, he selected Robinson, a UCLA-educated Army officer with a reputation for activism. Rickey knew the story of how Robinson had refused to bow to the military's Jim Crow laws and was court-martialed for insubordination—a trumped-up charge on which he was acquitted. Robinson was still a member of the NEGRO LEAGUES' KANSAS CITY MONARCHS when he received an offer from Rickey to meet in Brooklyn. Rickey had led Robinson to believe that he was starting a new Negro league team, but when Robinson arrived, he discovered Rickey's true plan: to integrate major league baseball.

During the signing meeting, Rickey predicted that opposing teams and many fans would resist the attempt to integrate the game, but he asked Robinson for a deal: for three years, Robinson would not retaliate against any of the taunts, beanballs, and spikings he would inevitably face. To this, Robinson reportedly asked Rickey, "Are you looking for a man without the guts to fight back?" Shouted Rickey: "I want someone with guts enough *not* to fight back!"

And so against the teeth of criticism from league officials, opposing players, and even mainstream publications such as *The Sporting News*, Robinson's journey began. In 1946 with the Dodgers' Triple-A farm club in Montreal, Robinson dominated the league. Then in 1947 in Brooklyn, he won baseball's first Rookie of the Year Award despite playing first base for the first time in his life.

Robinson basically repeated his 1947 performance in 1948, but in 1949 he broke loose. By that time, black players had joined other major league clubs, and Robinson's deal with Rickey to keep his temper in check expired. That's when Robinson enjoyed his greatest season, leading the league in batting and stolen bases, playing a stellar second base, helping his team to the World Series, and winning the MVP.

Aside from integrating the game, Robinson also helped bring to baseball a new level of excitement. He would dance and dart off the base, trying to rattle the pitcher; he'd go from first to third on an infield hit; he'd steal home—the kind of baseball that had existed in the Negro leagues but that most major league fans and players hadn't seen since the days of COBB and SPEAKER.

To the Dodgers, meanwhile, Robinson brought a winning attitude. Brooklyn had finished a close second or third in four of the previous five seasons before Robinson arrived. With Robinson as their catalyst, however, the Dodgers captured six pennants in 10 years as well as Brooklyn's only World Series victory.

He called it quits after to the 1956 season at the age of 36, but even in retirement, he couldn't avoid the spotlight: Not when he publicly campaigned for Richard Nixon's presidential bid in 1960. Not when he received criticism for his vocal opposition to the war in Vietnam. Not when his son put him on the front pages again after being arrested on a drug charge in 1968, after which Robinson became a spokesman against drug abuse. And not when he publicly denounced major league baseball for its lack of black baseball managers and executives.

On October 24, 1972, the diabetic Robinson suffered a heart attack and died at his home in Connecticut. Close friends suggested that the constant pressure and responsibility of being a cultural icon conspired to take his life away at the age of 53.

What Robinson did for baseball can be easily documented. What he did for society at large is still being measured. Eric F. Goldman's study of the postwar period, *The Crucial Decade*, acknowledges the debt owed to Robinson: "Jackie Robinson's triumph, so widely publicized and admired, enormously furthered acceptance for the Negro in many fields of American life... [He] was the flashing symbol of an era in the national life when, for all minority groups, for all lower-status Americans, the social and economic walls were coming tumbling down." Baseball's color barrier, then, wasn't the only wall Robinson helped destroy.

Alex Rodriguez
"A-Rod"
Shortstop/third base, 1995–present
In the 1980s, CAL RIPKEN reminded the world that a shortstop can be big and slug home runs. Rodriguez almost made Ripken look like a light-hitting defensive specialist. He came up to the Mariners as a 20-year-old in 1995 and almost immediately established himself as a superstar, combining power, speed, and fielding skill like no one since HONUS WAGNER.

However, in spite of all the evidence attesting to Rodriguez's greatness—the repeated 100-plus RBI seasons, 40- and 50-plus home run seasons, one 40/40 campaign, multiple MVP Awards, and so on—it seemed for a while that all his critics could focus on were a couple of bad playoff series and his huge, $250 million contract. But you know, that's what happens when you sign the richest contract in American professional sports history, which is what he did after the 2000 season when he left the Mariners to sign with the Rangers. Sure, it wasn't fair to Rodriguez that he was practically expected to hit a home run in every at bat and lead his teams to the World Series championships every season. But when you're making $25 to $30 million per season, you're inevitably going to be a lightning rod for criticism when things go bad.

But that was in the past. Beginning in 2009, there came new reasons to hate A-Rod: the revelations that he had failed a drug test in 2003, despite past denials that he'd ever used steroids; and his association with Biogenesis, a "wellness clinic" in Florida that provided PEDs to numerous athletes including A-Rod. Fans who were predisposed to hating him now hate him more, and the rest of us disinterested observers can only shake our heads and wonder how much the drugs helped him at the plate and in the field. Baseball suspended Rodriguez for the entire 2014 season—a suspension that was affirmed by an independent arbitrator—putting his entire career in limbo. There will probably be no 700 home runs for A-Rod—and almost certainly no Hall of Fame for a player who, by the numbers alone, stands as one of the two or three greatest ever to play his positions.

Pete Rose
"Charlie Hustle"
Infielder/outfielder, 1963–86
Manager, 1984–89

It's impossible to talk about Rose without mentioning the scandal that ended his career. But in fairness to him, let's focus on his on-field performance first, because the bottom line of his playing career is that he helped his teams win. He could play just about any position on the field, wherever his manager needed. He batted from both sides of the plate, so he was never at a platoon disadvantage. He never got hurt. And he always ran out every ground ball, every pop-up, even every base on balls. The results are phenomenal: three batting titles and ten 200-hit seasons, while leading the league variously in runs (four times), hits (seven times), and doubles (five times). In terms of career records, the numbers are equally amazing. He is baseball's all-time leader in hits (*see* 4,256), games (3,562), and at bats (14,053), and he is among the top ten in runs, doubles, and total bases.

But baseball isn't just about numbers; it's about winning, and Rose was hardly deficient in that area, either. From 1970 through 1976, his "BIG RED MACHINE" captured five division titles, four pennants, and two championships. After he joined the Phillies as a million-dollar free agent in 1979, it took only one year for the team to win its first-ever World Series. The 1983 team also won the pennant.

In mid-season 1984, he rejoined the Reds as a player-manager, where he was less successful on the field and where, a few years later, his real troubles began. Actually, the commissioner's office had known about Rose's problem—gambling—since around 1970, but did nothing about it. In 1989, however, assisted by an IRS investigation into income tax evasion against Rose, commissioner BART GIAMATTI hired a special investigator to examine charges that Rose: (a) consorted with known bookmakers and drug dealers; and (b) more importantly for baseball's sake, bet on baseball games, including games his own team had played. Regardless of the fact that Rose was accused of betting on his teams to win (as opposed to the BLACK SOX, who threw the 1919 WORLD SERIES in exchange for money from gamblers), such actions violated one of baseball's most sacrosanct policies.

Throughout the proceedings (and for more than a decade afterward), Rose steadfastly denied he ever bet on baseball. During the tumultuous summer of 1989, he even filed suit against the commissioner seeking to stop the investigation on various legal grounds. Rose was roundly criticized in the press for dragging out the ordeal, and in August, he agreed to a settlement: He would accept a lifetime ban from baseball if the agreement signed by both Rose and Giamatti would make no mention of the alleged baseball gambling. Then Rose could apply for reinstatement. However, Rose's troubles continued in 1990 as he pleaded guilty to tax evasion and served five months in an Illinois federal prison.

For a long time, Rose denied betting on baseball, and he attacked the results of the baseball investigation relentlessly. Most fans even seemed to have forgiven Rose. In 1999, he received the biggest ovation at major league baseball's celebration of its All-Century Team.

But in 2004, after years of denials, he finally came clean about his gambling. Just days before the Hall of Fame announced that year's inductees, his publisher released his autobiography, *My Prison Without Bars*, a self-serving tome that finally revealed his guilt. He hoped that the truth would set him free, as it were, but in fact it only made things worse. He seemed to show no contrition for his actions—the gambling, the tax evasion, the denials, the attempts to undermine the baseball establishment. Now, Rose appears no closer to achieving his goal of getting his ban lifted and enjoying a Hall of Fame induction.

Should he get into the Hall? For many years, my answer had been no. Rose broke a serious rule and had to pay the price. With time, however, I've softened my stance. Twenty-five years—and counting—of banishment is punishment enough, and I now think he should be eligible to be voted into the Hall. Former Commissioner Fay Vincent disagrees, believing that the lifetime ban is a deterrent for others who might think about betting on baseball. I think 25 years is deterrent enough. In addition, I think baseball should make a distinction between betting on a game and throwing a game. So unless it's ever proven that Rose bet on his team to lose and purposely threw a game, then I say it's time to forgive.

Amos Rusie
"The Hoosier Thunderbolt"
Pitcher, 1889–1901

Rusie had a tremendous effect on the game of baseball: He and his blazing fastball were partially responsible for the pitching mound being moved from 50 feet to its current distance of 60 feet, six inches from home plate in 1894 (*see* 1894: PITCHERS MOVE BACK 10 FEET).

Rusie pitched with such speed that his catcher even had to put a thin sheet of lead in his catching mitt to protect his hand. Rusie won 30-plus games four years in a row for the Giants, led the league in a variety of categories throughout his career, and became the standard to which all fastballers were measured for decades after his retirement.

Babe Ruth
Pitcher/outfielder, 1914–35

It's not very controversial to say that Babe Ruth was the greatest baseball player of all time. Other candidates have their merits; HONUS WAGNER, WILLIE MAYS, TY COBB, and even BARRY BONDS before the steroid allegations came to light have been put up as contenders, and each candidate can make a case. But my vote for "the greatest" goes to the Babe for several reasons.

First, he had a tremendous effect on the game by almost single-handedly reintroducing the home run as an offensive weapon. Until Ruth came along, baseball games were played and won with singles, stolen bases, the hit-and-run, and occasional extra-base hits. By showing the baseball world that an uppercut swing with a heavy bat held down at the knob could produce home runs on a regular basis, Ruth changed the sport forever. And it wasn't because of a new "RABBIT BALL," as some revisionists have claimed; he did it with the same "dead" ball as was already being used.

Ruth deserves the title of "baseball's greatest" on a second level as well: that of cultural icon. He was American sports' most famous athlete, known and loved by children and adults everywhere. Around the globe, Ruth *was* America, and stories have been told of Japanese soldiers during World War II shouting epithets about Babe Ruth to the Americans. Additionally, Ruth was the highest-paid athlete in the world, with a salary that reached a peak of $80,000 per season at the beginning of the Depression—a sum that exceeded the president's salary, which prompted Ruth to say, "Why not? I had a better year than he did."

Third, Ruth dominated the game on the field to an unbelievable extent. His entry in the *BASEBALL ENCYCLOPEDIA* is almost entirely bold-face (signifying a league-leading performance). I won't recount all his totals, but here are a few: 12 times leading the league in homers, six times in RBIs, eight in runs scored, 12 in slugging percentage, and so on. He is responsible for five or six of the top 10 offensive seasons of all time. And he didn't do all of this in a vacuum, either. He led his teams to 10 pennants, both as an outfielder and a pitcher.

Speaking of pitching, Ruth was also one of the best pitchers in the league before he shifted to the outfield in 1919. He led the league in ERA, shutouts, and complete games at various times during his two 20-win seasons in 1916 and 1917.

The strongest argument against Ruth as the greatest player of all time is that he competed before integration: he didn't have to face the best black and Hispanic pitchers, or have his statistics compared to the best black and Hispanic hitters. Some historians discount all baseball records before 1947 using that theory.

I agree with those historians up to a point. All records before 1947 do deserve at least a figurative asterisk. But it really isn't fair to the great stars of the pre-integration era to penalize them completely for something they had no direct control over. Certainly, some players of that era would not have dominated had they faced tougher competition. But I think the players who reached incredible heights of achievement would have dominated any era, and I put Babe Ruth in that category.

For more on Babe Ruth, *see* 1919: THE SOX SELL THE BABE and 1932: RUTH CALLS HIS SHOT. OR DOES HE?

Nolan Ryan
"Ryan Express"
Pitcher, 1966–93
The BABE RUTH of strikeout pitchers, Ryan is a biological marvel. No one in major league history ever threw harder—101 mph was his top measured speed—or longer—27 major league seasons—than Ryan. He struck out (*see* 5,714) and walked (2,795) more batters than anyone, he allowed the fewest hits per nine innings (6.56) ever, he holds the major league record with 383 strikeouts in one season (*see* 383), and he led the league in those categories throughout his career with the Mets, Angels, Astros, and Rangers. He also tossed a major league record seven no-hitters, the last two when he was over 40 years old.

He attributed his success to excellent conditioning, which kept him injury-free almost throughout his career. He retired with 324 wins (now tied for 14th all time) and 292 losses (third), and he was elected to the Hall of Fame in 1999 with nearly 100 percent of the vote. Off the field, he served as president and part-owner of the Texas Rangers for many years before retiring in 2013, then joined the Astros as a special assistant in 2014.

Curt Schilling
Pitcher, 1988–2007
The most accomplished big game pitcher of modern times, Schilling knew how to rise to the occasion. His post-season record is 11-2, and one of those losses came in 2004 when he had that injured ankle. Which, of course, was followed by the famous "BLOODY SOCK" game, one of the great moments in baseball history. But beyond that, Schilling was dominant in the 2001 postseason, when he won four games; went 3-0 in 2007; and had three great performances in four starts in 1993. His hallmarks as a pitcher were power and pinpoint control: He struck out a lot of guys and hardly walked anyone. He simply did not make mistakes. If I had to choose a pitcher to win the most important game of my life, Curt Schilling would be on my short list. Although the baseball writers have passed him over so far, he deserves induction into the Hall of Fame.

Mike Schmidt
Third baseman, 1972–89
Widely considered the greatest third baseman of all time, Schmidt nonetheless enjoyed a tumultuous relationship with his "fans" in Philadelphia, where he played his entire career. Blamed for Philadelphia's playoff losses in 1976, 1977, and 1978, Schmidt was regularly booed even while winning his eight home run championships and three MVP Awards. In fact, a friend who was there tells me that on the very day the club announced that fans had voted him the Greatest Phillie Ever, the boo-birds came out when Schmidt committed a early-inning error.

Still, he turned in amazing—if unappreciated—performances throughout his 18-year career. Defensively, he won 10 GOLD GLOVES and holds the NL records for single-season and career assists by a third baseman. Offensively, he smashed 548 career homers, including 30 or more 13 times, and led the league in slugging percentage five times and in RBIs four. Additionally, he led his Phillies to the postseason six times and delivered the franchise's first World Series victory in 1980.

Herb Score
Pitcher, 1955–62

For his first two seasons the majors, Score was a true baseball phenomenon—a left-handed fireballer who led the American League in strikeouts while winning 16 and 20 games with the Indians. But in early 1957, a line drive off the bat of the Yankees' Gil McDougald changed everything. It struck Score in the face and ended his season after only five games. He tried pitching again the following year, but lasted only 12 ineffective games. And though he hung on until 1962, the promising talent of his first two seasons appeared only in brief flashes. Whenever people speak of Herb Score, they always say, "What if...?"

Tom Seaver
"Tom Terrific"
Pitcher, 1967–86

More than anything else, Seaver was a winner. In his rookie season, 1967, he recorded a 16-13 won/loss mark with a Mets team that lost 101 games. Two years later, his 25 wins led the "Miracle Mets" to their first and most improbable World Series title and earned him his first of his three Cy Young Awards.

Atypical of a pitcher with his control, he notched 200 or more strikeouts nine straight seasons and once held the National League record with 19 whiffs in a single game (since broken by Kerry Wood). Throughout the '70s, Seaver averaged 18 wins per year and pitched mostly .600 ball on mostly sub-.500 teams. Traded to Cincinnati in midseason 1977, he still won 21 games and, a year later, led the Pete Rose-less Reds to the division title.

He returned to the Mets in 1983, ostensibly to finish out his career, but a clerical error placed him on waivers, and he wound up with the White Sox a year later. He played three seasons in the AL, and on the same day Rod Carew got his 3,000th hit, Seaver recorded his 300th victory in Yankee Stadium, just a few miles from where his career began.

Elected to the Hall of Fame on his first try in 1992, Seaver remains a true gentleman, admired by fans, other players, and the media. After spending some time as both a Mets broadcaster and team executive, he now operates a small winery in Napa Valley, California.

Ozzie Smith
"The Wizard of Ahs"
Shortstop, 1978–96

Probably the greatest fielding shortstop of all time, Smith was also one of baseball's most popular players. He played the game the way purists believe it should be played: with attention paid to the small but important things such as fielding, baserunning, bunting, contact hitting, hitting behind the runners, and so forth. Smith was, in fact, a modern-day Rabbit Maranville with better batting skills. (Their hitting statistics are actually pretty similar, but Maranville played much of his career when batting averages were inflated, which means Rabbit's .258 career average would be about .230 today.) They called Ozzie "The Wizard of Ahs," and his amazing plays for the Cardinals and Padres were a staple of highlight shows throughout the 1980s and into the 1990s. He made the Hall of Fame in his first year of eligibility in 2002.

Warren Spahn
Pitcher, 1942–65

The HANK AARON of pitchers, Spahn, like Aaron, had only a few years in which he was considered baseball's very best at his position. But, also like Aaron, his sheer number of excellent seasons is staggering. Because of World War II, Spahn didn't win his first game until the age of 25, but once he got on a roll, he was unstoppable. From 1947 through 1963 (17 seasons), he led the league in at least one major category (wins, ERA, strikeouts) in all but six seasons, and he made 14 All-Star teams. His career totals are phenomenal: 363 victories, the most by any left-hander, and 13 20-win seasons, which ties the NL record held by CHRISTY MATHEWSON and is the same number as STEVE CARLTON (6), TOM SEAVER (5), and GREG MADDUX (2) *combined.*

During the Braves' pennant-winning 1948 campaign, Spahn joined fellow 20-game winner Johnny Sain in an otherwise poor rotation, leading to the plaintive cry, "Spahn and Sain and pray for rain." By 1957, when the Braves made it back to the World Series, Sain was retired and Spahn was 36, which meant he only had six more good years left in him. Three years after that, Spahn pitched a no-hitter, and a year later, at the age of 40, he tossed another one. And when he retired from major league baseball after 1965, he pitched two more seasons in the minors. He finally sat still long enough for the Hall of Fame to induct him 1973.

Tris Speaker
"The Grey Eagle"
Outfielder, 1907–28

Is it me, or is Speaker the least-remembered truly outstanding player in baseball history? If there were a statistic that measured the ratio of greatness as a player (GAAP) to legends told about them (LTAT), then Speaker's would be off the charts. (On the opposite end of the spectrum, the leader would probably be David Eckstein.) Speaker combined power, speed, smarts, and fielding skills like almost no one before or since. He revolutionized the center field position by playing so close to second base that he sometimes participated in infield double plays and received catcher throws on steal attempts. He reasoned that playing shallow could allow him to cut off balls hit in front of him and his blazing speed could catch up with balls hit over his head. Of course, he got away with the strategy because he played most of his career during the DEAD BALL ERA, when few batters could regularly hit a ball 400 feet. Speaker, in fact, was one of those few.

Though he smacked only 117 homers during his career, he did slug an all-time record 792 doubles—many of which undoubtedly would have been homers if he'd played during the 1930s. He won only a single batting title because he played when TY COBB and George Sisler were at their peaks, but his career average is a phenomenal .345, and he collected 3,514 hits. Another great accomplishment was that he player-managed Cleveland to the 1920 pennant while batting .388 with a league-leading 50 doubles and a .483 on-base percentage (which, amazingly, didn't lead the league).

In the late 1920s, however, he was involved in a scandal that nearly got him kicked out of baseball. As recounted in Fred Lieb's book *Baseball as I Have Known It*, Speaker, Cobb, and Joe Wood were implicated in a plot to fix a game between Speaker's Indians and Cobb's Tigers in 1919. The prime evidence against them was a letter from Wood to Detroit pitcher Dutch Leonard strongly suggesting that Cleveland had thrown a ball game that would have helped Detroit capture second place ahead of New York. But when commissioner KENESAW MOUNTAIN LANDIS held a hearing to settle the charges, Leonard refused to appear, and Landis had no choice but to acquit Cobb, Speaker, and Wood. Hall of Fame voters had all but forgotten the taint by 1937 and elected Speaker by acclamation.

Turkey Stearnes
Outfielder, Negro leagues, 1921–41

A great outfielder and slugger in the NEGRO LEAGUES, Stearnes was finally elected to the Hall of Fame in 2000 after years of inexplicable snubs. Research has found that Stearnes ranks in Negro league annals among the top home run hitters of all time, behind JOSH GIBSON but ahead of OSCAR CHARLESTON and Mule Suttles. Stearnes said he never counted his long-balls: "I remember one year, my first season with Detroit, 1923. I think I hit about 50-some. But after I was up here about a year, I hit so many that that's the reason I didn't count them."

Why did it take so long for the Hall of Fame recognized him? Probably because he wasn't colorful like Gibson or COOL PAPA BELL or SATCHEL PAIGE. There were no stories about Stearnes scoring from second on a ground out or hitting a 650-foot home run out of YANKEE STADIUM. Bell always believed Stearnes belonged in the shrine: "If they don't put Turkey Stearnes in," he once said, "the shouldn't put anybody in." Stearnes died in 1979.

Casey Stengel
"The Old Perfessor"
Outfielder, 1912–25
Manager, 1934–65

Through six decades in baseball, Stengel was known as both clown and genius, prankster and innovator. During his playing days, he once doffed his cap to let a bird fly out. Another time, he supposedly disappeared into an outfield drainage hole, only to reappear in time to make a play. And he talked in a mangled English known as STENGELESE that delighted and confused all around him.

When he became a major league manager, he was saddled with lowly teams in Boston and Brooklyn, and he never got out of fifth place with those clubs. But when George Weiss was named the Yankees' general manager, one of his first moves was to hire Stengel—prompting scoffs and chuckles among baseball men. Stengel, however, proved everybody (but Weiss) wrong. He wove his magic to earn 10 pennants in 12 seasons, and it wasn't just the talent of the players that did it. Stengel had to deal with injuries and egos and mediocre-to-good pitching. Despite the appearance of a befuddled old man, he was always in control of his team.

But he couldn't control his owners, and the 1960 pennant would prove to be his last. "I was fired," he told reporters. "I'll never make the mistake of being 70 years old again." The Yankees fired Weiss for getting old, too.

The two rejoined forces in 1962 with the expansion Mets, aka the "AMAZIN' METS," with Stengel as its rumpled field leader. The 72-year-old had the perfect demeanor to sit through four consecutive dreadful seasons: patient, intelligent, grandfatherly, and above all, possessing a good sense of humor. A year after his retirement, the Hall of Fame inducted him, and Stengel then became a gracious and lovable ambassador for the game until his death in 1975.

Author Robert Creamer wrote his definitive biography, *Stengel: His Life and Times.* And if you want to read what made Stengel great as a manager, check out the book *Forging Genius: The Making of Casey Stengel* by Steven Goldman.

George Stovey
Pitcher, Negro leagues, 1886–91

The greatest Negro league pitcher of the 19th century, Stovey signed with the famous CUBAN GIANTS at the age of 20 but tossed only one game prior to switching to the Eastern League, a white minor league, before the COLOR LINE took hold. There, he posted excellent statistics and once struck out 22 batters in a game. After the season, Stovey, who was light-skinned, almost signed with the New York Giants before the club backed off for fear of angering CAP ANSON and other baseball racists. Stovey bounced around from team to team, including a season with Newark of the International League, where he and MOSES FLEETWOOD WALKER formed the first African-American battery in the history of organized baseball. Stovey died of a heart attack in 1937 as the last surviving African-American to play in organized white baseball until JACKIE ROBINSON.

Ichiro Suzuki
Outfielder, 1992–present, including Japanese league

Known by his first name, Ichiro made his debut at 18 for the Orix Blue Wave of Japan's Pacific League, but it took two more years to establish himself as a star. And when he did, he rewrote the Japanese league record books. He became a hitting machine, setting records for both hits and batting average and winning three straight league MVP awards and seven straight batting titles.

At the age of 27, he decided to come to America, where he joined the Seattle Mariners with much fanfare prior to the 2001 season. That year, Ichiro amazed fans on both sides of the Pacific with his contact hitting, tremendous speed, and incredible fielding skills. He led the league in hits, batting average, and stolen bases and became only the second player ever to win the American League's MVP and Rookie of the Year awards in the same year. In 2004, he rewrote American record books by breaking George Sisler's 84-year-old record for hits in a season. Ichiro finished with 262, besting Sisler by 5. He also broke WILLIE KEELER'S record for singles and became the first major leaguer to smack at least 200 hits in each of his first four seasons—since extended to 10 seasons before it ended in 2011.

In 2011, Ichiro achieved 3,000 hits as a professional—combined in both leagues. And he has a chance to hit 3,000 just in the major leagues, too. In fact, if he had played only in the majors, he might have challenged PETE ROSE'S hits record. Either way, when he's finished, he should earn induction into both the U.S. and Japanese Baseball Halls of Fame.

Frank Thomas
"The Big Hurt"
First baseman/designated hitter, 1990–2008
Winner of the 1993 and 1994 MVP Awards, Frank Thomas at his peak was, quite simply, baseball's best all-around hitter since TED WILLIAMS. That may sound like hype, but it's supported by evidence. He could hit for power and average, he drove in a ton of runs, and he had such great strike zone judgment that he posted on-base percentages in the mid .400s. A lot of other players could do those things but none as well as Thomas. He was never a great fielder, but at his peak with the wood in his hands, there was nobody better.

In the first edition of this book, I wondered whether Thomas's large size—he'd played football at Auburn and probably could have made the NFL—would make him susceptible to injuries and ultimately diminish his skills. In fact, Thomas began to break down in 1998, partly due to injuries. He played ten more years, but could stay healthy enough for only five of those years to really contribute to his teams. But when he was healthy, he was a monster with the bat.

Thomas gets credit as one of the few ballplayers in the 1990s willing to denounce the steroid use that had been going on around him. He spoke to George Mitchell for the MITCHELL REPORT and testified before Congress. He believes that not taking steroids cost him money during contract negotiations because his numbers weren't as superficially impressive as some of the players who used. But he regrets nothing. And the Hall of Fame rewarded him in 2014.

Joe Torre
Catcher/infielder, 1960–1977
Manager, 1977–2010
Torre has a lot in common with CASEY STENGEL. Stengel was an excellent player who went into managing at a young age after his playing career ended. He experienced little success in his first two stints as a manager, and it was a surprise to the baseball world when the Yankees hired him to be their manager. A lot of that applies to Joe Torre. He excelled as a player for many years—even winning the 1971 MVP Award as a Cardinals third baseman—and was hanging on with the Mets in 1977 when the team's manager was fired. Just 36 years old, Torre was offered the job and decided to retire as a player to devote himself to managing full time (but not before acting as player-manager for 18 games). He didn't accomplish much with the Mets and moved to Atlanta prior to the 1982 season, just in time to pilot that club to the N.L. West title. He lasted in Atlanta until 1984, did some broadcasting, then returned to the dugout with the Cardinals in 1990, where he languished between second and sixth place until getting fired mid-way through the 1995 season.

In late 1995, the Yankees called and offered him their opening. Fans and talk show hosts couldn't believe it: Joe Torre, with only one division title to his credit, managing the crown jewel franchise in American sports? "Clueless Joe!" shouted the New York tabloid headlines. There was no reason to believe Torre would succeed where Buck Showalter and countless others had failed. Yet succeed he did. Beginning in 1996, Torre and the Yankees began a run of success surpassed only by the Yankees of Stengel and MCCARTHY: 10 A.L. East division titles, six A.L. pennants, and four World Series victories.

Torre was known for a steady hand and calm demeanor—seemingly just the tonic for the craziness and high expectations that tended to surround GEORGE STEINBRENNER'S Yankees. Each year he didn't win the World Series brought more talk that Steinbrenner would fire him, but somehow Torre survived the axe until 2007.

Rube Waddell
Pitcher, 1897–1910

A stellar talent, Waddell could have been one of the greats. BRANCH RICKEY once said, "When Waddell had control—and some sleep—he was unbeatable." He had a blazing fastball and led the league in strikeouts six straight seasons—with a high of 349, which was 110 more than the second-place finisher. His greatest season was 1905, when he led the league with 27 wins, 287 strikeouts, and a 1.48 ERA. Except for the strikeout totals, however, his other seasons were good but not great; he won 20 four times, but because it was an era of three-man pitching rotations, 20 wins was not the standard for great pitching that it is today.

Waddell's problem, as Rickey implied, was that he was absolutely unreliable, and he may have been developmentally disabled in addition to alcoholic. For Waddell, making it to the ballpark was always a challenge. Being in a condition to pitch was another. Opposing players and managers used to try to break his concentration by giving him little toys. He played marbles with kids. He once disappeared from his team during spring training, only to be found leading a parade downtown. After years of putting up with him, A's manager CONNIE MACK finally got fed up and shipped him to baseball Siberia, the St. Louis Browns. Following a couple of undistinguished seasons with the Browns, Waddell died in 1914 from tuberculosis, which he contracted while trying to help residents of a Kentucky town brace against a flood. He was elected to the Hall of Fame in 1946 by an apparently sympathetic VETERANS COMMITTEE.

Honus Wagner
"The Flying Dutchman"
Shortstop, 1897–17

Wagner came up as an outfielder with the National League's Louisville franchise but moved to Pittsburgh when the other club folded after 1899. A few years later, he shifted to shortstop, and though already a star, Wagner blossomed into the biggest superstar in the game. The numbers themselves are amazing: eight batting titles, nine 100-RBI seasons, five stolen base crowns, six times leading the league in slugging, and on and on. But they don't tell the whole story. He loved to play the game, he loved to win, and he would and could do whatever it took to win. As a fielder, he was the greatest of his time. As a hitter and baserunner, only TY COBB was better. As a positive clubhouse influence, he was unmatched. He was more beloved by fans than anybody until RUTH. He was friendly with rookies and veterans alike, and he maintained his humility despite his fame.

"If I had a choice of all players who have played baseball," long-time Yankee boss ED BARROW, who guided Babe Ruth's career, once said, "the first man I would select would be Honus Wagner." And legendary manager JOHN MCGRAW said: "I consider Wagner not only as the number one shortstop, but had he played in any position other than pitcher, he would have been equally great at the other seven positions. He was the nearest thing to a perfect player no matter where his manager chose to play him."

Alas, the end of Wagner's career didn't go as smoothly as the middle of it. Wagner refused to sign a 1918 contract with Pittsburgh when owner Barney Dreyfuss demanded to cut his salary, citing "war conditions." Wagner was 44 anyway and ready to quit, and Dreyfuss decided he had no use for his great star anymore. The hard feelings between the two persisted, resulting in Wagner's near banishment from the game.

During the Depression, Wagner was living in poverty with his wife and two daughters. His sporting goods business had failed, and he was too proud to ask for charity. An article by sportswriter Fred Lieb describing Wagner's plight changed all that. Wagner got a job with the Pirates as a coach and gate attraction, and he spent the remaining years of his life with the game he loved. He was one of the first five men elected to the Hall of Fame in 1936. And when you're talking about an all-time all-star team, there's no doubt about who belongs at shortstop: The Flying Dutchman.

Eddie Waitkus
First baseman, 1941, 1946–55

Waitkus was an All-Star first baseman with the Cubs and Phillies, a good hitter who'd batted .292 in 1947 and .295 in '48. He had many fans, but none more devoted than 19-year-old Ruth Ann Steinhagen from Chicago.

Right after the first time she saw Waitkus play in 1947, she became so obsessed with him that she attended just about every Cubs game and talked about him incessantly, to the dismay of her parents, who never liked baseball. She clipped out newspaper articles and photographs and built a shrine to Waitkus in her room, sometimes carrying on conversations with the photos. Every man in her life—from her father to her boss to actors in movies—seemed to resemble Waitkus. When Waitkus was traded to Philadelphia before the 1949 season, she became despondent and had to leave her job. Waitkus knew nothing about this because she'd never tried to contact him, and if he walked near her after a game, she would back away and once almost fainted.

Early in 1949, the obsession caused her to buy a rifle from a pawn shop. "[I]f I couldn't have him," she told a court psychiatrist after she was caught, "neither could anyone else." When the Phillies came to Chicago, she checked into the team's hotel and sent him a note asking him to come to her room. He arrived at her door just before midnight on June 14, 1949. "What do you want to see me about?" he asked. Telling him she had a "surprise" for him, she turned and took the rifle out of her closet.

"For two years you have been bothering me," she told him, pointing the gun at him, "and now you are going to die." Calmly, she pulled the trigger and shot him in the stomach.

She had planned to kill herself next but said she lost her nerve. Instead, she called the hotel operator and asked for a doctor. Arrested and diagnosed as a schizophrenic, she spent three years in a state mental hospital.

Miraculously, Waitkus made a complete recovery. He missed only the rest of the 1949 season and came back to play a full schedule in 1950, helping the "Whiz Kid" Phillies to the National League pennant with a .284 average and 102 runs scored. He lasted five more seasons and retired with a career batting average of .285.

If Waitkus's story sounds familiar, it's because Bernard Malamud used it as the basis for his acclaimed novel THE NATURAL, although he changed the details of the crime and the motivations of the shooter

Moses Fleetwood Walker
"Fleet"
Catcher, 1884

JACKIE ROBINSON was not, technically, the first black man to play in the major leagues. He wasn't even the second. Those honors go to Moses Fleetwood Walker and Welday Wilberforce Walker, two brothers who played in 1884 for the Toledo club of the American Association, which was then considered a major league. Fleet, the more successful of the two, was a rarity among ballplayers: college educated, intelligent, and black. However, neither brother performed impressively that season: Moses, an excellent defensive catcher, batted .263 in 42 games, while Welday, an outfielder, played in just six games with a batting average of .182. Both were released from the team at the end of the season. Both encountered overt racial harassment from opposing fans and players throughout the season, but neither accused their club of racism. And they continued their baseball careers with teams in other professional (minor) leagues. Blacks playing alongside whites was, in fact, an occasional if uncommon occurrence until 1894, when, thanks in part to CAP ANSON, the COLOR LINE became entrenched.

Walker's life encompassed more than just his short time in baseball. After leaving the game, he received patents for four inventions, wrote a book on the repatriation of blacks to Africa, and even ran an opera house, of all things. But he also spent some time in jail for theft and was tried and acquitted for his role in a knife fight. For more on this fascinating man, check out David Zang's 1998 book *Fleet Walker's Divided Heart: The Life of Baseball's First Black Major Leaguer.*

Paul Waner
"Big Poison"
Outfielder, 1926–45

One of the few men to win a batting title in his rookie season, Waner was a hitting machine who finished his career with 3,152 career hits, which ranked him fourth on the all-time list when he retired. He could have had 3,153 hits, but on the occasion of his 3,000th, he asked the official scorer to change an infield hit to an error so that he could truly earn the hit. Playing for the Pirates in spacious Forbes Field, he didn't have home run sock, but his doubles and triples totals and his yearly slugging percentages in the .500s indicate he had excellent power.

Not only was Waner a terror at the plate and in the outfield, he could also attack the bottle. CASEY STENGEL once said, "He had to be a very graceful player, because he could slide without breaking the bottle on his hip." There is a famous story that he quit drinking one year at the request of his manager. By midseason, however, he was batting just .240, so the skipper brought him some liquor, and Waner's batting stroke returned.

Brooklyn Dodger fans nicknamed Waner "Big Poison," which didn't refer to a giant deadly concoction but rather, according to RED SMITH, was Brooklynese for "Big Person." Since Waner was only 5-8 and 153 pounds, one can only assume the term was meant figuratively.

Waner had a brother Lloyd, who, like Paul, is in the Hall of Fame (but, unlike Paul, doesn't belong). Poor Lloyd had a tough act to follow, and fans didn't help by nicknaming him "Little Poison" even though he was an inch taller than his brother.

John Montgomery Ward
Pitcher/shortstop, 1878–94
Manager, 1884, 1890–94
Ward owns perhaps the most impressive résumé in baseball history. The Penn State graduate came to the National League in 1878 as a pitcher, compiling his greatest season a year later when he led the league in victories (47) and strikeouts (239), while guiding Providence to the pennant. When not on the mound, he also played the outfield and the middle infield. His arm went bad in 1884, so he moved full-time to shortstop and became the league's top fielder as well as an excellent baserunner, stealing as many as 111 bases in a season.

Meanwhile, he was elevated to manager and was one of the most innovative of his era. He helped popularize the hit-and-run and railed against the sacrifice bunt, both positions contrary to the accepted wisdom of the time. He also wrote one of the first books teaching baseball strategy, called, simply, *Ward's Baseball Book* (which is available today as a free ebook).

During nights and off-seasons, he earned a law degree at Columbia, which prepared him for his next set of duties: those of labor leader. He helped form the short-lived PLAYERS' LEAGUE, which was the first real challenge to the baseball establishment and helped institute a number of reforms that restricted some of the owners' control over the players. He was elected to the Hall of Fame in 1964, which was about 25 years after he should have made it.

Buck Weaver
Third baseman, 1912–20

Poor Buck Weaver. In 1920, he was only 30 years old and having the best season of his career when he was suspended and later banned from baseball for not revealing his team's plot to throw the 1919 WORLD SERIES. It's possible that, with the LIVELY BALL ERA just beginning, Weaver would have fashioned a Hall of Fame career. But instead, he had chosen to protect his teammates and didn't divulge the knowledge that other White Sox players were conspiring with gamblers to fix the championship. Weaver always maintained that although he knew about the plot, he always played his best, and the numbers seem to back him up. For the Series, he batted .324 with four doubles, a triple, and no errors (on the other hand, he had no RBIs despite batting third in the lineup throughout the games). After the banishment, he applied for reinstatement every year until his death in 1956. The commissioner's office denied his request every time.

Earl Weaver
Manager, 1968–82, 1985–86

One of the most successful managers of all time, Weaver led Baltimore to six division titles, four pennants, and a World Series victory. He also had six second-place finishes, and he didn't finish lower than fourth until his final season at the helm, when the Orioles brought him out of retirement for one last go-around. Combative and often abusive toward umpires, Weaver was ejected from a league-record 91 games. But he was also perhaps the most innovative manager of his time. He was the first to keep detailed records of batter-pitcher matchups to help him choose pinch hitters and relievers. He helped develop the best pitching staffs of his era, who combined for almost two dozen 20-win seasons and 10 Cy Young Awards. And, he took platooning to new heights. His approach to the game was called the "BIG BANG THEORY": play for the big inning.

After his first retirement, he wrote one of the classic works on baseball managing, *Weaver on Strategy*, which has influenced a generation of managers, writers, and fans. In it, he listed ten "laws" that encapsulated his approach to managing, among them:

- "If you don't make any promises to your players, you won't have to break them."
- "The easiest way around the bases is with one swing of the bat."
- "Your most precious possessions on offense are your twenty-seven outs."
- "Don't play for one run unless you know that run will win the ballgame."

Sol White
Infielder/manager/executive/historian, Negro leagues, 1887–1926
With many NEGRO LEAGUE players, writers often like to use white major leaguers as comparable reference points: We'll write that POP LLOYD was the black HONUS WAGNER, for example, or JOSH GIBSON was the black BABE RUTH, and so forth. But with Sol White, there really is nobody comparable to him. Though no stats were kept during his playing days, White was a star performer who played on or managed some of black baseball's dominant teams, including the CUBAN GIANTS, Cuban X Giants, and Philadelphia Giants, as well as over half a dozen other teams, including a few other Giants. He also played an important role in the formation of the early organized Negro leagues, and he wrote *The History of Colored Base Ball* in 1906, the first book of its kind and an important reference even today. He died in 1948, and finally in 2006 a special Hall of Fame committee decided to induct him into the shrine. It should have come much sooner.

Smokey Joe Williams
Pitcher, Negro leagues, 1897–32
Many people who have studied the issue call Williams the greatest NEGRO LEAGUE pitcher ever. Even SATCHEL PAIGE, Williams's only rival for that distinction, said, "Smokey Joe could throw harder than anyone." And one manager, the great CUMBERLAND POSEY, said Williams was as fast as WALTER JOHNSON and LEFTY GROVE. In fact, Williams pitched exhibition games against Johnson, PETE ALEXANDER, Chief Bender, and other white Hall of Famers—and beat them all.

Legend has it that Williams struck out 25 batters in one 12-inning ballgame and 27 in another 12-inning contest, although the latter was played under some rickety portable lights. The Hall of Fame took its sweet time honoring Williams, who died in 1951, when it inducted him in 1999.

Ted Williams
"The Kid," "The Splendid Splinter"
Outfielder, 1939–60
Ted Williams was a mediocre fielder and baserunner who had trouble staying healthy. He led his team to only a single pennant and flopped in his only World Series. Still, Williams is one of the greatest players of all time because he was arguably the greatest hitter of all time. Throughout his career, Williams led the league at least twice in every major offensive category except hits and triples. He won two TRIPLE CROWNS, seven batting titles, and four RBI and home run championships—all with the greatest batting eye in history, as evidenced by this amazing fact: From his second season in 1940 until he retired in 1961, he led the league in on-base percentage *every single season he was eligible*, three times surpassing the .500 mark and five other times over .490.

Alas, despite his greatness, he won just two MVP Awards when he really should have won four. In the 1941 SEASON, when he batted .406 and led the league in runs, homers, walks, on-base percentage, and slugging, he lost the award to JOE DiMAGGIO. The Yankees won the pennant, DiMaggio led the league in RBIs, and he was a better fielder, which are three points in his favor. But consider this: DiMaggio batted .408 during his famous 56-game hitting streak and .357 overall, which means that during his other 83 games he batted just .321. Williams, on the other hand, batted .406 *over the entire season* with more homers and 13 more runs scored. But Joe was the media darling who played in the Big City with the glamorous Yankees, while Ted played with the also-ran Red Sox.

The following season, Williams won the Triple Crown with a .356–36 HR–137 RBI season but lost another MVP, this time to Yankee second baseman Joe Gordon. Williams finally captured the MVP in 1946 when his Sox won the pennant. But in 1947, when he won his second Triple Crown, he lost the MVP by a single point when a Boston writer who hated Williams left him off his award ballot entirely.

Ted won his second MVP in 1949, but the following season he broke his elbow in the All-Star game and his hitting was never the same. Even with the bad arm, he still managed to win three more batting titles, but his power and run-producing abilities were diminished, as he topped the 30 mark in homers and the 100 mark in RBIs only once each during his final 11 seasons.

A true American hero, Williams missed five seasons to pilot fighter planes in World War II and Korea, which cost him his chance at 3,000 hits and 650 home runs. As it was, he finished with 2,600 hits and 521 total homers—the last home run coming in the final at bat of his career, a great moment that is described movingly in John Updike's famous essay "HUB FANS BID KID ADIEU." Williams's life story, meanwhile, has been the subject of several recent books, none more interesting than Williams's own autobiography, called *My Turn At Bat*. It belongs in every baseball library.

Williams's death in 2002 set off one of the most bizarre controversies in modern memory as two of his children waged a legal battle over his remains. His daughter wanted to give him a traditional cremation, while his son claimed that Williams had wanted to have his remains frozen and preserved cryogenically. After several years of court hearings (and legal bills), his son finally prevailed, and at last check, Williams's body—or possibly just his severed head—sits in the Alcor Life Extension Foundation in Arizona, a sad and gruesome end to a great American life.

Dave Winfield
Outfielder, 1973–95

One of the greatest all-around athletes to star in the major leagues, Winfield was drafted by teams from each major sport and chose baseball partly because the Padres guaranteed him a starting spot right out of college. A slugger with good speed and fielding skills, he became one of baseball's most consistently impressive players throughout the 1970s.

He joined the Yankees with much fanfare in 1981 after signing a free agent contract worth between $16 and $23 million (depending on cost-of-living escalators), which was the richest ever at the time. It was also the most controversial; Winfield's frequent clashes with Yankee boss GEORGE STEINBRENNER throughout the 1980s stemmed from Steinbrenner's dissatisfaction with that contract.

Although remarkably injury-free throughout most of his career, Winfield missed the entire 1989 season with a back injury that required surgery. But he came back to post several more slugging seasons and won his first World Series title with the Blue Jays in 1992. By the time he retired in 1995, he had banged out more than 3,000 hits with 465 home runs. He was elected to the Hall of Fame on his first try in 2001, where he became the first inducted player whose plaque features the cap of the San Diego Padres (Tony Gwynn was the second).

George Wright
Shortstop, 1871–82
Manager, 1879

The best player in the country at his peak, Wright starred on the legendary 1869 Cincinnati Red Stockings, along with his brother HARRY WRIGHT (*see* 1969: THE FIRST ALL-PROFESSIONAL TEAM). While Harry was the brains of the team, George was the offensive force: During Cincinnati's undefeated season, he batted .629 with 49 homers in 60 games. He also made the most money, earning $1,400 to his brother's $1,200. When the NATIONAL ASSOCIATION came together in 1871, higher salaries enticed the brothers to jump to the Boston team, where they won four of the five pennants in the Association's history. But when pitchers started throwing curves regularly, Wright's batting prowess dwindled to nothing. He tried managing but lasted only a season. Instead, he focused his energy on the burgeoning sporting goods market, where he made a good living. He died at age 90 in 1937, just after he'd been elected to the brand-new Hall of Fame.

Harry Wright
Outfielder/pitcher, 1871–75
Manager, 1871–93

A newspaper of his day called Wright "a baseball Edison. He eats base-ball, breathes base-ball, thinks base-ball, dreams base-ball, and incorporates base-ball in his prayers." All of which may be true, but baseball wasn't even his first love. Wright played CRICKET in his native England before coming to the States. Once he picked up the new game, Wright saw its potential and switched to the American game.

After earning raves as an innovative player and manager, he organized the 1869 Cincinnati Red Stockings, the first openly all-professional baseball club—an accomplishment that earned Wright the title of "Father of Professional Baseball" (*see* 1969: THE FIRST ALL-PROFESSIONAL TEAM). As a pitcher, Wright was a top junkballer, capable of retiring batters with trick pitches rather than heat. He managed in the NATIONAL ASSOCIATION and the National League until 1893, during which time he remained a respected and influential baseball figure. Among his many managerial innovations, Wright initiated the practice of fielders backing up one another. Wright also suggested that pitchers throw overhand instead of underhand and sidearm. He was selected to the Hall of Fame in 1953.

Carl Yastrzemski
"Yaz"
Outfielder/first baseman, 1961–83

Now that the numbers are in the books, it would be easy to denigrate Yaz's career. We may think of him as a slugger, but he hit fewer than 20 homers in all but eight of his 23 seasons. We may think of him as a high-average hitter, but he batted under .285 more than half his career. We may think of him as a good fielder—and in fact he did win seven GOLD GLOVES—but he played first base and DH for most of the second half of his career.

Despite all that, he was one of baseball's most respected players and most feared hitters throughout the 1960s and 1970s. Yastrzemski's best years came in the 1960s, when offensive totals were at their lowest levels since the DEAD BALL ERA. But 1967 stands as a season for the ages when he practically carried the team to Boston's first pennant in 20 years, earning Yaz a TRIPLE CROWN victory (.326 BA–44 HR–121 RBIs) and MVP Award. It became known as "THE IMPOSSIBLE DREAM."

By the '70s, he had lost some of his batting stroke, but he was still a team leader. However, Yaz's Sox lost another Series in 1975 (*see* 1975: THE SOX AND REDS PLAY A SERIES FOR THE AGES) and a thrilling pennant race in 1978 (*see* 1978: THE BOSTON MASSACRE). When he retired, Yaz was the only American League player who had tallied both 3,000 hits and 400 homers. He was elected to the Hall of Fame on the first ballot in 1989.

Cy Young
Pitcher, 1890–1911

The man for whom the pitching award is named, Young holds many significant career pitching records: wins (511), losses (316), innings (7,354), games started (815), and complete games (749); he's also pretty high up there in games pitched (906) and shutouts (76). He could amass such amazing numbers because he played in a time—the DEAD BALL ERA—when pitchers didn't have to throw hard every pitch, so teams could employ three-man staffs and good pitchers could throw 350 to 450 innings and get 40-plus decisions every season.

But that shouldn't minimize Young's accomplishments because, even though pitching was so different back then, Young was among the best at his craft for nearly all of his 22 seasons in the majors. Pitching the bulk of his career with the Red Sox and Cleveland Spiders, he led the league in victories four times, ERA twice, shutouts seven times, and a bunch of other categories numerous times as well.

Fans today know him by a familiar nickname, but many don't realize that "Cy" itself is short for another nickname, "Cyclone," which was bestowed upon Young when he was pitching for a minor league club in his hometown of Canton, Ohio, in 1890. "I thought I had to show all my stuff," recalled Young, whose real name was Denton, "and I almost tore the boards of the grandstand with my fastball. One of the fellows called me 'Cyclone,' but finally shortened it to 'Cy,' and it's been that ever since."

Despite all the pitching records, Young was not in the first group of enshrinees to the Hall of Fame in 1936. It's not because he was undeserving, however. Hall voters in those early days were split into two groups, one selecting players from the 19th century and the other players from the 20th. Since Young's career straddled both eras, he didn't receive enough votes by either faction to make it. He was instead elected a year later.

Dutch Zwilling
Outfielder, 1910, 1914–16

Zwilling was a pretty good hitter who led the FEDERAL LEAGUE in homers in 1914 and RBIs in 1915. But his real claim to fame is that he comes last in any alphabetical listing of major league ballplayers, including this one.

2
EXECUTIVES, MEDIA
& MORE

Daniel Adams
"Doc"
Pioneer
An early "Father of Baseball" who helped influence and standardize baseball rules during the middle of the 19th century. Research by author John Thorn—now the official historian of the Baseball Hall of Fame—has credited Adams with a much larger role than was previously thought. See the entry on ALEXANDER CARTWRIGHT for a lot more information.

Lee Allen
Historian
Author BILL JAMES, who has studied the issue for decades, gives Allen a lot of credit for the growth and quality of baseball research over the past 50 years. As the first official historian at the Hall of Fame in 1958, Allen compiled detailed biographical data about every major league ballplayer—the first time it had ever been done in a systematic way. He built up the Hall's library to what it is today—the largest and best baseball library in the world. He made major contributions to *BASEBALL ENCYCLOPEDIA*, the first comprehensive statistical record of the major leagues. And when he died in 1969, his effect on the sport was only beginning to be realized. Today, the literature of baseball is rich with fascinating biographies, analytical histories, statistical stud-

ies, and more. And not a few of these books owe their existence, whether directly or indirectly, to Lee Allen. Quite a legacy.

Mel Allen
Broadcaster
TV and radio voice of the New York Yankees from 1939 until 1964 (when he was inexplicably fired) and later the host of TV's "This Week in Baseball," Allen was one of baseball's most influential broadcasters who popularized baseball on the radio during its early years. When you hear somebody say "How about that!" or "That ball is going, going, gone!" you're hearing Mel Allen.

Roger Angell
Writer
Angell appeared frequently on KEN BURNS'S *BASEBALL* documentary, but he is best known for the beautiful articles about baseball that he contributes to *The New Yorker* magazine once or twice a year. Baseball fans should own at least one of his baseball books. *Season Ticket, Late Innings, Five Seasons,* and *The Summer Game* contain reprints of his New Yorker pieces, and *Game Time* and *Once More Around the Ballpark* are "greatest hits" collections. *A Pitcher's Story* tells the story of one season in the life of veteran pitcher David Cone.

What makes Angell so wonderful and necessary is that his writing combines charming, eloquent prose with a philosophy that can be summed up simply: He just loves the game. And as ugly cynicism in baseball grows at an alarming rate, Angell's words can provide just the tonic we need. One reading of an Angell book will remind you why you fell in love with the game in the first place.

Red Barber
Broadcaster
The voice of the Brooklyn Dodgers, Cincinnati Reds, and several other teams, Barber was one of the pioneers of baseball broadcasting on radio. He began his career in the mid–1930s, first with the Reds and later as the first baseball broadcaster in New York City. He was known for his unique expressions, many of which came from his Southern roots, such as "They're tearin' up the pea-pod," "It's brewing up into a real rhubarb," and "The bases are FOB—full of Brooklyns." After retiring from broadcasting, Barber enjoyed a successful

writing career, penning books on such subjects as the breaking of the COLOR LINE (*1947: When All Hell Broke Loose in Baseball*) and sports broadcasting (*The Broadcasters*). Barber died in 1993.

Ed Barrow
Executive

Barrow worked in baseball as a scout, manager, and general manager from the 1890s until 1945. Early in his career, he signed HONUS WAGNER. Later, he managed the Red Sox, where he approved shifting BABE RUTH from the pitcher's mound to the outfield—although, as Robert Creamer points out in *BABE: THE LEGEND COMES TO LIFE*, Barrow resisted strongly and only agreed after vehement arguments with Ruth and some teammates. Barrow's greatest success, though, came as general manager of the Yankees from 1921 to 1945, where he created the dynasty that ruled baseball until the 1960s. In New York beginning in the 1920s, he signed LOU GEHRIG, Tony Lazzeri, Bill Dickey, Lefty Gomez, Joe Gordon, and JOE DIMAGGIO, among others.

Like most general managers of his day, Barrow was infamous for underpaying his employees. In 1938, for example, DiMaggio asked Barrow for a $45,000 salary; Barrow responded by noting that the great Gehrig earned only $41,000. DiMaggio's reply: "Mr. Gehrig is underpaid." DiMaggio held out but finally relented and signed for $25,000 when his demands angered the Depression-era public. Meanwhile, Barrow's employers were millionaires.

Billy Beane
Outfielder, 1984–89
Executive

Beane, the player, qualifies as one of the biggest busts in the history of the amateur draft. Beane, the general manager, qualifies as one of the most successful team-builders in modern baseball.

As described in Michael Lewis's *MONEYBALL*, Beane was one of the most coveted amateur players in the nation when he was taken in the first round by the New York Mets in the 1980 draft. In high school, everything had come easy to Beane, but when he got to the minors, he wasn't able to adapt to the higher-quality pitching. Scouts loved him; he *looked* like the star ballplayer they all thought he would become. But Beane never succeeded at the plate, and he finished his major league career with a .219 average and 3 homers over parts of six seasons.

Before the 1990 season began, at the age of 28, Beane abruptly walked into general manager Sandy Alderson's office and asked for a job as a scout. Imagine turning down a chance to play on a major league team in order to drive around small towns scouting amateurs. It shocked Alderson so much that he gave Beane the job and kept a close eye on him.

It didn't take long for Beane to work his way up to assistant general manager, and when Alderson left the A's in 1997, Beane took charge. He still works as GM of the A's.

For the first decade of his tenure, the A's made the playoffs repeatedly despite one of the league's lowest payrolls. He did it the way a good investor operates: by buying low and selling high. For example, Beane believed that ace closers were overvalued. So he would sign an un-known or out-of-favor hard-thrower to be his closer, watch him suc-ceed, then trade or let him go when he became too expensive. This tactic worked with Billy Taylor, Jason Isringhausen, Billy Koch, and Keith Foulke.

Beane's most glaring failure as GM has been his team's inability to win in the post-season. Pundits claim it's because his teams rely too much on walks and home runs and can't play "smallball"—bunt, steal bases, hit and run, and so on. In fact, I think the reason his teams haven't won much in the post-season simply comes down to bad luck. In a short series, almost anything can happen, and blaming Billy Beane because Jeremy Giambi failed to slide or Miguel Tejada didn't take an extra base is just wrong. Still, the lack of significant postsea-son success is a stain on Beane's record and will remain so until his A's win at least a pennant or two.

Dr. James Beckett
Publisher

The guru of the baseball card market, Beckett's company publishes books and magazines featuring price guides for baseball and other sports cards. Beckett, with a Ph.D. in statistics, practically invented the modern baseball card market when he instituted the first national statistical price survey for the cards in 1976. Beginning in 1979, he oversaw the publication of the *Sport Americana* guidebooks, which provided the first comprehensive price guide to the entire history of baseball cards.

Since 1984, when *Beckett Baseball Card Monthly* was first published, the card-collecting hobby has skyrocketed into a multibillion-dollar industry, and Beckett Publications has added magazines and a website devoted to basketball, football, hockey, and other cards. Beckett himself, meanwhile, remains *the* authority in the market, and it's no coincidence that the card market exploded around the time his authoritative guides were published. He wasn't the sole reason for the astonishing growth, to be sure, but his contributions can't be dismissed.

Scott Boras
Agent
Boras played minor league baseball in the Cardinals' and Cubs' organizations, but never made it out of AA ball. So he turned to law and became an agent, where he has achieved off the field what he couldn't do on it. Today, he is clearly the most successful player agent in history—coveted by players, feared by team owners, and reviled by opposing agents whose clients have defected to Boras. Almost every huge, record-setting contract signed since 2000 has been for a Boras client: ALEX RODRIGUEZ'S $252 million deal with the Rangers, Barry Zito's $126 million deal with the Giants, and many more.

Those are just the superstars, players who could be said to deserve the money. Boras's most sublime skill has come with players who had no business getting contracts as big as they were. In the early 2000s, Boras victimized the Dodgers twice—first getting them to sign Darren Dreifort for $55 million over five years, even though Dreifort had suffered numerous injuries and only had put together a single productive season. Then he got the Dodgers to sign Kevin Brown for $105 million over seven years in spite of Brown's age and injury history. Both times, he seemed to convince the Dodgers that other teams were seriously competing for the players, when the other teams had probably dropped out of the bidding when the price got too high.

Some in baseball claim that Boras is somehow responsible for the rising salaries in the game. Not true at all. Was it Boras's fault that the Dodgers got so caught up in the negotiating frenzy to forget about the fragility of Dreifort and Brown? No, it's not. Boras is responsible solely for getting his players the money that owners are willing to pay—not one dime more or less. And he's the best in the world at it.

Harry Caray
Broadcaster

The radio voice of the Cardinals, Athletics, and, more famously, the Chicago Cubs, Caray broadcast baseball games from the 1950s through 1999, when he passed away. A fan favorite, his trademarks included the phrases "It might be... it could be... it is!" and "Holy cow!" (a phrase borrowed by Phil Rizzuto). He would also lead the crowd in singing "TAKE ME OUT TO THE BALL GAME" during the seventh-inning stretch.

Broadcasting is apparently genetic in the Caray family: son Skip broadcast Atlanta Braves games for many years, and grandsons Chip and Josh are also announcers.

There is one teensy, tiny knock on Harry Caray as a broadcaster: near the end, he may have, once in a while, on certain occasions, had one or two too many beers in the broadcast booth. I'm not saying he was drunk, but, well, um, he would forget players names, he would miss some of the action on the field, he would talk about things like traffic or the weather and ignore the game for minutes at a stretch. But that just made many fans love him all the more.

Alexander Cartwright
Pioneer

Cartwright is recognized as one of the founders of modern baseball. However, the preponderance of evidence suggests that, like ABNER DOUBLEDAY, Cartwright has been erroneously credited with a greater role than he actually deserves.

According to historian John Thorn, Cartwright, a bank teller by trade, was among those responsible for founding the first organized baseball club—the NEW YORK KNICKERBOCKERS—that played with a set of official rules, known as the KNICKERBOCKER RULES. One of those rules was the establishment of foul territory, whereas ROUNDERS and CRICKET—baseball's precursors—have no foul ground.

But contrary to what his Hall of Fame plaque says, Cartwright did not set the bases 90 feet apart nor establish nine innings per game and nine players per lineup. Those innovations came as much as a decade after the year (1845) when Cartwright allegedly wrote the rules. In fact, Thorn's exhaustive research credits DANIEL "DOC" ADAMS as the originator of many of those rules. While president of the

New York Base Ball Club, Adams played the same game as the Knick-erbockers—using Cartwright's alleged rules—in 1840. And that game, already known as "base ball," was essentially the same as one played as early as 1832—which means that Cartwright's game was being played for nearly 15 years before he supposedly invented it.

In 1848, Cartwright left New York to join the gold rush in Califor-nia. And for the next 14 years, Adams served as the Knickerbockers president and then as presiding officer of the NATIONAL ASSOCIA-TION OF BASE BALL PLAYERS. During that time, it was Adams, not Cartwright, who helped refine the game further by fixing the bases 90 feet apart and the pitching box 45 feet from home plate. Under Ad-ams's guidance, the rules were also changed to declare the winner of a game to be the team leading after nine innings—not, as the original Knickerbocker rules dictated, the first team to score 21 runs (which was possible because pitching and defense hardly existed).

What was Cartwright's role in all this? As stated earlier, he did help form the first organized baseball club with a written constitution that set some rules of the game, such as the diamond-shaped field (actu-ally a square), the idea of foul territory, and the change in the roun-ders rules that called for retiring baserunners by throwing the ball at them. Baseball historians and writers alive at the time of baseball's development, such as HENRY CHADWICK, never claimed that baseball had a spontaneous creation, and probably neither did Cartwright. They always wrote that baseball was an evolutionary descendant of those British games. The truth is, the game of baseball doesn't have a distinct starting point—not 1845 or 1839 or even 1832—nor does it have a single "Father of Baseball." What started Americans believing that baseball had a Divine Creator was ALBERT SPALDING'S infamous MILLS COMMISSION REPORT in 1907.

Henry Chadwick
Writer

A true baseball pioneer, Chadwick was the first reporter to cover the sport regularly for major newspapers. He developed the box score and the first scoring system, and he wrote the first books and guides on the sport. Many called him the "Father of Baseball," and he had strong ideas about how the game should be played, preferring "scien-tific" baseball—spray hitting, aggressive baserunning—over slugging; these strategies dominated baseball until the 1920s. Additionally, Chadwick helped popularize the game among fans with his writings.

To illustrate the evolution sports writing has experienced, here's a sampling of Chadwick's prose describing a game in 1869: "On October 26th the Red Stockings returned to New York from Troy, after defeating the strong nine of the Haymakers of that village by a score of 12 to 7, and on the afternoon of that day played the first game of a new series of contests with the Mutual Club. The Saturday previous they had opened play in the east with a noteworthy triumph over the Athletics in Philadelphia by a score of 15 to 8, and therefore they entered upon this contest flushed with two victories, that at Troy being the most creditable display." Imagine that appearing in *USA Today*.

Happy Chandler
Commissioner, 1945–51
The onetime senator and governor of Kentucky, Chandler was elected baseball commissioner following the death of KENESAW MOUNTAIN LANDIS in 1945. Though he lasted just six years in office, Chandler oversaw the sport's most important change: the breaking of the COLOR LINE. Chandler defied ownership by publicly supporting integration—a surprising position from a Southern politician. Although his role in JACKIE ROBINSON'S signing was probably not as big as he liked to take credit for, the fact is that his predecessor never would have allowed it. Chandler was justifiably proud of his accomplishment.

Charles Comiskey
"Commy," "The Old Roman"
Infielder/outfielder, 1882–1894
Manager, 1883–1894
Owner
The founder of the Chicago White Sox, Comiskey was instrumental in the formation of the American League. Before that, he had a 13-year career as a player and manager, during which he pioneered the strategies of shifting fielders for different hitters and having the pitcher cover first base on balls hit to the right. Later, under Comiskey's leadership, the White Sox won four pennants and two World Series. It might have been three if Comiskey's notorious parsimony hadn't given eight members of the his team a reason to accept money from gamblers to throw the 1919 WORLD SERIES in the event that became known as the Black Sox scandal.

Abner Doubleday
Civil War veteran

"The only thing Abner Doubleday started," said BRANCH RICKEY, "was the Civil War." Indeed, Captain Doubleday fired the first Union shots at Fort Sumter. Later, he commanded Union troops at the beginning of the Battle of Gettysburg. But he did not start the game of baseball—that is 100 percent myth.

Nowhere in his diaries or memoirs does he even *mention* the sport he supposedly invented in the spring of 1839 in Cooperstown, New York. In fact, it's doubtful he was even *in* that part of the state, since he was a student at West Point at the time. But ALBERT SPALDING'S infamous MILLS COMMISSION REPORT gave Doubleday sole credit for the game's invention, and the Hall of Fame is now located in the city of its supposed birth.

However, today, not even the Hall itself is defending the story anymore: "The DOUBLEDAY MYTH has since been exposed," reads the Hall's website. "Doubleday was at West Point in 1839, yet 'The Myth' has grown so strong that the facts will never deter the spirit of Cooperstown."

Postscript: In 2010, baseball commissioner BUD SELIG disgraced himself and his office—even further—by writing, in a letter to a fan, "I really believe that Abner Doubleday is the 'Father of Baseball.'" I don't know if he was just just trying to tell the fan what he wanted to hear or if he really believes it, but geez, Bud, ever heard of something called "facts"?

Theo Epstein
Executive

The youngest and most popular general manager in the history of the Boston Red Sox, Epstein was promoted to his position in 2002 at the age of 29. Epstein, with the full assent of his bosses, proceeded to rebuild the team based on SABERMETRIC principles advocated by BILL JAMES and others, and he even worked with James himself after the author was hired as a consultant. The resulting World Series victory in 2004 means Epstein, despite leaving Boston for Chicago after the 2011 season, will never have to buy his own beer in Boston ever again (*see* 2004: THE CURSE IS REVERSED).

Donald Fehr
Union leader

Fehr headed the MAJOR LEAGUE BASEBALL PLAYERS ASSOCIATION from 1986 until 2009, having previously worked under MARVIN MILLER as the MLBPA's general counsel. Combining Miller's tough negotiating skills with impressive legal acumen, Fehr led the Association through a numerous labor battles.

During the 1994 strike, he was probably as hated by the general public as his adversary BUD SELIG, but Fehr and the MLBPA had a more defensible position (*see* 1994: THE WORLD SERIES GETS KILLED). After all, the players were fighting to keep the owners from taking away something that had been agreed to by the owners themselves. Where Fehr and the players went wrong was that they underestimated the owners' collective resolve. The owners were itching for some kind of labor victory over the players after 25 years of defeats. Fehr turned off a lot of people with his seeming aloofness, and late in that strike, some in the media called for Fehr to take himself out of the negotiations because it was feared that the personal animosity between Fehr and the owners was getting in the way of a settlement. In fact, the obstacle wasn't the personalities but rather the reluctance on either side to change its views.

It's easy to resent the players for their huge salaries: they're getting paid millions to play a kids' game. But the players didn't *steal* that money—the owners gave it to them. You can't expect the players to give that away without a fight. That was Fehr's job. And whenever he took an unpopular stand—such as his slowness in recognizing the problem of steroid abuse—he did so because he represented the financial interests of 700-plus dues-paying union members.

Charles Finley
Owner

The controversial owner of the Oakland A's in the 1960s and 1970s, Finley helped institute the designated hitter, night World Series games, and colorful uniforms. To his fellow owners' chagrin, however, he also helped usher in the FREE AGENCY era when he reneged on his contract with CATFISH HUNTER; the subsequent union grievance resulted in Hunter being declared baseball's first free agent.

A master of promotion and a great judge of baseball talent, Finley was much less successful managing his employees. Although his A's won three straight World Series from 1972 to 1974, they did it with feuds, fights, and two different managers. In fact, even before GEORGE STEINBRENNER made the practice fashionable, Finley led the league in hiring and firing managers. In the first ten years of his ownership, for example, he made 11 managerial changes. Charitably described as cheap, Finley sold his team and got out of baseball rather than succumb to the demands of free agents seeking high salaries.

Ford Frick
National League president, 1934–51
Commissioner, 1951–65

Frick is best known as the man who put a figurative ASTERISK next to ROGER MARIS'S record 61-homer season because it occurred in 162 games, not the 154 that BABE RUTH played in (*see* 61). Frick was a former sportswriter who ghost-wrote for Ruth in the 1920s and was associated with baseball for 43 years. So the asterisk isn't his only legacy.

As National League president, he helped ease JACKIE ROBINSON'S entry into baseball when he was confronted by a rumor that St. Louis Cardinals would go on strike rather than play against Robinson. Frick issued this ultimatum: "I don't care if half the league strikes. Those who do will... be suspended, and I do not care if it wrecks the NL for five years. This is the United States of America, and one citizen has as much right to play as another."

During Frick's reign as commissioner, which began in 1951, baseball underwent several sweeping changes: four major franchise shifts, including the 1958 WESTWARD EXPANSION by the Braves, Dodgers, and Giants; the addition of four new teams, changing the dynamics of baseball for the first time since the AL was formed in 1901; and the explosion in television and radio revenues during the 1950s. Yet the Robinson matter notwithstanding, Frick was a notorious yes-man who himself took little part in any of the monumental events that shaped his tenure. He let the real power brokers—the owners—have nearly free rein over the game; in those pre-union days, he was just what the owners needed.

He entered the Hall of Fame in 1970. Eight years later, the Hall created an award in his honor that is presented annually to broadcasters to honor their contributions to the game. Recent winners include

Dave Niehaus, Tony Kubek, Jon Miller, and, in 2011, TIM MCCARVER..

Bart Giamatti
National League president, 1986–88
Commissioner, 1989–89
One-time president of Yale University, Giamatti fulfilled a lifelong dream by becoming a league president in 1986 (he wanted to become American League president and settled for the National League job) and baseball commissioner two years later. His joyous enthusiasm for the game kept his reign focused on what he believed was best for baseball and made him popular among owners, fans, and the media. The players may have had a different opinion after Giamatti, in the most lasting decision of his short tenure, handed PETE ROSE a suspension from baseball for betting on baseball. As a result, Rose today remains barred from the Hall of Fame. Just nine days after announcing that momentous decision and 154 days after taking the office, Giamatti, a chain smoker, died from a heart attack at the age of 51.

William Hulbert
National League president, 1876–82
Hulbert owned the Chicago franchise of the NATIONAL ASSOCIATION—a loosely run league notoriously devoid of discipline that lasted only a few years. Hulbert wanted to create a league with schedules and rules, so he and a few other team owners formed the National League in 1876. Though he was not the first NL president—Morgan Bulkeley, a politician, was—Hulbert took over the reins of the league when Bulkeley failed to show up for an important league meeting. Under Hulbert's tight control, the fledgling league prospered. Hulbert, known for a time as "The Savior of the Game," died in 1882. Somehow, Bulkeley—who lasted less than one season as head of the League and had zero power—has been in the Hall of Fame for more than fifty years while Hulbert, who masterminded the whole deal, wasn't honored until 1995.

Bill James
Writer
The most influential baseball writer in recent times, James is largely responsible for revolutionizing the way people approach baseball statistics. Through his *Baseball Abstracts*, which he published from 1978

through 1988, James examined and analyzed countless statistical questions, such as the true value of the stolen base and the importance of walks, and he introduced new methods of judging ballplayers through the practice of SABERMETRICS, a term coined by James himself.

Among his other body of work, he wrote what I and many others consider the quintessential baseball history book—*THE BILL JAMES HISTORICAL BASEBALL ABSTRACT*; every fan should own a copy. Another great book is *Whatever Happened to the Hall of Fame?*, the first thorough examination of that institution.

Some mistakenly believe James is responsible for the explosion in statistics you see during a game: "Batting average on Tuesday afternoons," "Home runs against left-handers in day games after night games," and so forth. But that's an injustice to James. In fact, his precedent-setting statistical analyses and general approach to the game have positively influenced—directly or indirectly—an entire generation of baseball fans and writers, myself included.

One of his most recent breakthroughs is the "WIN SHARES" system, which is sort of a holy grail of baseball statistics. It combines the entirety of a player's contributions to his club—batting, baserunning, pitching, and fielding—into a single number. It's a fascinating tool that is already being used by sabermetricians everywhere. Today, James continues to deliver top-notch baseball analysis and research in book form, on his website, and as a consultant with the Boston Red Sox.

Ban Johnson
American League President, 1901–26

Johnson was working as a sportswriter when he and CHARLES COMISKEY took over the Western League, a minor league, in 1893. Seven years later, Johnson decided to take on the baseball establishment by changing the league's name to the American League and a year later proclaiming the AL to be a "major league"—touching off a war between the two leagues for players and fans (*see* 1901: THE AMERICAN LEAGUE WAR). When the truce was called after the 1904 season, Johnson emerged as the big winner: He wielded the greatest influence over the three-man National Commission that ruled baseball until the commissioner's office was established in 1920. Stern and unyielding, Johnson always did what he felt was best for the league.

For example, he banned liquor from ballparks and meted out harsh penalties against players engaging in "rowdyism." To enforce the rules, he backed his umpires vehemently at a time when on-field officials often received little support or protection from league offices.

When KENESAW MOUNTAIN LANDIS was installed as baseball's autocratic commissioner, Johnson's power disappeared. Without the control he was accustomed to, Johnson retired from the game in 1926.

Bill Klem
Umpire, 1905–41
"I never missed a call in my heart," Klem once said. With this attitude, Klem excelled at an always-tough job—made even tougher by the fact that, when Klem broke in, only one umpire officiated a game. Even after baseball added more umpires, Klem spent much of his career exclusively calling balls and strikes. A pioneer in the use of hand signals, he once kept the players in suspense after a close play. "What is it?" a player finally asked. "It ain't nothing till I call it," Klem replied.

Bowie Kuhn
Commissioner, 1968–84
Kuhn presided during perhaps baseball's most dramatic and controversial period: the FREE AGENCY era. At his election to the post, Kuhn was working at the New York law firm that served the National League. As commissioner, his legal training would be called upon often. The dismantling of the RESERVE CLAUSE, coming soon after the landmark Supreme Court case *Flood v. Kuhn* (*see* 1972: LABOR UNREST AND *FLOOD V. KUHN*), defined his tenure—as did the 1981 STRIKE that canceled 52 games.

Kuhn made lots of enemies: He suspended WILLIE MAYS and MICKEY MANTLE from participating in baseball-related functions because of their associations with Atlantic City casinos; he made several shortsighted decisions that helped facilitate the downfall of the reserve clause; he handed down suspensions to powerful owners GEORGE STEINBRENNER and TED TURNER; he allowed the TV networks to schedule all World Series games at night; and he created a controversial playoff system for the 1981 strike-torn season that angered fans and owners.

His tenure was, in fact, marked by more losses than victories, and owners ousted him in 1984 when they decided they wanted a businessman-CEO to lead a restructured baseball "corporation" into the future—which led to the selection of PETER UEBERROTH as commissioner. One of his frequent adversaries, CHARLIE FINLEY, had this to say about Kuhn: "If Bowie Kuhn had a brain in his head, he'd be an idiot."

Kenesaw Mountain Landis
Commissioner, 1921–44

Only a handful of men influenced major league baseball more than Kenesaw Mountain Landis. Prior to becoming baseball's first commissioner, he had worked as a federal judge who vaulted to fame though a number of antitrust decisions—many of which were outrageous enough to get overturned by higher courts. But in 1920, baseball needed an authoritarian figure to preside over the game in the wake of the 1919 BLACK SOX SCANDAL and the death of RAY CHAPMAN. So owners turned to Landis, who had refused to make a ruling on an antitrust case against major league baseball several years earlier.

Wanting to provide fans with the appearance of total propriety, the owners granted Landis nearly absolute power—a decision the owners soon came to regret. Landis's first act was to reaffirm the expulsion of the eight members of the Black Sox. He banished many more players for illegal or alleged illegal acts, suspended BABE RUTH for post-season barnstorming, and granted free agency to several hundred minor league ballplayers who were being crushed under the weight of the oppressive farm system. And despite public denials, he supported baseball's policy of denying blacks entry into major league baseball.

When Landis died in 1944 after 23 years on the job, the owners were publicly sad but privately relieved. They then promptly rewrote the bylaws to limit the commissioner's power. To many owners' dismay, BRANCH RICKEY took advantage of Landis's death to open the national pastime to people of all races.

Ernest J. Lanigan
Historian

The 20th century's most influential *unknown* baseball figure, Lanigan set the stage for modern statistical analysis. Working in the 1910s and 1920s, he invented or popularized such statistics as runs batted in, slugging percentage, ERA, and others. He was the first man to compile career statistics of all major league players. He helped create the BASEBALL WRITERS ASSOCIATION OF AMERICA, and he wrote or edited countless articles and books on baseball statistics and history. In 1946, when he was 73, Lanigan became director and then Historian of the Hall of Fame. During his tenure, Hall of Fame attendance increased dramatically. Author BILL JAMES, in his book *Whatever Happened to the Hall of Fame?*, says, "[T]he effect of his work on how people saw the game, how we see the game even today, can hardly be overstated."

Connie Mack
Owner/manager, 1894–1950

From the team's inception in 1901 and for the next 50 years, Cornelius McGillicuddy, or Connie Mack, owned and managed the Philadelphia Athletics—always dressed in a suit and tie, even while on the field. Mack oversaw the development of some of baseball's all-time greats, including EDDIE COLLINS, "HOME RUN" BAKER, MICKEY COCHRANE, JIMMIE FOXX, and LEFTY GROVE. And he put together some of the greatest teams in history, including the 1909–1911 and 1929–1931 clubs.

But because he was also a part owner, winning pennants was only Mack's *second*-greatest concern; profits were always number one. And so he would sell his stars while at the peaks of their careers to raise cash for his struggling bottom line. Still, he remained one of the best-loved figures in the game for most of his six decades in baseball, renowned for his gentle manner and always respectful attitude toward players and umpires. Because a man generally will not fire himself from a job, Mack continued to own and manage the Athletics until the age of 88, establishing unbreakable records for games managed (7,878), victories (3,776), and losses (4,025).

Larry MacPhail
Executive

A true visionary and power broker, MacPhail left a legacy to professional sports that will continue as long as games are played. Among his innovations: night games, radio broadcasts, air travel, and old-timers' days. In addition, he built pennant winners for three different franchises—Cincinnati, Brooklyn, and the Yankees—all while apparently trying to suppress a volatile temper that got him fired from two jobs.* MacPhail stands at the top of a baseball-loving family tree that continues today: Son Lee MacPhail served as AL president from 1974 until 1983, and grandson Andy MacPhail worked as a general manager for the Twins and Cubs (and is rumored to be a possible successor to BUD SELIG as commissioner). It's unlikely that anyone will ever exert more influence over the business of professional sports as Larry MacPhail.

Baseball lore: MacPhail was so, um, unstable that he hatched a plan to kidnap Kaiser Wilhelm at the end of World War I. In the 1940s, he got so drunk after winning the World Series that he quit his job as general manager and punched a newspaper writer.

Marvin Miller
Union leader, 1966–84

With few notable exceptions, no man did more during the last 50 years to revolutionize American sports than Marvin Miller. A longtime officer with the United Steelworkers' Union, Miller was elected head of the MAJOR LEAGUE BASEBALL PLAYERS ASSOCIATION (MLBPA) in 1966, when the burning issue on players' minds was their pension plan. They didn't care that the RESERVE CLAUSE kept their salaries ridiculously low while the owners made exorbitant profits. And they didn't care that baseball's system of resolving players' grievances was illegal and immoral. Marvin Miller *taught* them to care, and in so doing, he gained for all professional athletes higher salaries and overall equitable treatment.

Miller's excellent memoir, *A Whole Different Ballgame*, gives a complete and honest explanation of all the events that marked his tenure: the 1972 and 1981 players' strikes, the numerous collective bargaining agreements he helped negotiate, the renowned 1972 FLOOD V. KUHN Supreme Court battle, the landmark 1975 arbitration case that granted free agency to ANDY MESSERSMITH and DAVE MCNALLY, his seemingly weekly fights with commissioner BOWIE KUHN, and other historic events.

Miller also tells a funny story that illustrates the players' naiveté with labor-related matters when the union was getting started in the mid–60s: After they chose the liberal Miller as their leader, the players said they wanted him to balance the political scale by choosing a conservative as chief legal counsel; they suggested that Miller consider an out-of-work politician who was known to be a big sports fan. His name was Richard Nixon, a man who was certainly no friend to labor. Needless to say, Miller made it a condition of his appointment that he be allowed to choose his own counsel.

Is Miller to blame for all that is wrong in sports? For the greed, the disloyalty, the labor strife? Some have traced everything negative back to Miller, but that's simply misplaced. The money in sports is there. The question is, should the players get it, or should the owners? Remember, it's the owners who year after year shell out the multimillion-dollar contracts to players. Miller simply gained the same freedom for baseball players that the rest of us have in our daily jobs: the right to work elsewhere if we're unhappy in our present job. He should get credit, not blame.

Does Miller belong in the Hall of Fame? Of course he does. Will he ever make it? Maybe now that he has passed away. He was snubbed so many times that he asked to remove his name from consideration at all. In 2007, when a Hall committee featuring grudge-holding former executives passed him over and instead voted for the hapless Bowie Kuhn (!), the committee proved itself wholly unfit for its job. I don't blame Miller for wanting out of the system after being treated so shabbily. Miller died in 2012, which means, of course, that the Hall will most likely exercise its finely honed sense of timing and induct him posthumously and against his apparent wishes.

Robert Murphy
Labor leader

A former lawyer with the National Labor Relations Board, Murphy led a short-lived movement in the 1940s to improve working conditions for baseball players. After forming the American Baseball Guild (ABG), he came close to organizing a strike by the Pittsburgh Pirates to demand more equitable treatment. But it fell apart because not enough players—many of whom were anti-union and afraid of the owners—supported the efforts. The ABG died soon after, but not before effecting some important changes. It established a pension plan for retired ballplayers, got the owners to provide meal money while on the road and during spring training (once called "Murphy Money"), helped raise the minimum major league salary to $5,000, and set the stage for the more successful MAJOR LEAGUE BASEBALL PLAYERS ASSOCIATION that would be headed by MARVIN MILLER two decades later.

Rob Neyer
Writer

This book is filled with so many old or deceased writers, I feel it's important to recognize one of the best baseball writers of modern times who's going to be around for decades to come: Rob Neyer. He started his career as a research assistant for BILL JAMES, then went off on his own to become one of the founding baseball bloggers with ESPN.com—before they were even called bloggers. He was never a beat writer. Instead, Neyer analyzes the game mostly from his living room and his computer, delivering sharp insights and necessary analysis with a deep historical perspective. He's also the author of several books on baseball history that are both entertaining and thought-provoking, including *Rob Neyer's Big Book of Baseball Legends* and *Rob Neyer's Big Book of Baseball Lineups*. Now working for FOXSports.com, Neyer is the go-to writer for an entire generation of stats-savvy fans.

Daniel Okrent
Writer

Okrent, along with five baseball fan friends, invented the first fantasy baseball league in 1979 at a now-defunct New York restaurant called La Rotisserie Française; they named their league the "ROTISSERIE LEAGUE" in its honor. Today, fantasy sports is a multi-billion-dollar enterprise. And out of that, Okrent achieved only fame (or infamy, depending on your point of view), not money. And he never even won his league, either.

Walter O'Malley
Owner

The most hated man in the history of Brooklyn, O'Malley was responsible for airlifting the Dodgers from the New York borough to Los Angeles, a maneuver the Brooklyn faithful have never forgiven. The bankruptcy attorney rose to power in the Dodgers organization in the 1940s and took over completely by 1952 after a power struggle with co-owner BRANCH RICKEY. O'Malley was one of the first owners to recognize the potential of television, making the Dodgers perhaps the most watched team in America in the 1950s. He saw the untapped potential of the West Coast and convinced Giants owner Horace Stoneham to move their clubs to California during baseball's 1958 WESTWARD EXPANSION. And he wielded tremendous influence over league officials during a time of a weakened commissioner's office. When he came to L.A., he demanded and received a sweet deal that included 300 acres of choice land just a few miles from downtown. There, he built DODGER STADIUM using his own money—the better to make a profit from concessions and parking.

The biggest difference between O'Malley and most of the other owners was always the fact that O'Malley made his entire living from baseball while most of his brethren treated baseball as a hobby. This put O'Malley a step ahead at all times and helped him cement a huge legacy that included the once-profitable team that played ball in front of three million paying fans every year. After O'Malley's death in 1979, control of the club shifted to his son Peter O'Malley, who continued at the helm until the sale of the club to News Corp. in 1997 and in 2011 began to talk about buying it back.

Pete Palmer
Writer/statistician
Palmer has been involved in baseball statistical analysis since the 1960s and joins BILL JAMES as the two men who have done the most in recent times to redefine people's approach to baseball stats. Palmer has served as a consultant to the official statisticians of the American League, but his *magnum opus* is *The Hidden Game of Baseball*, in which he introduces a revolutionary method of evaluating ballplayers called "Linear Weights." The system involves a complicated formula of weighting a player's contributions—on the field, on the mound, and at bat—and comparing them to the league average player at that position. Such a methodology theoretically allows for an unbiased comparison of players from all eras and all ballparks. The formula has some flaws—especially when it comes to evaluating fielding—but overall, it offers a very illuminating view of what it takes to win ballgames. *The Hidden Game* is an intriguing work, and if you can find a used copy somewhere, it's worth buying.

Cumberland Posey
Outfielder/owner, Negro leagues, 1911–46
A NEGRO LEAGUE giant, Posey was part CONNIE MACK, part BRANCH RICKEY, part WILLIAM HULBERT. The college-educated Posey led the legendary HOMESTEAD GRAYS almost from their inception, as a player, manager, and owner. During that time, the Grays established a great dynasty, winning more than 80 percent of their games most years, against both white semipro teams and Negro

league competition. Posey was an excellent judge of talent, discovering or developing many of the biggest stars in the leagues, such as SMOKEY JOE WILLIAMS, COOL PAPA BELL, BUCK LEONARD, and JOSH GIBSON.

Posey ambitiously tried to establish a tightly controlled league system similar to the major leagues, with schedules and stable franchises. But this was in the 1930s, when business conditions were hardly favorable to new ventures. His East-West League failed, so Posey went back to leading the Grays through the loose-knit system of league games combined with barnstorming, continuing as a Negro league power broker until his death in 1946.

Joe Posnanski
Writer

Posnanski combines modern sensibilities—a love of advanced stats, an appreciation for the new medium of sports blogging—with classic storytelling skills, a wonderful sense of humor, and a reporter's nose for news. His blog and podcast (aka "Poscast") are musts for serious sports fans, and his articles in *Sports Illustrated*, where he became senior writer in 2010 after working as a newspaper reporter and columnist for many years, continued that magazine's great tradition of stellar sportswriting. Now he works for NBC Sports, and his writing is very worth your time. If you haven't jumped on the Pos bandwagon by now, it's time. You'll love what you read. And the great thing is, he should hopefully continue to do his thing for the next 30 years.

Shirley Povich
Writer

Sports editor of the *Washington Post* at the age of 21, Povich wrote about baseball and other sports for that paper beginning in 1924. He was one of the first writers to disdain the hero-worship and cliché-driven prose employed by so many of his brethren. He helped usher in the practice of in-depth, analytical sportswriting, covering not just the whos and whats but the whys and hows. When you learn from the local sportswriter *why* your team lost the game—because, say, a baserunner had been faked out by the opposing shortstop during a critical play—you're learning that partly because of Shirley Povich.

Branch Rickey
Executive

Rickey revolutionized baseball in two huge ways. As general manager of the Cardinals, he invented the FARM SYSTEM, a collection of minor league teams owned by a major league team for the purpose of providing talent for the big club. Rickey believed that there is "quality in quantity," and he turned out to be right. By 1940, the Cardinals controlled 33 different minor league teams and would win nine pennants from 1926 through 1946. Rickey's system produced some of the greats of the game, including ROGERS HORNSBY, DIZZY DEAN, and STAN MUSIAL, as well as fellow Hall of Famers Joe Medwick, Jim Bottomley, Chick Hafey, and others. If a measure of genius is how soon others copy your innovation, it's clear that Rickey qualifies, because soon after the Cardinals achieved success, every other team began to create its own farm system.

By the 1940s, Rickey had moved to the Brooklyn Dodgers, where he made his second great impact on the game of baseball, affecting American society in the process. Rickey risked his career to break major league baseball's 60-year-old COLOR BARRIER by signing JACKIE ROBINSON. While certainly a noble move, some have argued that it was really about money. Rickey wanted to increase Dodger attendance, they argue, by appealing to the growing black population in New York City. Or, they say, he wanted to use the untapped talent of the NEGRO LEAGUES to win pennants for the Dodgers and earn money for himself. Maybe it was simply because he wanted to right an injustice. The real answer almost certainly encompassed all of the above. By fighting to open up major league baseball to an entire race of people, Rickey also had an effect on society as a whole for, according to a number of social historians, the coming of Robinson helped accelerate the civil rights movement.

On a smaller scale, Rickey turned the Dodgers into real winners. With Robinson and a succession of other talent of all races, Brooklyn became the National League's most successful franchise in the immediate postwar era.

Forced out of the Dodgers' front office in a power struggle with WALTER O'MALLEY, Rickey joined the Pittsburgh Pirates, where he built a winner out of a lowly franchise in less than a decade. After leaving Pittsburgh, Rickey challenged the baseball establishment again by becoming the point man for the CONTINENTAL LEAGUE in the early 1960s. That league failed, but it did force the baseball powers into their first expansion since the turn of the century. Rickey died in 1965 at the age of 84.

Arnold Rothstein
Gambler

Rothstein was running an infamous gambling parlor in New York, dealing mainly in horse racing, when he became involved in the scam that would cement his reputation forever: the throwing of the 1919 WORLD SERIES by eight corrupt players. Rothstein was the money man, fronting the cash to pay off the players. Although only a portion of the payout made it to the players, Rothstein hit the jackpot, adding to his already considerable fortune.

Rothstein got off scot-free in the whole affair while the players paid for it with their careers. But ultimately, Rothstein hardly fared better in life. In 1928, hours after winning $600,000 on the presidential election, Rothstein was shot to death during a poker game.

Vin Scully
Broadcaster

A broadcasting giant, Scully has been the voice of the Dodgers since the 1950s. The Fordham University graduate took over broadcasting duties when RED BARBER quit (or was fired, depending on what you read) in a contract dispute, and Scully continues today as probably the most recognizable voice in baseball. Scully has an easygoing delivery and great command of the language, and, unlike most broadcasters, he often works alone, without a color commentator. He has a great eye for the nuances of the game, and virtually everyone in baseball will agree that there's never been a finer baseball broadcaster.

Bud Selig
Owner
Commissioner, 1992–2015

A used car salesman by trade, Selig purchased the bankrupt Seattle Pilots in 1970 and moved them to Milwaukee to become the Brewers. There, in a small-market setting, he invested in a good farm system, made some smart trades, and fielded such stars as Robin Yount, Paul Molitor, Pete Vuckovich, Ben Oglivie, and others, culminating in a 1982 World Series appearance. In the 1990s, however, Selig said the team was losing millions of dollars every year. Selig blamed his misfortune on the sport's existing labor structure, so when he got the chance to take the helm of the baseball ship, he grabbed it.

After helping oust commissioner Fay Vincent, Selig reigned as "acting commissioner" during the 1994 STRIKE, earning a $1 million salary in that capacity, which was almost 50 percent higher than any previous commissioner. What did he do to earn that money? He got all of baseball to believe that the future of the sport hinged on the success or failure of its small-market franchises.

Because his Brewers and a handful of other teams claimed to lose money, Selig helped shut down baseball in 1994. He got the *profitable* teams to buy his argument because they knew that they could make even *more* money under the labor plan Selig envisioned—and they were desperate for a labor victory over the players. "Buddy" wasn't alone, of course. He had some power-hungry allies throughout ownership circles, especially White Sox owner Jerry Reinsdorf and Marlins boss Wayne Huizenga. Whenever another owner tried to suggest a more reasonable course of action than to jam an unfair labor agreement down the players' throats, Selig and the gang would shut him up.

Selig proved himself to be the master of the conference call, a consensus-builder extraordinaire (when the consensus revolved around money), and, as we all will remember him, the man who did what World Wars and natural disasters couldn't: cancel the World Series.

After serving as "acting" commissioner for several years, ownership made it official in 1998, and he finally sold his interest in the Brewers in 2004. By the time his tenure expired (it was supposed to be in 2009 but actually happened in January 2015), Selig had presided over an industry that weathered countless storms under his watch. Let's take a quick accounting of the biggest issues he faced and decisions he approved:

- Two more expansion teams (Arizona and Tampa Bay)
- League realignment into three divisions
- Wild card playoffs
- Interleague play
- At least three labor negotiations
- Calling an end to the 2002 All-Star Game with the score tied when teams ran out of pitchers

- Disastrous Congressional testimony about baseball finances in which Selig had to be reminded that he was sworn to tell the truth
- The steroids scandal and his subsequent efforts to clean up the game through drug testing and punishment

There's clearly a lot more. The book *In the Best Interests of Baseball: The Revolutionary Reign of Bud Selig* by Andrew Zimbalist does a great job cataloging all that Selig did for the game, both good and bad.

Though I'm not a Bud Selig fan, one inescapable fact can't be disputed: during his tenure, the business of baseball thrived. Overall revenues nearly quadrupled compared to the early 1990s, and attendance in the 2000s reached record highs. Team owners continue to lavish huge contracts on players because the business is so healthy.

How much of that success is because of Bud Selig, and how much of it is in spite of Bud Selig? We'll never know for sure. But when Selig left office in 2015, he left the game in excellent financial shape.

Dr. Harold Seymour
Writer

Seymour was the first scholar to treat baseball history as part of American history. Co-authored with his wife Dorothy (whose contributions weren't known until many years after the fact), Seymour's famous two-volume examination of the game, *Baseball: The Early Years* and *Baseball: The Golden Age*, pioneered the study of sports history at a time when serious academia considered such a topic frivolous. He said that when he first decided to write about baseball in a historical context, his peers at Cornell University in 1941 were skeptical, and Seymour had to convince them of baseball's legitimacy as a subject for serious scholarship. The Seymours' books are universally regarded as the best starting points for baseball researchers who want to learn more about the game's origins, its early stars and controversies, and so on. Harold and Dorothy Seymour are, in fact, known as "Baseball's Biographers" to today's researchers.

Red Smith
Writer

A true sportswriting legend, Smith started writing in 1927 and became the most respected sports journalist of his time; in 1979, he became the first sports columnist to win the Pulitzer Prize. Equally renowned for his wit and his opinions, he used his columns in the *New York Herald Tribune* and the *New York Times* to celebrate, disparage, and eulogize several generations of sports heroes and villains. He attacked pomposity, personified by Smith's favorite target, BOWIE KUHN. And he supported the underdog, backing MARVIN MILLER and the Players Association, for example, when most in baseball saw the labor movement as somehow harmful to the game. Smith, who saw everybody in baseball from RUTH to REGGIE, led a fascinating life, described movingly in Dave Anderson's biography *Red*.

Albert Spalding
Pitcher, 1871–77
Executive/businessman

A true pioneer and entrepreneur in the grand American spirit, Spalding made several important contributions to baseball. First, he was a great pitcher, probably the greatest of his time. From 1871 through 1875 in the National Association and 1876 in the National League, he topped all pitchers in victories. Second, he played a large role in the formation of the National League by writing its constitution and by lending needed credibility to the upstart venture. Third, when his arm gave out, he started the sporting goods company that continues to bear his name, and he began to issue the first yearly baseball guides. The business, which supplied balls and other equipment to the major leagues, made him one of baseball's wealthiest and most powerful men, as did his tenure as president of the Chicago franchise, probably the NL's most popular. Fourth, he helped save the National League during the PLAYERS LEAGUE revolt by launching a public relations campaign attacking the motives and financial resources of the rebels, which effectively doomed the new league.

And fifth, he was chiefly responsible for creating the myth that AB-NER DOUBLEDAY invented baseball. It was Spalding who ordered the formation of a commission to study the origins of the game, and it was Spalding who made sure the MILLS COMMISSION REPORT said that baseball was invented by an American and was *not* adapted from the British games ROUNDERS and CRICKET.

Today, the Spalding Sporting Goods Company is a multi-billion-dollar enterprise. And so is the sport Spalding helped popularize.

George Steinbrenner
Owner

"We plan absentee ownership. I'll stick to building ships," said Cleveland shipbuilding magnate George Steinbrenner in 1973 as the group headed by him purchased the Yankees from CBS. But that's not what happened at all. Steinbrenner loved to bask in the yellow glow of the New York tabloids and quickly became the opposite of what he promised: the most meddlesome owner in history.

He began his tenure auspiciously: suspended for two years after his conviction for making illegal contributions to Nixon's 1972 reelection campaign. He returned to plunge the Yankees into the new FREE AGENT market by signing CATFISH HUNTER, REGGIE JACKSON, and GOOSE GOSSAGE to bring the Yankees their first pennants in over a decade. Later, he signed DAVE WINFIELD to the richest free-agent contract in history, a 10-year contract worth $15 million—plus some cost-of-living escalators that Steinbrenner didn't realize would increase the deal to about $23 million.

That extra $8 million nearly proved to be Steinbrenner's undoing, for he immediately began to despise Winfield and his agents. Throughout the 1980s, while Winfield was building his Hall of Fame career, Steinbrenner fought with and belittled Winfield, and even broke the part of the contract that ordered Steinbrenner to donate $3 million to the ballplayer's charitable foundation.

Then, according to the commissioner's office, Steinbrenner went a step too far: On claims from a gambler named Howard Spira who said that Winfield had given him money to pay off his debts to mobsters, Steinbrenner hired private detectives to investigate the player and his foundation. As it turned out, the foundation was on shaky financial and ethical ground. But the investigation actually haunted Steinbrenner. Spira began to extort money from the Yankee boss, threatening to go public with the owner's actions in digging up dirt on Winfield. Steinbrenner gave Spira $40,000 to keep him quiet, then Spira spilled his story to the commissioner's office.

The investigation and hearing that followed were extremely one-sided; for example, Steinbrenner's lawyers weren't allowed to cross-examine many important witnesses. The results were predictable: commissioner Fay Vincent banished Steinbrenner for two years in 1990. According to John Helyar's account of the affair in his book *Lords of the Realm*, it seems apparent that the baseball establishment was out to get Steinbrenner for his many other sins—from outrageous free agent signings to boorish behavior off the field.

His Yankees fell into despair during the time of the investigation and suspension. But when he got back, he started to build a winner again—not just a winner, but a dynasty. He began to generate cash through wise business decisions and, unlike a lot of other teams, reinvested that cash back into his club to sign great players. The result is that in 1995 the Yankees began a run of success exceeded only by previous Yankee dynasties. Over the next 15 years, Steinbrenner's club won eleven division titles, seven pennants, and five World Series titles.

Before his death in 2010, Steinbrenner was frequently criticized for spending so much money on player salaries—over $200 million per season at its peak. But he demanded excellence and wouldn't stand for mediocrity. Would you rather he keep the money for himself, like other owners do? Or spend it to make his team as good as it can be?

Harry Stevens
Entrepreneur
An English immigrant steel worker, Stevens came upon the idea of improving ballpark scorecards in the early 1880s. He approached owners all over professional baseball with his new version, and many of them let his company sell the scorecard in their ballparks. Stevens branched out into food sales, and soon his business was the largest around. Among his many innovations, Stevens invented the most popular ballpark treat: the hot dog. And even today, his name adorns the shirt backs of ballpark vendors across the country.

Ted Turner
Owner
The heir to a billboard company, Ted Turner transformed his father's modest advertising firm into a powerful all-media conglomerate through marvelous foresight and manic energy. One of his prescient moves was to purchase the downtrodden Atlanta Braves, who were a mainstay of his fledgling cable TV channel but were threatening to

move out of town. Flamboyant and opinionated, Turner immediately set out to buy a winner. In the aftermath of the ANDY MESSERSMITH free agency decision, Turner was the only owner to make a serious offer to the star pitcher, signing him to a $1 million multiyear deal. In a feat of promotional bravado, Turner issued Messersmith jersey number 17 and "nicknamed" the player "Channel." What a coincidence that Turner's cable station was Channel 17! The league president put an immediate halt to the blatant commercialism.

Turner broke a great many other rules and traditions, angering the stolid baseball men who had reigned for decades and earning Turner a one-year suspension at one point (which allowed Turner to skipper his yacht *Courageous* to an America's Cup victory). It was Turner who, in the 1980s, along with GEORGE STEINBRENNER, received most of the blame for escalating baseball's salary structure by offering huge contracts to free agents.

Turner merged his company with Time Warner in the 1990s and pretty much divested himself from baseball at the time, although his name lived on with the Braves ballpark at the time: "Turner Field." (The Braves are now working to move to suburban Atlanta so they won't be in Turner Field much longer.)

Peter Ueberroth
Commissioner, 1984–89
Ueberroth built his fortune in the travel agency business and his reputation as the leader of the most successful Olympics in history. Then, fresh off the 1984 Los Angeles games, Ueberroth succeeded BOWIE KUHN as baseball commissioner. *Time*'s Man of the Year immediately negotiated a liberal settlement to end an umpires strike that threatened the World Series, and the owners got a glimpse of the CEO they'd just hired: He knew how to lead, how to make decisions forcefully, and, most of all, how to make money.

As he did with the Olympics, he priced corporate sponsorships much higher than ever before, he increased revenue from merchandising, and he negotiated the largest TV contracts in history—filling the owners' coffers like never before. He also preached "fiscal responsibility" to the owners, which, according to an independent arbitrator, was a code phrase for "Don't sign free agents to large, multiyear contracts"—a clear violation of federal anti-collusion labor laws. The owners got busted for collusion, and the resulting ruling from an independent arbitrator cost the owners hundreds of millions of dollars.

Ueberroth's other pet project was getting rid of the illegal drug problem that was consuming baseball in the early to mid-1980s. He meted out harsh penalties to players caught with drugs, and he even tried to unilaterally institute a drug testing policy, which got shot down by the union. (If it had been implemented, we certainly wouldn't have had the steroid problem. Sigh.)

Ueberroth lasted only five years on the job, apparently unable to put up with "the 26 idiots," in his words. The owners were also eager to get rid of the man who had made them carloads of money; one owner would later say that Ueberroth was "more interested in his own image and where *he* was going." There was much talk that Ueberroth was going to run for political office, but aside from a short-lived run for the California governorship in 2003, he has kept a relatively low profile.

Bill Veeck
Owner

Whenever you read Bill Veeck's name in a book or article, the word "maverick" is always nearby: "Bill Veeck, the maverick owner of the St. Louis Browns..." And it's not a misnomer. Veeck was always an innovator, always ahead of his time. Veeck learned his trade first-hand as the son of a Chicago sportswriter who went on to become the Cubs' president. The young Veeck, in fact, came up with the idea of planting ivy along the outfield walls in Wrigley Field. During his long career, he owned three different teams—the Indians, Browns, and White Sox (twice)—and he brought his unique brand of leadership to each one. In Cleveland, he integrated the American League with the signing of LARRY DOBY in 1947 and, later, SATCHEL PAIGE, helping to secure a pennant in 1948 and drawing over 2.6 million fans, the most ever at the time. With the Browns, he sent midget EDDIE GAEDEL to the plate in a grand publicity stunt, but he couldn't revive that moribund franchise. As White Sox owner, he delivered the team's first pennant since the 1919 BLACK SOX SCANDAL and introduced the first exploding scoreboard.

Most of his tactics were frowned upon by his fellow owners, who felt baseball should remain classy and dignified. Veeck, on the other hand, saw baseball as entertainment for the masses. He staged stunts and promotions almost daily, like pregame circus acts, postgame fireworks, the time he let fans manage a game from the stands, and his "Disco Demolition Night," which caused his team to forfeit when marijuana-stoned fans stormed the field.

A law school graduate, he urged the commissioner to do something about the RESERVE CLAUSE built into every player's contracts—in 1940, or 30 years before CURT FLOOD. He also claimed that he tried to buy the lowly Phillies and stock the club with NEGRO LEAGUE stars—half a decade before BRANCH RICKEY and JACKIE ROBINSON broke the COLOR LINE. (There's no hard evidence other than Veeck's word that he ever really made this attempt.) Veeck, who died in 1986, told his life story in *VEECK AS IN WRECK*, universally regarded as one of the finest sports autobiographies ever.

3

TIMELINE OF IMPORTANT EVENTS

1744
The first reference to "base-ball"
In 1744, an English book publisher named John Newberry (for whom the modern Newberry Award is named) came out with *A Little Pretty Pocket-Book*, which not only is considered the first ever children's book but also contains the first known printed reference to "base-ball." This is just one more piece of evidence that baseball was not sprung from the mind of ABNER DOUBLEDAY or ALEXANDER CARTWRIGHT or anyone else.

1839
Doubleday invents baseball? Not exactly.
ABNER DOUBLEDAY was a cadet at West Point in 1839, yet according to the MILLS COMMISSION REPORT sponsored by ALBERT SPALDING, Doubleday somehow had time to trek up to Cooperstown to invent baseball. Didn't happen. But it makes for a good story. *See also* DOUBLEDAY MYTH.

1845

The Knickerbockers make the rules.

In 1845, ALEXANDER CARTWRIGHT, DOC ADAMS, and a bunch of their friends wrote down the KNICKERBOCKER RULES, the first modern rules of baseball and formed the NEW YORK KNICKERBOCKERS, the most famous club of the era.

1869

The first openly all-professional team.

It has long been accepted as fact that the 1869 Cincinnati Red Stockings were America's first professional *baseball* team—and by extension, America's first professional *sports* team. Major league baseball teams even put patches on their uniforms in 1994 commemorating the "125th Anniversary of Professional Baseball." But as this book points out in many other places, such a notion is simply baseball mythology, not fact. Men were getting paid to play the game for a decade prior to the advent of the Red Stockings. Most were members of ostensibly "amateur" teams and were forced to take the cash under the table, but published reports do exist of games played as early as 1864 where proceeds from ticket sales were divided among the players. What the 1869 Red Stockings can rightfully claim is that they were the first team to openly recruit players with generous cash payments. In an era of ubiquitous free agency, the team hired players for between $600 and $1,400 for a 10-month schedule of games against clubs from New York, San Francisco, and just about everywhere in between. Led by brothers HARRY WRIGHT and GEORGE WRIGHT, the Red Stockings dominated the nation with a 60-0 record, beginning a strong tradition of Cincinnati baseball that continues today.

1871

The first professional baseball league.

The NATIONAL ASSOCIATION OF BASE BALL PLAYERS was founded in 1871, creating the first professional baseball league.

1876

The National League is born.

On April 22, 1876, the NATIONAL LEAGUE OF BASEBALL CLUBS played its first game ever, a 6–5 victory by Boston over Philadelphia. The Chicago White Stockings, led by pitcher ALBERT SPALDING and owned by NL co-founder WILLIAM HULBERT, captured the League's first pennant.

1884
The first World Series, technically.
The first sanctioned postseason series between the champions of the rival National League and AMERICAN ASSOCIATION—called the World's Series—took place in 1884. In earlier seasons, pennant winners had met informally to play exhibition games, but the 1884 Series was the first to be officially approved and scheduled by league offices. In it, the NL's Providence Grays, behind the pitching of "OL' HOSS" RADBOURN, swept all three games from the AA's New York Metropolitans. Postseason championships continued until the AA folded in 1891, then reappeared as the Temple Cup Series that pitted the top two National League finishers against each other. Lack of fan interest killed the Temple Cup after four years of lopsided series. Then, two years after the AMERICAN LEAGUE'S FORMATION in 1901, baseball's czars reestablished interleague championships with what most fans consider the FIRST MODERN WORLD SERIES IN 1903.

1894
Pitchers move back 10 feet.
1894 marked the second full season after the pitching mound was moved to its present distance of 60-feet, six-inches from home plate. AMOS RUSIE, "the Hoosier Thunderbolt," was partially responsible for the shift, because at the previous 50-foot distance, his fastballs were practically unhittable. As pitchers were still getting used to the new distance in 1894, batting totals soared to a level they wouldn't reach again for decades. That season, Billy Hamilton scored 192 runs and Hugh Duffy batted .440—both still all-time single-season records. In addition, four players hit .400, three players recorded on-base percentages of over .500, and the entire league batted .309.

1901
The American League War.
The American League had been a minor league called the Western League prior to 1900. But with the 1901 expiration of baseball's NATIONAL AGREEMENT, which regulated player contracts and franchise locations and allowed the National League to monopolize major league baseball, founder BAN JOHNSON declared the AL a "major"

league and touched off a bitter war between the two organizations. He encouraged his franchise owners to raid existing National League ball clubs for players.

Since NL owners kept a tight rein on player salaries, the AL had little trouble getting many NL veterans to jump leagues. The most conspicuous defector was Phillies star second baseman NAPOLEON LA-JOIE, who broke his contract to join CONNIE MACK'S Philadelphia Athletics. The NL sued to regain Lajoie's services, taking their case all the way to the Pennsylvania Supreme Court. And although the Court ruled against the AL and ordered Lajoie returned to the Phillies, Johnson wouldn't be defeated so easily. He simply transferred Lajoie to the AL's Cleveland franchise and forbade Lajoie from entering or playing in Pennsylvania, where Lajoie could have been arrested. This victory exemplified the AL's persistence, and in the fall of 1902, the war-weary leagues called a truce and signed a revised National Agreement. After a rocky start, they've been coexisting, more or less happily, ever since.

1903
The first modern World Series.
In 1903, American League's Boston Pilgrims (now Red Sox) upset the haughty Pittsburgh Pirates of the National League five games to three in the first modern World Series. The idea of a postseason series was proposed by Pirates owner Barney Dreyfuss, who challenged Pilgrims owner Henry Killilea near the end of the season; all it took to seal the deal was a handshake. The unexpected victory by the American League upset the peace that had ended the 1901 AMERICAN LEAGUE WAR. And the following season, manager JOHN MCGRAW of the pennant-winning New York Giants, whose ownership did not recognize the treaty between the two leagues and was angry at the AL for having placed a rival franchise in New York, refused to entertain any notions of staging another postseason contest. By 1905, tempers had subsided and the Series was allowed to continue—which it did uninterrupted until the 1994 STRIKE, when a bonfire of greed and power conspired to take the World Series away from us.

1908
Merkle's Boner.
The legendary pennant chase between the Pirates, Cubs, and Giants in 1908 was decided in part by a notorious mistake by rookie Fred

Merkle. Here's what happened. The three teams were neck-and-neck-and-neck throughout most of the season, leading up to a September 23 game between New York and Chicago at the Polo Grounds. With the score tied 1–1 and darkness falling in the bottom of the ninth, the Giants had runners on first and third with two out. Shortstop Al Bridwell singled to center to score what everybody thought was the winning run.

Believing the game was over and trying to avoid the onslaught of screaming fans onto the field, the runner on first—poor Fred Merkle—ran straight to the dugout without touching second base, a common practice in those days. Alert Cubs second baseman Johnny Evers, who knew the rule book, retrieved a ball (though it probably wasn't the actual game ball, which was lost in the melee of swarming fans), got the attention of umpire Hank O'Day, and tagged second base. O'Day ruled Merkle out on the force play, but because it was dark and the field was overrun with fans, the game was called a tie.

The Giants protested the decision, and NL president Harry Pulliam ruled that the game would be replayed at the end of the season if it affected the pennant race. It did. The two teams met again in the final game of the season in an epic battle between CHRISTY MATHEWSON of the Giants and Chicago's Mordecai "Three-Finger" Brown, won by the Cubs 4–2.

For the rest of his playing days, Merkle would be reminded of his bonehead play and accused by ignorant fans of blowing the pennant for the Giants. In fact, Merkle was simply following baseball tradition, and Giants manager JOHN MCGRAW never blamed Merkle.

What most fans didn't know was that Evers had tried to capitalize on the same kind of blunder in a game earlier in the season, but umpire O'Day had disallowed his protest; when it came up again, O'Day was ready to rule in Evers's favor.

1910

A disputed batting race.

At the beginning of the 1910 season, the Chalmers Automobile Company announced it would award a new car to the major league player with the highest batting average; since few people owned cars, this was a coveted prize (*see* CHALMERS AWARD). As the season wore on, it became a two-man race: the Tigers' much-hated TY COBB versus Cleveland's beloved NAPOLEON LAJOIE. Both played the final weeks of the season at a sizzling pace—Cobb 25 for 47, Lajoie 30 for 54—but Cobb had the upper hand on the season's final day, .383 to .376. Cobb sat out the Tigers' last game to protect the batting title, knowing that Lajoie would have to go 8 for 8 during his team's doubleheader against St. Louis—a near-impossibility. Cobb was wrong, and the impossible happened: Lajoie actually did go 8 for 8, including 7 bunt hits, which aroused much suspicion since Lajoie possessed little speed.

A scandal soon erupted when it was discovered that the Browns' manager had instructed his third baseman to play extra deep on Lajoie and allow him to drop in those bunts. The incident forced the St. Louis manager from his job, and AL president BAN JOHNSON declared that a "discrepancy" had been discovered in the batting records and credited Cobb with an extra 2 for 3 and, consequently, the batting title. (It is this 2 for 3 which modern baseball historians have subtracted from Cobb's batting record, thus giving him 4,189 career hits and a career .366 batting average instead of the previously established 4,191 and .367; *see* .366 and 4,191) To avert the controversy, Chalmers awarded automobiles to both Cobb and Lajoie, but thereafter decided to give the cars to league MVPs as determined by a panel of baseball writers rather than by simple mathematics.

1918
The Great War disrupts baseball.
In 1918, to support the nation's war efforts, the U.S. government ordered a military draft of all able-bodied men not involved in "essential" work, and baseball was a casualty. (I know—baseball not essential? What bureaucrat decided that?) The government gave the leagues until Labor Day to finish the season, plus two more weeks to play the World Series—in effect canceling 25 regular season games. The government's 1918 policy contrasts sharply with its policy during World War II, when President Roosevelt, in the so-called "GREEN-LIGHT LETTER," asked baseball to continue to play its games in order to maintain the morale of the country and the troops.

1919
The Black Sox scandal.
Near the end of the 1919 season, a group of gamblers including former major leaguer Bill Burns and former boxing champion Abe At-

tell—supported by money-man ARNOLD ROTHSTEIN—conspired to fix the World Series by promising $100,000 to eight Sox players: pitchers EDDIE CICOTTE and Lefty Williams; infielders BUCK WEAVER, Chick Gandil, Swede Risberg, and Fred McMullen; and outfielders Happy Felsch and "SHOELESS JOE" JACKSON. The players accepted the offer—although they didn't received all the money that was promised and Weaver claimed that he never took a dime—and played poorly in the first few games: hitting batters with pitches, making errors and poor baserunning judgments. But as recounted in Eliot Asinof's landmark book *EIGHT MEN OUT* (and the movie of the same name), after Game 5, the gamblers seemed to renege on the deal and refused to pay up. The players supposedly tried to salvage the Series, but the gamblers may have threatened to kill Williams and his family, forcing him to pitch poorly in the deciding game. (Note: This threat is recounted in the book and movie, but it was probably false. See the entry on *Eight Men Out* for more.)

Allegations and rumors of fixed games actually permeated the entire decade, and there was even some talk that the Reds had won the 1919 pennant because of the suspicious play of Giants players HAL CHASE and Heinie Zimmerman, who allegedly "laid down" for second-place New York. Throughout the decade, players consorted openly with gamblers to supplement their meager baseball incomes. The baseball powers did little to stop it, apparently fearing the publicity might hurt gate receipts. That was the environment that spawned the Black Sox: greed supported by quiet tolerance.

After the World Series and into the 1920 season, accusations swirled against the Sox, led by the columns of sportswriter Hugh Fullerton, but many dismissed the allegations as grumbling by the losing team. Then late in the season, as the Sox battled Cleveland and New York for the pennant, a Chicago grand jury convened to investigate the charges. In September, Cicotte, Jackson, and others confessed to the grand jury; they were coerced into confessing with empty promises that no action would be taken against them. Immediately suspended by the league, the players sat out the final week of the season as the decimated Sox lost the pennant to the Indians by two games. In June 1921, just before the criminal trial was to begin, the players' grand jury testimony mysteriously disappeared, and the Sox were acquitted due to lack of evidence.

Meanwhile, in the wake of the scandal, major league baseball searched frantically for ways to restore public confidence in the game—and to keep ballparks filled. The result: the installation of all-powerful commissioner KENESAW MOUNTAIN LANDIS, a former federal court judge who'd made his name earlier in the decade with some famous antitrust cases. One of Landis's first official rulings was to uphold the suspensions of the eight players: "Regardless of the verdict of juries," wrote Landis, "no player who throws a ballgame, no player that undertakes or promises to throw a ballgame, no player that sits in conference with a bunch of crooked players and gamblers where the ways and means of throwing a game are discussed and does not promptly tell his club about it, will ever play professional baseball!" That last part covered the suspension of Weaver, whose "guilty knowledge" doomed him.

Eight Men Out, which was the first book to give a complete account of this story, places much of the blame on White Sox owner CHARLES COMISKEY, who allegedly paid his players the lowest salaries in the league. And why didn't the players demand a trade or hold out for more legitimate money? Because baseball players of Comiskey's time were bound by the RESERVE CLAUSE, which forced a player to play ball for his current employer or not play ball at all. The White Sox were underpaid compared to what other players were making. But if they quit, they couldn't play for anyone. If you thought you were underpaid by your employer, you could find another job. The White Sox, and every other player until FREE AGENCY came in 1975, did not have our freedom. If you had to work for your employer or else not work at all, wouldn't you be tempted to resist in some way? None of this *excuses* the actions of the Black Sox; it merely tries to explain them.

It seems unthinkable that such an event could occur today, with the big money the players are making. But is it? Legal and illegal gambling is a multibillion-dollar industry in this country, and greed will always remain high on the list of American sins. It is therefore imperative that baseball, and other sports, keep gamblers as far as possible from the game. That means meting out harsh punishment to those who are proven to have bet on baseball. The integrity of the sport, of all professional sports, is at stake.

The Sox sell the Babe.
A day after Christmas, 1919, the Red Sox sealed the fate of their franchise when owner Harry Frazee sold BABE RUTH to the Yankees for $125,000 and a $300,000 loan with FENWAY PARK as collateral. This has become the most mocked blunder in American sports history.

And it came about not necessarily because Frazee needed the money to finance one of his Broadway productions (popularly believed to be the musical "No No Nanette"), but mostly because Frazee was sick of putting up with the demands of his overgrown child star. After the 1919 season, in which Ruth broke the single-season home run record with 29, Ruth demanded a raise that would double his salary. This came after repeated holdout threats and childish behavior that irked Frazee. The owner was sick of it. He was also broke. Owning a major league team back then was not the license to print money that it is today. Even though the Sox had won World Series in 1916 and 1918, they were constantly under financial pressures. And Frazee wasn't the kind of owner who loved baseball. He was a Broadway entrepreneur first, baseball owner second. In addition, Ruth was clearly outgrowing Boston. He wanted bigger and better things. It was inevitable that he would leave Boston at some point.

Why the Yankees, Boston's archrival? Because of a feud with American League president BAN JOHNSON, Frazee had only a limited number of trading partners. Nobody in the NL would deal with him, and in the AL, his only options were New York and Chicago. New York offered big money, and Frazee took it.

Retroactively, the decision to sell Ruth has been blamed for cursing the Red Sox's fortunes for generations to come. But this "CURSE OF THE BAMBINO" did not have to be. If Frazee had invested his money back into his club through new player acquisitions, then maybe the Sox could have competed in the 1920s. If subsequent owner Tom Yawkey had hired smarter general managers or had embraced integration rather than resisting it, then they could have competed in the 1930s or 1950s. If the Sox had been a little luckier in 1946, 1967, 1975, or 1986, then nobody would ever have talked about a curse.

Instead, the Sox went 86 years between World Series victories. Not the longest drought—the Cubs are at 106 years as of 2014—but long enough to cause pain and suffering in New England.

1920
Tragedy on the diamond. And so much more.
1920 was a momentous year in baseball. BABE RUTH, in his first year as a Yankee, shattered the single-season home run record with an astounding 59. The baseball world was shocked by the suspensions of the BLACK SOX. And, on August 16, Cleveland shortstop RAY

CHAPMAN was killed by a pitched ball—the only on-field death of a player in major league history. The tragedy did more than cut short a life; it also changed baseball forever.

Here's what happened: On a 1–1 count, Carl Mays of the Yankees threw a high fastball to Chapman. "Chapman seemed rooted to the spot," wrote Joe Vila of the New York Sun. "He made no move either with his head or feet to get out of the way and the ball, pitched with all of Mays' strength, struck him squarely on the left temple." Chapman slumped to the ground, then, like a well-trained batter, got up and took two steps toward first base. Reporters said they could see Chapman's left eye hanging from its socket. The shortstop collapsed again and was rushed to a hospital but died within a few hours. Back in Cleveland a few days later, newspaper accounts described Chapman's funeral as "the largest in years."

In the wake of the shocking death, the league ordered umpires to keep fresh baseballs in play at all times, to make it easier for batters to see the ball. Although spitballs, which had been banned a year earlier, weren't a factor in Chapman's death, it was these two changes—not a new "lively" ball—that were most responsible for the increase in batting totals in the early 1920s. For batters, it was the difference between hitting a gray, discolored ball with a loose cover that had been used for the last five innings and hitting a new, white ball that has just been put into play. August 16, 1920, in effect, marked the end of the DEAD BALL ERA and inaugurated the LIVELY BALL ERA.

Baseball's longest game.

The longest baseball game in major league history took place on May 1, 1920, when the Boston Braves and Brooklyn Superbas (later the Dodgers) played 26 grueling innings. Opposing pitchers Leon Cadore and Joe Oeschger actually went the distance for their teams, although you have to wonder why they bothered: the game was finally called due to darkness with the score tied 1–1. Brooklyn would lose a 13-inning contest to the Phillies the following day, thus playing the equivalent of 4-1/3 games but finishing only one of them.

The longest game in *professional* baseball history (majors and minors) lasted 33 innings, with the Triple-A Pawtucket Red Sox defeating the Rochester Red Wings 3–2 in a 1981 game that was completed 35 days after it started. The two teams began playing on the evening of April 18th and continued for 32 innings locked in a 2–2 tie until 4 a.m., when the International League president halted the game. On

June 23rd, when the two teams met again, the marathon mercifully ended on an RBI single by Pawtucket's Dave Koza in the bottom of the 33rd.

1930
The Year of the Hitter.
1930 was the peak season of the LIVELY BALL ERA, during which batting averages and slugging totals reached all-time highs. In 1930, Hack Wilson of the Cubs smacked 56 home runs with a record 190 RBIs, Bill Terry batted .401, Chuck Klein had 445 total bases, the Phillies had a league-worst 6.87 ERA, and six teams had composite batting averages over .300. And that was just the National League.

1932
Ruth calls his shot. Or does he?
One of the most famous moments in baseball history came in the 1932 World Series, when BABE RUTH came to bat in the fifth inning of Game 3 having already hit one home run in the game. But he had misjudged a fly ball the previous inning to allow the tying run to score, and the Cubs players and fans were really letting him have it. When he took the first two pitches for called strikes, the razzing got louder and more abusive. Ruth stepped out of the box. What happened next is the stuff of legend. Ruth either (a) pointed his index finger at pitcher Charley Root and the Cubs dugout to indicate he still had one strike remaining, (b) pointed his middle finger at the Cubs players to let them know what he thought of their abuse, or (c) pointed to center field to indicate where he was going to slug Root's next pitch. Whatever the truth, Ruth slammed Root's next pitch over the outfield fence in the general area where he did or did not point, helping the Yankees to victory in that game before finishing the Series sweep in Game 4.

But did he really call his shot? The Associated Press thought not; its story the next day was headlined "Ruth Enjoys Razzing Cubs / Raises His Fingers To Show Strike Count, Then Hits Homer." Cubs pitcher Burleigh Grimes agreed, saying Ruth "[held] up his finger as if to say, 'I've got one left.'" But Hall of Fame sportswriter Fred Lieb wrote that LOU GEHRIG, who'd been on-deck when it happened, had told him, "What do you think of the nerve of that big monkey calling his shot and taking those two strikes and then hitting the ball exactly where he pointed?" Meanwhile, Ruth, ever the showman, liked to claim he did call his shot, but former Dodgers outfielder Babe Herman said he heard Ruth once say to Root years later, "I know I didn't [point], but it made a hell of a story, didn't it?" It sure did.

In 1999 actual home movie footage of Ruth was discovered, and it showed Ruth pointing in the direction of... either Root, the center field fence, or the Cubs dugout. It didn't really resolve the issue. (The movie is still an amazing artifact.)

1933
The first All-Star Game.
In the early 1930s, Chicago Tribune sports editor Arch Ward had an idea: gather the best players in each league to play an exhibition game. He got the baseball powers to agree, and in 1933, the first game was held at Comiskey Park, just in time for an aging BABE RUTH to hit the first All-Star home run. It was a truly star-studded game: 20 future Hall of Famers suited up.

Baseball's version is, I think, the best of all major sports' all-star games, but it has had its share of controversy, most of which has involved the selection of players. For the first 14 years, all players were chosen in a poll of major league managers. In 1947, league officials decided to let the fans select the eight-man starting lineup (excluding pitchers) in league-wide balloting. But in 1957, a Cincinnati newspaper printed an all-star ballot with Reds players marked at every position and encouraged fans to mail it in, which resulted in the selection of seven Reds to the lineup. The commissioner's office became incensed at the abuse of its system, an abuse that was practically inevitable because the league had failed to put any controls on the voting. Two of those Reds were replaced, and thereafter the league decided to hand over the selection of all-stars to a poll of players, managers, and coaches.

In 1970, the league decided to return the vote to the group for whom the game is supposedly dedicated: the fans. Even so, every year complaints arise that "deserving" players have been left off the team while popular stars who have been injured, slumping, or otherwise "unworthy" are annually selected. But the point of the All-Star game is to select not the player who is having the best half of a season but rather the player who is a "star," and part of being a star is being popular among fans. Sure, the voting could be modified a little bit to be more fair to great players who toil for bad teams with low attendance. But there's no reason to get too upset about these things.

The most infamous thing that ever happened at an All-Star Game came in 2002 when commissioner BUD SELIG was forced to halt the game with the score tied because the teams had used all their pitchers. Although I think Selig had no good options and made the right decision, the image of the commissioner shaking his head and throwing up his hands in exasperation—at his home ballpark!—was such an appropriate metaphor for his personality and leadership as commissioner. The upshot of the game was an overreaction that exemplifies Selig's fecklessness: He expanded the rosters to 32 players (now 34) and ruled that the winning league would gain the benefit of home field advantage in that season's World Series so that players would actually try to win. The tie was a fluke, and now we're stuck with the unnecessary and, in the case of the home field advantage rule, unfair consequences.

1938
The double no-no.
Johnny Vander Meer wasn't a *great* pitcher. His top win total was 18, he won in double figures only six times, and he finished his career with a record of 119 wins and 121 losses. He also walked 100-plus batters six times. But for two games in 1938, Vander Meer was literally unhittable, and therein lies his fame. On June 11, the Reds pitcher shut down the Boston Braves without allowing a hit, and he came back four days later to no-hit the Brooklyn Dodgers in the first night game ever at Ebbets Field.

This, to me, is the one *potentially* breakable record that never will be broken. By comparison, some records aren't even *potentially* breakable because the game has changed so much. For example, all of CY YOUNG'S marks, including his 511 career victories and 749 complete games, are way out of reach, as is Ed Walsh's 20th-century record for innings pitched in a single season, 464. They pitched in the DEAD BALL ERA, when pitchers could conserve their pitching energy knowing home runs were rare. But Vander Meer's record for consecutive no-hitters will stand forever because a person would have to pitch *three* straight no-nos—a feat which is possible but absolutely improbable.

1939
The luckiest man speaks.

On May 2, 1939, LOU GEHRIG took himself out of the New York Yankees' lineup for the first time in over 15 years, ending his record-setting streak of 2,130 consecutive games played (*see* 2,130). On that day in Detroit, Gehrig was batting just .143 in 28 at bats, and he seemed to know his playing days were numbered. "I haven't been a bit of good to the team since the season started," he told reporter James P. Dawson. "It would not be fair to the boys, to JOE [MCCARTHY, New York's manager], or to the baseball public for me to try going on.... Maybe a rest will do me some good. Maybe it won't. Who knows? Who can tell? I'm just hoping."

There was speculation at the time that Gehrig was simply tired, that he might return when the weather turned warm. But weeks later, the news from the Mayo Clinic ended all conjecture, ruined all hope: Gehrig suffered from amyotrophic lateral sclerosis, a debilitating disease that robs muscles of their strength (now commonly known as LOU GEHRIG'S DISEASE).

On July 4 of that year, Gehrig gave what his biographer, Ray Robinson, called "baseball's Gettysburg Address." Most people know only one line of that famous speech on Lou Gehrig Day, when he said good-bye to over 61,000 fans at YANKEE STADIUM. Here are some of the highlights of the speech:

> Fans, for the past two weeks you've been reading about a bad break. Yet today, I consider myself the luckiest man on the face of the earth.... When you look around, wouldn't you consider it a privilege to associate yourself with such fine looking men as are standing in uniform here today? Sure I'm lucky.... When you have a father and a mother who work all their lives so you can have an education and build your body—it's a blessing. When you have a wife who has been a tower of strength and shown more courage than you dreamed existed—that's the finest I know. So I close in saying that I might've been given a bad break, but I've got an awful lot to live for. Thank you.

1941
Williams and DiMaggio thrill baseball.

1941 was the season of two of baseball's most famous feats—TED WILLIAMS'S .406 batting average and JOE DiMAGGIO'S 56-game hitting streak (*see* .406 and 56). DiMaggio's feat helped lead the Yankees to the pennant, while the perennially underachieving Red Sox finished seven games out despite Williams' heroics. Although Williams led DiMaggio in batting average by 49 points, DiMaggio won the MVP. Voters were unaware of this fact: Williams actually out-batted DiMaggio .410 to .408 during DiMaggio's streak.

1945
Baseball begins its redemption.
Unofficially, 1945 marked the low point in baseball history, when most of the good players were at war and baseball had to do with 4Fs, washed up has-beens, and even a one-armed outfielder named PETE GRAY. Nothing against Gray—his story is inspirational. But these are the major leagues we're talking about.

But after the season was over, baseball redeemed itself: JACKIE ROBINSON signed with the Brooklyn Dodgers, becoming the first African-American to sign a major league contract in over 60 years and breaking baseball's notorious color line.

1947
Robinson breaks the color barrier.
On April 15, 1947, Jackie Robinson played his first major league game, breaking forever the COLOR LINE in major league baseball. Not only did Robinson stand up to the racial epithets, beanings, and death threats, he also played well enough in 1947 to win the first Rookie of the Year Award and lead the Dodgers to the World Series. That is hands down the greatest rookie season in the history of American sports.

1951
The Shot Heard 'Round the World.
1951 marks the year of one of the greatest pennant races of all time, which led to one of the greatest games of all time, and which culminated in one of the greatest moments of all time. That it happened between two of baseball's greatest enemies just makes it all the more fun.

The Brooklyn Dodgers had led their crosstown rival New York Giants most of the season, by as much as 13-1/2 games as late as August 12.

Sportswriters said it would take a miracle to win the pennant. But the Giants, led by manager LEO DUROCHER and rookie WILLIE MAYS, rallied for the next six weeks with an amazing run of victories. And by the time the dust settled on the season, the two teams were tied atop the league standings, forcing a three-game playoff to determine the league champion.

The clubs split the first two games, with the deciding Game 3 to be played at New York's POLO GROUNDS. With intimidating Don Newcombe on the mound, the Dodgers took a 4–1 lead to the bottom of the ninth. Alvin Dark and Don Mueller bounced singles through the infield to put two aboard and bring the tying run to the plate. MONTE IRVIN popped out, but Whitey Lockman doubled in a run to make it 4–2. Dodgers manager Charley Dressen had seen enough of Newcombe. He signaled to the bullpen for Ralph Branca to come in.

Maybe if the game were being played today, when statistical analysis in all forms is available to anybody who wants it, the game would have ended differently; instead, Dressen chose the one Dodger pitcher with the greatest chance of losing the game—for Branca had already allowed one home run to Thomson two days earlier and another during the regular season, and all told, Branca had lost five other games to the Giants in 1951.

Even so, the Dodgers could have avoided pitching to Thomson because first base was open and slumping Mays was on deck. But because conventional baseball wisdom says never to intentionally put the winning run on base, Thomson saw two fastballs. The first was right over the plate, and Thomson took it for a called strike. The next one was a little higher and a little more inside, but Thomson swung away. Here's what the Giants' radio audience heard from announcer Russ Hodges: "Branca throws... There's a long fly, it's gonna be, I believe... the Giants win the pennant! The Giants win the pennant! The Giants win the pennant! The Giants win the pennant! Bobby Thomson hits into the lower deck of the left field stands... The Giants win the pennant! They're going crazy! They're going crazy!" Watch the film of the event and you can see that Hodges is right: the whole ballpark went crazy, including all of the Giants players. Pandemonium ensued as Thomson rounded the bases, with JACKIE ROBINSON watching carefully to make sure he touched them all. He did, and the Giants won 5–4.

The next day, the New York Daily News labeled the home run the "Shot Heard 'Round the World," from Ralph Waldo Emerson's "Concord Hymn" about the shots that started the Revolutionary War:

> By the rude bridge that arched the flood,
> Their flag to April's breeze unfurled,
> Here once the embattl'd farmers stood,
> And fired the shot heard 'round the world.

Reality returned when the Giants lost the World Series to the Yankees a few weeks later, but for Thomson, fame and joy would be everlasting.

The Shot Heard 'Round the World was a great moment in baseball history, but was it legitimate? In 2001, journalist Joshua Prager wrote an article in The Wall Street Journal (and later a book, *Echoing Green: The Untold Story of Bobby Thomson, Ralph Branca and the Shot Heard Round the World*) revealing that in 1951, the Giants employed a spy to sit above the centerfield fence at the Polo Grounds to steal signs from the catcher and relay the information to the batters. Was it cheating? At the time, there was no rule specifically banning such tactics, but of course, that's a technicality; it was bad sportsmanship. Did Thomson know what was coming and did it help him? For the Journal article, Thomson told Prager, "My answer is no. I was always proud of that swing." But the way he answered the question leaves a little wiggle room. But here's the big question: Does it really matter? No.

1954
The Catch.
In the eighth inning of Game 1 of the 1954 World Series between the Giants and the Indians, the score tied and two Indians on base when first baseman Vic Wertz sent a Don Liddle pitch to the deepest part of center field. In any park other than New York's POLO GROUNDS, it would have been an easy home run, giving the Indians a 5–3 lead. Instead, WILLIE MAYS made a running, over-the-shoulder, back-to-home-plate catch that has been preserved on countless highlight reels and works of art. The Giants went on to win that game in extra innings on the way to a four-game Series sweep.

1955

"Next year" finally comes.

1955 is the year informally known in Brooklyn as "Next Year"—in other words, the year the Dodgers finally won the World Series and no longer had to say "Wait till next year!" It was a tense, exciting series, a seven-game victory over the Yankees. Dodgers pitching hero Johnny Podres won two games, including an eight-hit shutout in the finale, and Brooklyn center fielder Duke Snider belted four homers. The Series turned on a running grab by left fielder Sandy Amoros of a slicing liner off the bat of YOGI BERRA. The catch saved two runs and preserved Podres's Game 7 victory.

1956

Perfect.

On October 8, 1956, Yankees journeyman pitcher Don Larsen pitched what was for decades the only no-hitter in postseason baseball history. Roy Halladay joined Larsen in that pantheon in 2010, but Larsen actually did even better than a no-hitter—he tossed a perfect game. It came in Game 5 against the Dodgers. Because the Dodgers had roughed up Larsen in Game 2, he was a surprise choice to pitch Game 5 with the Series tied at two games apiece. But his no-windup delivery stumped the Dodgers all day long. Only one batter reached a three-ball count, and only a few balls even came close to falling for hits. The last batter, pinch hitter Dale Mitchell, took a called strike three to end the game on a pitch that was probably high and outside. But umpire Babe Pinelli, who would retire right after the Series, didn't want to let the game go any further. As catcher YOGI BERRA and the rest of the Yankees ran out to hug Larsen, Pinelli wept. "Sometimes a week might go by when I don't think about that game," Larsen once said, "but I don't remember when it happened last."

1958

The westward expansion.

Following the 1957 season, Brooklyn Dodgers owner WALTER O'MALLEY and New York Giants boss Horace Stoneham relocated their teams to Los Angeles and San Francisco, respectively. O'Malley had begun making plans years earlier when Brooklyn officials refused to build him a new ballpark; Stoneham moved because his club had been suffering from poor attendance in a rickety ballpark. Brooklyn fans have never forgiven O'Malley for uprooting their beloved team, since the move was obviously driven by greed—unjustified greed, in their minds, since the Dodgers franchise was already among the league's most profitable. L.A. fans, on the other hand, have nothing but respect for Mr. O'Malley.

1960
Maz's blast beats the Yanks.
One of the all-time great World Series, won by the Pirates over the Yankees in seven games. Although the Yankees had outscored the Pirates in the first six games 46 to 17—including scores of 16–3, 10–0, and 12–0—the scrappy Pirates hung on till the end. Game 7 was an immensely thrilling contest, perhaps the most exciting game in Series history: A total of 10 runs were scored in the final two innings, including a bottom-of-the-ninth, game-winning home run by Bill Mazeroski off Ralph Terry to give the Pirates an improbable 10–9 victory.

1961
Baseball expands.
The season of baseball's first expansion since the American League's inception in 1901. In 1961, two teams were added to the AL: the Los Angeles Angels and the Washington Senators (which took the place of the old Senators, who had just moved to Minnesota to become the Twins; a decade later, those new Senators would themselves move out of Washington to begin life anew as the Texas Rangers—got all that?). The National League would expand in 1962, adding the New York Mets and the Houston Colt .45s (soon to become the Astros).

As happens in most expansion seasons, pitchers suffered and hitters flourished. ROGER MARIS set the major league record with 61 home runs while teammate MICKEY MANTLE slugged 54 (*see* 61). And first baseman Norm Cash of the Tigers recorded his greatest season: a .361 average with 41 homers and 132 RBIs. He later admitted he used a corked bat all season—apparently reasoning that the weakened pitching wasn't enough of an advantage.

1968
The Year of the Pitcher.
1968 was the peak season of the pitcher's era, during which strikeouts were high and ERAs low. In 1968, DENNY MCLAIN won 31 games, BOB GIBSON had a 1.12 ERA in 304 innings pitched, CARL

YASTRZEMSKI led the AL with a paltry .301 batting average, DON DRYSDALE fashioned his streak of 58 2/3 scoreless innings, and both leagues had composite ERAs under 3.00. In another unlikely event typifying the strange season, GAYLORD PERRY of the Giants no-hit St. Louis one day, and the Cardinals' Ray Washburn followed suit with a no-hitter of his own against San Francisco the very next day. Following that year, the strike zone was reduced and pitching mounds were lowered.

1969
Modern baseball takes shape with more expansion and divisions.
The year of baseball's third expansion, which added four more teams: the Montreal Expos and San Diego Padres in the NL, the Kansas City Royals and Seattle Pilots (which became the Milwaukee Brewers) in the AL. To accommodate what had just become 12-team leagues, Eastern and Western divisions were formed and a round of postseason playoffs were added. The AL would increase by two more teams in 1977—with Seattle and Toronto—while the NL would wait until 1993 to reach 14 teams by adding Colorado and Florida. For the 1994 season, the two leagues split anew, adding a Central Division and yet another round of playoffs. And in 1998, Tampa Bay and Arizona joined the league.

1972
Labor unrest and Flood v. Kuhn.
In 1972, baseball players went on strike for the first time ever. They stayed out for 13 games and forced the cancellation of a week's worth of games.

More significantly, 1972 was also the year the Supreme Court rejected CURT FLOOD'S lawsuit challenging baseball's reserve clause, known as *Flood v. Kuhn*. In 1969, the thirty-one-year-old Flood, a three-time All-Star, had filed suit against baseball after refusing a trade from St. Louis to Philadelphia. "After 12 years in the major leagues," Flood wrote to commissioner BOWIE KUHN, "I do not feel that I am a piece of property to be bought and sold irrespective of my wishes. I believe that any system that produces that result violates my basic rights as a citizen and is inconsistent with the laws of the United States." He later wrote that he challenged baseball to "stop 24 millionaire owners from playing God with thousands of ballplayers' lives." With the backing of the MAJOR LEAGUE BASEBALL PLAYERS

ASSOCIATION and its head, MARVIN MILLER, Flood took his case all the way to the Supreme Court, knowing that he would be blacklisted from baseball and would almost certainly never play again.

Handling Flood's case was former Supreme Court Justice Arthur Goldberg, who argued that baseball's RESERVE CLAUSE violated federal antitrust laws. Supreme Court history was against them: In 1922, the Federal League challenged major league baseball on antitrust grounds and lost; then in 1953 a player named George Toolson lost his challenge to baseball when the Court refused to hear his case. In both instances, the Court had ruled that baseball was a sport, not interstate commerce, and therefore not subject to antitrust laws—even though the Court had in the past ruled that football and other sports *were* subject to those laws.

Resistance to the lawsuit came from all sides: from the owners, of course, but also from other players and the media. All believed that the reserve system was the "backbone" of baseball. The fact that it treated players as "property to be bought and sold" made little difference to them.

In the trial leading up to the Supreme Court, Flood's team called a number of witnesses, including former (and future) owner BILL VEECK, Hall of Famers JACKIE ROBINSON and HANK GREENBERG, and former major league pitcher Jim Brosnan. Later, Flood became convinced that if active major league stars had testified on his behalf, they would have demonstrated the solidarity of the players and helped the case immeasurably. But in the end, the illogical 1972 decision by Justice Harry Blackmun came out against Flood, upholding the Federal League case by saying that Congress had jurisdiction over the matter: "Remedial legislation has been introduced repeatedly in Congress but none has ever been enacted. The Court, accordingly, has concluded that Congress as yet has had no intention to subject baseball's reserve system to the reach of antitrust statutes." Basically, the Court passed the buck.

Although Flood had lost, his case became a great consciousness-raiser for players and reporters who had blindly accepted the reserve system. As Miller would later write in his autobiography, *A Whole Different Ball Game*, "Flood didn't actually change the game, though he was a positive influence and an example for others who did." In 1975, arbitrator Peter Seitz's ruling in the Messersmith–McNally case disbanded the reserve clause—thanks in no small part to the courage of Curt Flood.

1973
A DH is born.
1973 marked the first season of the designated hitter in the American League, when Ron Blomberg of the Yankees became the first-ever DH to bat. League officials instituted the change hoping that it would increase attendance, and it did—but only briefly. In 1972, the average AL team drew 953,000 fans; in 1973, that total grew to 1.1 million—a substantial increase of 15 percent. But the next year, attendance dropped by 3 percent, followed by a year of zero growth. It took the 1975 WORLD SERIES—in which no designated hitter batted—for baseball become really popular again.

1974
Aaron passes the Babe.
On April 8, 1974, HENRY AARON did what, a decade earlier, few thought could ever happen: He broke BABE RUTH'S all-time record for career home runs. Aaron had hit 40 homers in 1973 to finish the season with 713, just one shy of Ruth's mark. He hit number 714 on Opening Day in Cincinnati, and, to capitalize on the promotional value, Braves management wanted to keep him out of the next games so that Aaron would break the record at home. Commissioner BOWIE KUHN intervened and ordered the Braves to put him in the lineup, but Aaron gamely waited until he made it home to break the mark.

Every pitcher in the league dreaded facing Aaron; nobody wanted to be *the one*. Fate smiled upon Al Downing of the Dodgers. Aaron faced Downing in the fourth inning of a 3-1 game, with a runner on first. Fifty-two thousand fans greeted Downing's first pitch—a change-up in the dirt—with a chorus of boos. Downing's next pitch was supposed to be a tailing fastball, but it didn't tail. Aaron swung and ripped it over the left field wall, and just like that, the chase was over. He rounded the bases quickly and meaningfully, and Aaron's mother and father, as well as the whole Braves team, mobbed him at home plate. Atlanta relief pitcher Tom House, who'd been in the Braves bullpen in left field, handed the baseball to Aaron. It was a generous move, since at least two people were offering $25,000 for the home run ball.

Yet through it all, Aaron says he couldn't enjoy it much because, although he received thousands of complimentary fan letters, he also received hundreds of death threats from racists. Somehow, he was able to put those out of his mind and do a difficult job—hitting 90-mph fastballs out of the park—in front of sold-out crowds. "I don't want them to forget Ruth," he once said. "I just want them to remember me." We do.

1975

The Big Red Machine reaches its peak.

Another momentous year, which included a historic team, a storied World Series, and an arbitrator's ruling that changed the face of baseball. Let's start with the historic team: the Cincinnati Reds, who featured five future Hall of Famers, steamrolled the competition on the way to 108 wins, and became known as the "BIG RED MACHINE." In the post-season, they faced—and ultimately beat 4 to 3—the Boston Red Sox in a spectacular World Series. Five games were decided by one run and two went into extra innings, including the legendary Game 6 (see the next entry).

The Sox and Reds play a series for the ages.

Perhaps the greatest game ever played, Game 6 of the 1975 World Series introduced a whole new generation of fans to baseball. Three days of rain in Boston interrupted the World Series with the Reds leading the Red Sox three games to two. With each day's delay, fans and players grew more excited with anticipation, and in the end, nobody was disappointed. Boston took a 3-0 lead on a Fred Lynn home run in the bottom of the first. Cincinnati tied it in the fifth on a walk and three hits, then took the lead in the seventh when George Foster doubled home two runs. Cesar Geronimo slammed a home run to pad the lead to 6-3, but in the bottom of the seventh, Boston pinch hitter Bernie Carbo, little known before the Series, came to the plate with two on and two out.

Earlier in the Series, Carbo had banged a home run in a losing effort, and here in Game 6, he did it again—this one a three-run shot to tie the game. The Sox loaded the bases in both the ninth and 10th innings to no avail, and in the top of the 11th, Dwight Evans made a spectacular game-saving catch of potential home run by JOE MORGAN. Then, in the bottom of the 12th, catcher Carlton Fisk blasted one of the most memorable home runs in Series history to win the game for the Sox. It was a high fly down the left field line, over the

GREEN MONSTER; the only question was whether it would stay fair or hook foul. In one of the most widely seen baseball highlights, television cameras captured Fisk waving his hands to body-English the ball into staying fair.

Unfortunately for Boston, Game 7 proved the ultimate anticlimax. The Sox took a 3–0 advantage but lost the lead, the game, and the Series when Morgan blooped a single to drive Ken Griffey home with the winning run in the ninth inning. As had happened in 1946 and 1967—and would occur again in 1986—the Sox had lost a thrilling seven-game World Series.

Many baseball historians credit the 1975 World Series with rescuing baseball from the foundering attendance that had plagued the sport for the previous two decades. Yearly attendance figures seem to support that conclusion. From 1960 through 1975, major league attendance per team actually dropped by one quarter of one percent (although overall attendance increased by 10 million because of the addition of eight new clubs). After the spectacular Game 6, 75 million fans watched Game 7 on TV, the highest total to watch any sporting event in American history up to that time. And over the next five years, attendance per team rose by an average of 5 percent per year—the largest sustained period of growth since the immediate postwar period. Another reason for the growth was the aging of baby boomers. They had abandoned baseball during the 1960s because of everything else that had been happening during that turbulent decade. But by the mid-1970s, they were ready to return to the game they'd grown up with. For a lot of them, the 1975 World Series was the event that rekindled their interest.

A stunning arbitration decision.

Which leads to the final item on the list for 1975: the decision by arbitrator Peter Seitz to grant FREE AGENCY to ANDY MESSERSMITH and DAVE MCNALLY. This changed not only baseball but the entire sports landscape in America forever. For the better. Read the entries on Messersmith and McNally for more.

1978

The Boston Massacre.

Baseball's "Boston Massacre" refers to the four-game series between the Red Sox and Yankees in the midst of the great 1978 pennant race. Boston led New York in the standings by as many as 14 games as late as July 17. But when the Yankees visited FENWAY PARK on September 7 to begin a four-game series, Boston's lead was down to four. With just 24 games to play, the Red Sox had a chance to get rid of the Yankees once and for all; the Yankees could pull even with a sweep. Then the massacre began: 15–3 in the first game, 13–2 in the second, 7–0 in the third, and 7–4 in the finale—all Yankee victories. It wasn't just the home runs and doubles that killed the Red Sox; it was also the 11 errors. The Yankees would go on to lead the division by 3-1/2 in mid-September, but the Sox went on a tear with 12 wins in their last 14 games to tie the division race on the final day, setting up a one-game playoff in Boston. Weak-hitting shortstop Bucky Dent—known forever in Boston as "Bucky F-----g Dent"—proved the hero for New York as he slugged a three-run homer to give the Yankees a 3–2 lead on the way to a 5–4 victory, giving Sox fans yet another reason to cry.

1981

The Strike.

In 1981, baseball players went on strike for the second time in baseball history, causing more than 50 games per team to be canceled. The main issue of the strike was FREE AGENCY. The owners wanted compensation whenever one of their free agents signed with another team; the PLAYERS ASSOCIATION felt that such a policy would gut the whole concept of free agency. The confrontation came down to a battle of wills. Owners thought the players weren't strong enough to maintain their unity, but the players were, in fact, unified by their anger at ownership's arrogance. The owners did have a trump card: They had secured a strike insurance policy from Lloyd's of London and could afford to lose some money. But once the insurance ran out, the owners caved in. With MARVIN MILLER as their chief negotiator, the players retained their unrestricted free agency and other concessions earned during earlier negotiations.

The real losers were the Cincinnati Reds and St. Louis Cardinals. Commissioner BOWIE KUHN had decided to split the season in half, with the first-half "quarter-pennant" winners facing the second-half winners in each division to determine the participants for the League Championship Series. The Reds and Cardinals had baseball's two best overall records but saw no postseason action because they hadn't won either of the quarter-pennants. Because of that stupid decision, and because he was viewed as unhelpful in resolving the labor stoppage, Kuhn's days in office were numbered. Fans, on the other hand, forgave baseball quickly. In 1982, attendance grew by more than a million fans compared to the 1980 season.

1983
The Pine Tar Incident.
Probably the weirdest mini-scandal in recent major league history, replete with late-inning heroics, allegations of cheating, a near brawl, and BILLY MARTIN. What would a minor scandal be without Billy Martin? It was July 24, 1983, New York vs. Kansas City in YANKEE STADIUM. Relief ace GOOSE GOSSAGE was on the mound for the Yankees, protecting a 4–3 lead in the top of the ninth. With two outs and a runner on, third baseman GEORGE BRETT smashed a fastball over the fence to give the Royals an apparent 5–4 lead. To everyone's surprise, Martin, the Yankee manager, ran out his dugout carrying a rule book, trying to contain his glee. He had known for weeks that Brett was putting pine tar—a sticky black substance that helps a batter's grip—higher on his bat than the 18 inches the rules allowed. He was waiting for the right moment to spring the news on an umpiring crew, and this was it. After measuring the pine tar on Brett's bat using the width of home plate, umpire Tim McClelland ruled the home run illegal and called Brett out. Because he represented the third out of the inning, the Yankees had apparently won the game.

Then Brett came storming out of the dugout! In a wild rage, barely restrained by players and coaches, Brett embodied pure, unadulterated anger. Even though the game was supposed to be over, the umpires ejected Brett, manager Dick Howser, coach Rocky Colavito, and pitcher GAYLORD PERRY, who tried to hide the bat. The umpires were able to confiscate the bat only because, as it was getting passed from Royals player to player, the last man in the line didn't have anybody to give it to.

The Royals protested to the league office: "Broadway wouldn't buy that script... it's so unbelievable," huffed Howser. Four days later, AL President Lee MacPhail agreed with Howser. He overruled his umpiring crew, a rare occurrence, and allowed the home run. He declared that even though the pine tar was technically illegal, it didn't violate the "spirit of the rules." The Yankees were outraged. "It sure tests our faith in leadership," moaned Yankee czar GEORGE STEINBRENNER (of all people). Martin howled that the rule book was "only good for when you go deer hunting and run out of toilet paper." But MacPhail had the power, and his decision stood.

Now there was the matter of completing the game, which was still in the ninth inning. The completion was scheduled for August 18, and the Yankees decided they would charge regular admission, even for fans who had tickets to the first game! Enraged fans protested, and two lawsuits were filed declaring the team's policy illegal. In response, the club changed its policy but failed to announce it, so only 1,200 fans showed up to watch nine minutes and 41 seconds of baseball. Hal McRae struck out to end the ninth, and the Yankees went down in order in the bottom of the inning, giving the Royals a hard-fought 5–4 victory.

1986

A postseason for the ages.

Three of the most exciting postseason series of all time all occurred within one calendar month in 1986. In the NL playoffs, the Mets defeated the Astros 4 games to 2 in a series that included: a 1–0 opening game; a 2–1, 12-inning contest; and a series-deciding, 16-inning game in which seven runs scored after the 13th inning (see below). The ALCS was just as exciting: the Red Sox were one strike away from elimination in Game 5 but won that game and the next two to beat the Angels. In the World Series, it was the Mets who were one strike away from elimination only to miraculously come back in the bottom of the twelfth in the sixth game (see below). The Mets then came back again in Game 7 to ruin Boston's hopes of winning its first World Series since 1918.

NLCS Game 6, Mets vs. Astros.

The 1986 NLCS pitted the Mets against the Astros, a pair of teams with excellent pitching: eventual Cy Young Award winner Mike Scott and all-time strikeout leader NOLAN RYAN anchored the Astros, and 1985 Cy Young winner DWIGHT GOODEN headed a deep Mets staff. In Game 6, pitching would be at a premium. The Mets led the series 3–2, but Astros lefty Bob Knepper shut down the Mets on two hits and took a 3–0 lead into the ninth inning. Then things fell apart as Knepper allowed two runs and relief ace Dave Smith allowed another, sending the game to extra innings.

Both relief corps did their jobs until the 13th, when the Mets scored a run on two singles and a walk. In the bottom of the 13th, though, Billy Hatcher hit the biggest home run of his life to prolong the game. Three innings later, the Mets notched three more runs, giving them a seemingly insurmountable 7-4 lead going to the bottom of the 16th. But Houston showed remarkable resilience: A one-out walk to pinch hitter Davey Lopes. A single by Bill Doran. Another single by Hatcher, scoring Lopes. Then, with two outs, Glenn Davis brought the Astros to within a run with an RBI single. Two on base, one run down, Houston an out away from elimination. Ready to pitch Game 7, if Houston could win Game 6, was Mike Scott, who'd already shut down the Mets twice. "I really don't want to see Scott until April," thought Mets manager Davey Johnson.

Johnson got his wish. Mets reliever Jesse Orosco struck out Kevin Bass, and the Mets were on their way to their first World Series since 1973.

World Series Game 6, Mets vs. Red Sox.

The Red Sox led the Mets three games to two going into Game 6 at Shea Stadium—one victory away from their first World Series championship since the days of BABE RUTH. With ROGER CLEMENS on the mound, the Sox held a 2–0 lead until the fifth, when a walk, a steal, an error, and a ground ball double play brought home two Mets runs. Each team scored single runs later and the game went to the 10th inning tied, 3–3.

Then the fireworks happened. First, Dave Henderson slammed an 0–1 pitch into the left field stands, giving the Sox a 4–3 lead. Then, with two out, WADE BOGGS doubled and scored on a single to pad Boston's advantage. After the first two New York batters flied out to start the bottom of the 10th, reporters began to make their way to Boston's clubhouse for postgame interviews. The champagne was chilled and ready. Pitcher Bruce Hurst was about to be named the Series MVP. Sox owner Jean Yawkey, aging and frail, stood with commissioner PETER UEBERROTH, ready to receive the championship trophy.

But on the field, catcher Gary Carter singled to left. Pinch hitter Kevin Mitchell banged a hit to center. Ray Knight blooped a single to drive home Carter, sending Mitchell to third. Pitcher Bob Stanley replaced Calvin Schiraldi and promptly threw a wild pitch, bringing home Mitchell with the tying run. With millions of disbelieving Red

Sox fans watching, center fielder Mookie Wilson banged a soft ground ball to first baseman Bill Buckner, the ostensible third out that would send the game to the 11th. But gimpy Buckner, with bad knees and sore ankles, couldn't make the play! The ball bounced between his legs, Ray Knight scored, the Mets won, and Boston's frustration was prolonged yet again.

Buckner was immediately blamed for the loss, but it was Stanley who wild-pitched the tying run home, and it was Schiraldi who couldn't get the final out, and it was manager John McNamara who failed to put in a defensive replacement for Buckner (as he had been doing all season) and left Schiraldi in for 2-2/3 innings, and it was the whole Boston lineup that left 14 runners on base during the game.

Two days later, the Sox lost a tense Game 7, and the CURSE OF THE BAMBINO continued for 18 more years.

1988
Gibson blasts the Eck.
It was Game 1 of the 1988 World Series, featuring the seemingly overmatched Dodgers against mighty Oakland. The A's went to the bottom of the ninth leading 4–3 as Kirk Gibson, the Dodgers' left fielder, stood in the trainer's room, practicing his swing. Gibson had been the Dodgers' spark all season, and he would win the league's MVP despite underwhelming statistics. On this day, his ailing knees had forced him to the clubhouse for rehab, but he had himself shot full of cortisone so that if the situation presented itself, he could come out for one at bat.

On the mound for the A's to finish the ninth inning that night stood DENNIS ECKERSLEY, the league's best reliever, who'd notched 45 saves that season. Eck got the first two outs quickly. Then pinch-hitter Mike Davis worked Eck for a walk, and Gibson strode to the plate as a pinch hitter. The crowd erupted in cheers. He worked the count to 3–2, including one foul grounder that forced Gibson to limp to first base and another foul that nearly brought him to his knees, à la Roy Hobbs in the movie THE NATURAL. Then Eckersley tried a back-door slider, and Gibson swung.

The ball sailed high into the Los Angeles night and landed 10 rows into the right field bleachers. The game was over, the Dodgers had won, and Gibson's place in baseball history was secured. Even though

Gibson didn't play the rest of the Series, his spirit seemed to be there as the Dodgers went on to beat the A's in five games.

1989

Earthquake!

The Oakland A's swept the San Francisco Giants 4–0 in a 1989 World Series that will be forever remembered for the 7.1-magnitude earthquake that struck just before the start of Game 3. The quake killed 63 people and damaged the Oakland Bay Bridge, and many sportswriters and others urged the cancellation of the Series. Cooler heads prevailed, however, and after a delay of 12 days, the A's finished off the Giants.

1991

Morris comes up real big.

The 1991 World Series, in which the Twins prevailed over Braves 4 games to 3, is easily among the most exciting of all time. In five of the seven games, the winning run was scored in the eighth inning or later, and four of those were walk-off hits: Mark Lemke's RBI single in Game 3, Jerry Willard's pinch sacrifice fly in Game 4, KIRBY PUCK-ETT'S 11th-inning home run Game 6, and finally Gene Larkin's pinch single in Game 7 that clinched the series for Minnesota. And who can forget the gritty performance by grizzled veteran Jack Morris in the final game, when the 36-year-old workhorse threw a 10-inning shutout. Many people seem to believe that one game alone qualifies Morris for the Hall of Fame.

1994

The World Series gets killed.

The strike of 1994 canceled hundreds of games and wiped out the entire postseason. It was as close to a tragedy as anything baseball-related could get, for the 1994 season was shaping up to be one of the greatest ever. In the first year of the new divisional setup, the Cleveland Indians were marching toward the playoffs for the first time since the 1950s. Two storied teams—the Yankees and Dodgers—were leading their divisions. GREG MADDUX had sewn up his third straight Cy Young Award. Matt Williams and KEN GRIFFEY, JR. were making runs at ROGER MARIS'S single-season home run record. And FRANK THOMAS, Albert Belle, and JEFF BAGWELL were vying for baseball's TRIPLE CROWN.

But even though the players were the ones who went on strike, it's hard to side with the owners. The issue—surprise!—was money. The owners were claiming that at least 10 teams were losing money, even though 1993 attendance had been the highest in history by a wide margin (even if you take out the expansion Colorado Rockies and Florida Marlins). It's hard to trust the owners' claims of poverty since most of the teams refused to show their books to the players. The solution to the owners' problems, they believed, lay in a revenue-sharing agreement that included a salary cap limiting players to 50 percent of the clubs' revenues. The players, who were already earning 58 percent of the revenue, disputed the owners' claims, and they did not want their salaries artificially restricted; in all honesty, what self-respecting employee would? According to labor law, the owners could unilaterally implement their labor system if good-faith bargaining produced no results. Even though they knew the players would never agree to a salary cap, the owners took a year and a half to develop their plan and presented it to the players in June. The players believed they had no choice but to strike. They struck in August, but they could have hurt the owners even more by striking in late September, just before the playoffs and after they'd received all their paychecks. Instead, they picked a date that could have saved the postseason if the owners hadn't been so adamant in their demand for a salary cap. Making matters worse, the owners inexplicably reneged on a scheduled pension payment.

On September 14, acting commissioner Bud Selig issued a statement that did the unthinkable: cancel the World Series. Here's part of that decree:

> Whereas, the MLBPA has consistently been unwilling to respond in any meaningful way to the Clubs' need to contain costs and has consistently refused to bargain with the Clubs concerning a division of industry revenues with the players or any other method of establishing aggregate player compensation; ...

> NOW THEREFORE, BE IT RESOLVED that:

> In order to protect the integrity of the Championship Season, the Division Series, the League Championship Series and the World Series, the 28 Clubs have concluded with enormous regret that the remainder of the 1994 season, the Division Series, the League Championship Series and the World Series must be canceled and that the Clubs will explore all avenues to achieve a meaningful, structural reform of Baseball's player compensation system in an

effort to ensure that the 1995 and future Championship seasons can occur as scheduled and uninterrupted.

Several interesting things about that statement. Two owners refused to sign it: Cincinnati owner Marge Schott didn't sign because she felt the season should have gone on with replacement players from the minor leagues; and Baltimore owner Peter Angelos, a former labor lawyer, wouldn't sign because he objected to the negative wording of that first paragraph. That paragraph shifts all the blame to the players when the owners were just as hardline as the players about the salary cap. For most of the strike, the two sides didn't even meet, but union chief DONALD FEHR said repeatedly that he would have met anytime, anywhere, but that the owners rarely called him.

The situation worsened in December, when owners declared an impasse in the negotiations and imposed a labor system that included not a salary cap (which they had fought so hard for earlier) but rather a LUXURY TAX, in addition to an end to ARBITRATION and a restricted form of FREE AGENCY. The players would have none of it and challenged the owners' action in court.

The strike dragged on through spring training with owners seemingly willing to use replacement players in real major league games. Bargaining was going nowhere; even an attempt by President Clinton proved fruitless. Two days before the season was set to begin, in a decision by Justice Sonia Sotomayor (now on the U.S. Supreme Court), a federal court ruled that the owners had broken labor law by implementing its labor system. Owners were ordered to re-institute the old labor agreement, and the major leaguers returned for a season that began three weeks later than usual. Fans struck back by boycotting major league baseball. Finally, late in the season, the two sides hammered out a deal that preserved free agency and arbitration and added a toothless luxury tax.

The disparity between high-revenue and low-revenue clubs never has gone away, but the relationship between labor and ownership has improved dramatically, and today things look bright for baseball on the labor front.

1998

The Season that Saved Baseball.

Some called 1998 the greatest baseball season ever. It certainly was one of the most important. When the season began, memories of the 1994 STRIKE still lingered among baseball fans. The prior year, attendance had been down, and the World Series between the Indians and Marlins failed to excite regular fans. But 1998 seemed to erase the malaise. MARK MCGWIRE deserves the initial credit. In 1997, he threatened the single-season record of 61 home runs, held by ROGER MARIS (*see* 61), but had fallen short. In 1998, all of baseball was watching him closely, and he got out of the gate quickly, with 11 home runs by April 30. Sammy Sosa joined McGwire in the home run race with a record 20 in the month of June, and all summer long the two captivated the nation as they battled for the lead. But it never seemed to be a competition; each player seemed to revel in the accomplishments of the other.

As they approached 61, people who had abandoned the sport became fans again. McGwire's at bats were being broadcast on national TV, and the question throughout the nation was "How many did Mac hit?" Ultimately, of course, both McGwire and Sosa blew past the record, with McGwire finishing at a wondrous 70 with five homers in the final weekend (*see* 70). Even McGwire said he was in awe of his accomplishment.

The New York Yankees, meanwhile, had staged a chase of their own: the single-season record for team victories. And they dominated teams in the same way McGwire and Sosa had dominated pitchers. The Yanks finished with 114 regular-season wins, the American League record, then swept through the postseason and won the franchise's 24th World Series. The only thing missing from the 1998 season was a classic pennant race. The Giants and Sosa's Cubs did battle for the final wild card spot, but every other playoff spot was clinched so early that September was spent watching McGwire and Sosa. Fans didn't seem to mind.

Postscript: In 2010, McGwire revealed that he'd been using steroids throughout the 1998 campaign (and at other times), confirming a rumor that had permeated baseball since 1998. Does this revelation taint the joy of 1998 for you?

Ripken ends his streak.

On September 20, 1998, even though he was healthy and able to play, CAL RIPKEN decided to end the greatest consecutive-games streak in baseball history (*see* 2,632). "I was going to take the last day of the season off in Boston," he told reporters, "but I thought about it a long time and decided if this is going to end, let it end where it started in Baltimore." In the game, rookie Ryan Minor became the answer to a trivia question when he took over for Ripken at third base, and the Orioles lost to the Yankees 5-4.

2001

Bonds hits 73.

Just three years after MCGWIRE and Sosa thrilled the baseball world with their co-chase for the single-season home run record, BARRY BONDS made his own run. But this time, it came without the excitement and fanfare that accompanied the earlier chase. A few reasons for it: One, the fans were tired out; there's only so much emotion they have to give to a big event like that. Two, the chase was interrupted by the 9/11 attacks, and fans were not focused on baseball. Three, Bonds was known as selfish toward his teammates and unfriendly toward fans and reporters. And four—possibly most important—Bonds was the poster boy for baseball's burgeoning steroid scandal; a lot of people thought his performance was illegitimate.

But what a performance it was. Not only did Bonds blow past McGwire's home run record to finish with 73 (*see* 73), he also broke a record held by BABE RUTH and once considered untouchable: the mark for slugging percentage. In 1920, Ruth slugged .847, and in 2001, Bonds pushed the record to an astounding .863. And he did it even as he broke yet another single-season record by drawing 177 walks.

By September, the fear of pitching to Bonds became ridiculous, for he was being walked repeatedly, often in the first inning and almost always when there was a runner on base. The situation reached its apex—or nadir, depending on your perspective—during a three-game series in Houston in early October. Bonds came into the series sitting on 69 home runs, and Houston manager Larry Dierker seemed determined not to let him tie the record against the Astros. In the first game, Bonds walked twice and was hit by a pitch as the Giants won 4-1. In the second, he walked three times in an 11-8 San Francisco victory. And in the final game, he again walked three times, and it wasn't until the score was 9-2 Giants in the ninth inning that Bonds saw a good pitch, which, inevitably, he turned on for his 70th home run. (I recall Dierker being savaged in the media and by the fans—who had paid good money to see Bonds swing the bat—for this irrational fear of Bonds. Possibly as a result of being perceived as overly fearful of one player and unreasonably faithless in his own pitchers, Dierker was fired after the season, even though the Astros had just won the division.)

Still, Bonds saw enough good pitches down the stretch to reach and then break the record at home against the Dodgers during the last weekend of the season; he finished with 73 (*see* 73). If you lived in the San Francisco Bay Area at the time (as I did, and do), breaking the record was a huge deal. But for the rest of the country, you could almost feel the collective yawns as Bonds made his mark.

2003
Pedro flames out.
By 2003, the Red Sox had been the Yankees' whipping boys for 83 straight years—ever since Harry Frazee sold BABE RUTH (*see* 1919: THE SOX SELL THE BABE) But for a few moments in Game 7 of the 2003 American League Championship Series, it looked as if the Sox were finally going to slay all those demons. They led 5-2 in the eighth inning and were just six outs away from not only going to the World Series, but beating the Yankees in New York to do it. And the man leading the charge was one of the best pitchers of his generation: PEDRO MARTINEZ. Confidence was running high in Red Sox Nation.

Then hell broke loose.

It was well known in baseball circles that, by that point in his career, Martinez's effectiveness dropped off significantly after he reached 100 pitches. And so everybody was surprised that he came out to pitch the eighth inning. Yet there he was, giving up a one-out double to DEREK JETER.

Surely, Boston fans believed, manager Grady Little would replace him with Mike Timlin or Alan Embree, as he had been doing all year.

Nope. Martinez stayed in and gave up an RBI single to Bernie Williams. Now the score was 5-3, runner at first.

Surely Little would replace Martinez now!

Nope. Hideki Matsui roped a ground-rule double. Still 5-3, runners on second and third.

SURELY LITTLE WOULD REPLACE MARTINEZ NOW!

Nope. Martinez stayed in, and Jorge Posada dropped in another double, tying the score at 5-5 and sending the YANKEE STADIUM fans into a frenzy.

Finally, mercifully, Little replaced Martinez with Embree, and the bleeding stopped.

Although the Sox still had a chance to win the game, everybody knew in their hearts the Yankees would win. And in the bottom of the eleventh, when Aaron Boone (aka "Aaron F-----g Boone") hit the first pitch he saw from Tim Wakefield over the fence to win the game and send the Yanks to the World Series yet again, the Red Sox's misery continued.

2004
The Curse is reversed.
After Game 3 of the 2004 American League Championship Series, it looked like the Red Sox would go home losers yet again and the CURSE OF THE BAMBINO would continue. The Yanks had just won that game 19–8, giving them a seemingly insurmountable 3–0 lead in the series. No team in baseball history had ever come back from that deficit, but the Red Sox players appeared undaunted: They wore t-shirts that said "Why Not Us?"

And it worked. In Game 4, David Ortiz kept hope alive with a 12th-inning, walk-off home run after the Sox had earlier tied the game in the ninth against the previously invincible MARIANO RIVERA. In Game 5, Rivera blew another save, and Ortiz again drove home the winning run, this time on a single in the 14th.

The Sox had forced a Game 6. But after all those extra innings, Boston's pitching staff was in shambles. Their best starter during the season was CURT SCHILLING, yet he was nursing a seriously injured ankle. It was only after Boston's team physician performed an experimental surgical procedure that Schilling was deemed healthy enough to pitch. And boy did he rise to the occasion. With blood seeping through his sock (*see* "BLOODY SOCK"), Schilling threw 99 pitches over seven innings, allowing just four hits and one run. The game ended with the Sox winning 4–2. No team down 3–0 had ever forced a Game 6, let alone a Game 7, and now the two bitter rivals were heading to a final-game showdown that only die-hardiest of Sox fans would ever have predicted.

Game 7 proved to be the ultimate anticlimax for everyone outside Red Sox Nation. Boston scored six runs in the first two innings and cruised to an easy 10–2 win. After all those years of watching the Yankees stomp out their dreams, the Red Sox were returning the favor in historic fashion.

In a cosmic sense, it seems like the only way the Red Sox were ever going to "Reverse the Curse" was to overcome the longest possible odds. And coming back from three games down was about as long as the odds could possibly be.

2010
Perfection times two. And almost times three.
PERFECT GAMES are rare and celebrated events. Yet in the spring of 2010, you could barely turn on the TV without watching one. First, on May 9, A's pitcher Dallas Braden retired all 27 Tampa hitters to record just the 19th perfect game in major league history. Just 20 days later, Philadelphia's Roy Halladay threw a perfecto of his own, wiping out the Marlins.

And before fans could even catch their breath, Armando Galarraga of Detroit got 27 consecutive outs against the Indians on June 2 for the third perfect game of the—wait, what just happened? Did first base umpire Jim Joyce really call safe on the last out of the game, an infield grounder by Jason Donald? He did, he blew it, and he knew it, costing Galarraga a place in the record books. Within hours—minutes?—fans appealed to commissioner BUD SELIG to overrule his umpires, but there was no way the timid Selig was going to do something bold like that. Galarraga, for his part, handled the disappointment with class: he immediately forgave Joyce and never once acted angry. So instead of simply joining the record books, Galarraga's gem made it into the history books. His "Imperfect Game" is going to be remembered for a lot longer than almost any actual perfect game.

The Giants win the Series! The Giants win the Series!
The New York/San Francisco Giants are one of baseball's most storied franchises, and for the first 50+ years of major league history, they were also one of the most successful. But since moving to San Francisco, they had won zero World Series despite coming oh-so-close in 1962 and 2002. But in 2010, they reversed their fortunes with an unlikely team led by a young pitching staff featuring two-time Cy Young Winner Tim Lincecum, a veteran lineup featuring castoffs Aubrey Huff and Juan Uribe, and the rookie phenom Buster Posey. In the playoffs, they specialized in edge-of-your-seat games: they had five one-run victories in the division series and league championship series. Even the World Series against the Rangers had its share of tense moments, though on paper the Giants won in five games. San Francisco had always been a 49ers town, but beginning in 2010, it also became a Giants town. (And the Giants' victories in the 2012 and 2014 World Series cemented that fact.)

2011
Baseball's most exciting pennant finish.
The wildest, most thrilling night of regular season baseball ever, when two Wild Card berths were decided within a matter of minutes. The seeds of the excitement were planted a month earlier, when the Braves led the Cardinals in the Wild Card standings by as many as 10-1/2 games and the Red Sox led the Rays by almost as much. But both leaders collapsed and both upstarts rallied. By the final day of the season, the races were all tied up, and the pressure was on to win.

In the American League, the Sox took a 3-2 lead over the Orioles in a rain-delayed game in Baltimore, while the Rays trailed the Yankees 7-0 in the eighth. It looked all over for Tampa Bay, but then the Rays scored six times in the eighth, then once more in the ninth on a down-to-the-final strike homer by Dan Johnson. (Was Yankee manager Joe Girardi even trying to win? He refused to put in Mariano Rivera because New York had already clinched its playoff spot, and he didn't want to overtire their relief ace.) Meanwhile, in Baltimore, the Orioles refused to roll over against Boston. With two outs in the ninth and facing closer Jonathan Papelbon, they smacked back-to-back doubles to tie the game, then plated the winning run one batter later. Three minutes later, before Boston could even fully absorb what had just happened in Baltimore, the scene abruptly shifted to Tampa, where Rays third baseman Even Longoria thrust a dagger into the heart of Red Sox Nation by smacking a game-winning home run in the bottom of the 10th. One moment the Sox were going to the playoffs, literally the next they were going home for the winter.

Over in the National League, the action was only slightly less dramatic. The Cardinals blew out the Astros 8-0, so the Braves had to win to keep pace and force a one-game playoff the next day. And it looked like they would do it when they took a 3-2 lead into the ninth with their rookie fireballer Craig Kimbrel on the mound. But Kimbrel allowed the tying run on a single, a pair of walks, and a sacrifice fly. Because the Braves had stopped hitting, it was inevitable that the Phillies would eventually win the game, which they did in the 13th inning. And so it was the Cardinals, not the Braves, who won the Wild Card that season, capping off one of the most improbable comebacks in modern baseball history. And their come-from-behind antics weren't even finished. See the next entry.

The Cardinals record an epic comeback.

If you read the previous entry, you know about the Cardinals' improbable comeback to win the N.L. Wild Card over the Braves. But that was just the appetizer for this amazing team. The next course involved defeating the favored Phillies in the Division Series in five games, with the final game a tense 1-0 squeaker featuring one of the greatest post-season pitching duels ever: Chris Carpenter vs. Roy Halladay.

In the L.C.S., it "only" took the Cardinals six games to dispatch the favored Brewers; the final game was an undramatic 12-6 drubbing. Then finally, the main course: the World Series, in which again the Cards were the underdogs against the hard-hitting Texas Rangers. The teams traded victories early in the series, but then Texas took control and led three games to two heading to game six. In that game, the Rangers led 7-4 in the eighth and 7-5 in the ninth, with their fireballing closer Neftali Feliz on the mound. He got Ryan Theriot to strike out swinging, then allowed a double to Albert Pujols and a walk to Lance Berkman. Allen Craig struck out looking for the second out of the inning, and David Freese fell behind 1-2. One strike away from the Rangers' first World Series victory, Feliz tried to blow a fastball by Freese, but Freese caught up to it and launched it 350 feet off the right field wall for a game-tying triple. They went to the 10th, and the Rangers again took a two-run lead. And again the Cardinals were down to their last strike, but this time it was Berkman who tied the game. The Rangers failed to score in the 11th, and Freese, the 9th-inning hero, led off for the Cardinals. On a 3-2 count, he swung hard and sent the ball over the left-field fence to cap off one of the greatest games in baseball history. Hyperbole? Let us list some of the reasons it ranks so highly:

- It was the first time in postseason baseball history that a team scored in the eighth, ninth, 10th and 11th innings of a game.
- It was the first World Series game in history in which a team was one strike away from elimination twice and still won.
- It was the first World Series game in which the winning team trailed five separate times.
- It was the first World Series game in history in which two players (Texas's Josh Hamilton and St. Louis's Freese) hit go-ahead home runs in extra innings.

It's anticlimactic to note that there was a game the next day, which the Cardinals won 12-6 to earn its 11th World Series championship.

4

TEAMS, LEAGUES, AND OTHER GROUPS

A, AA, AAA

The three levels of minor-league baseball, also referred to as SINGLE-A, DOUBLE-A, and TRIPLE-A. All major league franchises have at least one affiliate at each level. There is also a ROOKIE level, and there are several independent leagues that operate without major league affiliations.

All-American Girls Professional Baseball League
Women's league, 1943–54

The AAGPBL was a World War II-era alternative to major league baseball. With most young men, including the best ballplayers, fighting the war, Cubs owner/chewing gum king Philip Wrigley worried that fans might not want to see minor league 4-Fs in major league uniforms. He recruited former major league ballplayers to act as managers, and invited women from all over the country to try out for the new league. It began play in 1943 with just four teams, and to most fans, it was just a novelty. The teams had flowery-sounding nicknames such as the Daisies, Chicks, and Belles, and the players wore short dresses instead of baseball pants. "In the beginning," said star shortstop/catcher Lavone "Pepper" Davis, "a lot of people came out to laugh and the guys to look at the legs."

But the league gained an enthusiastic following, and it gradually increased to 10 teams. Salaries increased from $50 or $75 per week to as much as $600 per month, which was close to what some major leaguers of the time made. Unlike their male counterparts, however, the women had to follow strict rules of conduct. Makeup was to be worn at all times. Drinking and smoking were prohibited in public. A chaperone joined them at any public engagement. And they had to attend charm school. On the other hand, they acted like major leaguers in at least one important way: "I had a boyfriend in every town," said Davis.

By 1954, however, interest waned, and the league folded. Women's professional baseball remained all but forgotten until the release of the box office smash *A League of Their Own* in 1992 and the 1994 formation of the Colorado Silver Bullets, a women's team that played men's minor league and semipro teams throughout the country.

Will there ever be a woman in the major leagues? Doubtful. But here's what would have to happen: girls would have to start playing baseball, not softball, at an early age. That would create a large pool of available players, some of whom may be skilled enough to make it to men's college teams and professional leagues. The first woman would probably face a JACKIE ROBINSON-like ordeal to do it, but it would be worth it. I'm all for anything that will help baseball evolve—assuming it's not just a publicity stunt.

American Association
Major league, 1882–91
The original AA was the most innovative league of its time, if you look at it from a player's and fan's perspective (as opposed to an owner's perspective). To entice NATIONAL LEAGUE players, AA owners rejected the NL's RESERVE CLAUSE, and the AA was the first league to hire full-time umpires, allow beer sales, and schedule games on Sundays. The AA and NL coexisted peacefully for 10 years, and even played several postseason series against each other. But the poorly managed AA couldn't keep up with the more powerful, established NL. Following the 1891 season, the NL absorbed four AA clubs and effectively disbanded the rest of the Association.

American Association
Affiliated minor league, 1902–1962, 1969–1997

For most of the 20th century, the American Association was an TRIPLE-A minor league affiliated with major league baseball, with teams throughout the Midwest. After the 1997 season, however, the league disbanded, and its teams joined other Triple-A leagues, including the PACIFIC COAST LEAGUE and the INTERNATIONAL LEAGUE, which are both still in existence.

American League
Major league, 1901–present

Also known as the Junior Circuit, the AL was founded in 1901 by BAN JOHNSON, a former sportswriter who gathered for the new venture several prominent players, managers, and executives from the long-established National League. The new league was not, however, embraced immediately by the baseball powers. Instead of recognizing the value of a two-league system, the haughty NL owners saw the AL as a threat to their bank accounts, leading to two years of feuds and roster raids—a skirmish known as the AMERICAN LEAGUE WAR. By 1903, the two leagues had declared peace by signing the NATIONAL AGREEMENT. Since that time, of course, the two-league system has become a standard practice, and the AL has thrived.

Thanks in part to the dominant Yankee teams of 1920 through 1964, the AL has won more than half of all World Series played. With the demise of the Yankee dynasty after the 1964 season, the AL experienced a crisis: Owing to the earlier integration, the NL boasted most of baseball's best players, while the AL was losing fans. To liven up games and increase fan interest, the league implemented the designated hitter rule in 1973 (*see* 1973: A DH IS BORN), which had the effect of adding about one run per game per team. It was supposed to be an experiment, but everybody loved it—except the purists—and now we're stuck with it.

Arizona Diamondbacks
National League West team, 1998–present

The city of Phoenix and the state of Arizona as a whole had been waiting years to get their chance at a big league team. They had been the home of spring training for decades and had proved their ability to support baseball over and over. They finally got their chance in 1998. It only took four years for the team to field a World Series winner when the 2001 club, led by RANDY JOHNSON and CURT SCHILLING, shocked the Yankees in seven games. It's the fastest championship run of any expansion team in baseball, beating the Marlins by a year.

Atlanta Braves
Formerly Boston, Milwaukee
National League East team, 1871–present
Having set up shop in 1871, the Braves are the only franchise to have fielded a team in every season of professional organized baseball. They began their history as the Boston Red Caps and were also known as the Red Stockings and Rustlers before settling on Braves in 1912. The new nickname proved popular with fans, especially when the 1914 "MIRACLE BRAVES" captured the pennant and World Series after languishing in last place as late as July 4.

Alas, postseason play eluded the team for the next 34 years, during which time the perennial last-place finisher even changed its name to the Bees in a futile attempt to stimulate foundering attendance. In 1948, after the Braves name was restored, the team reached the World Series—but fell to the Indians in a six-game championship.

Failing to attract enough fans in a city with two teams, the club moved to Milwaukee in 1953, in effect beginning baseball's westward expansion that would also include the Dodgers and Giants moving to California. From 1957 through 1959, led by HENRY AARON, Eddie Mathews, and WARREN SPAHN, the Braves won two pennants, came close on a third, and beat the powerhouse Yankees in a thrilling World Series.

Flagging attendance again forced a move in 1966, this time eastward to Atlanta, where media mogul TED TURNER purchased the team in 1976. Due to cable television, the Braves became one of baseball's richest and most popular teams. Yet the team languished near the bottom of the standings for most of the first 15 years of Turner's reign. But beginning in 1991, the club embarked on a period of dominance not seen since the Yankees dynasty of the 1950s. Managed by BOBBY COX, Braves won a division title every season from 1991 to 2005, and in 1995, the club brought home the first championship in Atlanta history.

Baltimore Orioles
Formerly Milwaukee Brewers, St. Louis Browns
American League East team, 1953–present
In 1953, the St. Louis Browns moved to Baltimore because the owners realized they couldn't make money in a two-team city, where the Browns always played bridesmaid to the Cardinals. The club's new owners changed its nickname to pay homage to the old NATIONAL LEAGUE ORIOLES of the 1890s, and it wasn't long before a thorough rebuilding process built a pennant contender worthy of JOHN MCGRAW'S old club.

From 1960 until the mid-1980s, the O's contended more often than not. And in the late 1960s, led by feisty manager EARL WEAVER, they put together one of the most talented teams in history. With a succession of 20-game winners on the mound, the Orioles had the league's best pitching staff. In the field, BROOKS ROBINSON anchored the league's best defense. And at the plate, sluggers like FRANK ROBINSON and Boog Powell followed Weaver's "BIG BANG THEORY." The club won pennants from 1969 through 1971 and again in 1979 and 1983, plus two more division titles. Alas, the great Orioles won just two World Series, and only one during Weaver's tenure, in 1970. The second championship came in 1983, when a new crop of stars—led by MVP shortstop CAL RIPKEN and steady slugger Eddie Murray—beat Philadelphia's aging "Wheeze Kids" in five games. Then injuries and ill-advised forays into the free agent market decimated the club, and in 1988, the club hit rock bottom, losing a record 21 straight games to start the season.

After moving to their new home, ORIOLE PARK AT CAMDEN YARDS, in 1992, the Orioles became one of baseball's most profitable teams. But after a few years of winning, poor ownership and bad personnel decisions has doomed the club to mostly second-division finishes—until 2014, when the Buck Showalter-led Orioles surprised the world and won the A.L. Eastern Division title for the first time in 17 years.

Baltimore Orioles
National League team, 1892–1900
The old Orioles came into being in 1892 and disappeared when the National League reorganized in 1900. During their first two years, they won just 106 out of 277 games, a .383 winning percentage. For five of the six years in between, however, they dominated baseball,

becoming the game's most storied franchise until BABE RUTH transformed the Yankees.

With seven future Hall of Famers, the Orioles captured three pennants and two second place finishes, and in the postseason Temple Cup series—which pitted the league's top two finishers—the Orioles won twice. The Hall of Fame roster: WEE WILLIE KEELER in right field, Joe Kelley in left, Dan Brouthers at first, Hughie Jennings at short, JOHN MCGRAW at third, Wilbert Robinson behind the plate, and NED HANLON in the dugout. They supposedly popularized "inside baseball"—the hit-and-run, squeeze, double steal, sacrifice, etc.—which dominated the game until the 1920s (actually, all those strategies were in use long before the Orioles, but when the legendary McGraw claimed his Orioles invented or popularized them, people believed him).

What the Orioles can rightfully claim is that they were the dirtiest team in history. McGraw used to brag about cutting from first to third behind the umpire's back, about holding a runner on third by grabbing his belt loop, about berating and spiking umpires, about vicious, bloody brawls. Owned by the same "syndicate" that had purchased the Brooklyn team, the Orioles saw all their good players move to Brooklyn in 1899, and the Orioles were gone a year later.

The American League placed a franchise in Baltimore in 1901, but when AL President BAN JOHNSON desired a club in New York, he ordered Baltimore transferred north. That team became the Yankees, and Baltimore was deprived of major league baseball until 1954.

Baseball Writers Association of America (BBWAA)

The union of newspaper and magazine journalists who cover baseball was established in 1908 to improve travel conditions for writers and promote uniform scoring standards. The organization was founded by ERNEST J. LANIGAN, and today it has grown into a powerful force: Members vote on the major postseason awards—the MVP, Cy Young, and Rookie of the Year awards—and Hall of Fame selections.

Boston Red Sox
American League East team, 1901–present

A charter member of the American League, the Red Sox (alternately known as the Americans, Pilgrims, Puritans, or Somersets) were, until

1918, one of baseball's proudest franchises. They won World Series in 1903, 1912, 1915, 1916, and 1918, and they boasted such stars as CY YOUNG, TRIS SPEAKER, Harry Hooper, and Smokey Joe Wood. The latter three championships came partly because of a young pitching phenomenon named BABE RUTH. Then owner Harry Frazee needed money, so he sold all his stars until Ruth was the only one remaining—then he sold Ruth, at that point the single-season record-holder for home runs, for $100,000 cash and a $300,000 mortgage on FENWAY PARK (*see* 1919: THE SOX SELL THE BABE). It was the worst move in baseball history. Not only did Ruth become the greatest player in the game, but the Red Sox fell out of contention for 25 years. During that time, the club went through two ownership changes, the last by a young, wealthy logging magnate named Tom Yawkey.

When Yawkey took over the team in 1933, the Sox had reached absolute rock bottom: They had finished the 1932 season 43–111, 64 games out of first. Within five years, Yawkey purchased or traded for some of the AL's brightest stars—including LEFTY GROVE, JIMMIE FOXX, and Joe Cronin—and the Sox joined the first division. But the Yankees proved too strong until 1946, when the TED WILLIAMS–led Sox finally won a pennant, only to lose a seven-game World Series to the Cardinals. Later, they put together some devastating offensive clubs; the 1950 team—with only a half-season from the injured Williams—scored 1,027 runs. The 1948 and 1949 teams weren't far behind offensively, yet none could bring the pennant home to Fenway.

CARL YASTRZEMSKI took over for Williams in left field in 1961 and almost single-handedly delivered a pennant six years later with the "THE IMPOSSIBLE DREAM." team. But another seven-game Series loss kept Boston fans wanting more. The 1975 club, sparked by Rookie of the Year/MVP Award winner Fred Lynn and fellow rookie Jim Rice, captured the pennant, but by this time, a pattern was established: a pennant followed by a seven-game World Series loss. In 1978, after leading by 7-1/2 games in late August, they lost the division on the final game of the season, a one-game playoff against the hated Yankees (*see* 1978: THE BOSTON MASSACRE). The pattern returned in 1986, when Bill Buckner got the blame for a near-tragic Game 6 loss (*see* 1986: WORLD SERIES GAME 6, METS VS. RED SOX).

In 2003, with progressive new ownership in place, they were just six outs away from beating the Yankees and heading to the World Series when they suffered an infamous flameout (*see* 2003: PEDRO FLAMES

OUT). A year later, they were down 3–0 in games to the Yankees in the ALCS before mounting the greatest comeback in baseball history and stormed to their first championship since 1918 (*see* 2004: THE CURSE IS REVERSED). Three years later, they won another World Series, and in 2013, they won yet another. And now nobody talks about the "CURSE OF THE BAMBINO" anymore.

Cactus League

Nickname for the SPRING TRAINING league that plays in Arizona, as compared to the league that plays in Florida, which is called the Grapefruit League. While teams have been training in Florida and other parts of the Southeast since the 1880s, Arizona spring training began in the mid-1940s when BILL VEECK bought the Cleveland Indians and decided to train near his home in Tucson.

Chicago Cubs
National League Central team, 1876–present

A charter member of the National League, the Cubs have represented Chicago since the 1870s, at first calling themselves the White Stockings. From 1880 to 1890 and 1901 to 1918, the team perennially challenged for the pennant and won nine of them. Their biggest regular-season success came in 1906, when the team, led by the TINKER TO EVERS TO CHANCE double play combination and a great pitching staff, won an all-time record 116 games. World Series victories in 1907 and 1908 and pennants in 1910 and 1918 followed, and the club moved into brand-new WRIGLEY FIELD in 1912. The team slumped until 1929, when a high-powered offense led by Hack Wilson and new arrival ROGERS HORNSBY drove the team to the pennant. They reached the World Series again in 1932 and 1935 but lost the championship each time, increasing their string of Series losses to five.

Since then, returning to the postseason has been a rare and celebrated event; a 1945 pennant, in the midst of World War II, has proved to be their last. But they have come close: in 1969, they led the NL East for much of the season before falling to the "MIRACLE METS"; in 1973, they finished five games out after leading for much of the season; in 1984, now owned by the Chicago Tribune Co., which purchased the club from the Wrigley family in 1981, the Cubs lost the NLCS after winning the first two games of a five-game series; in 1989, another NL East title was wasted in an NLCS loss to the Giants. In 2003, they nearly did it, but the BARTMAN INCIDENT led to their downfall again.

Chicago White Sox
American League Central team, 1901–present

In 1900, crafty owner CHARLES COMISKEY challenged the incumbent National League Cubs for the attention of baseball-crazy Chicagoans when he moved his American League team from St. Paul to Chicago. Though the AL didn't become a "major league" until 1901, the move was an unqualified success. The club won the AL's first two pennants, slumped, then captured the 1906 pennant to challenge the cross-town Cubs on the field. Despite a pathetic offense, the "Hitless Wonder" White Sox used their dominant pitching to best the Cubs, who had won a record 116 games during the regular season, four games to two. The Sox didn't win another pennant until 1917, when recent arrivals EDDIE COLLINS and "SHOELESS" JOE JACKSON led the club to 100 victories and a World Series championship. The title would prove to be their last for a long, long time.

In 1919, the Sox dominated the American League but lost a stunning World Series upset to the Reds. Throughout the 1919 WORLD SERIES, rumors abounded that gamblers had gotten to the Sox, and afterward the rumors turned out to be true. The Black Sox scandal rocked the game, leading to numerous reforms, including the formation of the commissioner's office. More than that, it shattered the White Sox franchise because eight Chicago players were kicked out of baseball.

They didn't recover to post a pennant winner—or even a serious contender—until the 1950s. In March 1959, BILL VEECK purchased controlling interest in the club from the Comiskey family. On the field, the club celebrated the change as the "Go-Go Sox," led by the double play combination of LUIS APARICIO and Nellie Fox and outfielder MINNIE MINOSO, captured the AL pennant, only to lose to the Los Angeles Dodgers in a six-game Series. Veeck sold the club, then re-purchased it in 1976, but they didn't finish in first place until 1983, after Veeck had sold to financiers Jerry Reinsdorf and Eddie Einhorn. They won another division title in 1993 with first baseman/MVP FRANK THOMAS. But it wasn't until 2005 that they made it back to the World Series and erased the demons of the Black Sox with a 4–0 annihilation of the hapless Houston Astros.

Cincinnati Reds
National League Central team, 1876–present

Professional baseball came out of the closet in Cincinnati in 1869 with a club that went undefeated (*see* 1869: THE FIRST ALL-PROFESSIONAL TEAM). They approached those heights again in 1882 when the Reds, now members of the AMERICAN ASSOCIATION after five years in the National League, captured the AA pennant by 11 1/2 games. Thirty-seven years passed before another pennant, and this time, the club captured the World Series. But it was a tainted title, as the 1919 WORLD SERIES would best be remembered for the scandal that erupted a year later: the expulsion of eight Chicago players accused of fixing the Series.

A decade later, LARRY MACPHAIL took over the club presidency, introducing night baseball and hiring RED BARBER as a full-time radio play-by-play man. The combative MacPhail lasted only a few years, but he did his job. Attendance soared, and so did the club. They won pennants in 1939 and 1940, capturing the latter World Series with the pitching of 1939 MVP Bucky Walters and the hitting of 1940 MVP Frank McCormick (probably the two least-known MVP winners ever, except Zoilo Versalles).

No Reds team made another pennant run until the late 1950s. They did make big news, however, when they succumbed to the McCarthyism that was sweeping the nation: the team removed the word "Reds" from home jerseys—where it had been for 45 years—and changed the name to "Redlegs," a stupid move lasted until 1961. After the "Reds" name was restored, the club captured a pennant in 1961, then went dry for the rest of the decade.

After moving to Riverfront Stadium in 1970, the Reds drove to new heights. Led by a star-studded cast, the "BIG RED MACHINE" won six division titles, four pennants, and two championships, including the thrilling 1975 WORLD SERIES. Free agency and retirements dismantled the team, but in the mid-1980s, PETE ROSE returned to his home to break the all-time record for hits and to player-manage. The team finished second several times and seemed poised to break out in 1989, but that was the year Commissioner BART GIAMATTI investigated charges that Rose had broken a long-standing rule by betting on baseball. The Reds' title hopes disappeared when Rose was booted out of the game. Under new manager Lou Piniella in 1990, however, the Reds streaked to the pennant and swept a stunned A's team in four straight to win the Series.

They moved out of Riverfront Stadium and into the beautiful downtown Great American Ballpark in 2003. And beginning in 2010, the Joey Votto-led Reds have been perennial postseason participants but haven't advanced very far (as of 2014).

Cleveland Indians
American League Central team, 1900–present
The Indians franchise has gone through probably the most dramatic shifts of any team in baseball. They've had long stretches of greatness, long stretches of mediocrity, and even longer stretches of ignominy. Until the late 1960s, the Indians were one of the American League's winningest teams—not in terms of pennants, because they only won three, but in terms of total victories. They started out as the Cleveland Blues, filling the void left in that city when the NL's CLEVELAND SPIDERS disbanded after the horrific 1899 season. In 1902, the club received NAP LAJOIE as part of the spoils of the 1901 AMERICAN LEAGUE WAR but couldn't win a pennant with arguably the game's greatest second baseman. They did change their name to "Naps" in honor of their star, but when Lajoie left after the last-place 1914 season (the team's only last place finish until the 1970s), fans voted to change the team's name to Indians. The new nickname purportedly paid homage to slugging outfielder Lou Sockalexis, an American Indian who'd starred briefly for the Spiders in the 1890s before drinking himself out of baseball and into the grave in 1913.

A trade for TRIS SPEAKER began the rebuilding process, and by 1917, the club returned to pennant contention. They reached the World Series in 1920, overcoming the tragic death of shortstop RAY CHAPMAN to capture a thrilling pennant race. That Series provided two events never before seen in baseball's ultimate stage: an unassisted triple play (by Bill Wambsganss) and a grand slam (by pitcher Elmer Smith). Even more unlikely: a Cleveland championship, something the city wouldn't see again for 28 years.

By 1948, all of baseball's stars had returned from the War, and ace pitcher BOB FELLER was at the top of his game. With shortstop Lou Boudreau playing and managing, the BILL VEECK-owned Indians captured the pennant after beating the Red Sox in a one-game playoff. In the Series, Cleveland topped the Boston Braves in six games behind the great pitching of another Bob, future Hall of Famer Bob Lemon. Possessing the best pitching staff in baseball, the Indians won another pennant in 1954—this time besting the Yankees with an

American League–record 111 victories (since topped by the 1998 Yankees). But the Giants swept them in the Series, and Cleveland didn't return until 1995.

The Indians earned their "lovable loser" tag in the 1970s because of 20 straight seasons of second-division finishes. The movie *Major League* and its sequel did nothing to enhance the team's image. It took general manager John Hart and a revolutionary personnel strategy to do that: Hart signed his young players—including Jim Thome, Kenny Lofton, and Sandy Alomar, Jr.—to long-term contracts, in most cases before they became stars. In 1994, the team moved into a new stadium, Jacobs Field (now Progressive Field), where they sold out nearly every game and began to earn the adulation of their fans again. They made it to the World Series in both 1995 and 1997, but lost to the Braves and, improbably, the Florida Marlins, respectively. Since then, they've made a couple of postseason appearances that haven't amounted to much (as of 2014).

Cleveland Spiders
American Association team, 1887–1890
National League team, 1891–1899
A solid if unspectacular team for its first decade of existence, featuring Hall of Famers CY YOUNG and Jesse Burkett, the Cleveland Spiders in 1899 reached a level of crappitude unmatched in baseball history. What happened was, the club was owned by the same group that owned the St. Louis Cardinals, so the Spiders' best players—including Young, Burkett, and Bobby Wallace—were scuttled to St. Louis to assist in a pennant race with Brooklyn—which, not coincidentally, was also a "syndicate" team. The Spiders finished the season 20–134 for a .134 winning percentage, 84 games behind Brooklyn, and they drew so few fans at home that they played 112 road games in order to pay the bills. After the farcical season, National League officials mercifully eliminated Cleveland and three other clubs to form an eight-team league. The owners' shenanigans eased the formation of the rival American League.

Colorado Rockies
National League West team, 1993–present
In part to keep Congress from enacting antitrust legislation against major league baseball, and in part to mine the virgin western territory of Colorado, National League owners in 1991 awarded expansion

franchises to the cities of Denver and Miami. Then-Rockies owners Jerry McMorris and John Antonucci paid $95 million for the privilege. With baseball's realignment in the 1994 season, the Rockies vaulted into contention for the NL West title, the earliest an expansion team had ever contended for a division title or pennant. The club even appeared in the postseason as a wild card in 1995. That was also the year their new home, COORS FIELD, opened.

For the next 12 years, the Rockies played mostly mediocre baseball, rarely contending for anything—until 2007. That year, the Rockies put together a stretch run for the ages. On September 15, they were 76–72 and in last place in the N.L. West. Then they won 14 out of their final 15 games, including an extra-inning one-game playoff against the Padres to capture the Wild Card. And they stormed through the playoffs, winning seven straight games and thrilling their fans. (I wish I could report that they continued their hot streak in the World Series, but alas, the Red Sox swept the Rockies in four straight.)

Continental League

An attempted third major league proposed by Branch Rickey in the early 1960s, the Continental League was formed in response to major league baseball's philosophy of slow growth and limited expansion, which effectively shut out most of America. The New York Mets and Houston Colt .45s were to be Continental League franchises, but Rickey's inability to receive the necessary financial backing doomed the league, and the two clubs instead entered the National League.

Cuban Giants
Negro league team

In 1885, as Jim Crow rules began to take over white organized baseball, this famed baseball club was formed by the headwaiter at a Long Island summer resort, who gathered other black waiters to provide entertainment for the hotel's guests. When the resort closed for the winter, the Athletics, as they were then called, went on a barnstorming tour against amateur, semipro, and even some major league teams, winning most contests. Later that season, the club took on some new players and a benefactor, who financed the team, shifted their home base to Trenton, New Jersey, and changed the name to the Cuban Giants. According to a famous story, the players didn't want fans and opposing players to think of them as simply a bunch of waiters, so they pretended they were foreigners, Cubans, and spoke gibberish on the field to seem authentic. They chose "Giants" because the National League's New York Giants were the most popular white club.

As the first salaried black team, the Cuban Giants dominated early black baseball much as the 1869–70 Cincinnati Red Stockings did in the white leagues. SOL WHITE, an early player, executive, and historian of black baseball, says the Cuban Giants weren't considered a novelty act: "Their games attracted the attention of the base ball writers all over the country, and the Cuban Giants were heralded everywhere as marvels of the base ball world. They were not looked upon by the public as freaks, but they were classed as men of talent.... They closed the season of 1886 with a grand record made against National League and leading college teams."

The club joined a number of NEGRO LEAGUES during the early years, but they refused an opportunity to join the all-white Eastern League in 1887 because the move would have cost them money. Still, the Cubans remained at the top of the black baseball world until the end of the century. The team that replaced them on top was the Cuban X Giants, who actually had no affiliation to the originals but simply usurped the name to capitalize on the popularity of the originals. The originals then became known as the Genuine Cuban Giants. I'm sure that didn't cause any confusion among baseball fans of the time.

Detroit Tigers
American League East team, 1901–present
This club has been known by a single nickname—the Tigers—since its inception in 1901, making it the only long-time major league team that can claim such a distinction. In the beginning, the Tigers had trouble winning games and drawing fans, but the arrival of TY COBB in 1905 began to turn things around. By Cobb's first full season in 1907, when he led the league in almost every offensive category, the Tigers had won their first pennant—a close race decided by just a half a game because Detroit never made up two rainouts. They won the pennant again in 1908 by the same margin because of a rainout that was never made up; under today's rules, they would have to play those missing games. In 1909, there was no dispute as Detroit captured its third straight pennant by three-and-a-half games. Cobb and his teammates, however, failed in all three of those World Series, losing to the Cubs in 1907 and 1908 and to the Pirates in 1909.

Throughout the rest of his career, Cobb would win a number of batting, slugging, RBI, and other offensive titles, but no more pennants. In fact, the Tigers didn't return to the pennant hunt until 1934, when the G-Men—HANK GREENBERG, Goose Goslin, and Charlie Gehringer—plus catcher/manager MICKEY COCHRANE carried the team to the World Series. The Tigers suffered their fourth straight Series loss when the Cardinals won Game 7 by a score of 11–0, but a year later, they were back, this time beating the Cubs in six games to capture the team's first World Series championship. They split World Series in 1940 and 1945, losing to the Reds and beating the Cubs.

The Tigers didn't win again until 1968: THE YEAR OF THE PITCHER. With 31-game winner DENNY MCLAIN and 17-game winner Mickey Lolich, the team stormed to the pennant and squeezed past the Cardinals in a seven-game Series. Sixteen years later, the team dominated baseball again. They started that season 35–5 and never looked back on the way to 104 wins and a 4–1 World Series victory. Unlikely hero Willie Hernandez, with 32 saves in 33 opportunities, won the MVP and Cy Young Awards, and the middle infield tandem of Lou Whitaker and Alan Trammell took over as the best double-play combination in baseball.

The Tigers reached the playoffs in 1987 but then fell of the baseball map for the next decade and a half, finally hitting rock bottom in 2003 when they posted the worst record in American League history: 43–119. It seemed hard to believe that the Tigers could ever recover from that debacle, but just three years later, they made it to the World Series—a turnaround matched only by the "MIRACLE BRAVES" of 1914. And they made it to the Series again in 2012, only to be upset by the Giants in a four-game sweep. Now, thanks to a new ballpark, a deep-pocketed owner, and the brilliance of Justin Verlander and Miguel Cabrera, the Tigers figure to stay in postseason contention for a while

Double-A

Designation for the middle child of minor league baseball, two steps ahead of rookie leagues and two steps below the majors. Representing cities from Portland, Maine, to Wichita, Kansas, Double-A leagues include the Texas, Eastern, and Southern Leagues.

Federal League
Major league, 1914–15

The Federal League was a short-lived challenge to major league baseball's monopolistic two-league system. It set up operations in 1914 and offered higher salaries to entice players from the established leagues. They were able to get HAL CHASE, Lee Magee, and DUTCH ZWILLING, among others, but failed to attract enough stars or fans for the league to continue. Although then–Federal Judge KENESAW MOUNTAIN LANDIS refused to rule on its case, the Federal League mounted a legal challenge against major league baseball, alleging antitrust violations, that reached all the way to the U.S. Supreme Court. In a landmark 1922 ruling, the Court struck down the Federal League's challenge, illogically maintaining that major league baseball did not constitute interstate commerce and was thus immune from federal antitrust laws. This decision was upheld three more times in history, including in the famous 1972 *FLOOD V. KUHN* decision that, despite the players' loss in court, helped opened the gates to free agency.

Grapefruit League

Nickname given to the SPRING TRAINING league that plays in Florida, as opposed to the CACTUS LEAGUE, which plays in Arizona.

Homestead Grays
Negro league team

The most famous of all NEGRO LEAGUE franchises, the Grays got their start as a group of black Pittsburgh steelworkers in 1910. CUMBERLAND POSEY joined the team in 1911, took over the managerial reins in 1916, and became club owner by the 1920s. Initially an independent team, the Grays boasted such stars as future Hall of Famers MARTIN DIHIGO, SMOKEY JOE WILLIAMS, OSCAR CHARLESTON, COOL PAPA BELL, and others. Beginning in 1929, the Grays, based alternately in Washington, D.C. and Pittsburgh, moved from one Negro league to another until finally settling in the Negro National League in 1935. By 1937, with JOSH GIBSON and BUCK LEONARD leading the way, the Grays won nine straight NNL pennants. The deaths of Posey and Gibson in 1946 and 1947 sent the club into a slump, but they bounced back to win the 1948 and 1949 pennants. The integration of the major leagues, however, spelled doom for the Grays, as for all Negro league teams. They folded after the 1951 season.

Houston Astros
National League Central team, 1962–2012; American League West team, 2013–present

Originally conceived as an entry into the failed CONTINENTAL LEAGUE, the Houston Colt .45s (as they were then known) joined the NL during the expansion of 1962 and played home games in a hot, humid, bug-infested outdoor stadium. When the ASTRODOME opened in 1965, the club changed its name to honor the new home. In 2000, they moved to a retractable-dome that is today known as Minute Maid Park (corporate sponsorship subject to change without notice).

Though they've appeared in only one World Series, the Astros came close two other times, losing in the final game of the 1980 NLCS and in the exciting Game 6 of the 1986 PLAYOFFS. Poor ownership was one of the team's flaws; in the summer of 1992, for example, the team's owner rented out the Astrodome for the Republican National Convention for an entire month—forcing the Astros to play 28 straight road games.

Happily, that owner sold the team after the 1992 season, and with the advent of realignment for the 1994 season, the club began to challenge perennially for the pennant. Since 1997, they've won four division titles and two Wild Cards, and they made it to the World Series in 2005, which they lost to the Chicago White Sox.

As a condition for the sale of the team to a new owner in 2011, the Astros switched to the American League beginning with the 2013 season. And they celebrated the change by posting one of the worst won-loss records in recent memory, going 51-111 and finishing 13th out of 15th in attendance.

International League

A long-time minor league at the TRIPLE-A level that includes teams in New York (Buffalo, Syracuse, Rochester), Rhode Island (Pawtucket), Pennsylvania, (Scranton/Wilkes-Barre) , North Carolina (Durham, Charlotte), Virginia (Norfolk, Richmond), and Canada (Ottawa). The IL has been around since the 1800s, and at one time during the 1920s, they boasted a team that could have competed in the major leagues: the Baltimore Orioles, owned by the legendary Jack Dunn, who discovered, among others, BABE RUTH and LEFTY GROVE.

Junior Circuit

Nickname for the American League, so called because the AL is 25 years younger then the NL (compare SENIOR CIRCUIT).

Kansas City Monarchs
Negro league team, 1920–57

This famed NEGRO LEAGUE team was founded in 1920 and fielded a team almost continuously until 1957, an impressive feat during the eras of the Depression and World War II. Owned by J. L. Wilkinson, who was one of the few white owners of Negro league clubs, the Monarchs were successful both on the field and at the ticket window. They won or challenged for pennants during almost every season of their existence, and their all-time team roster reads like a roll call of Negro league all-stars: Bullet Joe Rogan, SATCHEL PAIGE, Cristobal Torriente, TURKEY STEARNES, COOL PAPA BELL, Willie Wells, BUCK O'NEIL, JACKIE ROBINSON, ERNIE BANKS, Elston Howard, and others.

Kansas City Royals
American League Central team, 1969–present

The Royals came to life during the 1969 expansion, partially as a way to quash the threats against baseball's antitrust exemption made by a Missouri senator, who was angry that CHARLIE FINLEY had moved the Athletics from Kansas City to Oakland a few years before. (Most of baseball's expansion, in fact, has come about because of Congressional threats or lawsuits.) Owned for most of its existence by Ewing Kauffman, a patent medicine magnate, the Royals drafted shrewdly and were able to field a winning team in just their third year of existence and a serious pennant contender in their fifth. Once Finley gutted the A's to break their string of five straight division titles, the Royals came to the forefront of the AL West, capturing division crowns from 1976 through 1978. The team could not, however, get past the Yankees in any League Championship Series.

After an off-year, the Royals returned to the postseason in 1980, this time defeating New York in the LCS to appear in their first World Series. That season, third baseman GEORGE BRETT, who is easily the greatest player in team history (and is now a team executive), came within 5 hits of batting .400, but an attack of hemorrhoids curtailed his hitting in the Series and the Royals lost to the Phillies in six games. They stayed in contention throughout the early 1980s, winning back to back division titles in 1984 and 1985. It was in 1985 that they finally captured a World Series, beating St. Louis in a Game 6 that turned on an umpire's blown call and a blowout in Game 7.

Today, the Royals face the pressures of being a small-market club. They say they can't afford big-name free agents, so the only way they can win is through clever trades and smart drafts. Yet despite producing such stars as Johnny Damon, Carlos Beltran, and Zack Greinke, they were generally hapless and pathetic for three decades. Until 2014, when to everyone's surprise, they eeked into the postseason, overcame a big deficit to beat the A's in the Wild Card playoff, and swept the Angels in the Division Series and the Orioles in the LCS. It was only when they faced the Giants in the World Series—losing in a thrilling Game 7—that the fairytale ride came to an end. But what a ride it was!

Little League

The organized baseball league for preteen boys and girls was established in 1939 by Carl E. Stotz in Williamsport, Pennsylvania—which is where the Little League World Series is now held every year.

The league's motto of "Character, Courage, Loyalty" has been challenged in recent years. In 1974, a court order had to force Little League teams to accept girls. In the late 1970s, when foreign teams began dominating LLWS competition, the governing body ruled that the final game had to pit a U.S. team against a foreign team rather than mixing all the teams randomly in one pool. And teams have been booted from the games or, in the case of the Philippines in 1992, stripped of their title when they've been found to have over-age players; the most notorious example in recent times is the case of Danny Almonte, the Dominican-born New Yorker who dominated the LLWS in 2001 and turned out to be two years older than his opponents.

Unfortunately for the children, many parents consider Little League games to be the means for their sons and daughters to fulfill their dying dreams; they pressure their children to win at all costs—at the expense of the children. Recently, in the wake of a spate of violent or abusive incidents at Little League fields around the country, some leagues began asking parents to sign contracts prohibiting them from yelling at umpires or opposing players and coaches. But this is a problem that goes beyond Little League, and Little League is not to blame. For youngsters around the world, in fact, there is no better way to learn baseball than to play Little League.

Los Angeles Angels of Anaheim
American League West team, 1961–present

An expansion team created in 1961, the Angels have been consistently good throughout their history, but have won only one World Series, which came in 2002. They came close in 1979, 1982, 1986, and 1995. It's hard to decide what was their biggest heartbreak, 1986 or 1995. In 1986 they were a strike away from the World Series when Donnie Moore surrendered a dramatic homer to Dave Henderson in Game 5 and the Angels went on to lost the next two. And in 1995 the Angels led the AL West for most of the season before fading toward the end and finishing in a tie with the Mariners, forcing a one-game playoff, which they lost to RANDY JOHNSON.

Still, many great players have suited up in Angels uniforms: Dean Chance won the 1964 Cy Young Award, Rod Carew had five .300 seasons, Don Baylor won the 1979 MVP Award, NOLAN RYAN set the single-season strikeout record in 1973, Tim Salmon was named 1993 Rookie of the Year, and Mike Trout has won both Rookie of the Year and MVP. But only in 2002 were they able to put it all together long enough to win, and even that took some luck and a dramatic comeback. They were trailing 5–0 to the San Francisco Giants in Game 6 and stood just nine outs away from losing the World Series. But they came back to score six runs in the seventh and eighth innings, then captured the title a day later in Game 7. Since then, they've invested in both free agents and homegrown players, and have repeatedly challenged for titles but have come up short every time (as of 2014).

Looking at their history, it appears as if the Angels have been through quite an identity crisis. See if you can follow me here: Their first year, when they were called the Los Angeles Angels, they played in Wrigley Field in Los Angeles, formerly a minor league ballpark. Then they spent three years in Dodger Stadium, which was called Chavez Ravine when the Angels were in town. In 1965, they moved to Anaheim Stadium and became known as the California Angels, but they changed to the Anaheim Angels in the 1990s after the Disney Company bought the franchise from actor-cowboy Gene Autry. Now they're known as the "Los Angeles Angels of Anaheim" and play in

Angel Stadium of Anaheim (singular "Angel" not plural "Angels"), which has also been known over the years as both Edison International Field and Anaheim Stadium. Whew!

Why did they choose the godawful name "Los Angeles Angels of Anaheim"? Because owner Arte Moreno believes it broadens their appeal to the entire Los Angeles area. Why "of Anaheim"? Originally, Moreno didn't want to include it at all, but he discovered that his deal with the city of Anaheim for the use of the stadium required the word "Anaheim" to be part of the official team name. Thus, the longest name in the history of major league baseball.

Los Angeles Dodgers
Formerly Brooklyn
National League West team, 1884–present
Founded in 1884, the Dodgers are, with the Yankees, Red Sox, and Giants, among baseball's most storied teams. But they haven't always been called the Dodgers. They went through a number of team nicknames—from Bridegrooms in the 1890s (because several of the team's players had married in the offseason) to Superbas (the name of a famous circus act) to Robins (in honor of manager/team president Wilbert Robinson)—before finally settling on Dodgers (short for Trolley Dodgers, which is what denizens of other New York boroughs derisively called Brooklynites) in the early 1930s.

The franchise joined the National League in 1890 after starting out in the AMERICAN ASSOCIATION, playing good ball throughout much of the decade. They didn't win a pennant until their owner, who co-owned the BALTIMORE ORIOLES, transferred all of Baltimore's best players to Brooklyn in 1899. After repeating their success in 1900, the club fell into turmoil. Charley Ebbets, who'd started his career with the team as a ticket seller, purchased majority ownership and clashed with his partners. They sank to last place in 1905 and remained in or around the cellar for most of the next dozen seasons. Meanwhile, the team moved into a new concrete and steel ballpark, EBBETS FIELD, to replace old, broken-down Washington Park.

In 1916, managed by Robinson, the team made it to the World Series, only to lose to the Red Sox. They won another pennant in 1920, this time losing to Cleveland in the Series. For the next 21 years, the team failed to qualify for the postseason, and club officials realized something drastic had to be done. They hired volatile general manager LARRY MACPHAIL from Cincinnati and gave him free rein. Through deft trades and brilliant money-making schemes—such as installing lights at Ebbets Field and promoting games on the radio with announcer RED BARBER—MacPhail built a pennant winner by 1941. The Dodgers lost that World Series to the Yankees, their third straight Series loss, and a year later, MacPhail was gone: off to war to fight the Germans.

Certified baseball genius BRANCH RICKEY then came aboard and began to build a dynasty. Signed by Rickey, JACKIE ROBINSON broke the COLOR BARRIER and returned the Dodgers to the World Series in 1947. Other great players followed Robinson to Brooklyn: ROY CAMPANELLA, Don Newcombe, Duke Snider, Gil Hodges. *THE BOYS OF SUMMER*, as they came to be called in the title of a well-known book, won pennants in 1949, 1952, and 1953—losing to the Yankees each time in the Series—before winning everything in 1955. They followed that with another pennant, and another loss to the Yankees, in 1956.

Meanwhile, a new man had taken over the club: WALTER O'MALLEY. O'Malley began his rise to head of the Dodgers franchise in 1941, when his employer, the Brooklyn Trust Company, took over partial ownership in bankruptcy proceedings. He invested his own money and became a part owner by the mid-1940s, but he knew almost nothing about baseball. He let co-owner Rickey handle that. With O'Malley handling the business and Rickey the players, the club flourished. But after years of disagreements, O'Malley forced Rickey out in a power struggle. O'Malley wielded great influence over other team owners, so his biggest accomplishment received hardly any opposition in ownership circles: his transfer of the Dodgers from Brooklyn to Los Angeles after the 1957 season to continue baseball's 1958 WESTWARD EXPANSION. Fans in Brooklyn weren't as generous, however, branding O'Malley a traitor.

After one bad year, the Dodgers returned to the World Series in 1959, beating the White Sox—the first time the Dodgers had faced anybody in the Series but the Yankees in 39 years. Behind the great SANDY KOUFAX–DON DRYSDALE pitching staffs of the 1960s, the club captured three more pennants and two Series victories. They lost three World Series in the 1970s but rebounded to win two in the 1980s, including the unlikely victory in 1988 starring Kirk Gibson that marks their last good postseason performance (*see* 1988: GIBSON BLASTS THE ECK).

The Dodgers used to be known for their remarkable stability in the front office and on the field, probably because the O'Malley family made their money almost entirely from baseball (unlike most owners, for whom baseball was, for many years, a hobby). But in 1997 the family sold the club to the Fox Corporation, and everything changed. They had a revolving door of managers and general managers, and they underachieved on the field.

Most notoriously, Fox sold the Dodgers to the ownership team of Frank and Jamie McCourt, parking lot magnates from Boston who made a major mess of the once-proud franchise. Originally, they invested in the club and led the team to some postseason success. But when the McCourts began divorce proceedings in 2009, it turned out that they were running the club into the ground. They evidently used the club as a family ATM by, among other things, "hiring" their sons as consultants and paying them over half a million dollars even though one son was employed by Goldman Sachs and the other was a student at Stanford. More hilariously (unless you're a Dodger fan), they paid a Russian spiritual healer hundreds of thousands of dollars to send positive thoughts to Dodger Stadium from 3,000 miles away. Really. In 2011, Major League Baseball had to take control of the Dodgers and find a buyer, after which the Dodgers declared bankruptcy. The soap opera finally ended in 2012 when a well-financed ownership group that included Magic Johnson purchased the team and immediately set about lavishing huge contracts on star players. They've become Yankees West, and it is fascinating to see it play out.

Major League Baseball Players Association

The official players union was established in 1965 with MARVIN MILLER as its first executive director. One of his first orders of business was to negotiate the league's first collective bargaining agreement, which raised the minimum salary from $6,000 to $10,000. Over the next decade, Miller and the union gradually gained more rights for the players, including better retirement benefits and ARBITRATION rights, before achieving the biggest prize of all: FREE AGENCY. For decades, the relationship between the union and the owners was contentious, to say the least, but in the past decade, the two sides have been able to work together to avoid further work stoppages. Let's hope it continues into the future.

major leagues

The self-defining term that refers to the country's best baseball leagues. In addition to the National and American Leagues, which received "major league" certification in 1876 and 1901, respectively, there have been a number of other major leagues in this country. The baseball establishment recognizes seven different leagues throughout history as "major":

League	Years
NATIONAL ASSOCIATION	1871–1875
NATIONAL LEAGUE	1876–present
AMERICAN ASSOCIATION	1882–1891
Union Association	1884
PLAYERS LEAGUE	1890
AMERICAN LEAGUE	1901–present
FEDERAL LEAGUE	1914–1915

Mexican League

The infamous Mexican League case occurred in 1946, but its ramifications were felt for decades. That was the year Mexican League officials attempted to elevate their league to "major league" status by luring American players south of the border with the promise of higher salaries. During the offseason, the league enticed six players whose contracts had expired, including minor stars Vern Stephens, Sal Maglie, and Mickey Owen, to play in Mexico—igniting a controversy that raged throughout the major leagues. Because baseball's powers considered the Mexican League a threat to their profit-making monopoly, commissioner HAPPY CHANDLER issued a harsh edict: Any player signing a Mexican League contract would be barred from American baseball for five years. Such a threat, of course, scared most ballplayers from leaving.

As it turned out, the Mexican League folded quickly due to poor organization and lack of funds—leaving those players who did sign with no place to go. One player, a youngster named Danny Gardella, fought back. With the help of lawyer Frederic Johnson, Gardella sued baseball on the grounds that the RESERVE CLAUSE that supposedly bound him to a club for life was "a conspiracy in restraint of trade." To the owners' dismay, Gardella won a judgment from the federal Court of Appeals. This threat forced baseball executives into action again, and Chandler declared amnesty toward all Mexican League players. Though Gardella's case was still valid, Danny needed to feed his family, so to avoid a protracted court battle, he accepted a settlement worth $60,000 and dropped the lawsuit. The next serious challenge to the reserve clause came just three decades later, when CURT FLOOD and MARVIN MILLER took their case all the way to the Supreme Court.

Miami Marlins
Formerly Florida Marlins
National League East team, 1993–present
Like the Colorado Rockies, the Marlins joined major league baseball for the 1993 season as part of the National League's third expansion. Blockbuster Video CEO Wayne Huizenga cajoled his way into favor with National League owners to secure the franchise for Miami in 1991, while St. Petersburg had to wait for another chance (which they got in 1998). During the expansion draft, Marlins officials selected mostly minor league prospects, apparently hoping to build a contender for the future, not the present. In 1993, the Marlins did manage to finish ahead of one team in their division—the pathetic Mets. In 1997, owner Huizenga got impatient. He ordered trades and spent big on free agents. It paid off when the club shocked the Giants and Braves in the National League playoffs, then pulled out a seven-game World Series victory over the Indians.

Huizenga's plan wasn't just to win the Series. He wanted the city to build him a downtown ballpark, and he must have thought that a winning team would help in that effort. It certainly didn't help his bottom line, as Huizenga claimed huge financial losses. The ballpark idea fell through, so Huizenga decided to sell the team, and to make the club more palatable to prospective buyers, he also decided to trade away all the team's high-salaried players. It seemed that the fire-sale would doom the Marlins to a decade of irrelevance, but in 2003, with an entirely new lineup, they were back in the World Series, this time beating the Yankees in six games.

In 2012, with a new ballpark, a new team name ("Miami Marlins"), and an awful team logo, the club spent big money and seemed to try to become a contender again. But after one bad season, they gave up and traded away some of their best players, leaving them once again near the cellar. It's clear why owner Jeffrey Loria is considered one of the worst in baseball

Milwaukee Brewers
Formerly Seattle Pilots
American League team, 1970–97; National League Central team, 1998–present

The franchise was founded prior to the 1969 season as the Seattle Pilots, which lasted one horrible, nearly bankrupt season (and which provided the fodder for JIM BOUTON'S classic memoir *BALL FOUR*). Current owner BUD SELIG then purchased the team and moved it to Milwaukee, where fans were desperate for major league baseball after losing the Braves in 1965. It took only nine years to field a division contender and thirteen years for a pennant winner. That came in 1982, when the slugging Brewers—known as "Harvey's Wallbangers" in honor of manager Harvey Kuenn—captured the AL pennant but lost to the St. Louis Cardinals in the famed "World Series of Suds." That's basically been the extent of the Brewers' success during their 40-plus years of existence. In 1998, Selig (now commissioner of baseball) transferred his club to the National League so that the two new expansion teams—Arizona and Tampa Bay—could enter the league. They've made the postseason a few times, but have been able to get only to the National League Championship Series (once) so far (as of 2014).

Minnesota Twins
Formerly the old Washington Senators
American League Central team, 1961–present

After 60 years in the nation's capital, Washington Senators owner Calvin Griffith bolted for the greener pastures of Minnesota. The Senators had been losing money, as well as a lot of games, and the people of Minneapolis–St. Paul were clamoring for a team. The change of scenery did wonders. A perennial also-ran in Washington, the Twins finished second and third in 1962 and 1963, then won the pennant in 1965, losing the World Series to Los Angeles. In 1967, the Twins led the AL until the last day of the season, when the "IMPOSSIBLE DREAM" Red Sox swept a doubleheader to beat the Twins by a single game. They followed with division titles in 1969 and 1970, led by slugger Harmon Killebrew and sweet-swinging Rod Carew, but couldn't top the Orioles in the LCS.

During the 1970s, the Twins finished third or fourth nearly every season, and owner Griffith was mostly responsible. He resisted the high salaries stars were making, and he traded away all his stars for low-cost alternatives. The team dropped to last place in 1982, the year they moved into the Hubert H. Humphrey Metrodome. Griffith finally sold the club in 1983 to banker Carl Pohlad. The most popular player in the history of the franchise, KIRBY PUCKETT, joined the team a season later, and in 1987, the Twins won another division title. Despite the lowest winning percentage of any American League pennant winner, the Twins won the World Series—their first ever—a seven-game victory over St. Louis in the first Series ever played indoors. By 1990, they were in last place again, but in 1991, they and the Atlanta Braves became the first teams ever to go from "worst to first" in a single season. In the 1991 WORLD SERIES, the Twins vanquished the Braves in one of the most thrilling championships in baseball history. Over the rest of the decade, the Twins fell apart, and in 2001, MLB owners actually voted to eliminate the Twins and Expos as part of a negotiating ploy with the players' union.

The "contraction" vote preceded a major turnaround in the club's fortunes, and soon the Twins became one of the league's winningest teams, though they haven't return to the World Series (as of 2014). In 2010, they did finally get the shiny downtown ballpark that Pohlad, for years before his death, had been agitating for. So now they have no excuse not to compete for the pennant every year.

minor leagues

The story of the minor leagues is like the story of what happens to a small town when Big Business moves in. Since the founding of professional baseball, minor leagues have existed and flourished throughout the country, usually in small cities like Pocatello, Idaho, and Durham, North Carolina, but sometimes also in places as big as Detroit and Miami. At one time, thousands of players in dozens of minor leagues performed for fans who otherwise had no contact with professional baseball. In order to survive, minor league teams would sign young players right out of high school or a small college, often local kids, and if they got good enough that major league scouts were interested, they'd sell the players to big league clubs. Attendance and player sales—that's how minor league owners made their money.

When major league owners began to realize that professional baseball could be a big moneymaker—and some owners realized it sooner than others—they started manipulating minor league teams to their advantage. Around the 1920s, the major leagues began to set limits on how much they would have to pay for minor league players. Then they set a hierarchy of leagues, depending mostly on sizes of the cities, like we see today. Back then, there were class A, B, C, and D leagues; now we have SINGLE-A, DOUBLE-A, and TRIPLE-A. A player would work his way up the minor league ladder, all the way to the majors.

Soon, savvy owners and general managers began to follow BRANCH RICKEY'S lead: They began setting up "FARM SYSTEMS" of minor league teams owned by major league clubs. The big club would sign agreements that would give them the pick of the litter from their minor league affiliates. At this point, minor league owners found themselves in trouble. Profits were sagging because they couldn't sell their best players on the open market to the highest bidders. And fans stopped coming to games because they had no bonds with the local players; once a player became good and popular, he'd get called up by a major league club. Of course, this wasn't the case everywhere. In leagues with little major league affiliation, like the PACIFIC COAST LEAGUE in the 1930s, for example, a lot of players became local heroes and attendance flourished; Buzz Arlett, for example, smashed over 400 minor league home runs, more than half with the PCL's Oakland Oaks. But for the majority of teams, it was all they could do to survive financially. So major league clubs took the inevitable step: They started to buy out minor league teams. That's the system we have today for almost every minor league team. The big club pays all the player salaries and a stipend to the small club for operating expenses. The minor league team's profits depend on attendance, which is tough because meaningful pennant races usually don't exist at the minor league level. If a player is hitting .350 with a bunch of home runs and his team is in first with two weeks to go, none of that matters to a big league club if it wants a player to come off the bench every six days to pinch hit.

There are a few independent leagues that are operating like the minor leagues of old, but those are the exception. Like the countless small towns that used to have a dozen corner stores before the Wal-Mart moved in, the minor leagues were ruined by corporate maneuvering.

Montreal Expos
National League East team, 1969–2004
The Expos owned probably the least exciting nickname in all of team sports, its source being the Expo 1967 World's Fair. Born during the 1969 expansion, the Expos continued a strong tradition of baseball in Montreal, where the minor league Royals had established a strong fan base. The club's first year was typical of an expansion team, as they

finished in last with a miserable 52-110 record, 48 games out of first. They got as close as three-and-a-half games behind the division leader in 1973, but they didn't break the .500 mark until 1979. Two years later, thanks to the players' strike that split the season in half, the Expos captured the second-half quarter-pennant and beat the Phillies to win the NL East title. They made it close against the Dodgers in the NLCS, but Rick Monday's home run in the top of the ninth in Game 5 broke Montreal's hearts. That was the closest they ever got to the World Series, although they were leading the division before the 1994 STRIKE hit.

In fact, the strike not only cost the Expos a chance at the postseason in 1994, but it also may have cost Montreal its team. Ownership soon began dismantling the club to save money, which led fans to stop paying attention. The situation got so bad during the 2000 season that new owner Jeffrey Loria couldn't or wouldn't even put the team's games on English-speaking radio or television; apparently, ratings were so low that no local stations wanted to pony up the money that Loria wanted. And with the government refusing to build a downtown ballpark, it was clear that the team's days in Montreal were numbered.

In 2001-2002, Loria decided he didn't want to own the Expos anymore, so he engineered a deal with Major League Baseball where MLB would buy the Expos and Loria would buy the Marlins. MLB then went searching for a new buyer and a new home for the Expos, which they found in Washington, D.C., resulting in the birth of the Washington Nationals.

National Association of Base Ball Players
Major league, 1871–75
As the first professional baseball league, the Association was formed in 1871 but was so disorganized it lasted only a few years. As the name suggests, power was in the hands of the players, rather than club owners. Players could jump their contracts with ease to go where the money was. Teams could join just by paying a $10 entry fee, so clubs popped in and out regularly. There was no set schedule; teams were expected to play each other five times per season, but they often did not. The volunteer umpires couldn't control the players, and the weak league office had little disciplinary power. Without proper financing, the league was doomed, and its demise in 1875 set the stage for the formation of the National League a year later.

National League
Major league, 1875–present

As with the birth of the American League, the National League came about in response to an outrageous season by the previously established league. With the AL, it was the 1899 season, which culminated in the disbanding of four National League clubs. For the NL, it was the NATIONAL ASSOCIATION'S 1875 season, dominated by the 71-8 record posted by HARRY WRIGHT'S Boston Red Stockings. The National League of Base Ball Clubs was the brainchild of Chicago White Stockings owner WILLIAM HULBERT, who decided early on that this would be an owner's league, not a player's league. The owners set limits on who could enter the league. They created a RESERVE CLAUSE to bind players to their clubs for life. They implemented regular schedules and paid independent umpires (though not full-time umpires; the AMERICAN ASSOCIATION started that). Morgan Bulkeley, a compromise candidate, was named the head of the League, but he really had nothing to do with anything; it was Hulbert's baby. In any case, when Bulkeley failed to show up for a meeting in 1877, he was ousted in favor of Hulbert, who ruled until his death in 1882.

During the NL's first 25 seasons, the League vanquished three rivals—the AA, Union Association, and PLAYERS LEAGUE. But League owners couldn't stop the American League from cutting into their monopoly beginning in 1901, which resulted in the AMERICAN LEAGUE WAR. The system of peaceful coexistence between the two leagues, which we take for granted today, was an acrimonious, hard-fought battle. Even still, players and managers in each league take a lot of pride in beating the other in World Series and All-Star Games.

One fact that gets trumpeted every year around July is that the NL once had a stranglehold on All-Star Games, winning the Midsummer Classic 21 out of 23 tries from 1963 through 1985. The reason for the dominance can almost certainly be traced to the fact that the NL was the first league to really embrace black and Latin players. Of the stars from the 1950s through the 1970s—from HANK AARON to JOE MORGAN—many were black or Latin, and most played in the National League. Over the last two decades, however, the AL has gotten even.

The AL and NL expanded in 1961 and 1962, respectively, then again in 1969, during the latter expansion splitting into four divisions. In 1977, the AL placed franchises in Seattle and Toronto, and in 1993 the NL finally agreed to expand by adding teams in Denver and Miami. In 1998, baseball expanded again, putting one new team in each league. The NL got the Arizona Diamondbacks and the AL got the Tampa Bay Devil Rays, but since that would have placed an odd number of teams in each league, the commissioner transferred the Milwaukee Brewers to give the NL 16 teams, vs. the AL's 14.

Another difference between the two leagues is that the NL has never implemented the designated hitter. The NL and Japan's Central League are the only two organized leagues in the entire world that haven't adopted the DH, a fact that ALers gleefully highlight to show how old-fashioned and hardheaded the NL is for not using the DH. NL fans, meanwhile, decry the adulteration of the game caused by the DH.

Negro leagues

Negro leagues were born from the desire for players of races other than white—mainly African-Americans and dark-skinned Latinos—to play baseball in organized leagues. As the COLOR LINE became entrenched in white "organized" baseball in the 1880s and 1890s, nonwhite ballplayers led by such luminaries as SOL WHITE and RUBE FOSTER made it their life's work to create and maintain leagues for the 10 to 20 percent of the American population shut out from the mainstream by institutionalized racism.

There was never just a single "Negro League," with a capital "l," but rather a half-dozen or more during the heyday. Some such leagues included the Negro National League, Negro American League, East-West League, Eastern Colored League, Negro Southern League, and others. The Negro American and Negro National Leagues were the most successful and annually pitted the pennant winners in a "Colored World Series." League seasons generally lasted only 70 or 80 games; the rest of a team's schedule was made up of exhibition games against barnstorming major leaguers, local semipro teams, and anybody else who wanted to challenge them.

The leagues were loosely organized, subject to the whims of the national or local economies. During the Depression, for example, a number of teams and leagues folded. Clubs depended on gate receipts to make payrolls, and because of that, Negro league play was probably the most exciting baseball played in the country. From the 1920s until the 1960s, by contrast, major league baseball was stuck in a rut. BABE RUTH had taught players how to hit home runs, so managers didn't ask for anything else. With few exceptions, the game was played station to station. Get a hit, draw a walk, wait for a home run. Boring! Negro league players, on the other hand, danced off bases, stole home, used the bunt-and-run. The players considered themselves professional entertainers, paid to put on a show. Flamboyant players like SATCHEL PAIGE would call in his outfielders while he struck out the side. COOL PAPA BELL would score from second on an infield out. JOSH GIBSON would hit mammoth home runs and throw out baserunners from his knees. It's no coincidence that major league baseball changed dramatically for the better in the 1960s and 1970s, after players like JACKIE ROBINSON, MINNIE MINOSO, WILLIE MAYS, Maury Wills, and dozens of others had made their impacts.

How good were the Negro leaguers in comparison to white players? John B. Holway, in his book *Blackball Stars*, presented some interesting data. His research showed that Negro leaguers and major leaguers played against each other 436 times, with the Negro leaguers winning 268 games for a .615 winning percentage. One could argue that the black players wanted to win more than the white players, but there's no evidence of that; these were professionals, on both sides of the diamond, and professionals don't like to lose baseball games, period.

People often wonder how Negro leaguers would have fared in the white major leagues. Holway wonders just the opposite: How would white major leaguers have fared in an integrated league? If they'd had to face a Satchel Paige or SMOKEY JOE WILLIAMS on a regular basis, argues Holway, Ruth and GEHRIG no doubt would have lost some homers, MATHEWSON and GROVE would have had higher ERAs, and COBB and HORNSBY would have lost some points off their batting averages.

When the major leagues were integrated, the Negro leagues hung around for a few years (and even signed a few white players), but they weren't financed well enough to function as regular minor leagues. By 1957, the last Negro league teams had disbanded.

The 1968 publication of Robert B. Peterson's book *Only the Ball Was White* rekindled interest in the Negro leagues. And in 1972 the Hall of Fame finally agreed to create a special committee to select Negro league players for enshrinement. Even that didn't go smoothly. At first the Hall's idea was to create a special display for Negro leaguers, which stoked a controversy at the time. "I was just as good as the white boys," proclaimed Paige. "I ain't going in the back door of the

Hall of Fame." A public furor ensued, the Hall was called racist, and commissioner BOWIE KUHN, in one of his more enlightened moments, helped convince the Hall that it should treat the Negro leaguers just like the other players.

The special committee on Negro leaguers originally selected nine players, including Paige and Gibson and Bell, and since then the VETERANS COMMITTEE has added TURKEY STEARNES, Willie Wells, SMOKEY JOE WILLIAMS, and numerous others (many of whom are in this book). Possibly the only truly deserving former Negro leaguer still missing from the Hall of Fame is BUCK O'NEIL, and the fact that he wasn't enshrined before his death is an outrage that selectors should be ashamed of.

New York Knickerbockers

The first organized baseball club, created in part by ALEXANDER CARTWRIGHT and DOC ADAMS in 1845. More of a social club than a sandlot or semipro team, the Knickerbockers influenced several significant rules changes, such as the diamond-shaped infield with bases 90 feet apart, three strikes per out, and three outs per inning. The club published and popularized the KNICKERBOCKER RULES, and their version of baseball, known as the "New York game," was adopted by the other baseball clubs that soon appeared—many of which played and lost to the Knickerbockers. Their first official game against a serious opponent took place on June 19, 1846, at the ELYSIAN FIELDS in New Jersey.

New York Mets
National League East team, 1962–present

The exodus of the Dodgers and Giants from New York in the late 1950s left the nation's largest city devoid of National League baseball. To say the 1962 Mets were able to fill that void would be generous. In losing a record 120 games, the "AMAZIN' METS" established a record for futility that has only once been in danger of falling (by the 2003 Tigers).

For the next six seasons, the team pretty much stayed in the cellar of the NL, except for 1966 and 1968, when they vaulted up to ninth. The next year was different. Led by TOM SEAVER and featuring a young NOLAN RYAN, the 1969 "MIRACLE METS" have become part of baseball folklore. They captured the NL East title in the first year of divisional play by winning 38 of their final 49 games, beating a Cubs team that has been unjustifiably accused of choking. (How can you choke when your opponent goes 38–11 to finish the season?) In the World Series against the mighty Baltimore Orioles, the underdog Mets parlayed strong pitching, timely hitting, and often-spectacular fielding into a 4 games to 1 victory.

Four years later, the team posted an unimpressive 82–79 record—their worst since 1968—but it was enough to win them the division title, although they lost the World Series to the Oakland A's. The club finished between third and sixth for the next decade before gearing up for another serious pennant run. Meanwhile, they'd traded Seaver, gotten him back, and then lost him via a clerical error in the front office.

Lucky for the Mets, they had a young phenom named DWIGHT GOODEN who would almost make fans forget Seaver. Gooden stormed onto the baseball world in 1984, wielding a blazing fastball and devastating curveball (which was nicknamed "Lord Charles" instead of "Uncle Charlie"). In 1985, when the Mets finished a close second to the Cardinals, Gooden had established himself as the best pitcher in baseball. The next season, with a stellar offense to go with the league's best pitching, the Mets were unstoppable. They won 108 games and finished 21-1/2 games in front of second-place Philadelphia. In the playoffs, the Mets won a thrilling series against Houston in the LCS and Boston in the World Series to bring home New York's second World Series title (*see* 1986: A POSTSEASON FOR THE AGES). The team finished second in 1987, then won the division again in 1988, though they lost to Los Angeles in the playoffs.

Team owners refused to stand pat, however, and they began trading away or losing to free agency several of the players who'd played small but significant roles on the 1986 club, and by 1991, the team had returned to the second division, and in 1993, despite a huge payroll, the Mets posted a wretched 59–103 record. It took seven years, but they returned to the World Series in 2000 to face the Yankees in a SUBWAY SERIES, but the Yanks were just too strong and beat the Mets in five games. They came within a game of returning to the World Series in 2006, leading fans to believe they'd be back. But in both 2007 and 2008, the club suffered historic collapses in September from which they still haven't recovered.

New York Yankees
Formerly Baltimore Orioles
American League East team, 1903–present
You can't argue with the numbers proving that the Yankees are the most successful franchise in the history of American professional sports: 40 pennants, 27 World Series titles, utter dominance of the league for a 45-year period, and a host of baseball's greatest players.

It wasn't always that way. When the Baltimore Orioles shifted to New York at the request of American League president BAN JOHNSON in 1903, the club—first known as the Highlanders because they played in a park in upper Manhattan—had trouble competing. They finished a close second in 1904, losing on the final day on a wild pitch by Jack Chesbro, and earned second-place finishes again in 1906 and 1910. Otherwise, fifth to eighth place finishes were more common. Then BABE RUTH came over from the Red Sox in the most celebrated deal in baseball history, Boston manager ED BARROW soon followed, and the dynasty began. (*See* 1919: THE SOX SELL THE BABE.)

Barrow knew the Red Sox club so well he was able to steal away half a dozen of its players to play for the Yankees. Almost immediately, the club started winning pennants, and didn't stop for decades: From 1921 through 1964, the Yankees finished lower than third only twice; during those years, they captured 29 pennants and 20 World Series, including four in a row once and five in a row another time.

Another significant achievement during the early years was the team's move into YANKEE STADIUM in 1923; they'd shared the Polo Grounds with the Giants for the previous 10 years. In the meantime, Barrow and, later, George Weiss produced or traded for most of the league's top players: Ruth, LOU GEHRIG, Bill Dickey, Lefty Gomez, JOE DiMAGGIO, Joe Gordon, YOGI BERRA, MICKEY MANTLE, WHITEY FORD, ROGER MARIS, and many more. According to Gordon, the reason for all the championships was simple: Yankees owner Colonel Jacob Ruppert paid some of the lowest salaries in the league, and players needed the Series bonuses to live.

It's not easy to select which of those Yankee teams were the most dominant: were they the Ruth-Gehrig teams of the late 1920s, or the Gehrig-DiMaggio teams of the late 1930s, or the Mantle-Berra teams of the 1950s, or the Mantle-Maris teams of the early 1960s? In terms of sheer dominance, it's hard to argue with the selection of postwar Yankees, managed by CASEY STENGEL. During the Stengel era,

1949–1960, the team won 10 pennants and seven World Series, plus four more pennants and two more championships after Stengel and Weiss were fired following the 1960 season.

The 1964 season marked a turning point in the franchise. Yogi Berra managed the team through tough injuries and sub-par performances, but they still won the pennant. Even so, Berra was fired as owners Dan Topping and Del Webb sold the club to CBS. CBS also dumped popular broadcaster MEL ALLEN and pretty much vomited on the proud franchise. The team dropped to sixth in 1965, then 10th in 1966—the club's first last-place finish since 1908.

Slowly, they began to creep out of the second division, but it wasn't until the team's purchase by a group headed by GEORGE STEIN-BRENNER in 1973 that the team made any serious waves. Unlike the previous owners, Steinbrenner wasn't afraid of spending money. He dipped into the new free agent market and came away with REGGIE JACKSON, CATFISH HUNTER, and GOOSE GOSSAGE. The team captured three consecutive pennants, 1976 through 1978, and World Series victories the latter two years. But turmoil off the field was rocking the club. Over the next decade and a half, Steinbrenner made 19 managerial changes; BILLY MARTIN alone had five different stints as manager. Steinbrenner engaged in loud, public feuds with many of his star players, notably Jackson and DAVE WINFIELD. And, after the 1981 pennant and subsequent loss to the Dodgers, the Yankees went fifteen years without a league title—the longest drought in club history since the pre-Ruth days.

That came to a screeching halt in 1996 when smart trades, a great farm system, some key free agent signings, and the calm leadership of manager JOE TORRE returned the Yankees to the World Series. They beat the Braves 4 games to 2 in 1996, took a year off, then produced one of the most dominant teams of all time. By some measures, the 1998 Yankees surpassed even the earlier Yankee teams in terms of greatness. Led by shortstop DEREK JETER, the club finished 114-48 in the regular season, the best ever in league history, plus 11-2 in the postseason. It was truly a team for the ages, with no weaknesses. The following year there was bound to be a little letdown, but not much. The team barely broke a sweat on its way to another World Series championship. In fact, from 1995 through 2012, they won four Wild Card berths, 13 division titles (including 10 straight), seven pennants, and five World Series. With revenues that can support a payroll of more than $200 million—usually the highest in baseball—the

Yankees will always be able to sign high-priced free agents, and they should avoid prolonged dry spells for years to come.

Oakland Athletics
Formerly Philadelphia, Kansas City
American League West team, 1901–present

One of the AL's charter franchises in 1901, the Philadelphia A's were managed and co-owned by CONNIE MACK for the first 50 years of the franchise's history, until he retired at the age of 88. During his reign, Mack fielded some of baseball history's greatest teams, including the 1911–14 teams that featured the famed "$100,000 INFIELD" and the 1929–31 teams starring JIMMIE FOXX, LEFTY GROVE, and MICKEY COCHRANE—clubs that won six pennants and four World Series between them. But Mack was equally famous for his periodic "housecleanings" that dismantled his teams through trades, sales, and cuts—often at the peak of a player's career. Consequently, A's history is replete with last place finishes.

After 1951, when manager Mack was forced out of the dugout by his three co-owner sons, both player quality and attendance plummeted. So, in 1954, the team—which finished an astonishing 60 games out of first—was sold and moved to Kansas City. When that owner died in 1960, the team was still floundering in last place. New owner CHARLES O. FINLEY took over and began to infuse the team with young talent. In 1968, Finley moved the A's to Oakland, where they experienced a renaissance in the form of five straight AL West titles (1971–75) and three straight World Series victories (1972–74), led by such stars as REGGIE JACKSON, ROLLIE FINGERS, and CATFISH HUNTER. But Finley was a tough man to work for, and the clubhouse atmosphere reflected it: bickering, fights, and feuds were common. Finley was also very cheap. At one point in the late 1970s, Finley was angry at the deal he had with the local radio station that broadcast the team's games; to try to force a new contract, he awarded the team's exclusive broadcast rights to the 10-watt FM station owned by the University of California, Berkeley. That lasted about a month, but Finley's parsimony did not. Unwilling to succumb to the demands of the FREE AGENT era, Finley sold off or traded nearly all his stars and, by 1977, the team had returned to the cellar. He finally sold the team in 1981 to the Haas family, heirs to the Levi Strauss company. By the end of the 1980s, excellence returned to Oakland as the MARK MCGWIRE– and JOSE CANSECO–led A's won AL pennants from 1988–90.

In the 1990s, the Haas family sold the team to a couple of Bay Area real estate developers, claiming that it was impossible for the club to make a profit in a two-team region. The club then sold or traded its stars and quickly returned to mediocrity. Beginning in 2000, however, they experienced another renaissance. Led by BILLY BEANE, the A's assembled a team of young pitchers, young hitters, and castoffs from other teams and made it to the postseason five times in the decade. But to their lasting disappointment, they never made it to the World Series, and so the rebuilding process had to begin anew. And it paid dividends in 2013 and 2014 when they again made it to the postseason but couldn't get out of the first round.

Pacific Coast League

A TRIPLE-A level minor league located throughout the western United States. Until the 1950s, when the Dodgers and Giants moved west, the PCL was the closest westerners got to big league baseball. In their home cities, the players were as celebrated as any major leaguers. The PCL produced many baseball greats: JOE DIMAGGIO, TED WILLIAMS, BILLY MARTIN, Ernie Lombardi, and many others. One of the PCL's greatest players, however, had only a brief major league career—Oakland's Buzz Arlett, who blasted a PCL-record 251 lifetime homers. (Arlett smashed 184 homers in other minor leagues, making him—not Crash Davis—the all-time minor league home run champion.) During the golden age of the PCL (1920–57), some of the league's teams included the San Francisco Seals, Oakland Oaks, San Diego Padres, Portland Beavers, Los Angeles Angels, Seattle Raniers, Hollywood Stars, and Sacramento Solons.

Today, the PCL is a misnomer: most of the states represented aren't even near the Pacific Ocean. Thanks to the consolidation of minor leagues that occurred in the 1990s, the PCL has teams as far east as Tennessee, Louisiana, and Iowa. But I don't blame them for not changing the name of the league. The PCL has such a great history, it wouldn't make any sense to throw that away.

Philadelphia Phillies
National League East team, 1876–present
The Phillies represented the city of Philadelphia in the National League for over 100 years before finally winning a World Series. This despite the fact that the Phils had their share of great players: Ed Delahanty, Elmer Flick, GROVER CLEVELAND ALEXANDER, Gavy Cra-

vath, Chuck Klein, Robin Roberts, Richie Ashburn, DICK ALLEN, and many others.

Then known as the Athletics, the Philadelphia club took part in the first game in National League history, a 6–5 loss to Boston on April 22, 1876. The loss typified a season in which the club went 14–45 and was expelled from the league for failing to play out their last western road trip. They returned to the League a few years later and posted a few second- and third-place finishes for the next 30 years but didn't field a pennant winner until 1915. They lost that World Series 4–1 to the Red Sox and promptly returned to the ranks of also-rans in the National League.

The blockbuster trade of Alexander to the Cubs before the 1919 season kicked off an era that saw the Phillies finish dead last 16 times and second-to-last another eight times over the next 30 years. The club reached its absolute nadir in 1928 when it posted a 43-109 record, a winning percentage of .283. The problem was the pitching staff. Hurt by the cozy BAKER BOWL, Philly pitchers posted the league's worst ERA every year from 1918 through 1934. But it wasn't just the ballpark that contributed to those ERAs: The 1930 Phillies, for example, allowed 8.36 runs per game at home and 7.03 on the road, both the highest totals of all time.

The Phils moved out of the antiquated Baker Bowl in 1938, but their march to respectability didn't begin until after the war. In 1950, a group of young players known as the "WHIZ KIDS," led by Ashburn, Roberts, Dick Sisler, and Curt Simmons, along with veterans such as reliever Jim Konstanty, EDDIE WAITKUS, and Harry Walker, captured the National League pennant, only to get swept in the World Series by the Yankees. The Phils fell out of contention again until 1964, when the Gene Mauch-managed club led the NL for much of the season and were six-and-a-half games in front of the Cardinals on September 21. In one of the greatest collapses in baseball history, the Phils dropped 10 straight games and lost the pennant.

The 1970s, by contrast, were good to the Phillies. Behind the pitching of STEVE CARLTON and the slugging of third baseman MIKE SCHMIDT and outfielder Greg Luzinski, the team captured three straight NL East titles from 1976–78 but couldn't make it past Cincinnati or Los Angeles to get to the Series. In 1980, everything went right. Carlton won his third of four Cy Young Awards and Schmidt his first of three MVPs as the team edged past the Astros to win

Philly's first pennant in 30 years. In the Series against the Royals, Schmidt drove in seven runs and Carlton won two games in leading the Phillies to their first-ever championship. They returned to the Series in 1983 and again a decade later but couldn't bring home another championship; the 1993 Series turned on the Phillies' blowing a five-run, eighth-inning lead in Game 4, losing 15–14.

In 2004, the Phillies moved out of the decrepit Veterans Stadium and into shiny new Citizens Bank Park, and within three years, they wrested the NL East title from the Braves and embarked on a run of success unparalleled in the team's history. They won five straight division titles from 2007 through 2011, two pennants, and, in 2008, the club's second World Series title.

Pittsburgh Crawfords
Negro league team, 1933–39

The HOMESTEAD GRAYS may have been the most *famous* Negro league club, but most historians agree that the Pittsburgh Crawfords put together the *greatest* team of all time. Imagine a major league team with RICKEY HENDERSON, WILLIE MAYS, GEORGE BRETT, JOHNNY BENCH, and WALTER JOHNSON. That's basically what the Crawfords had in 1935, whenCOOL PAPA BELL, OSCAR CHARLESTON, Judy Johnson, JOSH GIBSON, and SATCHEL PAIGE played on the same squad. They won 39 of 54 games that season and 36 of 60 a year later, but, without a RESERVE CLAUSE to bind players to the club like in the white leagues, most left to pursue better money elsewhere. By 1939, the entire team had moved to Toledo, but for that one shining moment, the Pittsburgh Crawfords fielded a team for the ages.

Pittsburgh Pirates
National League Central team, 1882–present

Known at first as the Pittsburgh "Alleghenies," then the "Innocents," the club has represented Pittsburgh since 1882, though not always with distinction. They became "Pirates" in 1891 after "pirating" a player from rival Philadelphia following the PLAYERS LEAGUE revolt of 1890. Otherwise nondescript in the 19th century, the Pirates reached their apex beginning in 1901. They'd picked up a host of players from the disbanded Louisville club, including HONUS WAGNER, and captured pennants in 1901, 1902, and 1903, although they shockingly lost the 1903 WORLD SERIES—the first modern Series—to Boston. The Pirates won their first Series in 1909 as Wagner outplayed Detroit's TY COBB in a battle of the best players in baseball at the time. They won another Series in 1925 and a pennant in 1927 but slumped for the next 30-plus years.

After the war, the team dropped out of contention altogether. In 1952, despite having the game's best slugger in Ralph Kiner, the team finished with a 42–112 record, 54-1/2 games out of first place. Baseball genius BRANCH RICKEY joined the team and signed ROBERTO CLEMENTE in 1954, among others, to lay the groundwork for future success, which came in 1960. The Pirates captured the pennant by seven games, and then beat the mighty Yankees in a thrilling World Series finally won on Bill Mazeroski's sudden home run in the final inning of the final game (*see* 1960: MAZ'S BLAST BEATS THE YANKS).

They returned to the Series 11 years later to face the equally mighty Baltimore Orioles. This time, Clemente was the hero, using the national stage to remind fans that he'd been one of the best players in the game for over a decade. With additional contributions from slugger Willie Stargell and a great pitching staff, the Pirates upset the Orioles in seven games.

The Pirates never finished lower than third throughout the 1970s, and in 1979, it was Stargell's turn to come to the fore. With the disco song "We Are Family" as the club's theme, "Pops" Stargell led the Pirates back to the World Series—a replay of the 1971 Series against the Orioles, which even ended the same way: a seven-game victory for Pittsburgh.

The 1980s were less successful, as the small-market club found it couldn't compete for the high-priced free agents other clubs were signing. By 1990, deft trades and a good farm system—built by the high draft picks earned from its last-place finishes—had returned the club to the top of the division. Outfielder BARRY BONDS won two MVP Awards and the Pirates won three straight division titles from 1990 through 1992. But they couldn't make it to the Series, and most of the team's expensive stars—Bonds, Bobby Bonilla, and Doug Drabek among them— left for more fame and cash.

After years of claiming that they couldn't compete for a title in their aging ballpark, the Pirates got their new digs in 2001: a gorgeous, open-air park overlooking the Allegheny River known as PNC Park. Universally renowned as a crown jewel of a ballpark, it's a wonderful place to catch a ballgame. And in 2013 and 2014, they actually fielded teams that were worthy of the park when they won spots in the postseason for the first time in over 20 years.

Players League
Major league, 1890

By 1885, baseball owners had been angering ballplayers for nine years in the National League and three in the AMERICAN ASSOCIATION. The biggest sore point was the RESERVE CLAUSE, which bound a player to his team for life, but the leagues also set limits on salaries, fined players arbitrarily, blacklisted the players who complained or demanded higher salaries, and refused to allow for a fair grievance system. So some NL players formed a union, the Brotherhood of Professional Base Ball Players, with JOHN MONTGOMERY WARD as its president. They set out to negotiate a labor agreement with the NL, demanding more equitable treatment in terms of salaries (but not an end to the already-entrenched reserve clause). The owners, however, rejected all negotiations and, in 1888, even introduced a plan to limit salaries further. The Brotherhood tried a different approach: They found some investors and created their own league, called the Players League, described by historian HAROLD SEYMOUR as "a democratic alliance of workers and capitalists in which both were to participate in the government and share in the profits of the enterprise."

Beginning play in 1890, the Players League rejected the reserve clause and instead made every player sign three-year contracts. Numerous stars defected to the league, including KING KELLY, BUCK EWING, CHARLES RADBOURN, Pete Browning, Dan Brouthers, and others. NL owners screamed and called the new venture an "outlaw" league. Rather than negotiate with it, they set out to destroy it.

Heading the NL's "War Committee" was ALBERT SPALDING, the most influential man in all of baseball. He set out on a massive public relations campaign, pointing out the weaknesses in the PL's setup. He got HENRY CHADWICK, the most famous sportswriter of his day, to speak out against it; he called the Brotherhood "revolutionaries" and "secessionists." The owners even appealed to the courts to compel players back to the NL, but the courts ruled against them.

Support for the players came from *THE SPORTING NEWS* and *The Sporting Life*, both popular weeklies. But it wasn't enough. To entice the players to return, NL had repealed its salary limitation plan and introduced other reforms. And fans were beginning to rebel against the chaotic state of the game, with three leagues now vying for attention on the field, in the papers, and in the courthouse. No league made money that year, but the Players League, with the most to both gain and lose, lost bigger. Typically grandiose, Spalding said, "Not in the 20 years' history of professional club organizations was there recorded such an exceptional season of financial disaster and general demoralization as characterized in the professional season of 1890."

The PL folded after the 1890 season, and the American Association disbanded a year later. Peace was declared, and the National League gained a monopoly over the game. It lasted only a decade before the American League challenged them.

rookie leagues

The rookie leagues are the lowest minor leagues, sort of a pre-SINGLE-A. They're usually where major league clubs send players they've just drafted out of high school; college draftees, by contrast, often bypass rookie leagues and go to Single-A or DOUBLE-A leagues, sometimes even TRIPLE-A. Rookie leagues typically play a shortened season, since most of their players are just getting out of school and aren't used to playing more than 30 or 40 games in a year. The Arizona and Gulf Coast Leagues are low rookie leagues, while the Pioneer and Appalachian Leagues are called "advanced rookie" leagues.

St. Louis Browns
American League team, 1901–52; now the Baltimore Orioles.
St. Louis was the most hapless franchise in baseball history, winning only one pennant during its entire existence—and that coming during World War II when baseball's best players were in the military. Only a few great players were ever members of the Browns; George Sisler is clearly their best. Among the others on the team's all-time roster: a one-armed outfielder (PETE GRAY) and a midget (EDDIE GAEDEL). When owner BILL VEECK sold the club to Baltimore investors in 1953, the Browns joined the Braves in the first franchise shifts since 1901. Those transfers were momentous for another reason: They marked the first time cities built stadiums to entice major league clubs. Prior to 1953, most stadiums were privately owned, and the idea that a municipality would build a ballpark simply to attract a major league club seemed unthinkable. Today, it happens all the time.

St. Louis Cardinals
American Association team, 1882–1891
National League Central team, 1892–present

One of baseball's oldest and proudest franchises, the Cardinals were founded in 1882 as an AMERICAN ASSOCIATION team by a beer magnate who hoped to use the club to promote sales of his ale. Also called the Browns, Perfectos, Maroons, Red Hats, and Red Socks, St. Louis joined the National League when the AA folded in 1891.

They didn't become good, however, until after general manager BRANCH RICKEY instituted baseball's first FARM SYSTEM in 1918. With the big league club getting the top players from dozens of minor league affiliates throughout the country, the Cardinals became a National League powerhouse, winning five pennants from 1926–34—the last few with the DIZZY DEAN-led "GAS HOUSE GANG"—and then four more with the STAN MUSIAL–led teams from 1942–46.

But Rickey's firing in 1942 marked the beginning of a down period for the team. Slow to integrate after the COLOR LINE was broken, the club didn't appear in the postseason between 1946 and 1964, when new owner August Busch, Jr.—another beer magnate—rejuvenated the team. World Series victories in 1964 and 1967 and a seven-game Series loss in 1968 were due largely to the strong play of All-Stars BOB GIBSON, Orlando Cepeda, CURT FLOOD, and Lou Brock, none of whom would have seen action before the color line was broken.

Over the next decade, the club lost several close pennant races and didn't see postseason action again until 1982 during the "World Series of Suds" against the team representing the nation's other beer capital, Milwaukee. The Cardinals, led by OZZIE SMITH and KEITH HERNANDEZ, captured that Series in a seven-game thriller. They returned to the championship in 1985 and 1987 but lost close ones; 1985 was the real heart-breaker because it turned on an umpire's blown call in the ninth inning of Game 6.

In the 1990s, the Cardinals produced spotty records and reached the postseason only once, but the 1997 acquisition of MARK MCGWIRE in a trade with Oakland put the Cardinals back on the baseball map, and in 1998, McGwire's chase for the home run record revitalized the team, the city, and the game as a whole. Beginning in 2001, ALBERT PUJOLS became the face of the franchise, putting up one spectacular season after another and making numerous trips to the postseason. In 2006, the Cardinals moved into a new incarnation of Busch Stadium and celebrated with an unexpected World Series victory—unexpected because the club won just 83 games that season, the lowest total for any baseball champion.

In 2011, the Cardinals won an even more improbable World Series: they went 23–9 after August 24 to make up a 10-1/2 game deficit and win the Wild Card; they eked out a thrilling five-game Division Series over the mighty Phillies; they squeezed past the Brewers in a six-game LCS; and in the World Series, they were a strike away from elimination twice in Game 6 before winning that and Game 7 against the heavily favored Rangers. (*See* 2011: THE CARDINALS RECORD AN EPIC COMEBACK.) They're well-managed and well-financed, their fans are supremely loyal, and they seem to be at or near the top of the standings year in, year out.

St. Paul Saints
Minor league team, 1993–present

St. Paul is where the spirit of the old minor leagues lives on. The club was co-founded by Mike Veeck, the son of legendary baseball executive BILL VEECK, and the younger Veeck brought his father's flair for showmanship to the club. Among the stunts St. Paul has featured: A pig riding a motorcycle wearing a Judy Garland outfit. Mimes doing instant replays. Call in Sick Day, in which they encouraged people to skip work and gave them sunglasses to hide behind. "In the early days as the St. Paul Saints' philosophical Director of Fun," says Veeck, "we did everything we could to not be the major leagues—and in the process spawned a renegade identity of our own and for all of independent baseball." Today, Veeck serves as a special advisor and comedian Bill Murray, supposedly, serves as Team Psychologist.

San Diego Padres
National League West team, 1969–present

Lobbying by sportswriter Jack Murphy was responsible for bringing major league baseball to San Diego in 1969—although "major league" was a term applied loosely to the team during its early years. They finished last for their first six seasons and didn't post a winning record until 1978. In 1974, with attendance foundering, club owner

C. Arnholt Smith decided to sell the club to investors from Washington, D.C., which had been recently abandoned by the team that became the Texas Rangers. At the last minute, McDonald's founder Ray Kroc bought the team to keep them in San Diego. For the next decade, the team made some ill-advised forays into the free agent market and never mounted serious competition for the pennant.

In 1984, however, with some good free agent pickups—including Steve Garvey, Graig Nettles, and GOOSE GOSSAGE, each of whom had won a number of pennants in the 1970s—plus batting champion Tony Gwynn, the Padres made it to the World Series. The powerful Tigers walloped them in five games, and the Padres went into another slump. In 1993, new owner Tom Werner, responding to declining revenues and a small fan base, traded away most of the team's high-priced stars in return for cheap youngsters. But then Werner sold the team and San Diego started winning again. They won the division in 1996 and then again in 1998, the former thanks to league MVP Ken Caminiti, the latter due to star pitcher Kevin Brown. In '98, they shocked baseball by getting past the Braves and making it to the World Series, where, as in 1984, they faced an unstoppable juggernaut, this time the New York Yankees. What the Padres need to do is make it to the World Series in a season when their opponent *isn't* one of the greatest teams of all time.

San Francisco Giants
Formerly New York
National League West team, 1883–present
Some 67 men who wore Giants uniforms, both players and managers, have been inducted into the Hall of Fame as of 2015—the most of any team in major league baseball. Included in that group are men who can arguably be called the greatest manager of all time (JOHN MCGRAW), the greatest pitcher (CHRISTY MATHEWSON), and the greatest overall player (WILLIE MAYS).

The team came into being in 1883, when tobacco merchant John Day acquired several players from the recently defunct Troy Haymakers and started a new National League team in New York. He also owned the successful New York Metropolitans of the American Association, and soon it became clear to him that the National League was the more profitable league. So he shifted his best players from the Mets to the "Nationals," laying the groundwork for a team that would capture the 1888 and 1889 pennants. After a dry spell in the

1890s, the Giants, as they became known, hired "Little Napoleon" McGraw to manage the team. For the next four decades, the team flourished. McGraw won his first pennant in 1904 but refused to play in a World Series against the rival American League. In 1905, tempers had subsided as the Giants remained at the top of the National League. Behind three shutouts by the amazing Mathewson, New York beat the Athletics for the franchise's first World Series championship. They lost the thrilling 1908 PENNANT RACE by a single game to the Cubs, but won three straight league titles from 1911 through 1913 and another in 1917. None of those pennants brought Series victories, however, and the team went into the 1920s having won six 20th-century pennants—more than any other team—but only a single World Series. That changed in the next two decades.

Led by fiery second baseman Frankie Frisch, the Giants began a string of four straight pennants in 1921, the first three of which pitted them in the World Series against their co-tenants in the Polo Grounds, the Yankees. The Giants won two of those four Series, then made it back in 1933 with a new crop of stars—including MEL OTT and CARL HUBBELL—and a new manager, Bill Terry, who had taken over for McGraw after his retirement in 1932. Terry led the team to three pennants and two World Series wins before stepping down in 1941.

Ott took over in the 1940s, playing and managing, but the teams didn't go anywhere. According to Brooklyn Dodger manager LEO DUROCHER, the Giants players were all too nice, and, of course, "NICE GUYS FINISH LAST." Ironically, Durocher replaced the ousted Ott in 1948, and three years later, after apparently teaching the players the benefits of being mean, led them on one of baseball's greatest-ever pennant chases, which culminated with Bobby Thomson's 1951 "SHOT HEARD 'ROUND THE WORLD." They lost to the Yankees in the Series, but with Willie Mays, their rookie center fielder that season, the team had promise. Mays led them to a 1954 Series victory, a 4-0 sweep of the powerful Indians.

Five years after moving to San Francisco with the Dodgers in the WESTWARD EXPANSION, the Giants won the 1962 pennant, which followed another legendary pennant race against the Dodgers. Over the next 30 years, the team captured two Western Division titles and one pennant but no more World Series. The 1993 season—following the arrival of superstar BARRY BONDS—was a big heartbreak. In the final year that each league had just two divisions, the Giants posted 103 wins but saw no postseason action because the rival Braves won

104. In 1997 the Giants staged another wondrous race with the Dodgers for the division lead, ultimately won by San Francisco owing to a thrilling three-game sweep in San Francisco with weeks to go.

In 2000, the club moved into its much-anticipated new home, Pacific Bell Park (now AT&T PARK), and a year later, Bonds blazed through the record books with his record 73 home runs (*see* 2001: BONDS HITS 73). In 2002, the Giants made it back to the World Series for the first time since 1989, and they were nine outs away from a championship before falling apart and losing. Eight years later, with a club led by pitching stars Tim Lincecum and Matt Cain, everything fell into place for the Giants, and they finally won the World Series that San Francisco had been waiting for (*see* 2010: THE GIANTS WIN THE SERIES!). Amazingly, they did it again two years later, with an utterly improbable four-game sweep of the Tigers. And even more incredibly, they did it yet again in 2014, beating the Royals in a thrilling seven-game series.

Seattle Mariners
American League West team, 1977–present
The Mariners came into being in the 1977 American League expansion to settle a long-standing lawsuit against major league baseball for the loss of the Seattle Pilots after the 1969 season. For most of its history, bad ownership, a small fan base, and a truly horrible stadium crippled the team's performance. In 1992, however, the team was purchased by an ownership group headed by the Japanese company Nintendo, and they seemed to dedicate the club to winning. They finally reached the postseason in the magical 1995 season, when Edgar Martinez, KEN GRIFFEY, JR., and RANDY JOHNSON carried the Mariners past the California Angels in a thrilling race. Then in the playoffs, Seattle stunned the Yankees in an exciting, five-game series. They didn't make the World Series, but they did accomplish something else: The team had excited the city so much that voters passed a referendum on building a new stadium. The following year, the club added yet another superstar, shortstop ALEX RODRIGUEZ, and a year after that, the team drew 3 million fans and returned to the postseason, though they lost to the Orioles in the playoffs.

In 1999 the team's new home, Safeco Field, opened to mixed reviews. Griffey complained that the ball didn't carry well and would cost him home runs, but fans seem to love the substantial upgrade over the Kingdome. Griffey's unhappiness during the season foreshadowed his offseason contract negotiations. With the Mariners already having traded Johnson prior to free agency, Griffey then decided, a year before *his* free agency, that he wanted to play closer to his home in Florida and would not sign with Seattle after the 1999 season. The Mariners had to trade him in order to get something in exchange for Griffey, but then he made it even tougher for Seattle by saying he would play only for Cincinnati, where his father was a coach. Seattle ended up trading him but in return received only a fraction of Griffey's actual value.

The Mariners lost Rodriguez to free agency after the 2000 season—if you're scoring at home, that's three of the greatest players of this generation leaving a single team within a two-year span—leading most fans to wonder how they would ever recover. But the very next year, they did more than recover: they dominated baseball and set a new record for team victories. They did it after making a huge international splash by signing one of the biggest stars in Japanese baseball: ICHIRO SUZUKI. In 2001, he won both the MVP and Rookie of the Year Awards and carried the Mariners to the postseason with his fast legs, uncanny batting eye, and rifle arm. However, the Yankees were too tough in the ALCS and dispatched the Mariners in five games. They haven't been back to the playoffs since (as of 2014).

Senior Circuit

Other name for NATIONAL LEAGUE, as distinguished from the American League, known as the JUNIOR CIRCUIT. The names are based simply on chronology: The NL was created in 1876, the AL in 1901.

Single-A

The second-lowest level of minor leagues, just above the ROOKIE LEAGUES. There are actually three types of Single-A leagues: A-Advanced, for young players just out of college or one or two years out of high school; A, which includes a mixture of new players and those promoted from less advanced leagues; and A-Short Season, which plays a season with about 75 games and is mainly for kids just out of high school. Teams in Single-A leagues mostly represent small and medium-sized cities, such as Appleton, Wisconsin, and Winston-Salem, North Carolina—although California's third largest city, San Jose, also has a club. Seven Single-A leagues are around today: the California, Carolina, and Florida State are Class A-Advanced; Midwest and South Atlantic are Class A; and New York-Penn and Northwest are Class A-Short Season.

Tampa Bay Rays
American League East team, 1998–present

Back in the late 1980s, the Tampa-St. Petersburg region badly wanted a baseball team. They had been hosting spring training for decades, apparently proving that they had enough fans. So city fathers decided, against the advice of baseball officials, to build a stadium, now called Tropicana Field, in the hopes that they could lure an existing team to the region. In 1989, it looked like the White Sox were going to take them up on their offer, but at the last minute, Chicago voters decided to build a new Comiskey Park. And in 1992, the San Francisco Giants announced they would be sold to a St. Petersburg ownership group, but major league baseball forced the Giants owner to sell to a local group instead. The 1993 expansion placed teams in Miami and Denver, bypassing Tampa Bay altogether.

After all these rebuffs, local officials filed suit against major league baseball, and *not* coincidentally, baseball decided to expand again and place a team in Tampa Bay. As it turned out, local politicians and the team's owners vastly overestimated the willingness of the citizenry to watch a bad baseball team in a crappy stadium. Gee, what a surprise. For years, while the Devil Rays struggled on the field, they also struggled to draw fans. They also made many terrible personnel decisions, and were baseball's biggest punchline.

In 2008, however, the Rays (as they were now called) made all of baseball eat its words. Just one year after losing 96 games, Tampa Bay stormed baseball and won the AL East title, beating both the Yankees and Red Sox despite a payroll that was just a fraction of their northern rivals. With low-cost youngsters at practically every position, the Rays crushed the White Sox in the division series and outlasted the Red Sox in the ALCS. The magic wore off in the World Series, which they lost to Philadelphia in five games. But the Rays are now a model franchise, with smart ownership and a resourceful front office, and although they still don't draw as many fans as other successful teams, they're a force to be reckoned with in the American League.

Texas Rangers
Formerly Washington Senators
American League West team, 1972–present

The Rangers joined the American League in the 1961 expansion as the new Washington Senators, who'd taken the place of the old Washington Senators, who'd just moved to Minnesota to become the Twins.* Before the 1972 season, team owner Bob Short decided to get out of Washington, and league owners approved the move to Arlington, Texas. Two years later, with volatile BILLY MARTIN at the helm, the Rangers finished in second place, five games out of first, the closest to the top they would finish until the mid-1990s.

In the interim, the club was purchased by a group headed by George W. Bush, who got the government to build the team a new ballpark in Arlington, now named Rangers Ballpark in Arlington. With a devastating offense, the Rangers vaulted to the top of the standings with division titles in 1996, 1998, and 1999. But each time, the club faced the Yankees in the playoffs and were destroyed.

Eleven years later, they were finally back in the playoffs with a club led by MVP Josh Hamilton and Cy Young Award contender Cliff Lee. This time, they faced the Yankees in the ALCS and treated the New Yorkers as if they were Little Leaguers, winning games by scores of 7-2, 8-0, 10-3, and, in the deciding Game 6, 6-1. It was Texas's first-ever trip to the World Series, and they played like it. Against the Giants, the Rangers allowed 20 runs in the first two games before settling down a bit and ultimately losing in five games (*see* 2010: THE GIANTS WIN THE SERIES!). And in 2011, the Rangers returned to the Series and were one strike away from winning it all in Game 6—twice!—before improbably blowing the game and ultimately the Series to the Cardinals. (*See* 2011: THE CARDINALS RECORD AN EPIC COMEBACK.)

*Make sense? There'll be a quiz tomorrow.

Toronto Blue Jays
American League East team, 1977–present

In the 1977 American League expansion, Toronto received the Blue Jays franchise after failing to lure the Giants away from San Francisco. After only a few lean years, the Blue Jays parlayed comprehensive scouting and excellent ownership—headed by the Labatt's Beer Company—to become one of baseball's best teams by the mid-1980s on the way to consecutive World Series victories in 1992–93. The best trade they ever made was the one that brought Roberto Alomar and Joe Carter to the Jays in exchange for Fred McGriff and Tony Fernandez. Alomar became baseball's best second baseman, Carter kept driving in 100 runs per season, and sweet-swinging John Olerud took McGriff's place at first base and challenged the .400 mark in 1993.

Through the 1990s, the Blue Jays were one of baseball's most profitable franchises, but as the decade ended, their dominance was just a memory. Today, despite some quality players and a competitive club, they have trouble drawing fans—a far cry from the salad days of 4 million-plus every year.

Triple-A

Designation for the highest level of minor league baseball, just a step below the majors. Today, two Triple-A leagues featuring 30 clubs in cities as large as Buffalo and as small as Pawtucket feed players to the majors: the INTERNATIONAL LEAGUE and the PACIFIC COAST LEAGUE.

Veterans Committee

The group that has historically been responsible for selecting players for the Hall of Fame who had earlier been shunted or were ineligible for selection by the BASEBALL WRITERS ASSOCIATION OF AMERICA (BBWAA). Actually, there is no official "Veterans Committee" because the Hall has changed the way it selects old-timers. The task is now divided into three separate committees: Expansion Era Committee, Golden Era Committee, and Pre-Integration Era Committee. But colloquially, it's all still considered the Veterans Committee.

Rules for elections and committee membership change every few years. As of 2015, for example, one committee includes Hall of Fame players JOE MORGAN and OZZIE SMITH, executives Pat Gillick and Roland Hemond, and media members Steve Hirdt and Tracy Ringolsby.

Historically, the Veterans Committee has had a checkered voting history, making some good and some bad moves. Among the best were the selections of HARRY WRIGHT, Goose Goslin, HOME RUN BAKER, JOHN MONTGOMERY WARD, and BUCK EWING, along with all the

NEGRO LEAGUE players (who weren't eligible for BBWAA election) and many from the early days of the game. Among the worst selections have been Waite Hoyt, Jesse Haines, Chick Hafey, Lloyd Waner, and a few others. Actually, to document all the selections of the Committee here is impossible; if you're interested, I would suggest reading the definitive book on the Hall of Fame, BILL JAMES'S *Whatever Happened to the Hall of Fame?*

In the past, the Committee was overly influenced by a couple of members who were able to push through the selections of an old teammate or friend. As pointed out in James's book, such eminently unqualified players as Haines, Hafey, Dave Bancroft, Freddie Lindstrom, Ross Youngs, and George Kelly were chosen chiefly because they were teammates of Frankie Frisch and Bill Terry, who were able to dominate the Committee in the early 1970s. Other recent choices, such as Nestor Chylak, Frank Selee, and Vic Willis—whose marks on baseball history are almost impossible to see without a microscope—are simply puzzling. And even though the various committees have inducted a great many players, they have shamed themselves by ignoring MARVIN MILLER, the father of the modern labor system, and BUCK O'NEIL, the man who did the most to keep the history of the Negro leagues alive in the modern age. At this point, with all they've done—good and bad—I think the various Veterans Committees just need to declare victory and go home.

Washington Nationals
Formerly Montreal Expos
National League East team, 2005–present
When the Montreal Expos ceased to be profitable—or profitable enough—owner Jeffrey Loria basically traded the team for the Florida Marlins, with Major League Baseball taking control of the Expos and looking to find a buyer. There was no shortage of interested parties, with groups representing everywhere from Monterrey, Mexico, to San Juan, Puerto Rico, to Portland, Oregon, trying to horn in on the action. Ultimately, baseball settled on the Washington, D.C., area, which rankled Peter Angelos of the Baltimore Orioles until he negotiated a favorable compensation plan to shut up.

The Nationals set up shop in 2005, playing their first three years in Washington's RFK Stadium before relocating to a beautiful publicly financed park in D.C. called Nationals Park. On the field, the team has pretty much stunk from day one, finishing last every season but

2007, when they finished second to last. But hope springs eternal: in the 2009 amateur draft, they selected fireballing phenomenon Stephen Strasburg, and a year later, they picked another much-heralded stud, Bryce Harper. Yet not long after striking out 14 hitters in what was called "the most hyped pitching debut the game has ever seen," Strasburg blew out his arm and required TOMMY JOHN surgery, sidelining him for at least a year. It was a rough way to start a career, and a terrible blow to a franchise that was still searching for respectability. Yet they made it all seem moot in 2012 when they improbably won the National League East thanks to Strasburg—who operated under a strict innings limit and was shut down before the end of the season—and the 19-year-old rookie sensation Bryce Harper. They won another division title in 2014 and now expect to contend every year.

Washington Senators
American League team, 1900–60
"First in war, first in peace, and last in the American League" went the saying about the Senators. But for all the talk about how bad the Senators were, they in fact finished last only 10 times in their 61-year history, a better ratio than the Athletics, Browns, or Phillies.

As one of the charter members of the American League, the Senators did start out poorly. In their first 11 seasons, they never finished higher than sixth. WALTER JOHNSON, arguably the greatest pitcher of all time, came aboard in 1907, but it wasn't until the 1920s that they were able to seriously compete for the pennant. In 1924, with 27-year-old boy wonder Bucky Harris playing and managing, the Senators captured their only World Series victory, a thrilling seven-game affair in which four games were decided by one run. Game 7 was legendary: with the score tied 3-3, the 36-year-old Johnson, on just one day's rest, entered in the ninth against the Giants and shut them down until the Senators could score in the 12th. Johnson wouldn't be so lucky the following year, when his poor Game 7 performance cost the Senators their second World Series. They made it to the Series again in 1933, this time losing to the Giants in five games.

Over their last 27 years in the nation's capital, the club challenged for a pennant just once and finished last six times. It was after World War II that the previously quoted expression came into popular use. In the late 1950s, owner Calvin Griffith believed a change of venue would help the struggling franchise. After the 1960 season, he got his wish:

The team moved to Minnesota, where it would win a number of pennants and division titles and two World Series.

Washington Senators
American League team, 1961-1971

Baseball men let the old Washington Senators leave to become the Minnesota Twins only because the 1961 expansion put a new team in the nation's capital. The new Senators were not, however, any better than their predecessors. They lost 100 games in each of their first four seasons, then improved by a few games for the next three years before returning to the cellar in 1968. In 1969, baseball immortal TED WILLIAMS joined the team as manager, and he went about teaching the players as much as he could about hitting. It worked. Nearly every player had a career year at the plate, and the team jumped to fourth place, posting its first winning record. The magic somehow disappeared after the season ended, however, and the team returned to the cellar. After a fifth-place finish in 1971, team owner Bob Short received the permission of his fellow owners to shift the club to Arlington, Texas, where they've been ever since.

5
PLACES

Astrodome

Baseball's first domed stadium, called the "Eighth Wonder of the World" when it opened in 1965 to house the Houston Astros, who changed their name from the Colt .45s to reflect their new home. The roof was originally made of clear glass and the turf of natural grass. But outfielders complained that the glare from the sun through the roof hampered their ability to catch flies, so part of it was painted white—which killed the grass, of course, leading to the introduction of ASTROTURF the following season. Masterminded by Astros' owner Judge Roy Hofheinz, the 'Dome also introduced to American sport the luxury box—now a moneymaking staple of every ballpark—and the electronic scoreboard. MICKEY MANTLE hit the first indoor home run during an exhibition game in 1965, and Maury Wills of the Dodgers was the first man to bat on artificial turf the following year. Contrary to popular belief, the Astrodome was not the world's first covered stadium. That honor goes to the ancient Colosseum in Rome, which was enclosed by an awning back in the days of gladiators and emperors.

AT&T Park

Even before it opened in spring 2000, San Francisco's AT&T Park (then called Pacific Bell Park) was being hailed as baseball's most beautiful field. The truth is, the 40,500 seat park itself is really not much more attractive than CAMDEN YARDS, COORS FIELD, PNC Park, or any of the other "new classic" parks built the past few decade by the famed architecture firm HOK. What does elevate AT&T Park above all others is what no other city can offer: San Francisco Bay. From the upper deck, you can see clear across the Bay to the Oakland skyline. At sunset, the colors are stunning. And the right field wall runs along the edge of the water, allowing left-handed sluggers to drop home run balls into what's called McCovey Cove. Beyond the aesthetic beauty, it's also just a great place to watch a ball game. The fans love it: The Giants still sell out almost every game.

Not only is the ballpark spectacular, it's the first baseball field since Dodger Stadium to be built mostly without public funding. The team's owners really had no choice. Voters of the Bay Area repeatedly turned down ballot initiatives to raise taxes to pay for a new stadium. Finally, in 1996, the club announced plans to build a park with private money, and voters in San Francisco overwhelmingly approved an initiative to re-zone the China Basin area of the city to support the ballpark. The team will be paying debts on the park for many years to come, but if it remains the cash cow it seems destined to be, the burden won't last too long. Now if only the rest of the sports world follow San Francisco's lead and force rich owners to build their own stadiums.

Baker Bowl

The unfabulous Baker Bowl housed the Phillies from 1895 until 1938, but to call it a major league ballpark would be an overstatement. It was so small that it seated only about 23,000 fans and it featured some of the shortest outfield fences in baseball. Gavy Cravath, for example, fashioned a pretty good career in the Baker Bowl as a DEAD BALL ERA power hitter: From 1913 to 1915, he hit 51 of his 62 home runs in Philadelphia. But its small size isn't really what separates it from a real major league stadium—it's the fact that the park was so poorly made that on two separate occasions, sections of the stands collapsed during games, killing a dozen people and injuring hundreds. That Philadelphia management didn't shut the place down after the first collapse is unconscionable.

Busch Stadium

Named for the late August Busch, former owner of the Cardinals and founder of the Busch Brewing Company (which makes Budweiser and other beers), the original Busch Stadium was home to the St. Louis Cardinals from 1966 until 2005. It held the distinction of being the first of the dull, multipurpose, artificial-turf, cookie-cutter stadiums built beginning in the 1960s, heralding a trend that included stadiums in Philadelphia, Pittsburgh, and Cincinnati. Thankfully, they're all closed now, replaced by lovely baseball-only ballparks, including the new Busch Stadium in St. Louis.

Candlestick Park

Before the Giants moved out in 2000, Candlestick Park was probably the worst ballpark in the major leagues. Why? It was ugly. It was inconvenient. During night games, the fog would often roll in and obscure the field. And being right next to the Bay, the howling wind made it freezing. Pitcher Stu Miller was called for a wind-aided balk in the 1961 All-Star Game (he was not blown off the mound, as you sometimes read). Routine pop flies were anything but routine when they reached the Candlestick jet stream. Staying the length of a night game was a real feat, and the team even handed out special buttons to fans who weathered a nighttime extra-inning game; called a "Croix de Candlestick," the buttons read, "I came. I saw. I survived." Prior to 1996, voters in both San Francisco and nearby San Jose had on several occasions turned down ballot initiatives to finance a new baseball-only ballpark for the team. Finally in 1996, the team decided to build its own ballpark, and now AT&T PARK is one of the most beautiful in the majors. Nobody misses Candlestick, and after the 2013 NFL season, even the 49ers moved out, leading to the complete demolition of Candlestick.

Cleveland Municipal Stadium

Certainly among baseball's worst stadiums, the park was replaced in 1994 by beautiful Jacobs Field (now Progressive Field) and demolished two years later to make way for the new Cleveland football stadium. "Cavernous" is probably the best way to describe Municipal Stadium. The park seated around 70,000, which, for a short time around the late 1940s and early 1950s, was a boon to the club. By fielding some of the league's best teams outside the Bronx, the Indians were able to finish first or second in attendance six times between 1947 and 1954. But as soon as the talent stopped arriving, so did the fans. And by the 1970s, Cleveland Stadium lay empty way more often than not. So even if they drew a very good crowd of 40,000 (a rarity), the place still looked almost half-empty. That's demoralizing to a team. Unlike when EBBETS FIELD or TIGER STADIUM or Baltimore's Memorial Stadium closed down, no tears were shed when the Indians left "The Mistake by the Lake."

Comiskey Park

The original Comiskey Park stood for 81 years as the home of the White Sox until local politicians bowed to the Sox ownership's request—*blackmail* is more accurate—to build a modern facility with luxury boxes and such; the owners had threatened to bolt to Tampa-St. Petersburg if their demand wasn't met. Never mind that old Comiskey was still a serviceable park with plenty of history, natural grass, 43,000 seats, and foul lines made of crushed, painted water hoses. Never mind that the public money from a new hotel tax spent on the new park could have been put to better use—like fighting crime, educating schoolchildren, or another trivial endeavor. The owners wanted their luxury box money, so old Comiskey Park was turned into a parking lot across the street from New Comiskey. If the money had to be spent, it at least should have been spent wisely. They could have built a classic-looking park like ORIOLE PARK AT CAMDEN YARDS or Jacobs Field, where old meets new to great success. Instead, the builders constructed a cookie-cutter park with a perfectly symmetrical outfield and front row upper-deck seats that are farther from home plate than the last row at old Comiskey. That's not progress.

Cooperstown

Upstate New York home of the BASEBALL HALL OF FAME MUSEUM AND LIBRARY, supposedly where ABNER DOUBLEDAY invented the game in 1839. We know now that the DOUBLEDAY MYTH is a lie, but that shouldn't detract from a fan's appreciation of Cooperstown as a tourist attraction. The place is named after its most famous resident, James Fenimore Cooper, author of *The Last of the Mohicans*.

The story of how Cooperstown got the Hall of Fame is interesting because it illustrates once again (as if such illustration is necessary anymore) how the simple desire for money can affect history. The idea belonged to a man named Alexander Cleland, who worked for a nonprofit foundation established by the heirs to the Singer Sewing Machine Company. Cooperstown had long been a resort community, but it, like the rest of the world, was hit hard by the Great Depression. Cleland suggested to the Clark Foundation, whose namesake lived in the town, that a museum based on baseball history would be a great way to attract tourists and spice up the local economy. As author BILL JAMES points out in his book *Whatever Happened to the Hall of Fame?*, Cleland projected that such an establishment could draw "hundreds of visitors a year."

He was only off by a factor of a thousand. With the backing of major league baseball and some money from the Clark Foundation, the Hall of Fame opened in 1939, steadily gaining in popularity so that today, 400,000 fans (well, about 300,000 fans and 100,000 bored spouses and children) pass through its gates. Which is no easy task, by the way, because the town is in a remote part of New York—at least four hours from New York City. But it's a beautiful drive and totally worth it.

Coors Field

The fourth in what has proven to be a successful line of classic baseball-only ballparks, Coors Field opened in Denver in 1995. Like ORIOLE PARK AT CAMDEN YARDS, Jacobs Field, and Rangers Ballpark in Arlington before it, Coors Field combines old and new with spectacular results. It's a 42,000-seat park with striking red-brick architecture and comfortable seats that are angled to face the pitching mound. While most of the seats are painted green, one row in the upper deck is Rockies purple, an indication that the row is exactly 5,280 feet in the air—truly mile-high seats. Right next door to the field, a restored Depression-era gasoline station acts as a ticket booth and souvenir shop. With a full set of luxury boxes and an entire city of baseball-crazy fans, Coors Field is a moneymaking machine for Rockies ownership. And the selling of the park's name to a beer company doesn't hurt the team's bottom line, either.

As predicted by everyone who even thought about it for more than two seconds, the high altitude and thin air enabled Rockies players at first to dominate the league's hitting categories, and no lead was ever safe. But in 2002, the team determined that it was the *dry* air of Denver, not necessarily the *thin* mile-high air, that was causing the offense to spike. So the club installed a room-sized humidor in which to store baseballs prior to their use in games, and it worked. Home runs now fly out of Coors at about the same rate as in other ballparks, and pitchers now have a fighting chance.

Dodger Stadium

Built in 1962, the stadium dubbed "Taj O'Malley" resides on a plot of land handed to Dodgers owner WALTER O'MALLEY by city officials when he moved the team from Brooklyn in 1957. Chavez Ravine, as it was known, had previously housed low-income families, many of whom initially refused to sell to developers only to relent when the pressure became too great.

O'Malley built the stadium with his own money, unlike most of today's parks—the better to reap the rewards of ticketing, parking, and concessions. And O'Malley realized from day one that there was money to be made in encouraging families to visit the park, so for many years, he priced tickets below most other teams' tickets. Consequently, the Dodgers almost always drew around three million fans every year, most of whom paid for parking and bought Dodger Dogs. In fact, according to a story from the 1960s, even if the team had charged no admission, they still would have made a good profit because of all the concessions and parking money. That's how to run a baseball team.

Ebbets Field

The home of the Dodgers when they played in Brooklyn, Ebbets Field is one of the most storied old ballparks. The site, on the corner of Flatbush and Bedford Avenues, was once a slum, four and a half acres of shanties and garbage pits in a section of Brooklyn called Pigtown because local farmers often brought their pigs there to feed. Charley Ebbets, the first owner of the Dodgers, purchased the land in 1912 and built a ballpark when the team's previous one, Washington Park, began to crumble. Ebbets built the new one out of iron and brick and concrete, and named it after himself.

It was a classic urban park, tucked into the neighborhood as if it belonged. The fans there practically became part of the game. One famous fan, Howling Hilda Chester, sat in center field and rang a cowbell incessantly. The Dodger Sym-Phoney sat in Section 8 and led fans in a Brooklyn-made song: "Leave Us Go Root for the Dodgers, Rodgers / That's the team for me. / Leave us make noise for the boist'rous boys / On the B.M.T. / Summer or winter or any season, / Flatbush fanatics don't need no reason." When they tore it down in 1960, three years after the Dodgers moved to Los Angeles, the whole town wept. The spirit of Ebbets Field lives on in today's "new classic" ballparks like Citi Field in Queens, Miller Park in Milwaukee, and others.

Elysian Fields

Around 150 years ago, the NEW YORK KNICKERBOCKERS were looking for a place to play ball. The social club was formed in 1845 by
ALEXANDER CARTWRIGHT and DOC ADAMS and consisted mostly of
gentlemanly city folk: merchants, stock brokers, insurance salesmen,
and other professional types. But there weren't many places in Manhattan to play, so they took the ferry to Hoboken, New Jersey, and set
down at a park known as the Elysian Fields. At first, the club would
just practice or play intrasquad games, but they still attracted attention. "Sometimes we had as many as a hundred spectators watching,"
said Adams. "The first professional English cricket team that came to
this country... used to come over and watch our game. They rather
turned up their noses at it, and thought it a tame sport, until we invited them to try it. Then they found it was not so easy as it looked."
The first official game between the Knickerbockers and another team,
the New York Base Ball Club, was played at the Elysian Fields on
June 19, 1846. The Knickerbockers played their reserves and lost 23–
1, but their real goal was to enjoy themselves and spread baseball
throughout the city. At that, they succeeded.

Fenway Park

Conventional wisdom has it that Fenway Park in Boston is the absolute epitome of major league fields. Nestled into the neighborhood
between TED WILLIAMS Way and Yawkey Way, Fenway features some
of the strangest outfield distances in baseball history. The right field
foul pole lies just 302 feet from home, but the fence slopes out so
that the wall in straightaway right is about 380 feet from the plate.
Deepest center field has a 420-foot measurement, but straightaway
center is 388 feet. And left field... home of The Wall, *aka* the GREEN
MONSTER. The sign on the 37-foot-high wall reads 315 feet, but Red
Sox officials have refused to grant anyone the opportunity to inde-
pendently measure it. Two rebel authors burst onto the field in 1975
and came up with 309 feet, five inches before they were hauled away
for trespassing. With aerial photography, the Boston Globe calculated
the distance as 304.8 feet. By any measurement, it's the shortest left
field in baseball. And since Fenway also boasts the league's smallest
foul territory, it's a classic hitter's park.

Both built in the 1910s, Fenway and Chicago's WRIGLEY FIELD are
baseball's two oldest ballparks. At times in the past few decades, Fenway's days appeared numbered. Some have wanted to build a new
ballpark with luxury boxes and 45,000 seats, but as of 2014, at least,

plans haven't gone far beyond that. One idea that has been floating around is to build a new Fenway (no doubt with the name of a corporate sponsor) that includes a Green Monster and the same cozy dimensions. I think that's a bad idea. The Green Monster is special because it had to be there owing to the shape of the plot of land upon which the park was built. You can't manufacture charm. Build a new Fenway if you must, but let it have its own unique characteristics.

Forbes Field

A classic old ballpark, Forbes Field served as the home of the Pittsburgh Pirates from 1909 until 1970, when the team moved to Three Rivers Stadium. The park was torn down but home plate is still there: It has been encased in glass and preserved in almost its exact location, which is now the University of Pittsburgh's Forbes Quadrangle (*almost* exact because the exact location is now a ladies room). Like most of the old parks, Forbes Field had character. When HANK GREENBERG played there in 1947, the team built a short fence in front of the left field scoreboard and "planted" it with chicken wire to increase home run production. Fans called it "Greenberg Gardens" that season, then changed the name to "Kiner's Korner" when Ralph Kiner slugged homers there from 1948 to 1953.

Griffith Stadium

The 50-year home of the Washington Senators, Griffith Stadium was where U.S. presidents traditionally threw out the first ball on Opening Day to inaugurate the season. Clark Griffith, the longtime owner of the Senators, humbly named the park after himself. The funniest thing that ever happened there—aside from the sorry play of the frequently last-place Senators—occurred during the park's first night game in 1941. According to author Philip J. Lowry in *Green Cathedrals*, the stadium's lights went out as the pitcher began his windup. When the lights came on again moments later, every outfielder and infielder, the batter, the catcher, and the umpire were lying flat on the ground, protecting themselves. The pitcher remained standing because only he knew he hadn't actually thrown the ball.

Hall of Fame

In the 1930s, baseball was in trouble. The Depression was cutting sharply into attendance, and the BABE RUTH juggernaut, which saved baseball in the 1920s, was winding down. Baseball needed something else. In 1931, the BASEBALL WRITERS ASSOCIATION formalized the MVP award, and two years later, sportswriter Arch Ward created the All-Star Game (*see* 1933: THE FIRST ALL-STAR GAME). Then some people from COOPERSTOWN, New York, the alleged birthplace of baseball, approached the commissioner with an idea: a museum honoring baseball's great players and innovators. The commissioner liked it, and so did the rest of baseball. When it opened in 1939, it was a single-room exhibit with plaques and pictures. Thanks to curator LEE ALLEN, who presided over the shrine from 1948 until his death in 1969, the Hall added an extensive library and expanded the museum, so that today the Hall features three stories and 50,000 square feet of exhibits to entertain and enthrall.

When you go there, you can start in the Hall of Fame Gallery, where bronze plaques of the game's immortals stand in tribute to their accomplishments. The Great Moments Room features artifacts and photographs from the game's top events. There's a screening room that shows baseball movies continuously. And other parts give detailed histories about the game's origins, ballparks, and innovations. Ultimately, you can visit the Hall of Fame Library for the greatest collection of baseball books and papers in existence. The place is open year-round except on Christmas and Thanksgiving. It gets really crowded during the summertime, especially during the induction ceremonies every July. It's a must-see for any baseball fan.

Kingdome

The Kingdome was constructed in the 1970s to lure a major league expansion team. The plan was a success (even the NFL moved a team into the stadium), but the resulting stadium was a dismal failure. In 1994, a number of ceiling tiles collapsed into the seats, closing the park for several months until all 40,000 tiles could be replaced (the Mariners were probably the only team happy about the 1994 STRIKE). But that was only the latest problem. From the beginning, the Kingdome was built on a shoestring budget of public money. The builders cut corners in the design and construction, scrimped on amenities such as comfortable seats, and basically created baseball's ugliest dome. In 1995, voters approved a referendum to build two new ballparks in Seattle, one for baseball and one for football. Safeco Field, the retractable dome baseball park, opened in 1999, and the city imploded the Kingdome in 2000 to the cheers of an entire city.

Negro League Hall of Fame

Like the one in COOPERSTOWN, another important museum for all baseball fans to see is the Negro League Hall of Fame, which opened in 1994 in Kansas City, Missouri. It's smaller than its major league brother but no less impressive. There, you can see pictures of and read about all the NEGRO LEAGUE greats, both the ones who have and who haven't been elected to that other Hall: BUCK O'NEIL, Double-Duty Radcliffe, Lou Dials, and numerous others. The museum isn't just about the racism the players faced, although that's part of it. It's also about the passion they felt for baseball, the sacrifices they made, and the fun they had. "Baseball fulfilled me like music," said O'Neil. "I played most of my life and loved it. I wasn't born too early. I was right on time."

Olympic Stadium

Built initially for the 1976 Summer Olympics, Montreal's Stade Olympique is perhaps the biggest ballpark fiasco in North American sports history. Because of internal Montreal politics, the park went horrendously over budget and wasn't even completed until more than a decade after the Olympics. Locals call the stadium "The Big Owe," because even decades later, the province of Quebec still owed up to $304 million in Olympics-related costs, including the stadium. The costs seemed to keep going up—and bad things kept happening. The retractable Kevlar roof that went up in 1987 broke two years later and was no longer retractable because constant rips in the material proved too costly to mend. And in September 1991, a 55-ton concrete beam fell off the structure, closing the stadium for the last weeks of the season. In 1998, the roof was removed altogether and the park became open-air again. Now that the Expos are gone, it just sits there without a main tenant.

Oriole Park at Camden Yards

The home of the Baltimore Orioles since 1992, this is the first in what became a long line of architecturally spectacular, baseball-only ballparks. Oriole Park at Camden Yards (its official title) is a throwback to an earlier generation of stadiums with all the amenities of modern ballparks like luxury boxes and sufficient parking. Built with $105 million in lottery and bond money, the whole thing covers 85 acres near the city's waterfront. Along the right field side sits the old warehouse for the Baltimore and Ohio railway company, now the Orioles' offices. KEN GRIFFEY, JR. was the first to hit the warehouse's brick facade on the fly, some 430 feet from home plate—a tempting goal for left-handed sluggers. Unlike the cookie-cutter ballparks built from the 1960s to the 1980s, Camden Yards features asymmetrical outfield distances and emerald green natural grass. It's the proud uncle of Rangers Ballpark in Arlington, Jacobs Field, COORS FIELD, AT&T PARK, and the other beautiful parks that have followed Camden Yards' lead. And there's no doubting its success: Baltimore sold out most of its games in its first few years of existence and still sells more than 30,000 for almost every game.

Polo Grounds

The Polo Grounds known to most fans today was actually the fifth version of the park. The other four existed between 1883 and 1911 but didn't survive for various reasons; Polo Grounds number 1, for example, was unexpectedly leveled in 1889 so that New York City could build 111th Street between 5th and 6th Avenues, and Polo Grounds number 3 burned to the ground in 1911. Polo Grounds number 5—the storied one—housed the New York Giants from 1911 through 1957, the Yankees from 1913 through 1922, and the Mets in 1962 and 1963.

The park was perhaps most famous for its strange outfield distances: 279 and 258 feet down the left and right field lines, respectively; 447 and 440 to the alleys; and 483 to deep center. These distances made possible two of baseball history's greatest moments: Bobby Thomson's 1951 "SHOT HEARD 'ROUND THE WORLD," which was really just a medium fly to left that went about 280 feet; and "THE CATCH" IN 1954, WILLIE MAYS'S running, back-to-the-plate grab of Vic Wertz's 440-foot drive to center in the World Series, which anywhere else would have been a home run. Even Dodgers and Indians fans would have to admit that these kinds of oddities account for most of baseball's charm. The same wrecking ball that leveled EBBETS FIELD in 1960 demolished the Polo Grounds four years later.

SkyDome (now the Rogers Centre)

Toronto's huge $C570 million (US$937 million in 2015 dollars) colossus, the SkyDome, as it was called when it was built, is a triumph of modern architecture. It features what at one point was the world's largest television screen, a 348-room hotel, a Hard Rock Cafe, a couple of other restaurants, a fitness club, 161 private luxury boxes, and an 11,000-ton retractable roof that uses hundreds of dollars worth of electricity just to open or close. It's certainly a great spectacle. But it's a terrible baseball park, for two reasons: (1) Baseball should be played on grass; SkyDome has the fake stuff, even though grass could theoretically grow since it could be exposed to direct sunlight when the roof is retracted. And, most importantly, (2) baseball is a game steeped in tradition, not modern accoutrements; the SkyDome is all about high technology and futuristic gadgets.

Tiger Stadium

For decades, the city of Detroit was involved in a weighty issue: to tear down or not to tear down venerable Tiger Stadium, stomping ground of TY COBB, Charlie Gehringer, Al Kaline, Kirk Gibson, and Jack Morris. Even though the team leased the ballpark rent-free from the city, owner Mike Ilitch wanted to build a new park along the order of ORIOLE PARK AT CAMDEN YARDS and Jacobs Field. He was even willing to pay the $175 million the park was supposed to cost, although the city had fork over the hundred or so million in land acquisition and preparation costs. And in 1994, he threatened to move the team out of Detroit if he didn't get his wish. For the longest time, Tiger fans and taxpayers wanted no part of it. Despite the opposition, Ilitch won and built Comerica Park for the 2000 season.

Maybe it was just Tiger Stadium's time. It had been built in 1912 in what turned into a pretty bad neighborhood. For all the opposition to the destruction of Tiger Stadium, fans had basically abandoned the place. Over the stadium's last few years of existence, the Tigers posted some of the worst attendance figures in all of baseball. Part of that can be attributed to the poor team that was on the field, but it's also a reflection of a broken down park. I'm not opposed to progress; I just don't think taxpayers should foot the bill. In the end, Ilitch paid $145 million and taxpayers contributed $115 million toward the new ballpark.

Wrigley Field

The grandest of the old-time ballparks, Wrigley Field belongs to the people of Chicago. Or at least it should. The park brims with charm and character—amazing for an inanimate object. But you can almost feel it! It starts when you get off the El at the Addison St. exit. On game day (and most games still take place under the sun, despite the installation of lights in 1988), the whole area is primed for baseball: t-shirt and newspaper vendors, locals, out-of-towners. There's not a bad seat in the house, from the third deck to the bleachers. If you're lucky, the wind is blowing out to center field and the home runs fly. When home run balls go out of the park and onto the street, there's a mad dash among the waiting kids to recover the ball. It's the only park where a ball can get stuck in the ivy-covered outfield walls—ivy conceived of originally by the young BILL VEECK in the 1930s. Across the street on Waveland and Sheffield avenues, the rooftops have makeshift bleachers so homeowners and their (sometimes paid) guests can watch the action. Even though the owners don't have luxury boxes to rake in the millions, they've never seriously tried to move out of Wrigley. It would be like the Catholics moving out of Notre Dame.

Yankee Stadium

Today we take for granted the big concrete and steel, 60,000-seat sports facilities. We call them stadiums, of course. But in the 1920s, they didn't exist. There were 30,000-seat ballparks, yes, but no gigantic stadiums as we know them today. Think of the old-time ballparks: WRIGLEY FIELD, FENWAY PARK, Shibe Park, EBBETS FIELD, POLO GROUNDS. Not a *stadium* among them (back then, TIGER STADIUM was known as Navin Field). Yankee Stadium—the "HOUSE THAT RUTH BUILT"—changed all that.

It was entirely fitting that the nation's largest city should serve as home for the most innovative entertainment facility of its time, and even more fitting that the country's most larger-than-life sports figure should have something to do with it. For it was BABE RUTH who put the Yankees on the baseball map by making them a good enough team to draw more fans than the rival Giants, to whom the Yankees had always played second fiddle. Possibly as a reward, the Yankees designed the Stadium for him, building a right field fence just 294 feet down the line so his clouts wouldn't have to travel too far to go out of the park. Meanwhile, left-center and center field were cavernous—490 to dead center, 395 to left center—dimensions that probably cost the right-handed-hitting JOE DiMAGGIO countless home runs. Yankee Stadium seated more than 70,000 fans when it opened, around twice as many as any other existing ballpark, and enabled the team to become the first club to draw more than two million fans.

Like all great ballparks, the Stadium had some pretty amazing quirks. From the 1930s until the extensive remodeling in 1974–75, three marble monuments honoring Ruth, Lou Gehrig, and legendary manager Miller Huggins stood in deep center field—in play. Once, while watching a long fly bounce around out of reach of his fielders, an exasperated CASEY STENGEL is purported to have shouted, "Ruth, Gehrig, Huggins, someone throw that ball in here NOW!" During the $100 million renovation, builders placed an inner fence in front of the monuments, shortening the outfield distance but also removing one of baseball's coolest quirks.

In the 1990s, team owner GEORGE STEINBRENNER began threatening to move the team out of Yankee Stadium (!) unless the city built him a new park. He lobbied and lobbied city leaders until he and his pal Mayor Rudy Giuliani convinced the city and state to build a new Yankee Stadium across the street from the old one. New Yankee opened in 2009, and it's a gem of a park. If you can afford the tickets.

6
FOLKLORE, LITERATURE & DIVERSIONS

"Alibi Ike"
Written by Ring Lardner
A hilarious short story from 1915 about a ballplayer who has an excuse for every situation. "His right name was Frank X. Farrell," begins the story, "and I guess the X stood for 'Excuse me.' Because he never pulled a play, good or bad, on or off the field, without apologizin' for it." They made a pretty funny movie out of the story in the 1930s starring Joe E. Brown and Olivia de Havilland.

"Amazin' Mets"
Nickname for the New York Mets ball club at its inception in 1962, first applied by CASEY STENGEL during the team's first spring training. At a press conference in April 1962, Stengel introduced the term in his unique brand of speaking known as STENGELESE: "And you can say this tremendous and amazin' new club is gonna be ready in every way tomorrow when the bell rings, and that's the name of my right fielder, Bell." The team's 120 losses—an all-time record—should indicate that it's an ironic nickname. But when the team won the World Series just seven years later, they became the "MIRACLE METS."

APBA

A classic, much-imitated baseball board game invented in 1931 by J. Richard Seitz that uses real players and statistics; it's also a computer game. Incidentally, although APBA stands for American Professional Baseball Association, loyalists pronounce it "app-bah."

asterisk (*)

The metaphoric symbol commissioner FORD FRICK placed in the record books next to ROGER MARIS'S single-season record of 61 home runs (*see* 61). Because the 1961 season consisted of 162 games—eight more than the season in which BABE RUTH established the previous record of 60 homers—Frick decreed that for the record to stand on its own, Maris would have to break it in 154 games. Unfortunately for Maris, he slammed his 61st homer in the season's final game, prompting Frick's infamous asterisk. Even though Frick never actually uttered the word "asterisk," the little star followed both Maris and Frick for the rest of their lives; Frick even titled his autobiography *Games, Asterisks, and People.*

Today, a lot of people want to asterisk the home run records set by MARK MCGWIRE and BARRY BONDS. To them, I say give it a rest. The steroid era happened, records were broken, and no asterisk can change it. *See also* 1961: BASEBALL EXPANDS.

artificial turf/AstroTurf

The fake grass first put into use in 1965 as sod for the first domed stadium, the ASTRODOME, and now used in other ballparks and stadiums. We have two men to thank for this abomination: Judge Roy Hofheinz and Dr. Harold Gores. Hofheinz, owner of the Astros and the Astrodome, hired the chemicals manufacturer Monsanto to create fake grass to replace the real stuff that kept dying inside the 'Dome. Dr. Gores actually invented it, but he didn't intend it to be used in today's stadiums. Gores was a New York educator who wanted to create an artificial surface to be used on the playgrounds of New York City. As chairman of the Educational Facilities Laboratories, Gores helped Monsanto develop the turf, which Monsanto marketed as ChemGrass in 1964. Because of its high cost, however, ChemGrass/AstroTurf never did fulfill its intended purpose, and instead went straight to college and professional stadia.

Controversy surrounds the fake stuff. Critics argue that it increases injuries and adulterates the game with sky-high bounces and ground-ball triples. As DICK ALLEN once said, "If a horse won't eat it, I don't want to play on it." But because real grass didn't grow in the early domed stadiums, many teams had choice but to adopt it. The teams that used turf in outdoor stadiums had no real excuse.

In the first edition of this book, I wrote "Alas, artificial turf is here to stay." But in the last half-decade, baseball has begun to purify itself. Numerous teams have torn down their artificial turf stadiums and moved into parks with real grass, and now the only teams still playing on artificial turf are the Blue Jays and Rays.

Babe: The Legend Comes to Life
Written by Robert Creamer
(Simon and Schuster, 1974)
The first exhaustive biography of BABE RUTH, written while HENRY AARON was chasing Ruth's home record. Acclaimed as one of the greatest sports biographies ever written, it was the first book on Ruth to dig past the myths and folklore, presenting a complete portrait of an extraordinary human being. For a more modern take on Ruth, try Leigh Montville's excellent biography, *The Big Bam*.

The Bad News Bears
The hilarious baseball film starring Walter Matthau and Tatum O'Neal about a band of misfit Little Leaguers. Matthau played a deadbeat who's forced to coach a pathetic little league team; O'Neal is the club's best player. For an entire generation of baseball fans, *Bad News Bears* remains one of the best-remembered movies of our youth.

BALCO
The Bay Area Laboratory Co-Operative (BALCO) was the company that supplied designer steroids, supplements, and other performance-enhancing drugs (PEDs) to baseball players and other athletes from the late 1980s to the early 2000s. BALCO and its boss, Victor Conte, got busted by federal authorities for conspiracy to distribute illegal steroids and money laundering. It was the investigation into BALCO that blew the lid off the PED scandal in baseball, leading to the MITCHELL REPORT, the conviction of BARRY BONDS for obstruction of justice, and, thankfully, drug testing in baseball that seems to have

mostly eliminated PEDs from the sport. At the very least, the *talk* of PEDs is way down, which is good for all of us.

Ball Four
Written by Jim Bouton
(Stein and Day, 1971; rev. 1981)

The great baseball book written by JIM BOUTON recounting the first season of 1969 Seattle Pilots expansion team. It gives an inside account of things such as contract negotiations and the off-field habits of players—both considered off-limits to the public in those days. In trying to tell the truth about what he saw, Bouton succeeded in angering the baseball establishment. The book jacket even brags that commissioner BOWIE KUHN told Bouton, "You've done this game a grave disservice."

These days, tell-all books are common, and the media seem to be all-knowing. But in the late 1960s, people didn't know that some players cheated on their wives, that every other word out of their mouths was profane, and that drinking was their second favorite sport. *Ball Four* is still in print, and even though some of the parts that were scandalous at the time might seem tame now, it's definitely worth reading.

Bang the Drum Slowly
Written by Mark Harris
(Alfred A. Knopf, 1956)

A wonderful baseball novel—a sequel to another terrific novel, *The Southpaw*—about left-handed pitcher Henry Wiggen, who throws the baseball "with his arm and his brain and his memory and his bluff for the sake of his pocket and his family." The 1973 movie version, starring Michael Moriarty and a young Robert De Niro, remains one of the best baseball movies ever. Neither of those actors actually *looks* like a baseball player, but the movie concerns itself more with the characters and the situations than with the game on the field.

Bartman Incident

It was Game 6 of the 2003 National League Championship Series, Cubs vs. Marlins in WRIGLEY FIELD. Chicago led 3–0 and stood just five outs away from heading to the World Series for the first time since 1945. Then Florida's Luis Castillo hit a foul fly ball toward the left field stands, and outfielder Moises Alou gave chase. As the ball came down, Cubs fan Steve Bartman along with everyone around him stood up to try to catch the souvenir, and Alou reached into the stands to attempt the catch. Bartman appeared to interfere with the ball's path, and the ball landed in the seats. Alou was ticked off at the fans, and the crowd booed Bartman, a lifelong Cubs fan who had no intention to interfere with the fielder. He did what any one of would have done. Yet after the play, the Cubs completely unraveled. Pitcher Mark Prior walked Castillo and threw a wild pitch. The next batter lined a single to bring in a run. Then on a routine grounder to short, the Cubs' Alex Gonzales muffed what could have been an inning-ending double play ball. It got worse for the Cubs, and it wasn't until eight runs had scored that the inning mercifully ended. With every hit and walk, the crowd booed poor Bartman even louder until finally security escorted him from the field for his own safety. When the Cubs lost Game 7 the next day, the Bartman Incident was all people could talk about. Although the players never really blamed him, Bartman was an easy scapegoat for the Cubs' utter failure to play good baseball that day and the next. Since then, he has kept a very low profile and has refused offers to cash in on his infamy. But I don't think fellow fans will completely forgive him until the Cubs win a pennant. *If* that ever happens.

baseball cards/bubble gum cards

A cardboard-backed card featuring photographs or paintings of ball-players. The first baseball cards were packaged with cigar and cigarette boxes and received limited distribution. In 1951, the TOPPS CO. began selling the cards in packages of 10 to 15 with a stick of bubble gum. The hobby grew only gradually for 30 years, then exploded in 1981 when two more companies, Fleer and Donruss, began selling similar cards. In the late 1980s, several more companies flooded the market; this glut caused a massive devaluation of all post-1980 cards while also increasing the value of earlier cards.

The world's most valuable card is a 1909 tobacco card of HONUS WAGNER, called the T206, of which there are about a dozen in existence; it has sold for as much as $2.1 million. The story behind that card has become part of baseball folklore, but recent research has debunked much of the tale. Legend has it that after the cards came out, Wagner ordered them removed from circulation because he didn't want his name associated with tobacco products. But in 1993, *Sportslook* magazine published an article saying that Wagner actually smoked cigars and chewed tobacco. In addition, Wagner's face can be seen on four other tobacco company cards from around that same time. What seems most likely, according to the article, was that Wagner threatened legal action against the tobacco company for using his picture without paying him any money.

Baseball Encyclopedia
(Macmillan, 1969)

The first comprehensive reference book on baseball, first published in 1969. Its original publication marked a watershed moment in the history of baseball by cataloging statistical and biographical data for everyone who'd ever played in the majors. It was the brainchild of David Neft, head of Information Concepts, Inc., whose team used original source material—including newspaper accounts of games—to compile data and correct errors, and they worked closely with LEE ALLEN of the Hall of Fame for the personal information. Even with a price tag of $25 and weighing in at 6-1/2 pounds, the book sold over 100,000 copies and is still beloved and revered by researchers.

Baseball Prospectus

Baseball Prospectus comprises a group of writers and researchers who produce some of the most cutting-edge sabermetric analysis in baseball today. They have a website and an annual season preview book that are must-reads for fantasy players and baseball lovers in general, and their writers have gone on to publish their own books. They've introduced or refined an alphabet soup of innovations including, among others, WINS ABOVE REPLACEMENT (WAR) and VORP, two statistics that evaluate a player's contributions to winning compared to a typical TRIPLE-A "replacement player"; and PECOTA, a seriously advanced tool to predict a player's performance from year to year. If you love baseball stats, you owe it to yourself to check out Baseball Prospectus.

Baseball-Reference.com

The world's most indispensable baseball website, period. Baseball-Reference.com is the product of Sean Forman, a former university mathematics professor who started the site in 2000 because, he writes, "I was disappointed with not being able to find historical baseball statistics on the web and I was not convinced that existing sites were effectively utilizing the hyperconnected environment of the web." The site was amazing to begin with, and has grown ever larger with ever more useful information. I could sit here and explain what's on the site, but it would be so much better for you to just check it out. If you've never been there before, leave yourself at least an hour to explore and learn. After checking out the player statistics and information that go back to 1871, I suggest visiting the Play Index, which lets you search through tens of thousands of major league games to find, say, every walk-off hit in postseason history, or every 30/30 season, or the most consecutive games with a strikeout, or practically any other tidbit you can think of. Best of all, the basic information is all completely free (though you can subscribe to the site to get more detailed Play Index information). Thank you, Sean Forman.

Baseball's Great Experiment: Jackie Robinson and His Legacy
Written by Jules Tygiel
(Oxford University Press, 1983)

The first comprehensive historical treatise on the breaking of the COLOR LINE by JACKIE ROBINSON. Still in print, Tygiel's learned study presents a full history of African-Americans in baseball, from MOSES FLEETWOOD WALKER to Robinson and beyond in a readable, enjoyable style. Tygiel, then a history professor at San Francisco State University, was perhaps the leading authority on the sociological implications of baseball until his death in 2008.

"Baseball's Sad Lexicon"

Baseball history's second-most popular poem,* written by Giants fan/ newspaper columnist Franklin P. Adams. Appearing in the New York Globe in 1908, the poem lamented the excellent work of the TINKER TO EVERS TO CHANCE double play combination of the Chicago Cubs, who won consecutive pennants over the Giants from 1906 through 1908 (the word "double" in line 6 refers to double play, not two-base hit):

> These are the saddest of possible words,
> "Tinker to Evers to Chance."
> Trio of bear cubs, and fleeter than birds,
> "Tinker to Evers to Chance."
> Ruthlessly pricking our gonfalon bubble,
> Making a Giant hit into a double—

> Words that are heavy with nothing but trouble:
> "Tinker to Evers to Chance."

Mostly because of this poem, Joe Tinker, Johnny Evers, and Frank Chance were inducted into the Hall of Fame as a group in 1946.

*Baseball's *most* popular poem, by the way, is "CASEY AT THE BAT."

"Big Bang Theory"

The managing style popularized by the Baltimore Orioles' EARL WEAVER. In leading his team to four pennants, Weaver disdained the sacrifice bunt and hit-and-run, choosing instead to let his batters hit away, get on base, and hit three-run homers. The thinking is that in the majority of ball games, the winning team scores more runs in a single inning than the loser scores in the entire game. As Weaver liked to say, "If you play for one run, that's all you're gonna get!"

"Big Red Machine"

Nickname given to the Cincinnati Reds teams of the early- to mid-1970s. Featuring Hall of Famers JOHNNY BENCH, JOE MORGAN, Tony Perez, and manager SPARKY ANDERSON and career hits leader PETE ROSE, the Reds won five division titles, four pennants, and two World Series from 1970 through 1976. Their best year was probably 1975: Morgan won his first MVP, Bench drove in 110 runs, Rose had 210 hits, the team won 108 games, and the club bested the Red Sox in one of the greatest World Series ever (*see* 1975: THE SOX AND REDS PLAY A SERIES FOR THE AGES).

The Bill James Historical Baseball Abstract
Written by Bill James
(1st edition: Villard, 1985; revised edition: Villard, 1988; "New" edition: Free Press, 2001)

Without a doubt the most insightful and fascinating baseball book I own and possibly the best overall history/statistics book ever written. This book combines two great premises. The first half of the book is a decade-by-decade look at baseball history, filled with anecdotes, explanations, and analyses of the important and not-so-important people and events. The second half is a position-by-position look at the greatest players of all time, using BILL JAMES'S groundbreaking methods of statistical analysis—including his latest and most consequential invention, WIN SHARES. Whether you've read James before or not, you will learn a lot from reading this book, and you will start to look at the game of baseball in a new and exciting way.

Billy Goat Curse

Why haven't the Chicago Cubs returned to the World Series since 1945? If you believe crazy people, it's because of a man named Billy Sianis, the owner of the Billy Goat Tavern in Chicago who was kicked out of a World Series game in 1945 at WRIGLEY FIELD because his pet goat, who he brought along for good luck, I guess, was bothering other fans. As he was being forcibly escorted from the grounds, he supposedly shouted, "Them Cubs, they aren't gonna win no more." Or maybe he later sent a telegram with a similar message; accounts are sketchy. In any case, the Cubs went on to lose that series and, as we know, haven't been back since. I can almost believe in the CURSE OF THE BAMBINO, but this weak hex? Give me a break.

Black Sox

Ignominious nickname given to the Chicago White Sox team that accepted money from gamblers to throw the 1919 WORLD SERIES. While it would seem that the Black Sox name was applied after the scandal was revealed, in fact, the team had earned that nickname even before the scandal. Club owner CHARLES COMISKEY was so cheap that at one point during the season, he began to make his players pay for the cleaning of their uniforms. Outraged, the players protested by not washing them, so they became known around the league as the Black Sox—not metaphorically but physically.

bleacher bums

Fans who sit in the bleachers, drink beer, get into fights, taunt opposing outfielders, throw back visiting team home run balls, and support the home team vehemently and loudly. While almost every team can claim its own group, baseball's quintessential bleacher bums reside in Chicago's WRIGLEY FIELD.

Bloody Sock

The artifact from one of this generation's most dramatic and important clutch performances. The sock belonged to CURT SCHILLING, who had suffered a serious ankle injury early in the 2004 POSTSEA-

SON and was not expected to return to action. When the Red Sox fell behind the Yankees three games to zero in the American League Championship Series, it looked like his season would be over. But then the Sox won Games 4 and 5, and they needed Schilling. Problem was, one of the tendons in his right ankle had broken loose from its protective sheath, and with every step, it was snapping painfully across the bone. "I couldn't push off," he told reporters. "It affected both my command and velocity."

Boston's medical staff tried various methods to make Schilling's ankle well enough so that he could pitch again in Game 6, including a special ankle brace and a custom-made shoe, but nothing worked. Then, team physician Dr. William Morgan had a brainstorm: he would suture the tendon directly to the skin to keep it from snapping around the bone. It had never been done, so Morgan practiced the procedure on a cadaver first, and the night before Game 6, he performed it on Schilling. The procedure seemed to work, but nobody knew how the sutures would hold up in a real game.

In Game 6 at YANKEE STADIUM, Schilling pitched brilliantly and the Sox won, but sometime in the first or second inning, a suture broke and caused blood to seep through his white sock. TV cameras homed in on the stain repeatedly, and more than one observer ascribed divine meaning to Schilling's gutsy performance by likening the bloody image to a stigmata.

The Sox went on to win Games 6 and 7, capping their miraculous come-from-behind victory over the Yankees and reversing the "CURSE OF THE BAMBINO." And Schilling's bloody sock stands as dramatic symbol of Boston's achievement.

bonus baby

A young prospect who gets a large sum of money as an incentive to sign with a major league team. Because of the high amount of money invested in them, bonus babies are treated more gingerly than non–bonus babies as they move up the minor league ladder. When this term first came into popular use, a $100,000 bonus was rare and noteworthy; today, multimillion-dollar bonuses for the top few picks in the yearly AMATEUR DRAFT are commonplace.

The Boys of Summer
Written by Roger Kahn
(Harper and Row, 1972)

Poignant bestseller about the Brooklyn Dodgers of the 1950s, who included, among others, JACKIE ROBINSON, ROY CAMPANELLA, and Duke Snider and won five pennants in eight years. The book examines the players' lives both in and out of baseball—the challenges, successes, and heartbreaks of not just a group of players but a group of men.

Bronx Bombers

Nickname given to the New York Yankees, first applied to the oft-pennant-winning teams of the RUTH-GEHRIG era, because YANKEE STADIUM is located in the Bronx. Don't confuse it with the nickname of boxer Joe Louis, who was known as the Brown Bomber.

Bull Durham

One of the funniest—and some say best—baseball movies ever made, starring Kevin Costner and Susan Sarandon about minor league life with the Durham Bulls of the SINGLE-A Carolina League. The film is notable for many reasons, not the least of which is the chance to hear Costner utter, *before* he spouted conspiracy theories in *JFK*, "I believe Lee Harvey Oswald acted alone!" Good sports movies are rare enough, but a good, hilarious sports movie is a true gem.

"Casey at the Bat"

The greatest and most famous baseball poem ever written, "Casey" first appeared on page 4 of the Sunday, June 3, 1888, edition of the San Francisco Examiner. Ernest L. Thayer, a Harvard friend of Examiner publisher William Randolph Hearst, penned the ballad under the pseudonym "Phin," and it was the only thing noteworthy he ever wrote. More than two dozen sequels and homages have appeared in the years since "Casey's" publication, including "Casey's Revenge," "Casey the Comeback," "Mrs. Casey at the Bat," "Casey's Son," "Casey's Daughter at the Bat," and others. But none is as good as the original. Here it is, in its entirety:

CASEY AT THE BAT
A Ballad of the Republic, Sung in the Year 1888

The outlook wasn't brilliant for the Mudville nine that day:
The score stood four to two, with but one inning more to play,
And then when Cooney died at first, and Barrows did the same,
A sickly silence fell upon the patrons of the game.

A straggling few got up to go in deep despair. The rest
Clung to that hope which springs eternal in the human breast;
They thought, "If only Casey could but get a whack at that—
We'd put up even money now with Casey at the bat."

But Flynn preceded Casey, as did also Jimmy Blake,
And the former was a lulu, and the latter was a cake;
So upon that stricken multitude grim melancholy sat,
For there seemed but little chance of Casey getting to the bat.

But Flynn let drive a single, to the wonderment of all,
And Blake, the much despised, tore the cover off the ball;
And when the dust had lifted, and men saw what had occurred,
There was Jimmy safe at second and Flynn a-hugging third.

Then from five thousand throats and more there rose a lusty yell;
It rumbled through the valley, it rattled in the dell;
It pounded on the mountain and recoiled upon the flat,
For Casey, mighty Casey, was advancing to the bat.

There was ease in Casey's manner as he stepped into his place;
There was pride in Casey's bearing and a smile on Casey's face.
And when responding to the cheers, he lightly doffed his hat,
No stranger in the crowd could doubt 'twas Casey at the bat.

Ten thousand eyes were on him as he rubbed his hands with dirt;
Five thousand tongues applauded when he wiped them on his shirt;
Then while the writhing pitcher ground the ball into his hip,
Defiance gleamed in Casey's eye, a sneer curled Casey's lip.

And now the leather-covered sphere came hurtling through the air,
And Casey stood a-watching it in haughty grandeur there.
Close by the sturdy batsman the ball unheeded sped—
"That ain't my style," said Casey. "Strike one!" the umpire said.

From the benches, black with people, there went up a muffled roar,
Like the beating of the storm-waves on a stern and distant shore;

"Kill him! Kill the umpire!" shouted someone on the stand;
And it's likely they'd have killed him had not Casey raised his hand.

With a smile of Christian charity great Casey's visage shone;
He stilled the rising tumult; he bade the game go on;
He signaled to the pitcher, and once more the spheroid flew;
But Casey still ignored it, and the umpire said, "Strike two!"

"Fraud!" cried the maddened thousands, and echo answered "Fraud!"
But one scornful look from Casey and the audience was awed.
They saw his face grow stern and cold, they saw his muscles strain,
And they knew that Casey wouldn't let that ball go by again.

The sneer is gone from Casey's lip, his teeth are clenched in hate;
He pounds with cruel violence his bat upon the plate.
And now the pitcher holds the ball, and now he lets it go,
And now the air is shattered by the force of Casey's blow.

Oh, somewhere in this favored land the sun is shining bright;
The band is playing somewhere, and somewhere hearts are light,
And somewhere men are laughing, and somewhere children shout;
But there is no joy in Mudville—mighty Casey has struck out.

color line, color barrier

Just as slavery is part of America's shameful past, so is the color line
part of baseball's. In the early days of professional baseball, blacks
played alongside whites in professional leagues throughout the country. Brothers Welday and MOSES WALKER even made it to the majors, albeit for only a single season. The practice reached a turning
point in 1887, however, following an incident in which Chicago
White Stockings' manager ADRIAN "CAP" ANSON, one of baseball's
biggest superstars, threatened to forfeit an exhibition game unless the
opposing team's black pitcher was removed. Anson backed down
when he learned that he'd lose his game money, but similar threats
began to come from other managers, and teams began to drop their
black players. By 1895, baseball's color line had become entrenched,
and blacks wishing to play professional ball were forced to join the
loosely organized NEGRO LEAGUES and play for substantially lower
salaries and prestige.

To hear baseball executives put it, however, no color line had ever existed. Just before his death in 1944, commissioner KENESAW MOUN-
TAIN LANDIS, who had ruled baseball with czar-like authority since

1921, declared: "There is no rule, formal or informal, no understanding subterranean or otherwise, against black ball players in the majors." As explanation for the absence of black players from major league rosters, owners claimed that they could find none who were qualified, and thus shifted the blame to the minor leagues: "Colored players have never been discriminated against in the major leagues," said Indians owner Alva Bradley. "They have simply never been able to get into the minor leagues to get the proper training for major league competition." The fact that the majors controlled the minor leagues shows just how hypocritical Bradley's argument was. And in any case, there are many stories about baseball owners and managers blocked, either by the league office or the other owners, from signing black men to play "organized" baseball. Legendary manager JOHN MCGRAW, for example, once tried to pass off an African-American as Native American but was found out.

In the 1940s, JACKIE ROBINSON and BRANCH RICKEY changed everything. But even after Rickey signed Robinson to play for the Dodgers' Montreal farm team, doubters still existed. To mask their racism, however, they looked for other reasons to denigrate Robinson. In 1945, *THE SPORTING NEWS* reported: "Robinson, at 26, is reported to possess baseball abilities which, were he white, would make him eligible for a trial with, let us say, the Brooklyn Dodgers Class B farm at Newport News, if he were six years younger." Of course, if Robinson had been white, he would have made it to the majors years earlier. Other doubters did not hide their racism. Before Robinson's first year in the majors, a number of Dodger players signed a petition asking Rickey not to promote Robinson to the big league club. Rickey ignored it. Then, during the 1947 season, rumors spread that the St. Louis Cardinals were threatening to strike rather than play against Robinson. National League president FORD FRICK threatened back: Anybody who refuses to play against Robinson, he wrote, will be banned from baseball. They didn't strike (and they have denied ever discussing a strike). Frick's threat and Robinson's determination made the "great experiment" a success. The first academic study of the breaking of the color line was *BASEBALL'S GREAT EXPERIMENT* by history professor Jules Tygiel.

cricket

One of the British games from which baseball evolved, cricket resembles baseball only in the sense that both sports use a bat and ball. Cricket originated in England before 1700 and is now played around the world, most prominently in former British colonies. In it, two 11-player teams take turns defending a wicket with a bat. A "bowler" throws the ball at the wicket, and the batsman swings at the ball to prevent it from striking the wicket. When he hits the ball, he scores runs for his team by running from wicket to wicket while the fielders retrieve the ball. If the ball strikes his wicket either directly or while he's running, he's out, and then the next batsman on his team takes his turn. Play continues until all 11 men are retired, and then the two teams switch sides; that's an innings (yes, plural). A game lasts just two innings, but sometimes it can go on for days.

"Curse of the Bambino"

The superstition—first named in *New York Times* article by George Vecsey following the Game 6 debacle in 1986 (*see* 1986: WORLD SERIES GAME 6, METS VS. RED SOX), then amplified in a 1990 book by Boston reporter Dan Shaughnessy—that purported to explain why the Red Sox didn't win a World Series after they sold Babe Ruth to the Yankees in 1919 (*see* 1919: THE SOX SELL THE BABE). The Sox had won the championship a year before that, and they had come within a single game of winning it in 1946, 1967, 1975, and 1986. But each time, Ruth's curse supposedly struck them down. Of course, Ruth had nothing to do with bad personnel decisions, unlucky plays, institutional racism, and the other actual reasons why Boston went without a championship so long. Among Boston diehards, the "Curse" may have simply become an easy excuse for preventable and accidental errors. When the Sox finally won the World Series in 2004, it took the "Curse" entirely off the table (*see* 2004: THE CURSE IS REVERSED). Which is good for Boston, good for baseball, and good for rational thinking in general (but bad for New York fans).

"Damn Yankees"

A 1955 Broadway musical, then a 1958 movie, based on Douglass Wallop's entertaining novel *The Year the Yankees Lost the Pennant*. Legendary choreographer Bob Fosse arranged the dance numbers, with lyrics and music by Richard Adler and Jerry Ross. The story concerns a Washington Senators fan who sells his soul to the Devil so that the Senators can beat the Yankees for the pennant.

Dead Ball Era

The era of baseball history from the turn of the 20th century until the 1920s, characterized by low batting averages, low run totals, and little power. The reason the Dead Ball Era begins around 1901 or 1902 is that both leagues had just changed the rules to count foul balls as strikes and pitchers began to throw spitballs and other trick pitches in earnest. Before that, .400 seasons were common. Between 1903 and 1921, there were only two seasons when batters topped the .400 mark—both coming after a new cork-center baseball was introduced in 1911. Overall, league batting averages hovered around .240 to .250 (vs. .260 today), league slugging percentages stayed around .320 (vs. .410 today), and league ERAs were below 3.00 (vs. 4.25 today). Strikeout totals were also low, and so were home run totals; a typical league-leading home run season would be 10 or 11.

Along with the foul strike rule, there were some other factors that created the Dead Ball Era. First, batters were trained to just make contact with the ball, not swing for the seats. That was the dominant strategy: bunt, beat out a single, sacrifice, steal, hit behind the runner, force an error. Most of the players could run well, and the majority of teams would steal more than 200 bases a year (vs. 115 today). Why risk a strikeout when you can claw your way on first base and usually steal the next one? The second, and probably most important, reason for the Dead Ball Era has to do with the ball. The SPITBALL, tobacco ball, emery ball, and all other ways to doctor a baseball were legal. Pitchers could do whatever they wanted with it, and their teammates could help out by spitting on the ball themselves. Additionally, umpires would usually only use one or two baseballs per game. If the ball went into the stands, the fans would toss it back and play would resume using that same ball. So even in broad daylight, the ball could be hard to see when it came out of the pitcher's hand. It's no wonder players concerned themselves with just putting bat on ball. The Dead Ball Era ended and the LIVELY BALL ERA began because of three unrelated events: the coming of BABE RUTH, the banning of the spitball, and the death of RAY CHAPMAN.

"Dem Bums"

Loving nickname Brooklyn Dodger fans bestowed upon their hometown team in both print and speech. And the Dodgers earned it. From the 1920s through the 1930s, the team finished in the second division more often than not, and then from 1941 through 1954, the Dodgers won five pennants, came nightmarishly close to four others, and lost all five World Series to the Yankees. Finally, in 1955, the Dodgers beat the Yankees in the Series, and the front page of the next day's Brooklyn newspaper showed a smiling transient with a banner headline, "Who's a bum?" *See also* 1955: "NEXT YEAR" FINALLY ARRIVES.

Doubleday Myth

In 1905, famed sportsman and entrepreneur ALBERT G. SPALDING decided to commission a study on the origins of baseball. Fervently patriotic, Spalding set out to prove that baseball was a uniquely American invention, not a descendent of the British games ROUNDERS and CRICKET, as was asserted by the legendary sportswriter HENRY CHADWICK. Instead of considering all the facts—including the obvious similarities between baseball and those much older British games—the MILLS COMMISSION REPORT relied on the dubious testimony of a elderly mining engineer named Albert Graves, who claimed to have witnessed the day ABNER DOUBLEDAY created the first baseball diamond in 1839 in Cooperstown, New York. Never mind the fact that Doubleday, a famous Union general during the Civil War, had never discussed the sport he had supposedly invented in any of his diaries. Spalding wanted an American genesis, and he got one. After his findings were announced, the son of ALEXANDER CARTWRIGHT protested that his father had been short-changed, so the Commission also recognized the contributions of Cartwright and the NEW YORK KNICKERBOCKERS. Unfortunately, the only person who didn't have anyone lobbying for him was the person who probably had more to do with transforming baseball into the game we know today: DANIEL "DOC" ADAMS.

Eight Men Out
Written by Eliot Asinof
(Holt, Rinehart and Winston, 1961)

A marvelous recounting of the Black Sox scandal and its legacy—the first book that attempted to tell the full story. John Sayles made a movie out of it in 1988, a film that has some flaws but pretty much does what it set out to do: re-create the 1919 baseball scene and try to explain why the players did what they did. In their retelling, Asinof and the filmmakers shift most of the blame for the scandal onto White Sox owner CHARLES COMISKEY, who treated his players like indentured servants. Certainly the players were greedy, in placing cash above integrity. Asinof's book strikes a good balance.

But how much of *Eight Men Out* is true? Most of us assumed that Asinof's book was historically accurate, but it turned out that there were some dubious elements thrown into the book, muddying the story for those of us who care about things like facts and the truth. What happened was, before his death, Asinof released all his notes, and researchers discovered some serious holes in the story, so it's not clear which parts were real and which were made up. Asinof also admitted to adding two fictional characters to the story. For example, in the book and movie, there's a scene where Lefty Williams, the pitcher, has his life threatened by a thug to keep him from pitching well. Turns out, Asinof inserted the thug and another fake character into the story so that if the story ever got made into a movie without his permission—or, more to the point, without paying him—he could claim copyright infringement. The outline of the story presented in *Eight Men Out* is true, but some of the details may not be. History is messy sometimes.

Elias Sports Bureau

The official statisticians of major league baseball, the Elias Bureau is responsible for verifying the accuracy of all baseball statistics.

fantasy league

A fictitious league in which players act as general manager/owners of virtual teams, accruing points based on how major leaguers perform in real life. (They're also known as ROTISSERIE LEAGUES, for reasons explained in that entry.) Over the last decade, the popularity of fantasy leagues has grown exponentially, and today millions play these games on the Internet. In most leagues, the teams compete for supremacy in categories such as team batting average, home runs, RBIs, stolen bases, pitcher strikeouts, ERA, wins, and a category called WHIP—the ratio of walks and hits to innings pitched; many leagues offer some other categories, too. It's a fun game to play, but it really changes the way you follow baseball, and a lot of critics argue that it's ruining fans. They have a point. Fantasy league players are only interested in individual stats, not team victories, which detracts from what baseball is: a team sport. Some people think that's bad for baseball, but I think baseball will survive.

Field of Dreams

Field of Dreams is a magical fantasy about an Iowa farmer named Ray who builds a baseball diamond in his cornfield because a voice tells him "SHOELESS" JOE JACKSON will play in it (*see* "IF YOU BUILD IT, HE WILL COME"). The film, which received an Academy Award nomination for best picture, and the book upon which it's based, W. P. Kinsella's *Shoeless Joe*, tackle issues that are much weightier than baseball: dreams, passion, father-son relationships. I still get chills during the movie when Burt Lancaster's character tells Ray (played by Kevin Costner) what he would want with a single wish. And I love when James Earl Jones's character gives a moving speech about baseball's role in American culture. And even though it occasionally lapses into bouts of hokeyness, the movie maintains a charm and whimsy that keep you engaged until the last scene.

The book *Shoeless Joe* is deeper and more powerful than the movie. One interesting difference between the two is that in the book, the author that Ray is supposed to find is not the fictional Terence Mann but the very real J. D. Salinger. Marvelously written, *Shoeless Joe* is the favorite baseball novel of a whole generation of fans, although it does have its share of critics: Katherine A. Powers of the Boston Sunday Globe called the book "appallingly sentimental." I would call it "refreshingly sentimental."

"Gas House Gang"

The nickname for the Cardinals teams in the 1930s, featuring such colorful characters as Frankie Frisch, LEO DUROCHER, DIZZY DEAN, Pepper Martin, and Joe Medwick. With Durocher as the ringleader and Martin as the clown, the Cardinals made themselves famous for scrappy play and childish pranks. Once, after a tough loss, player-manager Frisch called a team meeting during which he lambasted his players with insults and profanity. Then he asked if anyone had any questions. During the heavy silence that followed, only Martin was brave enough to raise his hand: "I was just wondering," he asked Frisch innocently, "whether I ought to paint my midget auto racer red with white wheels or white with red wheels." Even Frisch had to laugh.

The first Gas House Gang, according to author Paul Dickson, was a band of thugs who prowled the Lower East Side of Manhattan near a number of large gas tanks in the 19th century. The term came to be applied to the Cardinals because, according to one legend, they were a notoriously rough team that once played a game in against the Giants in soiled uniforms, reminding a New York writer of the famed thugs.

The Glory of Their Times
Written by Lawrence Ritter
(Macmillan, 1966)

A landmark book, the first of its kind: the baseball oral history. Ritter's book is a collection of interviews with more than two dozen ballplayers from the first third of the century, including Hall of Famers Edd Roush, Goose Goslin, and PAUL WANER. It's a great insight into the early days of baseball, full of terrific stories and honest opinions. It's also a wonderful place to learn about the legendary ballplayers who died before their stories could be told. In *The Glory of Their Times*, Sam Crawford talks about TY COBB, Tommy Leach about HONUS WAGNER, Chief Meyers about CHRISTY MATHEWSON. Ritter says he got the idea for the book in 1961, when Cobb died at the age of 74, and he decided that somebody should, before it was too late, tell the stories of some of the men who influenced the game that has affected American society so much. Ritter's book succeeded so well that there have been dozens of imitators, with more coming out each year.

"Good field, no hit"

Scout Mike Gonzalez's famous assessment of catcher MOE BERG in a terse telegram to his superiors. The phrase now gets used all the time, usually to pass judgment over a middle infielder with an invisible bat.

The Great American Novel
Written by Philip Roth
(Holt, Rinehart and Winston, 1973)

One of the greatest novels about baseball, this work by megabestselling author/baseball fan Philip Roth takes you on a surreal and hilarious trip through the Pioneer League, the fictional third major league that enthralled fans before World War II. Definitely worth spending time with.

"Green-light letter"

The letter written by President Franklin Roosevelt to baseball commissioner KENESAW MOUNTAIN LANDIS in 1942 urging professional baseball to continue despite America's involvement in World War II. During World War I, by contrast, President Wilson had ordered all nonessential industries halted, and because baseball fell under that category, the 1918 season was cut short. Roosevelt felt differently: "I honestly feel that it would be best for the country to try to keep baseball going," he wrote in the letter. "There will be fewer people unemployed and everybody will work longer hours and harder than ever before. And that means that they ought to have a chance for recreation and for taking their minds off their work even more than before.... Here is another way of looking at it—if 300 teams use 5,000 or 6,000 players, these players are a definite recreational asset to at least 20,000,000 of their fellow citizens—and that in my judgment is thoroughly worthwhile."

Green Monster

FENWAY PARK'S 37-foot-high wall in left field, painted green since 1947. Before that, the wall featured a number of giant billboards, the most famous being a Gem razor blade sign reading "Avoid 5 O'Clock Shadow" and a Lifebuoy soap sign saying "The Red Sox Use It." The Green Monster is baseball's most famous wall (which is more of a distinction than it sounds), and it's obviously one of Fenway's greatest charms. But it may have cost the Sox a number of pennants. Here's why: With such an inviting home run target, the team traditionally stacked its lineup with power hitters, forsaking the all-around players who are the real keys to winning baseball. Additionally, left-handed pitchers are said to be intimidated by the Wall, so the Sox historically had trouble developing them. If you go to Boston, though, don't call it the "Green Monster"; there, it's called The Wall.

"Hit 'em where they ain't"

WEE WILLIE KEELER'S famous proclamation describing the secret of his success as a hitter. Keeler was the king of the 19th-century slap hitters, a five-foot, four-and-a-half-inch outfielder who choked way up on the bat. Consequently, 86 percent of his 2,932 hits went for singles.

Hot Stove League

A term for a mythical league that's in season during the winter months, consisting not of athletes but of regular folks who like to sit around a hot stove and talk baseball.

"The House that Ruth Built"

One of the nicknames for YANKEE STADIUM. The Yankees shared the POLO GROUNDS with the more popular and successful Giants until BABE RUTH joined the club. Once the Yanks became better than the Giants, JOHN MCGRAW'S club kicked out the American Leaguers. If it weren't for Ruth, there's no telling where the Yankees would be playing. Another interesting thing about the Stadium is that traditional folklore says that the park was built to suit his batting style, with a short right field fence for him to slam home runs over. I don't doubt the accuracy of that story. But the amount Ruth was helped is usually overplayed by journalists and writers. For his career, in nearly the exact same number of games for each, Ruth slugged 239 doubles and 347 home runs at home, 269 and 367 on the road. The truth was, he could hit anywhere.

"Hub Fans Bid Kid Adieu"

Written in 1960 originally for *The New Yorker* magazine, this great essay by John Updike gets reprinted in almost every baseball anthology. As well it should. It describes the last game in TED WILLIAMS'S career, a day that was "overcast, chill, and uninspirational" but that nevertheless produced one of baseball's most remarkable moments: the home run hit by Williams, aka "The Kid," in his last major league at bat. Updike viewed the action from a box seat through the eyes of a loving fan, not as a cynical sportswriter sitting in press row. The result is a much-recommended piece full of beautiful prose and surprising turns.

"If you build it, he will come."

The opening line of the great baseball movie *FIELD OF DREAMS*, taken from W.P. Kinsella's novel *Shoeless Joe*. It's spoken by a disembodied voice that only the main character, Ray, can hear. The "it" is a ballpark, which the Voice asks Ray to build out of his cornfield. The "he" is something for viewers and readers to find out. (The end credits list "The Voice" as one of the characters. The actor who plays "The Voice"? None other than "Himself.")

"The Impossible Dream"

The term applied to the 1967 Red Sox's miraculous season, in which they advanced from a ninth-place finish in 1966 to capture the American League pennant in a thrilling race. CARL YASTRZEMSKI received—and deserved—much of the credit for the team's surge. In winning the majors' last TRIPLE CROWN, Yaz dominated the month of September: In the final two weeks, with the Sox in a tight pennant race with the Twins and Tigers, he batted .523. And on the final day, against those Twins, he went 7 for 8 as the Sox eked out a one-game pennant victory. Against St. Louis in the World Series, he batted .400 with three homers, but he couldn't stop BOB GIBSON'S Cardinals by himself. In a fitting end, Yaz singled to lead off the ninth inning of Game 7 with the Cards ahead 7–2. The next batter, Ken Harrelson, erased Yastrzemski on a double play grounder. Thus the city of Boston awoke from its dream.

"Joltin' Joe DiMaggio"

A popular song, circa 1941, celebrating the man who captivated the nation with his 56-game hitting streak (*see* 56). The tune, written by Alan Courtney and performed by Les Brown and his Orchestra with Betty Bonney on vocals, streaked to number 12 on the pop charts just weeks after DiMaggio's streak ended.

Ken Burns's *Baseball*

The 18-1/2 hour PBS documentary that provided fans with their only baseball-related entertainment during the fall of 1994. With labor unrest having canceled the World Series (*see* 1994: THE WORLD SERIES GETS KILLED), *Baseball* garnered some of the highest ratings in the history of public television. Burns, whose previous documentary effort, *The Civil War*, earned equally strong accolades, divided *Baseball* into nine episodes, or innings, covering the game's 150-plus years. Among several recurring themes, the documentary explored baseball's tumultuous labor relations and its transcendent problems of race, and almost an entire "inning" is devoted to the Negro leagues and the breaking of the color barrier.

It was comprehensive, engaging, sometimes funny, and uncompromising. Purists quibbled with some of its minor historical inaccuracies. Other critics knocked the documentary's often languorous pace. But even they would have to admit that such pacing suited its subject matter perfectly.

In 2010, Burns continued the series with a "tenth inning" covering the events since 1994, such as the strike, steroids, the rise of the Yankees, the success of the Red Sox, and so on. Interspersed throughout all ten episodes are commentaries from writers (such as ROGER ANGELL and DANIEL OKRENT), former players (e.g., BUCK O'NEIL and Bill Lee), and other noteworthy baseball fans (from actor Billy Crystal to Harvard professor Doris Kearns Goodwin). The information is presented so effectively, and the style is so effortless, that, despite its flaws, it can quite simply be called the *Citizen Kane* of sports documentaries.

Knickerbocker Rules

The rules created by the NEW YORK KNICKERBOCKER Baseball Club of 1845, led by ALEXANDER CARTWRIGHT and DANIEL "DOC" ADAMS. For his part, Cartwright is in the Hall of Fame, where his plaque says that he was responsible for setting the bases 90 feet apart and establishing nine men per team and nine innings per game. I have no idea where they made that up, because the actual Knickerbocker rules don't say anything about 90, nine, or nine. Rule number 8 says that the game will "consist of 21 counts, or aces"—that means the first team to 21 runs. Rule number 6 discusses the size of each team, but it doesn't give any actual numbers; it just says, "If there should not be a sufficient number of members of the Club present at the time agreed upon to commence exercise, gentlemen not members may be chosen in to make up the match"—basically, ringers are allowed if needed.

And the part about 90 feet? Rule number 4 does say that the distances from home to second and first to third should be 42 paces. If you assume three feet per pace, that calculates to 30 yards between bases, or 90 feet. At last! Something that's accurate about Cartwright's Hall of Fame plaque! Sorry, no. As author John Thorn has pointed out while debunking the Cartwright story in *Total Baseball*, a "pace" in 1845 was defined as 2-1/2 feet, not three. Thorn quotes Webster's 1832 and 1853 dictionaries to prove it: "Pace: The space between the two feet in walking, estimated at two feet and a half." Three feet per pace didn't get established until well into the 20th century, which means that the base paths under the Knickerbocker Rules were actually about 75 feet long.

Some things that the Knickerbocker Rules did establish were the idea of foul territory, three strikes per out, and three outs per inning. Over the next 17 years, while Doc Adams presided over the Knickerbocker

Club, he and his clubmates changed the rules to create a nine-inning game, establish 90 feet between bases, and place a pitcher's box 45 feet from home. For more on the propaganda that we've been fed about the origins of baseball, see ABNER DOUBLEDAY, the DOUBLE-DAY MYTH, and the MILLS COMMISSION REPORT.

Lively Ball Era

An oft-told baseball story is that sometime around 1920, major league executives acted in concert with baseball manufacturers to "liven up" the ball. Their supposed aim was to increase flagging attendance in the wake of the BLACK SOX SCANDAL. With this new ball, BABE RUTH slammed 54 then 59 home runs, shattering the major league record, and for the rest of the decade, batters went wild and, more importantly, attendance soared. It's hard to find a baseball history book that does *not* tell this story as if it were undisputed truth. There's only one thing wrong: It's just not true! No writer who espouses this theory has any evidence to prove it. That's because the ball used from 1920 to 1926 was not in any substantial way different from that used from 1911 from 1919. The REACH COMPANY, which manufactured balls for both leagues (although SPALDING SPORTING GOODS put its name on the NL's balls), did use a higher-quality yarn after World War I, but it had little, if anything, to do with the inflated averages; and even if it did have an effect, it was not done intentionally to fatten batting averages and boost attendance. This "RABBIT BALL" gets blamed simply based on the fact that offensive totals increased. But that's like accusing somebody of murder when the only evidence you have is the dead body.

Actually, three important factors were responsible for the outrageous hitting totals of what became known as the Lively Ball Era: the banning of the spitball; the death of RAY CHAPMAN in 1920 (*see* 1920: TRAGEDY ON THE DIAMOND); and the coming of Babe Ruth. The outlawing of the spitball came before the 1919 season because there was a fear that a pitcher might lose control of the ball and kill someone. Well, someone did die the following season, but it wasn't because of the spitball. Chapman's death from an underhand fastball by Carl Mays inspired major league executives to order that umpires keep fresh white balls in play at all times; prior to that, the same one or two balls were used throughout the game, and by the later innings, that ball would get spit on and covered with dirt and mud. Ruth, who had already broken his own home run record before Chapman's death, helped usher in the new era by showing the baseball world that home runs were possible. Before he became a full-time hitter, baseball games were won with "scientific" spray hitting and stolen bases (*see* DEAD BALL ERA). Ruth and his uppercut swing became so popular that legions of baseball players started copying him. Add to that the small size of most ballparks, and of course you're going to have an increase in home runs.

What proof is there that no lively ball was introduced? A lot more than the proof that a lively ball *was* introduced. Throughout the 1920s, journalists and league offices launched a number of investigations into the alleged "rabbit ball" theories, and all of them came to the same conclusion: that the balls used after 1920 had the same weight and size and bounce and used the same materials (except for the yarn, which didn't make much of a difference) as the ball that had been used in the past decade. In addition, the manufacturer and league officials gave sworn depositions to that effect. Much-respected NL president John Heydler said, "At no time have the club owners ordered the manufacturer to make the ball livelier. The only stipulation the club owners have made about the ball is that it be the very best that could be made." The *Reach Baseball Guide* ran a full-page ad announcing, "We never experiment with our patrons. There has been no change in the construction of the CORK CENTER BALL since we introduced it in 1910." And the United States Bureau of Standards conducted extensive tests that came to the same conclusion.

So what we have is an easy-to-understand *effect*—the inflated batting numbers—with a very complex series of *causes*. In such instances of uncertainty, many people find it reassuring to believe that somebody, somewhere, no matter how manipulative and secretive, is in control of things. Certainly, batting totals zoomed out of sight, and at just about any other time in the game's history, such an explosion would have been met with some kind of official attempt to get control of things. Instead, what the league found was that fans loved it. Attendance per game increased by 21 percent in both leagues in 1920, and though it fluctuated for the next decade, the owners let their bottom lines do their talking, and the home run was there to stay. In 1926, Reach introduced the "cushioned cork center" to replace the plain old "cork center," but that change actually *hurt* the batters: league batting, on-base, and slugging averages went down in 1926. By the 1930 YEAR OF THE HITTER, however, an entire generation of players had honed the art of power hitting using thin-handled bats, and batting totals reached their peak.

The *de facto* end of the Lively Ball Era was the beginning of World War II. Throughout the 1930s, batting and slugging averages were still really high, but after the war, they seemed to go down to more "normal" levels. There's really no easy explanation for that change except to note that it was gradual and probably due to evolutionary forces rather than Babe Ruth's *revolutionary* force. (An excellent study of 1920s baseball, from which much of my information comes, is William Curran's *Big Sticks*.).

The Long Season
Written by Jim Brosnan
(Harper and Brothers, 1960)

Brosnan's controversial book about the life of a baseball player created a minor scandal at its publication because it discussed such taboos as drinking and sexual activity among ballplayers. Like its successor in that genre, JIM BOUTON'S *BALL FOUR*, Brosnan's book seems tame by today's standards. But you have to remember that in 1960, the press hadn't yet insinuated itself into every element of celebrity life. And in any case, *The Long Season* made its real impact not because of any sordid escapades, but rather because Brosnan is a smart thinker who had a lot to say about the game.

Lou Gehrig's Disease

Amyotrophic lateral sclerosis (ALS), the deadly disease that slowly but inevitably robs muscles of their strength. LOU GEHRIG, its most famous victim, succumbed to the illness on June 2, 1941. Today, 30,000 people suffer from this incurable disease.

Louisville Slugger

The name of the most famous bats in baseball, manufactured by the Hillerich and Bradsby Company. Pete Browning, a 19th-century slugger who played for Louisville of the American Association, was known to be fond of his bats, and when one of them broke during a game in the 1880s, John "Bud" Hillerich, the son of a local woodworker, approached Browning with the offer of making a bat for him. Browning was so successful and happy with his new bat that other players started requesting them. H&B rode that success to become the king of bat manufacturers, a position they hold today. Although there are at least six other bat companies in the United States, H&B has contracts with 70 percent of all major leaguers.

To keep up with the demand, its new factory in Louisville puts out 1.4 million bats per year, 10 to 15 percent of which go to the professionals. If you're in the vicinity, you can take a tour of the plant or go to the museum. You can see all the lathes working, and you'll be amazed that it takes as little as eight seconds to mold a bat. They'll even custom-make one for you with your own brand on it.

Mills Commission Report

In 1907, powerful sporting goods magnate ALBERT G. SPALDING created the Mills Commission ostensibly to examine the origins of baseball. In fact, the patriotic Spalding really just wanted to end all the "rumors" to the effect that baseball was not truly an American game. As he wrote, "While it is true that ball playing in many forms has been engaged in by most nations from time immemorial, it is a proven fact that the game now designated 'Base Ball' is of modern and purely American origin." Now that Spalding's mind had been made up, there was the little matter of those pesky "facts." So the commission, headed by A. G. Mills, who had succeeded WILLIAM HULBERT as president of the National League in 1882, scoured the land for someone who could provide them. They somehow found an elderly mining engineer named Abner Graves who claimed he was on hand the day a West Point cadet named ABNER DOUBLEDAY laid out the bases and positioned the fielders in a configuration like that of baseball. The many holes in Graves's claim can be found elsewhere in this book. Despite the obvious falsehoods, here is what the report found, in part:

> First—That Base Ball had its origin in the United States;

> Second—That the first scheme for playing it, according to the best evidence obtainable to date, was devised by Abner Doubleday, at Cooperstown, New York in 1839.

After these findings went public, the son of ALEXANDER CARTWRIGHT protested to Spalding that his father, who headed the NEW YORK KNICKERBOCKERS, should receive credit for the invention of the game. The young Cartwright was so successful that today almost all modern fans who give it any thought believe the Cartwright story (although a few—*I'm looking at you,* BUD SELIG—still think Doubleday had something to do with it). But as author John Thorn demonstrated in a chapter from *Total Baseball* called "The True Father of Baseball," the Cartwright story is also incorrect. Thorn gives the lion's share of the credit to DANIEL "DOC" ADAMS.

"Miracle Braves"

One of the first "miracle teams," the Braves of 1914 were a ragtag bunch of aging veterans and unknown kids. They'd finished 31-1/2 games out of first place in 1913, and were languishing in last place on July 18 the following season. But then they won 60 of their last 76 games (!)—one of the most amazing runs in the history of baseball—and captured the pennant by 10-1/2 games. In the World Series, they faced the mighty Athletics, winners of four AL titles in the previous five years. True to the fairy tale finish, the Braves swept the stunned A's in four straight. Their biggest star, Johnny Evers, captured the league's CHALMERS AWARD, and the team rewarded itself with a new ballpark the following season. Alas, despite the new home, the magic had disappeared. The Braves finished second in 1915, then third—a position in the standings they wouldn't reach again until after World War II.

"Miracle Mets"

Like the "MIRACLE BRAVES," the 1969 "Miracle Mets" shocked the baseball world with an amazing pennant run. The Mets franchise had been born in 1962 as the worst team of the 20th century, losing a record 120 games. Their next six seasons weren't much better, but in 1968 they did show some promise by climbing out of the cellar to finish ninth out of ten. Nobody expected the Mets to go anywhere in 1969, the first year of divisional play. But ace TOM SEAVER won 25 games to lead the league, and the team's pitching staff as a whole finished tops in the NL with a 2.99 ERA. Though just ordinary offensively, they had enough clutch performers that the Mets won 38 of their final 49 games and notched exactly 100 victories. They beat the Braves in the League Championship Series, and then faced the Baltimore Orioles in the World Series. Those Orioles were regarded as the greatest team in recent years. But they couldn't stop the miracle. Thanks to some big fielding plays and timely hitting, the Mets beat the O's in five games—cementing the 1969 Mets' position in baseball folklore.

Mitchell Report

The infamous report on steroid use in major league baseball, written by former U.S. Senator George Mitchell after a multiyear investigation. The report named 89 players as users of illegal performance-enhancing drugs (PEDs), including such stars as ROGER CLEMENS, BARRY BONDS, and Jason Giambi. And like everything else about the

PED scandal, it's depressing and incomplete. We still don't know how widespread PEDs were during the 1990s and early 2000s because no player was given immunity from punishment for speaking to Mitchell, and without such assurances, the union advised players not to participate. Only FRANK THOMAS, a vocal opponent of PED use, and Giambi cooperated with the investigation—and in Giambi's case, it was probably only because he was already involved in the BALCO CASE and had admitted to PED use in a grand jury hearing.

Available for a free download from the MLB.com website (but really, why would you want to?), the Mitchell Report runs 400 pages and includes lots of hoary accusations of players sending cash payments to dealers and getting shot up with PEDs in the locker room, and of team officials looking the other way even in the face of hard evidence of PED use. Nobody comes out looking good. Thankfully, the steroid days appear to be mostly over. Sure, there are drug test violations and occasional suspensions, but it's not the scourge it was around the turn of the 21st century.

Moneyball
Written by Michael Lewis
(W. W. Norton and Company, 2004)

The most important baseball book of the past 20 years, *Moneyball* traces the success of the BILLY BEANE-led Oakland A's from 2000 to 2003, when the club boasted one of the lowest payrolls but the highest winning percentage in the league. There is so much misinformation out there about what a "moneyball" team really does that every fan owes it to himself or herself to actually read the book. The way I understand it, "moneyball" doesn't mean that a team has to focus on one particular statistic such as on-base percentage or strikeout-to-walk ratio. Rather, it means that a team tries to exploit market inefficiencies to find undervalued commodities and get rid of overvalued commodities. For example, Beane believed closers were overvalued relative to their contributions to a club, so he would pick up a hard-thrower off baseball's scrap heap and hand him the closer role; if the pitcher succeeded, other teams might want him and he could be traded for more valuable assets. One might think that, because the A's never won a World Series, Beane's philosophy has been discredited. I believe just the opposite: that Beane was so successful (albeit unlucky in the post-season), front office executives throughout baseball started copying him and made it more difficult for him to find the inefficiencies he sought.

"Murderer's Row"

Nickname for the 1927 Yankees, who featured power up and down the lineup: BABE RUTH, LOU GEHRIG, Tony Lazzeri, Earle Combs—all of whom made it to the Hall of Fame—as well as a deadly pitching staff featuring Hall of Famers Waite Hoyt and Herb Pennock. The '27 team won 110 games in the regular season, then demolished Pittsburgh in the World Series in four straight games. Interestingly, the term "Murderer's Row"—which comes from the mythical death row in a prison filled with murderers awaiting execution—had been applied to a number of teams before 1927. But once Babe Ruth stepped in, the term became his team's alone.

"Mustache Gang"

One of CHARLIE FINLEY'S greatest strengths as an owner and businessman was his ability to generate publicity out of nothing. The "Mustache Gang" was an example. In the early 1970s, he gave bonuses to any A's players who would grow mustaches. In almost any other line of work, it wouldn't have been a big deal, but at the time, many teams forbade players to grow facial hair as a matter of policy. ROLLIE FINGERS, CATFISH HUNTER, REGGIE JACKSON, Joe Rudi, and other teammates took Finley's money, and the team became known as the "Mustache Gang." They would be forgotten today if they hadn't won three straight World Series from 1972 to 1974.

national pastime, the

Although baseball evolved in the mid-19th century from the British games CRICKET and ROUNDERS, people almost immediately bestowed upon the sport the mantle of "America's national pastime"; probably the first journalist to do so was William Trotter Porter, who ran *Spirit of the Times*, a leading sports journal. Poet Walt Whitman would say, "I see great things in baseball. It's our game—the American game. It will take our people out of doors, fill them with oxygen, give them a larger physical stoicism. Tend to relieve us from being a nervous, dyspeptic set. Repair losses and be a blessing to us." Famed historian Jacques Barzun had this to say: "Whoever would understand the hearts and minds of America had better learn baseball." And President Herbert Hoover said, "Next to religion, baseball has had a greater impact on the American people than any other institution."

The Natural
Written by Bernard Malamud
(Harcourt, 1952)

This classic baseball novel was made into an Oscar-nominated film starring Robert Redford in 1984. It's about the fairy tale life of Roy Hobbs, an aging outfielder with a sweet swing who makes it to the majors for one glorious season. The book has some dark and ominous twists, while the movie version changes the ending and lightens the mood. "It may or may not be a good picture, but it... certainly isn't my book," Malamud asserted. The movie version of *The Natural* is full of sentiment and schmaltz, but it's fun throughout. Not all viewers share my opinion.

Nice Guys Finish Last
Written by Leo Durocher (with Ed Linn)
(Simon and Schuster, 1975)

Generally regarded as one of the best baseball autobiographies, this work remains a classic. In it, you can read Leo's side of 50 years of chaos and controversies, including his explanation of the title; in this book, you can read the explanation under the LEO DUROCHER entry.

nicknames

Even though few players have creative nicknames today (first letter/ first part of last name is about as creative as it gets: A-Rod, K-Rod, etc.), baseball history is brimming with great ones. Throughout this book, next to a player's name, I've included a nickname if it's appropriate. Here's a sampling of great nicknames for some other players:

"Sudden" Sam McDowell
"Smiling" Mickey Welch
"Bollicky" Billy Taylor
"Laughing" Larry Doyle
"Grunting" Jim Shaw
"Poosh 'Em Up" Tony Lazzeri
"Daffy" Dean (Dizzy's brother)
Bob Ferguson, "Death to Flying Things"
Pepper Martin, "The Wild Horse of the Osage"
Arlie Latham, "The Freshest Man on Earth"
Red Lucas, "The Nashville Narcissus"
Lou Novikoff, "The Mad Russian"
Russ Meyer, "The Mad Monk"

Eddie Yost, "The Walking Man" (check out his yearly walk totals)

Sal Maglie, "The Barber"

Camilo Pascual, "The Little Potato"

Lou Skizas, "The Nervous Greek"

Jimmie Wynn, "The Toy Cannon"

Dick Radatz, "The Monster"

Phil Regan, "The Vulture"

Dennis "Oil Can" Boyd

Hughie "Ee-Yah" Jennings

Odell "Bad News" Hale

Jim "Bad News" Galloway

Hazen "Kiki" Cuyler (pronounced "kai-kai," not "kee-kee")

George "Twinkletoes" Selkirk

Eric "Boob" McNair

Hugh "Losing Pitcher" Mulcahy

Walter "Boom Boom" Beck (one "boom" for the sound of a batter connecting with one of Beck's pitches, the other "boom" for the sound of the ball hitting the outfield wall)

Lynn "Line Drive" Nelson (a pitcher, not a hitter)

Johnny "Grandma" Murphy

Eddie "The Brat" Stanky

Jim "Abba Dabba" Tobin

Walter "No-Neck" Williams

Frank "Hondo" Howard

Jim "Mudcat" Grant

Jack "The Ripper" Clark

Ray Schalk, "Cracker"

Ernie Lombardi, "Schnozz"

Mike Epstein, "Superjew"

Many Native Americans were nicknamed "Chief"

$100,000 Infield

The Philadelphia Athletics' famed infield from 1911 to 1914, consisting of first baseman Stuffy McInnis, second baseman EDDIE COLLINS, shortstop Jack Barry, and third baseman HOME RUN BAKER. Together, they helped CONNIE MACK'S A's to three pennants and two championships in four years. The $100,000 referred not to what they were paid in those days of the oppressive RESERVE CLAUSE, but rather what they would have been worth to A's ownership if they had been sold on the open market (and don't think that idea hadn't occurred to Mack, who was notorious for periodic "housecleanings" where he would dismantle a team to raise quick cash). Much later, Baker and Collins—as well as Mack—would be reunited in the Hall of Fame.

Only the Ball Was White
Written by Robert Peterson
(Prentice Hall, 1970)
The first serious book about the NEGRO LEAGUES. When Peterson published this book, the Negro leagues were a part of baseball history that, like its great players, had been shunted to the fringes. Peterson succeeded in raising awareness about black baseball, and he helped get the Hall of Fame to start including Negro leaguers. Today, Peterson's book is out of date in many places, and other books—notably the ones by John B. Holway—have done more to set the record straight. But as an introduction to the players and the time, you can't go wrong with *Only the Ball Was White*.

Pride of the Yankees
The famous 1942 movie about LOU GEHRIG starring Gary Cooper as Gehrig and Teresa Wright as his wife Eleanor. It's a great piece of Hollywood, and some of it is actually true, telling the emotional story of the son of immigrants who makes it big in New York, then is struck down by a horrible, debilitating disease (*see* LOU GEHRIG'S DISEASE). Like most movies of that period, it's over-dramatic and overacted at times, but it's great entertainment.

"rabbit ball"/"juiced ball"
The "rabbit ball" or "juiced ball" theory is the conspiracy theory that tries to explain why batting and home run totals go up in a given year. Simply put, there is no evidence that the "rabbit ball" (so named because it hops off the bat) has ever existed. I don't know how much more forcefully I can say it. In 1987, for example, home run totals increased by 14.5 percent, and fans, players, and the media cried that the leagues had surreptitiously introduced a new "juiced" ball. But other than the batting totals, they had absolutely no evidence—no confession from a disgruntled RAWLINGS COMPANY employee, no leaks from the commissioner's office, no legitimate results from an investigation, no tests showing that the ball used in 1987 was any different from that used in 1986.

The exact same allegations sprang up in the 1920s to explain the tremendous batting successes of BABE RUTH, ROGERS HORNSBY, and others. And they've come up at various other times in baseball history, most recently in 1994 and again in 2000. (*See* LIVELY BALL ERA for a discussion of the 1920s batting revolution.) The truth is, however, that only three times in this century has the ball been altered: in 1910 with the introduction of the cork center, in 1926 when the cushioned cork center was invented, and in 1974 when the manufacturer switched from horsehide to cowhide. Only the first of those moves really affected major league batting totals.

But in the absence of evidence, conspiracy theorists like to create some. They claim that the ball is being manufactured differently, either secretly or at the behest of baseball officials. Ridiculous, a Rawlings spokesperson told me: "The balls we manufacture are the most consistent baseballs ever manufactured. And test results prove it." The balls weigh the same and have the same measurements as always.

One sub-theory is that the ball is "wound tighter." But if you wind the yarn tighter, then it stands to reason that you either have to make the balls smaller or you have to add more yarn to fill the existing size, which would make the ball heavier and negate the whole purpose of the tighter winding. In either case, the whole design of the baseballs would have to change, as well as the manufacturing process. Rawlings has not done that.

In spring 2000, major league baseball officials even toured the Rawlings plant to see how things worked, and they came away with the same conclusion: The ball is not the issue. Some possible explanations include the use of performance-enhancing drugs, the quality of pitching, especially in an expansion year, a smaller strike zone, and the predominant weather in league cities; home runs are easier to hit in hot weather than in cool weather. There are, in fact, quite a few legitimate theories for increased batting totals, many related to physics. But a "rabbit ball" isn't one of them.

Rawlings Company

The company that manufactures balls, gloves, uniforms, bats, helmets, and other equipment used by major league baseball teams as well as equipment for other sports. Founded by George and Alfred Rawlings, the company opened its doors in 1887 as a general sporting goods company, selling mainly hunting and fishing equipment. In

1906, the St. Louis Cardinals became the first team to contract with Rawlings for uniforms. In the 1910s, the company first began supplying major leaguers with gloves, and today, more major leaguers use Rawlings gloves than any other (*see also* GLOVE). Capitalizing on its standing as the premier glove manufacturer, Rawlings began sponsoring the GOLD GLOVE AWARD in 1957, the trophy for fielding excellence as selected by a panel of managers and coaches. Since 1977, Rawlings has supplied all the balls to major league baseball—totaling more than 60,000 dozen per year, all manufactured at a plant in Turrailba, Costa Rica.

Now and again, the Rawlings Company (which is a subsidiary of Jarden Corporation) is accused of "juicing" the baseball to help batting totals. But the idea that a publicly traded company—which has to answer to its shareholders, contractors, and the public at large—would engage in such a deception is patently ludicrous; *see* "RABBIT BALL" for more.

Reach Company

The first big baseball-related sporting goods company, Reach was founded by Ben Shibe, who went on to the own the Philadelphia A's, and A. J. Reach, an English-born baseball star of the mid-19th century. Reach standardized the manufacture of baseballs and earned the first contract to supply balls to the National League in 1876. Interestingly, the contract called for Reach to provide the balls free of charge; the company was banking that the title "official baseball of the National League" would give them some marketing clout over the competition. Then its biggest competitor, the SPALDING SPORTING GOODS COMPANY, began paying the League to use its baseballs, so Reach turned to the American Association. Little did people know that Spalding had actually contracted with Reach to produce the balls with the Spalding name on them.

In 1892, Reach was bought out by Spalding. As a marketing ploy, ALBERT SPALDING insisted that the buyout be kept secret and that Reach continue to manufacture and market products under its own label in direct competition with Spalding. When the American League was founded in 1901, AL president BAN JOHNSON offered Reach's Ben Shibe the contract to supply their baseballs if Shibe would back a Philadelphia franchise. Johnson may not have known at the time that Reach and Spalding were one and the same. In any case, Reach began an affiliation with the American League that lasted until

1976, when the RAWLINGS COMPANY took over. The funny thing is that for baseball's first century, countless writers and players throughout the years swore the balls were different. Actually, the only difference was the name on the ball and the color of the stitching: Reach ball stitches were red, Spalding blue.

Reach introduced baseball's two most significant innovations: the cork center in 1910 and the cushioned-cork center in 1926. The first change increased batting totals significantly; the second had no effect (*see* LIVELY BALL ERA).

retired jersey numbers

Here's a listing of some of baseball's most famous jersey numbers, all of which have been retired by the players' teams. One interesting thing about this list is that it offers insights into the choice of jersey numbers for some current players. For example, many young power hitters choose number 44 because of HANK AARON. STEVE CARLTON may have selected 32 because of that other talented left-hander, SANDY KOUFAX. Ruben Sierra and several other Puerto Rican players have worn number 21 to honor ROBERTO CLEMENTE. And speedy outfielders with power often wear number 24 in honor of WILLIE MAYS—such as KEN GRIFFEY, JR., when he played in Seattle and BARRY BONDS when he was with Pittsburgh.

No.	Player/Manager	Team(s)
1	BILLY MARTIN	Yankees
1	Pee Wee Reese	Dodgers
1	OZZIE SMITH	Cardinals
3	BABE RUTH	Yankees
3	Harmon Killebrew	Twins
4	LOU GEHRIG	Yankees
4	MEL OTT	Giants
5	JOE DIMAGGIO	Yankees
5	BROOKS ROBINSON	Orioles
5	JOHNNY BENCH	Reds
5	HANK GREENBERG	Tigers
5	GEORGE BRETT	Royals
6	Al Kaline	Tigers
6	STAN MUSIAL	Cardinals

7	MICKEY MANTLE	Yankees
8	YOGI BERRA	Yankees
8	JOE MORGAN	Reds
8	CARL YASTRZEMSKI	Red Sox
9	TED WILLIAMS	Red Sox
9, 44	REGGIE JACKSON	A's, Yankees
14	ERNIE BANKS	Cubs
17	DIZZY DEAN	Cardinals
19	BOB FELLER	Indians
20	MIKE SCHMIDT	Phillies
21	ROBERTO CLEMENTE	Pirates
21	WARREN SPAHN	Braves
24	WILLIE MAYS	Giants
30, 34	NOLAN RYAN	Angels, Rangers, Astros
32	SANDY KOUFAX	Dodgers
32	STEVE CARLTON	Phillies
33	HONUS WAGNER	Pirates*
37	CASEY STENGEL	Yankees, Mets
39	ROY CAMPANELLA	Dodgers
41	TOM SEAVER	Mets
42	JACKIE ROBINSON	Dodgers, MLB**
44	HANK AARON	Braves, Brewers
44	WILLIE MCCOVEY	Giants
45	BOB GIBSON	Cardinals
72	Carlton Fisk	White Sox

*Honus Wagner didn't actually wear a number on his jersey while an active player. The #33 is what he wore as a Pirates coach much later in life.

**In 1997, the 50th anniversary of the breaking of the color barrier, major league baseball decided to retire Jackie Robinson's 42 in perpetuity for all ball clubs. It was a surprising and entirely appropriate tribute to Robinson as both a ballplayer and a hero. Every ballpark now honors Robinson with a blue number 42.

Retrosheet

An organization that's doing some of the best research a fan of baseball history could ask for: its volunteers are compiling box scores and play-by-play data for every game in major league history and making the information available free to view on the web and download for your own use. I was surprised to learn that, until Retrosheet, there was very little game-level information for about the first 75 to 100 years of baseball history. At this writing in 2011, the Retrosheet team has published game logs going back to 1871, box scores going back to about 1920, and play-by-play data to about 1950. And they're continuing to augment the data, so who knows what they'll uncover in a few years. It truly is a bonanza for baseball historians and buffs.

Rotisserie League

Name of the first FANTASY BASEBALL LEAGUE, invented in 1979 at a now-defunct New York restaurant called La Rotisserie Francais. Six baseball fans, including authors DAN OKRENT and Steve Wulf, invented the game that, over the next three decades, would sweep America and permeate every other professional team sport.

rounders

One of the games from which baseball evolved (CRICKET is the other), rounders was invented in England and has been played for centuries. It's played with a bat, a soft, rubbery ball, and three "bases," which are actually four-foot sticks poking out of the ground, between two teams of eight or more players. There's no foul territory. Batters are put out when the defense catches the batted ball on the fly or on one bounce or when a defensive player hits a runner with the ball when he's running to a base. The team bats until all its members are retired, then they switch sides. It's a great game for people of all ages because it doesn't require loads of skill. Pitchers don't throw fast—they just toss it in—and batters are only expected to make contact, not drive the ball 350 feet.

"Say hey!"

WILLIE MAYS'S trademark saying. He had a personalized license plate with those words, and he titled his autobiography *Say Hey!*

"Say it ain't so, Joe"

The alleged cry made by a youngster to "SHOELESS" JOE JACKSON as Jackson made his way from the courthouse after testifying before a Chicago grand jury in the early stages of the 1919 BLACK SOX SCANDAL. Although it makes for a good story, this probably never happened. Reporters of that time would often embellish their stories, and perhaps a child within earshot of a journalist shouted something— perhaps "It ain't true, is it, Joe?"—from the crowd, but Jackson said he never heard it. "I guess the biggest joke of all," Jackson later told a reporter, "was that story that got out about 'Say it ain't so, Joe.' It was supposed to have happened... when I came out of the courtroom. There weren't any words passed between anybody except me and a deputy sheriff.... He asked me for a ride and we got in the car together and left. There was a big crowd hanging around in front of the building, but nobody else said anything to me."

Society for American Baseball Research (SABR)

Founded in 1971 by Bob Davids, SABR (pronounced "saber") is baseball's premier research organization. Each year, they publish numerous research journals and other books containing articles about baseball history—usually a previously unknown research topic or unremembered part of history. They also hold a yearly convention in a major league city with guest speakers, contests, and other big events. Clearly, SABR has significantly advanced the research of the game's history. Memberships cost just $65 a year, which includes its yearly publications, discounts on baseball books, and more. If you want to join, visit SABR on the Internet at http://www.sabr.org.

Spalding Sporting Goods Company

Founded by ALBERT SPALDING while still enjoying a successful and popular career in baseball—first as a pitcher, then as a manager—the Spalding Company ruled the American sporting goods market in the late 19th century. With Spalding's name, the company marketed bats, balls, uniforms, gloves, and equipment for every other sport. In fact, as William Curran makes clear in his book *Big Sticks*, Spalding licensed the manufacture of that equipment to other companies, putting his name on the finished product as a marketing gimmick. Then he began to buy out his competitors but let their products "compete" with his (*see* REACH COMPANY). Today, that might be grounds for an antitrust lawsuit. In the 1890s, it was good business.

Spalding, of course, diversified the company into other sports, introducing the world's first basketball in 1894 as well as the first American football, golf club, golf ball, and tennis ball. Now affiliated with the Even-Flo baby products company, Chicopee, Massachusetts–based Spalding is a billion-dollar company.

The Sporting News

Founded in 1886 by Canadian-born Al Spink, TSN became known as the "Bible of Baseball" because of its in-depth coverage of the sport, including editorials, feature stories, team notes, and complete box scores through much of the publication's history. As part-owner of St. Louis's Sportsman's Park, Spink and his partners tried to lure a major league team to his city. They succeeded in getting the Browns of the AMERICAN ASSOCIATION to moved in, then Spink set about to compete with baseball's other weekly publication, Francis Richter's *The Sporting Life*. After just three years, Spink's weekly surpassed TSL in both circulation and advertising dollars.

It was a true family affair as brothers, sons, a sister-in-law, and, later, grandsons joined the organization. What really helped the paper succeed, however, was the reporting by such luminaries as Ring Lardner and Fred Lieb; many of America's best baseball writers wrote for TSN. Even though TSN covered other sports, baseball was always its number one priority. But after World War II, as professional football and basketball gained popularity, TSN began devoting nearly equal time to a variety of activities under the direction of the publication's most illustrious and forward-thinking leader, J. G. Taylor Spink. He also helped create the GOLD GLOVE AWARD. With Spink at the helm, TSN also entered the book publishing business with yearly preseason guides, record books, and histories.

Today, TSN is an all-purpose sports weekly and website that still offers comprehensive baseball coverage—without the box scores, which they eliminated a number of years ago. The Hall of Fame even offers the J. G. Taylor Spink Award "for meritorious contributions to baseball writing," whose recipients include RED SMITH, Jim Murray, Damon Runyon, Grantland Rice, and dozens of others.

spring training

The two-month tune-up players go through every year before the season starts. As you no doubt already know, spring training actually starts in February, when pitchers and catchers report. Other players arrive at their teams' camps in Florida or Arizona over the next few weeks, although there are always a few holdouts unhappy with their contracts or players stuck in their home countries with visa problems. For a long time, Florida, where spring training originated, hosted the lion's share of major league clubs, who played in what's called the GRAPEFRUIT LEAGUE, with the rest of the teams based in Arizona's CACTUS LEAGUE. However, in recent years, many clubs have moved west, and so there are now 15 clubs in each state.

Spring training traces it roots to 1870, when, according to HAROLD SEYMOUR'S *Baseball: The Early Years*, the Chicago and Cincinnati clubs started formal camps in Louisiana. Florida hosted its first spring training in 1888. Once it was just a way for players to get warmed up for the season. Now, spring training has become a real money-making tool for clubs, and cities have been constructing new ballparks to entice clubs to shift their home base.

Stengelese

The peculiar brand of double-talk and hilarious verbiage uttered by CASEY STENGEL, Hall of Fame manager and noted linguist. Casey wasn't a buffoon. He was a great story-teller who loved to make people laugh. Here's a sampling of his memorable words:

- "I don't know if he throws a spitball, but he sure spits on the ball."
- "I was pitching batting practice and they told me not to throw so hard. I wanted to impress the manager, so I threw as hard as I could. Then hitters commenced hitting balls over buildings. Then I threw harder and they hit the ball harder. Then, I told the manager I was really an outfielder."
- "If we're going to win the pennant, we've got to start thinking we're not as good as we think we are."
- "The secret of managing is to keep the guys who hate you away from the guys who are undecided."
- "Most people my age are dead."
- "They say some of my stars drink whiskey, but I have found that the ones who drink milkshakes don't win many ballgames."
- "When a fielder gets a pitcher into trouble, the pitcher has to pitch himself out of a slump he isn't in."
- "There comes a time in every man's life, and I've had plenty of them." (The quote that appears on his gravestone.)

- "You could look it up." (His most quoted line.)

stickball

A game played mostly in big cities using a stick or broom handle for a bat and a small rubber ball. Since it's played on the streets between big buildings, the players have to come up with a unique set of ground rules regarding foul ground and extra base hits. A lot of major leaguers grew up on stickball, and in more innocent times, some stars—WILLIE MAYS among them—were known to play the game with neighborhood kids even after they'd made the majors.

Strat-O-Matic

One of the most realistic and comprehensive baseball board games, Strat-O-Matic celebrated its 50th birthday in 2011 and still has legions of fans. Created by Hal Richman, Strat-O-Matic is a cards and dice game that simulates almost every element of a baseball game. Armed with a set of cards, fans can replay entire seasons of baseball and create their own dramatic moments. It started as a baseball board game and has expanded to football, hockey, and basketball and offers both offline and online versions. It's a great fun, and it's not just for kids.

Subway Series

A World Series played between New York teams, so that travel could theoretically be done by subway. There have been 14 Subway Series and three other World Series between teams from the same metropolitan areas, also called City Series or, in the case of the Giants and A's in 1989, the Bay Bridge Series. The following table lists the teams and winners:

Year	Winner	Loser
1906	White Sox	Cubs
1921	Giants	Yankees
1922	Giants	Yankees
1923	Yankees	Giants
1936	Yankees	Giants
1937	Yankees	Giants
1941	Yankees	Dodgers

1944	Cardinals	Browns
1947	Yankees	Dodgers
1949	Yankees	Dodgers
1951	Yankees	Giants
1952	Yankees	Dodgers
1953	Yankees	Dodgers
1955	Dodgers	Yankees
1956	Yankees	Dodgers
1989	Athletics	Giants
2000	Yankees	Mets

"Subway Series" also describes preseason exhibition and interleague series between the two New York teams. Most other teams that have nearby neighbors have similar series; in Los Angeles, for example, the games between the Dodgers and Angels are called the Freeway Series.

"Take Me Out to the Ball Game"

Written by Jack Norworth, the same person who wrote "Shine on Harvest Moon," "Take Me Out to the Ball Game" became baseball's anthem shortly after its publication in 1908. This song is sung in every major league park during the seventh-inning stretch. In KEN BURNS'S *BASEBALL* documentary on PBS, he played more than 200 versions of the song.

30-30 Club

A mythical club for any player who slugs 30 homers and steals 30 bases in one season. Ken Williams of the St. Louis Browns first earned the distinction in 1922, but nobody remembers him. It took WILLIE MAYS and Bobby Bonds to make 30-30 famous. But because so many players—from Howard Johnson to Brandon Phillips—have entered the club since the mid-1980s, it has lost quite a bit of its exclusivity. A much more exclusive club is 40-40, with only four members: JOSE CANSECO, BARRY BONDS, ALEX RODRIGUEZ, and Alfonso Soriano.

Tinker to Evers to Chance

The infield double play combination of the Chicago Cubs from 1903 to 1910. Made famous by Franklin P. Adams's poem "BASEBALL'S

SAD LEXICON," the trio of Joe Tinker, Johnny Evers, and Frank Chance (with Harry Steinfeldt at third base) led the Cubs to four pennants and two World Series victories. All three are in the Hall of Fame, but how good were they? Adams seems to have thought they were something special. But maybe it was just because the Cubs' pennants came at the expense of Adams's Giants. Let's look at the stats. From 1903 to 1910, the Cubs as a team never led the league in double plays, and only once did they lead the league in the percentage of double plays turned per baserunner allowed. Strong argument for calling T–E–C overrated—an opinion that many baseball fans now hold.

But let's look at the big picture. The Cubs' pitching staff was always or nearly always the best in the league. During that eight-year period, they led the league in team ERA six times (with a low of 1.73), in lowest opponents' batting average seven times (low of .207), and in lowest opponents' on-base percentage six times (low of .272). Since batters rarely got on base, the double play combo got few chances to record a DP. And even when they did allow baserunners, the opposing team's manager knew he was going to have a tough time scoring them against such stingy pitchers. What would he do? Sacrifice. Steal a base. Hit and run. Anything he could to get that man to second base and avoid the double play. That's the way baseball was played during the DEAD BALL ERA. You can't fault Tinker, Evers, and Chance for failing to turn the DP when they probably got so few opportunities.

So maybe, Tinker to Evers to Chance was not the world's greatest double play combination. But they won all those pennants—they had to be pretty damn good. What was the greatest double play combination in terms of fielding prowess? Impossible to say, but I can name some contenders. The 1999 Mets had a pretty good one: Rey Ordoñez to Edgardo Alfonzo to John Olerud. The 1984 Tigers had Alan Trammell to Lou Whitaker to Darrell Evans. The White Sox of the 1950s had LUIS APARICIO to Nellie Fox to Earle Torgeson. And the Dodgers of that same era had Pee Wee Reese to JACKIE ROBINSON to Gil Hodges.

Topps Company

The chewing gum company that grew into the nation's preeminent BASEBALL CARD manufacturer. Topps was founded in 1938 by Abram, Ira, Philip, and Joseph Shorin, who at first marketed regular gum and then, after the war, Bazooka bubblegum. In 1951, the company put out its first set of baseball cards—two individual 52-card sets designed to be used in some kind of game. The next year, they released a 407-card set with player stats and personal information similar to the cards sold today. That set, which contains rookie cards of both MICKEY MANTLE and WILLIE MAYS, is today worth hundreds of thousands in good condition; the Mantle card alone has sold for as much as $275,000 in mint condition.

Topps wasn't the first card manufacturer. Tobacco companies sold cards with players' pictures on them for many years, and right after the war, the Bowman Company marketed baseball cards. In fact, Bowman competed with Topps until 1955, when Topps bought them out. For the next 25 years, Topps held a monopoly on the product, and the company became synonymous with bubble gum cards of all types, including other sports and even cards relating to movies and music groups. In 1981, two competitors entered the market: Fleer and Donruss. Their cards also included sticks of bubblegum inside their packs. Topps sued over patent infringement, claiming that other companies weren't allowed to sell sports cards with gum. Fleer and Donruss simply took the gum out of the packs and avoided the lawsuit.

Over the next decade, several other card manufacturers—including Upper Deck, perhaps the most successful of the bunch—entered the market, and card collecting became a business rather than a quaint hobby. Where once there was only a single card set issued each year, there now are more than 30 sets and subsets from nearly a dozen manufacturers. In addition, there are numerous magazines devoted to sports cards, many of them published by card guru JAMES BECKETT. Topps alone says that it distributes over a billion cards each year.

"Van Lingle Mungo"

For my money, this is the most interesting and fun baseball song of them all. Written by jazz musician Dave Frishberg in 1969, the song consists solely of the mellifluous names of old ballplayers—including Bob Estalella, ROY CAMPANELLA, Danny Gardella, and more—set to a jazzy tune. Van Lingle Mungo himself was a mediocre pitcher from the 1930s who would be largely forgotten today were it not for Frishberg's song. Frishberg likes to tells a story of the day he and Mungo appeared together on the Dick Cavett Show, where Frishberg was asked to sing the song. "Backstage," says Frishberg, "Mungo asked me when he would see some remuneration for the song. When he heard my explanation about how there was unlikely to be any remuneration for anyone connected with the song, least of all him, he was genuinely downcast. 'But it's my name,' he said. I told him, 'The only way you can get even is to go home and write a song called Dave Frishberg.' He laughed, and when we said goodbye he said, 'I'm gonna do it! I'm gonna do it!'"

You can buy this song online. You'll love it.

Veeck as in Wreck
Written by Bill Veeck
(New York: G. P. Putnam, 1962)
BILL VEECK'S wonderful, critically acclaimed autobiography, *Veeck as in Wreck* tells the story of a master showman, perhaps the most innovative baseball executive ever. Unlike most owners of his day, Veeck set out to bring entertainment—not just baseball—to the masses. He loved to stage promotions and publicity stunts; his signing of midget EDDIE GAEDEL is his most famous, but the book tells of a dozen more. His freewheeling attitude angered the Establishment, and you can read about that, too. After nearly 50 years, the book is still worth owning.

"Wait till next year!"
The perennial cry of an also-ran. Brooklyn Dodger fans are most famous for this wail because from 1941 through 1953, they lost five World Series to the mighty Yankees. The Dodgers finally beat the Yanks in the 1955 WORLD SERIES, but when they lost again a year later, Dodger fans chanted, "Wait till *last* year!"

"Whiz Kids"
Nickname of the 1950 Phillies, who won the National League pennant with a starting lineup of players all around 30 years old or younger. With Robin Roberts, Curt Simmons, and MVP Jim Konstanty on the mound and Richie Ashburn, Del Ennis, and Eddie Waitkus in the field, the Kids squeezed past the Dodgers by two games to win the pennant but lost the World Series to the Yankees in four straight. Years later, the 1983 Phillies marched to the pennant with a band of aging veterans led by PETE ROSE, JOE MORGAN, Tony Perez, and STEVE CARLTON. They were called the "Wheeze Kids."

"Who's on First?"

The great comedy routine made famous by Abbott and Costello. If you've never heard it, there's no way this book can do it justice, because even after several listenings, it's still really funny. The premise is that Abbott is the manager of a team and Costello wants to join as a catcher, but before that, he has to learn the players' names. Here's the lineup:

> First base: Who
> Second base: What
> Third base: I Don't Know
> Shortstop: I Don't Care or I Don't Give a Damn
> Left Field: Why
> Center Field: Because
> Right Field: (not mentioned)
> Pitcher: Today
> Catcher: Tomorrow

After Abbott and Costello popularized it on the radio, they included the skit in their movie *The Naughty Nineties*.

"Willie, Mickey, or the Duke?"

The question much-discussed among New York City baseball fans in the 1950s. Nobody ever had to ask the first part: Who is the best center fielder? Based on both career stats and single-season highs, it's pretty clear that the real battle comes down to WILLIE MAYS or MICKEY MANTLE, with Duke Snider out of the running. But in the mid-1950s, the answer wasn't so simple. Although Mays and Mantle could steal bases, Snider led them all in homers and RBIs during the five years they played together. Defensively, Mays was spectacular but Mantle and Snider were near-perfect. In terms of pennants, Mantle won four, Snider three, and Mays two. In MVPs, Mantle captured two, Mays one, and Snider was shut out. The Willie-Mickey-Duke question is only one reason why New York City was the capital of baseball from the end of World War II until 1958.

Yogi-ism

A term for the various mangled sayings that purportedly came from the mouth of the great YOGI BERRA. For his baseball mind, the Hall of Fame catcher was a near genius. He played the most difficult defensive position flawlessly, and he managed several pennant winners.

But as a thinker... that's another story. Here are some choice quotes attributed to Mr. Berra:

- "Ninety percent of this game is half mental."
- "A nickel ain't worth a dime anymore."
- "If you can't imitate him, don't copy him."
- When asked his cap size in spring training: "I don't know. I'm not in shape yet."
- "You can observe a lot by watching."
- "We made too many wrong mistakes."
- "You've got to be careful if you don't know where you're going, because you might not get there."
- "It ain't over until it's over."

That last line is Berra's most famous, and he even titled his autobiography after it. But in his book *Yogi: It Ain't Over...*, he writes that he doesn't think he said "even 10 percent" of what has been attributed to him. He does admit to saying, "It ain't over until it's over."

7

RECORDS, STATISTICS & AWARDS

.366

TY COBB'S career batting average, the highest in baseball history. When he retired, he was believed to have batted .367, but after examining the records of Cobb's era, researchers have determined that Cobb was wrongly credited with a 2-for-3 game, and so Cobb's lifetime hits total were lowered from 4,191 to 4,189 and his batting average adjusted to .366 (*see* 1910 BATTING RACE).

For many years, major league baseball resisted such statistical changes. "The passage of 70 years," said commissioner BOWIE KUHN in 1981, "...constitutes a certain statute of limitation as to recognizing any changes in the records with confidence of the accuracy of such changes." In 1995, however, major league baseball changed its policy by endorsing the statistics book *Total Baseball*, which lists 4,189 and .366 as Cobb's official totals, among other changes. These kinds of revisions do strike a chord with baseball fans. "Some of these numbers acquire a kind of a poetry to them," Hall of Fame librarian Tim Wiles told The Wall Street Journal in 1995. "When somebody takes them away or changes them and says we've improved baseball record keeping, it's someone else's loss." But John Thorn, *Total Baseball's* co-editor at the time and now the Hall's historian, believes historical accuracy is more important. "To me," he says, "that's the equivalent of saying that if we disinterred Napoleon and found that contrary to all written reports he was not five-foot-two but six-foot-two, we should keep this a secret." I agree with Thorn, that truth should win out over fiction. Nevertheless, I think it's great that a controversy so trivial can stir up such passion among baseball fans.

.406

TED WILLIAMS'S batting average in 1941, the last time a player has batted over .400 for a season (*see* 1941: WILLIAMS AND DIMAGGIO THRILL BASEBALL). On the final day of the season, his batting average stood at .39955, which rounded up would have given him a .400 mark.* His manager asked Williams if he would like to sit out the team's double-header to protect his average. Williams refused. "If I'm going to be a .400 hitter," he said, "I want to have more than my toe-nails on the line." He responded with a 6 for 8 afternoon, raising his average to .406.

Can somebody do it again? In the 1990s, batting totals skyrocketed, but only one player mounted a serious assault on the .400 mark: Tony Gwynn, who was batting .394 when the 1994 STRIKE hit. I'm not going to predict that we'll never see another .400 hitter, but it seems awfully unlikely.

*But does rounding up really count? If you have 99 cents, you can't say you have a dollar. By the same token, .39955 is less than .400, so it shouldn't count, in my opinion. It's good Williams made the decision he did.

.426

Highest single-season batting average in the 20th century, achieved by NAPOLEON LAJOIE in 1901. This figure has been discounted in three ways: First, 1901 was the inaugural season of the American League, which had been a minor league the previous year, so the caliber of pitching was below that of the National League. Second, the AL had not yet adopted the foul strike rule, making it easier to get a hit. And third, the Macmillan *BASEBALL ENCYCLOPEDIA*, based on their inter-pretation of the statistics, credited Lajoie with a .422 average. If you go by that source, ROGERS HORNSBY has the century's highest batting mark, .424 in 1924.

.440

Highest single-season batting average in baseball history since the pitching mound was moved to its current distance of 60 feet six inches from home plate. Hugh Duffy achieved this mark in 1894, the second season after the mound was moved back from 50 feet (*see* 1894: THE PITCHERS MOVE BACK 10 FEET). As the pitchers adapted to the new distance, the entire National League batted .309. Duffy's high average wasn't a fluke; he also led the league in RBIs with 145 and tied in homers with 18. For this stellar season, the Boston outfielder received a salary increase of $12.50 per month ($310.89 in today's dollars).

0.96

This is the record for the lowest single-season ERA since the pitching mound was moved to its current distance of 60 feet six inches from home plate. Lefthander Dutch Leonard achieved this mark in 1914 while pitching for the Red Sox; in addition to the amazing ERA, Leonard had a 19–5 record and allowed just 139 hits in 224 innings pitched. Even for the DEAD BALL ERA, it was pretty impressive. In some record books, this statistic is listed as 1.01, which for a long time was considered the record. But after researching the season stats, the team from *Total Baseball* discovered some statistical anomalies and credited Leonard with 0.96.

1.12

Single-season ERA record for a pitcher with more than 300 innings, held by St. Louis's BOB GIBSON. In the 1968 SEASON, known as "The Year of the Pitcher," Gibson pitched the Cardinals to a pennant with a 22–9 won-loss record, only 7.4 baserunners per nine innings, and 268 strikeouts. It's easy to figure out how he won 22 games. The question is: How did he lose nine? Thanks to Retrosheet and Baseball-reference.com, it's easy to find out: Eight of his losses came when the Cardinals scored two or fewer runs; even still, his overall record in those games was 9–8, including four 1-0 shutout victories. When the Cards gave him three runs or more to work with, his record was an astounding 13–1. In games decided by one run, Gibson went 7–5 with two no-decisions.

7

Record number of no-hitters thrown by NOLAN RYAN, an unbreakable career record if ever one existed. As if any more proof is needed that Ryan was not a normal human being, he tossed the last two nonos when he was over 40 years old.

Here's a game log of all his no-hitters:

Date	Score	Key Stats
May 15, 1973	Angels 3, Royals 0	3 walks, 12 Ks
July 15, 1973	Angels 6, Tigers 0	4 walks, 17 Ks
Sept. 28, 1974	Angels 4, Twins 0	8 walks, 15 Ks
June 1, 1975	Angels 1, Orioles 0	4 walks, 9 Ks
Sept. 26, 1981	Astros 5, Dodgers 0	3 walks, 11 Ks
June 11, 1990	Rangers 5, A's 0	2 walks, 14 Ks
May 1, 1991	Rangers 3, Blue Jays 0	2 walks, 16 Ks

44

Number of games in PETE ROSE'S 1978 hitting streak, which tied the National League record originally set in 1897 by WEE WILLIE KEE-LER but was 12 short of JOE DIMAGGIO'S major league record (*see* 56).

56

Record number of consecutive games in JOE DIMAGGIO'S famous 1941 hitting streak (*see* 1941: WILLIAMS AND DIMAGGIO THRILL BASEBALL). DiMaggio batted .408 with 15 homers and 56 RBIs during The Streak, which lasted from May 15 to July 16. It was finally stopped in Cleveland by pitchers Al Smith and Jim Bagby in front of a crowd of 67,468, which at the time was the largest crowd ever to see a major league night game. Third baseman Ken Keltner made two great fielding plays to rob DiMaggio, and Bagby induced him to ground into an inning-ending double play in his last at bat. The failure may have cost DiMaggio a tidy sum of cash: He was supposedly in talks with the Heinz company to receive a $10,000 endorsement deal if he had extended the streak one more game (Heinz 57, get it?).

59

Number of consecutive scoreless innings pitched by Orel Hershiser in 1988, breaking DON DRYSDALE'S 20-year-old record of 58-2/3 innings. Hershiser set the mark during his last game of the season by pitching a 10-inning shutout. To give Hershiser the opportunity to break the record, the Dodger "offense" failed to score during the nine regulation innings. Coincidence? Or were they purposely trying not to score to let him set the record? We may never know

61

ROGER MARIS'S home run total for 1961, which stood as the single-season record until MARK MCGWIRE'S PED-fueled 1998 SEASON. Although Maris no longer holds the record, his pursuit of BABE RUTH'S then–34-year-old record remains one of baseball's more lamentable stories. Maris had joined the Yankees in a 1960 trade with Kansas City and quickly became one of the top players in baseball; he even won the 1960 MVP award with a 39-homer, 112-RBI season. But nothing portended the assault on the record the following year. He and teammate MICKEY MANTLE staged a year-long contest to see who would get there, much like McGwire and Sammy Sosa 37 years later.

But Maris had several things going against him, as far as Yankee fans and the rest of baseball were concerned: He was not nearly as popular as Mantle. He batted only .269. He had Mantle protecting him in the batting order (never mind that Ruth had LOU GEHRIG batting behind him). He did it against the diluted pitching of baseball's first expansion year. And worst of all, he did it in baseball's first 162-game season, eight games longer than the season in which Ruth had set the record (*see* ASTERISK). Yankee fans responded by alternately booing and cheering him, and the media coverage grew ever more intense and, at times, hostile—all of which drove Maris, a very private man, even further into his shell. MVP voters recognized his achievement when they awarded him the 1961 MVP Award not only for the 61 homers but also for his 142 RBIs and league-leading 132 runs. But for Maris, it wasn't enough. He lost much of his hair during that historic season; he admitted later that he also lost his spirit.

62

Single-season record for saves, set by Francisco "K-Rod" Rodriguez in 2008, surpassing Bobby Thigpen's previous record of 57. How did he do it? The Angels played in 110 games decided by three or fewer runs and won 71 of them—totals that not only led the league in 2008 but also were the highest totals in a decade. If anyone's going to break K-Rod's record, they're going to need a lot of luck.

70

The monumental home run total reached by MARK MCGWIRE during his magical (at the time) 1998 SEASON. McGwire bested ROGER MARIS'S record of 61 by nearly a 15 percent margin (*see* 61). To put that in perspective, a pitcher would have to notch 440 strikeouts or a hitter 218 RBIs to break those single-season records by the same percentage margin. McGwire hit his first home run of the season off Ramon Martinez of the Dodgers on March 31, then averaged one every 7.27 at bats for the rest of the campaign. Home run number 62, the one that broke the record, came off Steve Trachsel of the Cubs on September 8. Then, like a world-class sprinter, McGwire finished the season with a strong kick: five home runs in the final weekend, with home run number 70 off Montreal's Carl Pavano on September 27. McGwire did it with the national media spotlight shining on him at every turn, with Sammy Sosa riding on his tail, and with pitchers so afraid of him that they walked him 162 times, which was the second-highest total in history to that point.

73

The current single-season record for home runs, set by BARRY BONDS during his incredible but steroid-tainted 2001 CAMPAIGN. During that wondrous season, Bonds bested MARK MCGWIRE'S previous record by three home runs (73-70) and surpassed BABE RUTH'S 80-year-old record for slugging percentage by 16 points (.863-.847)... all while drawing 177 walks, which was also a record (soon to be shattered by Bonds himself)

Bonds saved the record-breaking homers for the Giants' archrivals, the Los Angeles Dodgers, who came to San Francisco for a three-game series to end the season. Number 71 came off starter Chan Ho Park in the first inning of game 1. He followed that with number 72 in the third, also off Park.

Two games later, he launched home run number 73 into the right field pavilion off the Dodgers' Dennis Springer. That ball became the stuff of legend, not just because of the record. In the stands, Giants fan Patrick Hayashi emerged from a scrum with the ball in his hands, and he immediately became famous around the country. But then another fan, Alex Popov, claimed that the ball had been grabbed from his mitt. Video evidence seemed to support Popov's position, and, as is the American way, a legal tussle ensued. Just about every objective observer believed that the ball should be sold at auction and the proceeds split 50/50. Instead both Popov and Hayashi insisted on going to court, where a judge ruled... you guessed it... that the ball should be sold at auction and the proceeds split 50/50! To make matters worse, the ball ended up selling for much less than the $3 million a collector had paid for Mark McGwire's 70th home run ball, and it's doubtful that the proceeds even covered Hayashi's and Popov's legal costs.

130

RICKEY HENDERSON'S stolen base total in 1982, the single-season record. While breaking Lou Brock's previous record by 13 steals, Henderson also had the dubious distinction of getting caught trying to steal 42 times—a modern-era major-league record.

190

Single-season record for RBIs, achieved by Hack Wilson in the 1930 SEASON, the peak year of the LIVELY BALL ERA. Some baseball researchers maintain that Wilson should have 191 RBIs, due to discrepancies in the historical record, but major league baseball (and *Total Baseball*) recognizes 190 as the official number.

Unless the baseball powers decide they're not making enough money and extend the season by a few more games, this mark has almost no chance of being broken. Here's one reason why: Too many batters hit home runs and not enough just try to get on base. If you had a lineup filled with contact hitters without much power—guys like ICHIRO—along with a single big power hitter like Ryan Howard or ALBERT PUJOLS, then you might see a serious challenge to the record because that power hitter would always come up with men on base. As it is today, even shortstops hit 30 home runs, and the cleanup hitter simply doesn't get enough RBI opportunities.

Sure, every now and then a top slugger puts together such a great first half that it seems they might challenge Wilson's record. For example, Juan Gonzalez in 1998 and MANNY RAMIREZ in 1999 had around 100 RBIs at the All-Star break, but both tailed off in the second half. As it was, each posted amazing RBI totals—157 for Gonzalez, 162 for Ramirez—just not enough to challenge Wilson.

383

Single-season record for strikeouts in the modern era (since 1900), achieved by NOLAN RYAN while with the California Angels in 1973 , which broke SANDY KOUFAX'S 1965 mark by a single strikeout. In 1999 and 2001, RANDY JOHNSON made something of an assault on this record by notching 364 and 372 strikeouts. Other than Johnson and his superhuman arm, however, no pitcher has seriously challenged Ryan's record, and there is very little chance of the mark being broken. Pitchers just don't throw enough innings, and there is too great a risk of injury due to overuse that no manager is going to risk a $20 million arm on a record like this.

511

All-time record for victories by a pitcher, held by CY YOUNG. During his storied career, Young recorded 316 losses—also the highest total in history. Both records are absolutely unbreakable. Why? Because pitching has changed so much. Back in Young's day, pitchers completed about 95 percent of their starts, and with a three-man rotation, they started between 40 and 50 every year. Today, pitchers complete less than 10 percent of their starts, and with a five-man rotation, they start only about 32 games per year. Breaking the record simply will never happen.

714

BABE RUTH'S career home run total. When he retired, Ruth was more than 300 home runs ahead of the number two man, and for many years, nobody thought the record would ever be broken. HANK AARON changed that.

755

HANK AARON'S career home run total, tops among all American players until BARRY BONDS came along—and if you ask many purists, 755 should remain the record in America. (Japan's SADAHARU OH finished his career with 868 home runs.) Twenty years ago, almost any baseball expert would have called this record nearly unbreakable. But the steroid era changed baseball, and now both ALEX RODRIGUEZ and ALBERT PUJOLS have a realistic chance of breaking Bonds's record, too.

762

The current record for home runs in a career, held by BARRY BONDS and set in 2007. Home run number 756—the one that broke HANK AARON'S record—came at home against Washington pitcher Michael

Bacsik, and the last one of Bonds's career came against Ubaldo Jimenez in Colorado.

Like Bonds's chase for the single-season home run record six years earlier (*see* 2001: BONDS HITS 73), the chase for 756 was about as joyless and plodding as a trip to the dentist. Outside of San Francisco, nobody in baseball wanted to see the record broken because they didn't believe that the steroid-tainted Bonds had any right to appear in the record books. Commissioner BUD SELIG, a friend of Aaron's, pointedly refused to attend Bonds's games. Some commentators even urged Bonds to reach 754 or 755, then retire immediately. But if they thought Bonds would even consider doing that, then they clearly knew nothing about the man. He was about the most driven, insular superstar of our generation. He acted as if he truly did not care what other people thought of him, and it showed in the way he treated reporters and even some teammates.

So Bonds had steroids, and Aaron put up with racist death threats when he was chasing Ruth. Maybe someday, a player will break the record without any BS. Let's all root for ALBERT PUJOLS.

2,130

Number of consecutive games played by LOU GEHRIG over 14 seasons from May 31, 1925, when he took over for WALLY PIPP, until May 2, 1939, when he removed himself from the lineup (*see* 1939: THE LUCKIEST MAN SPEAKS). Gehrig, who earned the nickname "Iron Horse" during the streak, remained in the Yankee lineup despite several injuries and at least one bout of lumbago—and played at a level above 99 percent of ballplayers for most of that time. This mark stood as one of baseball's "unbreakable" records until September 1995, when CAL RIPKEN surpassed it. Nearly 50 years passed between Gehrig and Ripken. It's probable that at least that much time will pass before someone else approaches this amazing figure.

2,632

The number of consecutive games played by CAL RIPKEN during his momentous streak, which lasted from 1982 to 1998, when Ripken removed himself from the lineup for the Orioles' final home game (*see* 1998: RIPKEN ENDS HIS STREAK). When you really think about it, doesn't it seem strange that we celebrated so joyously a man whose feat was simply that he showed up for work every day? That was the attitude Ripken himself seemed to have. He didn't seem much interested in records; he just wanted to do his job and play baseball. And he did it for 17 years without ever spraining his ankle, hurting his back, or, as actually happened to another poor player, poking his eardrum with a Q-Tip.

4,191

TY COBB'S career hit total at his retirement in 1928. Further research into the disputed 1910 BATTING RACE has credited Cobb with just 4,189 hits, knocking his career average down to .366 (*see* .366).

4,256

PETE ROSE'S career hit total, tops in major league history. Can this record be broken? Sure, why not? There's no player active today with a realistic chance of breaking this mark, unless you count the hits ICHIRO SUZUKI had in Japan. To break this record, you would need another player like Ichiro or Rose: a hitting machine who could crank out 200-plus hits per year every year for more than 22 years. Highly unlikely but definitely within the realm of possibility.

5,714

All-time record for strikeouts by a pitcher, achieved by NOLAN RYAN during his incredible 27-year career. Since Ryan's career began in an era when pitchers completed most of their starts and routinely notched 300-inning seasons, it is doubtful that anyone will ever even approach Ryan's mark. The top strikeout pitcher of the last generation, RANDY JOHNSON, pitched until age 45 and still finished 839 strikeouts behind.

BABIP (batting average on balls in play)

In the late 1990s, while trying to figure out a better strategy for drafting a FANTASY BASEBALL team, a semi-anonymous fan named Voros McCracken made a controversial and counterintuitive discovery that rocked the SABERMETRICS world: pitchers have very little ability to prevent hits on balls put into play by the batter. In other words, there is little difference between Clayton Kershaw and Wade Miley when a batter hits their pitches. What actually distinguishes the best pitchers from the rest is their ability to get strikeouts and to prevent walks, home runs, and hit batters—the only things that are entirely under the pitcher's control. This is counterintuitive and controversial because it has long been believed that some pitchers have an inherent ability to induce weak ground balls and lazy fly balls. What McCracken discovered is that once the ball leaves the bat, it's a combination of luck and the quality of the defense that determines whether an out is recorded, not the quality of the pitcher.

McCracken made this insight because he discovered that the batting average on balls in play (BABIP) allowed by most pitchers fluctuates significantly from year to year. He reasoned that if a pitcher allows a .350 BABIP one year and a .250 BABIP the next, then the difference must be attributable to something other than the pitcher's skills. Otherwise, BABIPs would be mostly stable from year to year for everyone from the best pitcher to the worst.

This conclusion became more or less accepted in the sabermetric community right away, though non-sabermetricians have had a hard time believing it. But all you have to do is look at almost any pitcher's BABIP from year to year to see the light. Here's a few pitchers I've chosen at random, along with their BABIPs for a random five-year period in their careers:*

Pitcher	Years	Yr 1	Yr 2	Yr 3	Yr 4	Yr 5
Greg Maddux	1995–99	.244	.280	.280	.262	.324
Randy Johnson	2000–04	.326	.315	.289	.348	.264
Clayton Kershaw	2010–14	.275	.269	.262	.251	.278
Jamie Moyer	1997–01	.275	.285	.291	.301	.249
Mark Beuhrle	2001–05	.242	.277	.296	.295	.290

As you can see, some pitchers' BABIPs fluctuate up to 80 points from year to year, while others' fluctuate only about 5 points. But taken as a whole, the fluctuation is statistically significant and indicates that there is something more at work than curveballs and sliders.

Using this knowledge, McCracken developed new ways to evaluate pitchers' effectiveness, which he called DIPS, or defense-independent pitching statistics, and which are now the building blocks upon which modern sabermetric analysis is based. For his part, BILL JAMES, the godfather of sabermetrics, understood the insight immediately and kicked himself for not having discovered it.

As for McCracken, he did some consulting work for the Red Sox, but is not producing original research for publication and is not really a public figure.

*Thanks to Fangraphs.com for the data.

batting average (BA)

The standard statistic by which batters are judged, first used in 1880. Here's the simple formula:

Hits / At Bats

Hugh Duffy achieved the highest batting average in major league history in 1894 with a .440 mark, and TY COBB is the all-time career leader with a mark of .366.

Batting average is actually a very poor measure of a player's total offensive performance, since it excludes all the other things that score runs for a team—extra base hits, walks, stolen bases, and so forth. Some people lionize a .300 hitter, but if a player hits .300 with little power and few walks, that's an empty .300. A much better simple statistic on which to judge a hitter is his ON-BASE PERCENTAGE.

batting championship, batting title

The mythical award given to the league leader in BATTING AVERAGE. TY COBB holds the major league record for the most batting titles: 11, including seven in a row (if you count the disputed 1910 BATTING RACE).

Chalmers Award

Baseball's earliest official most valuable player award, the Chalmers Award was originally instituted in 1910 to reward the major leagues' batting champion. But after the controversial 1910 BATTING RACE, Chalmers changed its policy and awarded the prize—a Chalmers automobile—to the player in each league selected most valuable by a vote of sportswriters. The winners were:

1911: Wildfire Schulte (NL) and TY COBB (AL)
1912: Larry Doyle and TRIS SPEAKER

1913: Jake Daubert and WALTER JOHNSON

1914: Johnny Evers and EDDIE COLLINS

After those awards, the Chalmers Company had fulfilled its five-year commitment to the award, and the honor was discontinued. Within a few years, the Chalmers company itself was discontinued. The MVP idea regained steam in the 1920s and was institutionalized in the 1930s.

Cy Young Award

The idea for the Cy Young Award came out of the belief that pitchers should be honored separately from position players. In one of his few positive accomplishments, commissioner FORD FRICK helped orchestrate the new award, which initially honored one pitcher in both leagues, as selected by the BASEBALL WRITERS ASSOCIATION OF AMERICA. Frick instituted the award partly because pitchers received little representation in the MVP voting. So it's ironic that the first Cy Young winner was the man who also won that year's MVP AWARD: Brooklyn's Don Newcombe in 1956.*

After Newcombe won, his career pretty much fell apart, making him the first victim of the so-called Cy Young Jinx. Supposedly, the Jinx strikes pitchers the year after they win, and a cursory look at the record gives that theory some credence. Some infamous Jinx victims include Bob Turley, Mike Marshall, Steve Stone, Pete Vuckovich, LaMarr Hoyt, and John Denny. However, superstitions aside, it's pretty easy to figure out why the Jinx struck these guys: they were above-average pitchers who had one great season that was good enough to win them the award. It's hard enough to have a *good* season, let alone a *great* season, and it's unfair to expect these pitchers to have consecutive great seasons. Pitchers like SANDY KOUFAX, STEVE CARLTON, Jim Palmer, TOM SEAVER, ROGER CLEMENS, GREG MADDUX, PEDRO MARTINEZ, and RANDY JOHNSON—all multiple award winners—were legitimately great pitchers from whom great seasons were expected. The Cy Young Jinx is, in fact, simply a matter of a pitcher returning to his old self.

Back to the award history: At commissioner Frick's insistence, the first 11 awards were given to the best pitcher in both leagues. When he retired, the award was changed to honor one pitcher in each league, which is how we have it today; it never did make sense to have

Koufax compete with WHITEY FORD, but a lot of what Frick did made no sense, so we shouldn't be surprised.

At first, the voting structure was kind of screwed up: one writer in each major league city placed a single name on the ballot, and the pitcher who got the most votes won. MVP Award voting, on the other hand, features a weighted ballot on which writers place 10 names in descending order. In 1969, the screwed-up voting system victimized the BBWAA when Mike Cuellar and DENNY MCLAIN tied for the award with 10 votes apiece. After that, the voting changed to an MVP-like weighted system—voters placing three names on their ballots with five points going to the first-place pitcher, three to second place, and one to third place. That's how it is today, and it's a good system.

*Pitchers' eligibility for both awards has never been addressed by the BBWAA, and whenever a guy won both, griping could be heard all over the land. The gripers do have a point: Why should one group of players have the chance to win two awards, while everybody else can only win one? The flip side is just as frequent: When a pitcher has a dominant season, some writers refuse to vote for a pitcher; that's what happened to Pedro Martinez in 1999, when two writers left him off their MVP ballots entirely. The BBWAA can resolve the issue pretty easily—by rendering pitchers ineligible for the MVP Award—but for some reason, they haven't. And in 2011, Justin Verlander captured both awards for the first time since 1992, then Clayton Kershaw did the trick in 2014.

earned run average, ERA

As the basic statistical measure of a pitcher, ERA determines the average number of earned runs scored against a pitcher every nine innings; an earned run is a run that's deemed to be the pitcher's fault, while an unearned run, which is usually the result of a fielding error, is not. The ERA formula is simple, but you do need a calculator:

$$\text{Earned Runs} \times 9 \ / \ \text{Innings Pitched}$$

So, for example, a pitcher with a 3.50 ERA is expected to allow three and a half earned runs whenever he pitches a complete game. To be eligible for the yearly ERA championship, a pitcher must have thrown at least one inning for every game his team played, usually 162.

From a historical perspective, it's important to realize that baseball has changed so much that any listing of the top single-season and career leaders in ERA has no meaning. From 1876 through 1892, when the pitching box stood at between 45 and 50 feet from home, and again from the late 1890s through the 1910s, the best ERAs remained in the mid-1.00s and an ERA over 3.00 was poor. In the LIVELY BALL ERA, from 1920 through World War II, an ERA below 2.00 was a rare and phenomenal event. From the war until the 1960s, ERAs fell slightly, and in the mid- to late-1960s, they reached lows that hadn't been seen since the DEAD BALL ERA. From 1969 until about 1993, ERAs were pretty stable, with the league-leader occasionally below 2.00 and the league average around the mid 3.00s. During the Steroid Era, only a few pitchers posted ERAs in the low 2.00s; now, the league average is usually around 4.50.

fielding average

"There are three kinds of lies," said Disraeli. "Lies, damn lies, and statistics." No where is that adage more applicable than with the statistic of fielding average. People can twist it to transform, say, Prince Fielder into a great-fielding first baseman and Evan Longoria into a mediocre third baseman. To apply fielding average correctly, you have to look at it in conjunction with other fielding statistics. Let me explain.

First, here's how to calculate fielding average: Divide the number of clean fielding chances into the total number of plays a fielder makes:

$$(\text{Total Chances} - \text{Errors}) / \text{Total Chances}$$

The resulting number is the percentage of plays a fielder makes cleanly. For a first baseman, as an example, a fielding average below .995 is usually unacceptable unless he shows great range or has a great arm. And therein lies the fielding average dilemma: a mediocre fielder can actually have a great fielding average because he never takes enough risks to make errors. That is Prince Fielder in a nutshell. Meanwhile, a third baseman who gets to balls others don't can have a mediocre fielding average because he has more chances to make a mistake. That's Evan Longoria.

To look at it another way: You or I can stand anchored atop second base, and on every ball hit directly to us, we could make the play cleanly. That would give us a 1.000 fielding average, but it wouldn't make either of us a good second baseman. On the other hand, sometimes people discount this statistic entirely, and they're wrong, too. When considered with other stats such as total chances per game, assists per game—and with actual game observations—fielding average can help give a complete assessment of a player's ability.

Gold Glove

A yearly award sponsored by the RAWLINGS COMPANY that honors the best fielders in the league. Today, the award winners are selected by a poll of managers and coaches, who aren't allowed to vote for anybody on their own teams. The voting isn't perfect; an above-average defensive player with a good bat can usually beat out a defensive wizard who can't hit his weight, and sometimes a player wins based on his reputation rather than his skills. In fact, that's what happened in 1999, when RAFAEL PALMEIRO won the Gold Glove even though injuries had confined him to the designated hitter position for almost the entire season. Overall, however, it's a great award, and it honors a part of the game that is often overlooked.

"Mendoza line"

The mythical "line" that separates decent hitters from bad hitters. The de facto Mendoza line is .200, even though Mario Mendoza—the Mendoza in question—hit .215 over his nine-year career with the Pirates, Mariners, and Rangers. GEORGE BRETT gets credit for the originating the term when he said, "The first thing I look for in the Sunday papers is who is below the Mendoza line." Exactly what Mendoza did to earn such notoriety remains a mystery. Thousands of other players have hit worse than the poor guy. If Brett had been a National Leaguer, for example, he might have named it the "LeMaster line."

MVP Award

This is the most-coveted of all post-season awards, voted on annually by a panel of members of the BASEBALL WRITERS ASSOCIATION OF AMERICA (BBWA). Record books often list Frankie Frisch and LEFTY GROVE as the first official MVP winners, both in 1931. But that's just the first BBWAA award; MVP awards as voted on by sportswriters actually date back to the CHALMERS AWARD. A few years after Chalmers stopped awarding its autos as prizes, the leagues picked up the idea. American League president BAN JOHNSON wanted his league's winners, selected by a poll of sportswriters, to have their names engraved on a monument to be built in the nation's capital. The National League, by contrast, offered $1,000 cash for its winners. These League Awards, as they were called, were handed out from 1922 until 1928 for the AL and 1925 until 1929 for the NL. They fell out of favor for a number of reasons: the AL's monument was never built; MVP winners started demanding more money from their teams; and the AL disallowed repeat winners, which made a sham of the award because it shut out the league's best player—BABE RUTH—after he'd won once.

In the absence of League Awards, *THE SPORTING NEWS* began selecting MVPs. The BBWAA started up in 1931, which is the award we recognize today. TSN continued to hand out its awards in direct competition with the BBWAA, and in the early years, the TSN award may have been more prestigious. For several years in the late 1930s and 1940s, the BBWAA and TSN unified their awards, but then they split again, and today, the honors compete with each other—although now it's the BBWAA trophy that means more.

With a few minor changes, the voting structure in the 1930s is basically what we have today: two writers in each major league city rank 10 players on their ballots, the first place winner receiving 14 points, second place getting nine, third place eight, and so on. The record for MVP victories is seven, held by BARRY BONDS, followed by several Hall of Famers who won three each, including JOE DiMAGGIO, MICKEY MANTLE (who could have won five or six), MIKE SCHMIDT, and others.

There has long been controversy about what constitutes an MVP winner. Is he the league's overall best performer? Or is he the player who was most valuable to his team? Does his team's position in the standings have any effect? How can a player be valuable to a last-place team when they could have finished last without him? MVP voters have never addressed these questions meaningfully. For example, in 1958 and 1959, they selected Ernie Banks, even though his team never contended for the pennant, because he was the best player in the league. But in 1947, Bob Elliot of the second-place Braves captured the award over Ralph Kiner and Johnny Mize, who dominated the league's offensive categories but didn't play on pennant contenders. TED WILLIAMS lost out on about three awards because his teams didn't win the pennant (and because many writers hated him). And DiMaggio won at least one award when he didn't deserve it simply because his name was Joe DiMaggio. (There's also a controversy about pitchers winning MVP Awards; see CY YOUNG AWARD for more on that.)

So what does it take to be the MVP? Let's look at the statistics. Generally speaking, of course, you have to play on a pennant contender. In the history of the modern MVP award (from 1931 through 2010), only a handful of players won despite playing on non-contenders (most recently ALEX RODRIGUEZ in 2003). For many years, pitchers had a good shot at winning, but these days, voters have pretty much stopped voting for them (except Justin Verlander in 2011 and Clayton Kershaw in 2014). It does, however, help to play a key defensive position like catcher or shortstop because you can win even if you don't have the best batting totals. The single most important offensive statistic is RBIs: around 33 percent of all MVP winners also led their league in RBIs; in fact, 11 MVPs led their league only in RBIs (although in the past decade, RBIs alone have been less important). The least important offensive statistic? Stolen bases; only three stolen base leaders have won the MVP. Finally, it helps to be a nice guy: The media's dislike of Ted Williams probably cost him a couple of awards. More recently, Mo Vaughn won the 1995 award over Albert Belle in no small part because Vaughn is a likable guy while Belle is not. A whole book could be written about the MVP award.

on-base percentage (OBP), on-base average (OBA)

The measure of the number of times a player gets on base via hit, walk, or hit by pitch, expressed as a percentage of his total number of plate appearances:

$$\text{(Hits + Walks + Hit by Pitch) / (At Bats + Walks + Hit by Pitch + Sacrifice Flies)}$$

This statistic should replace batting average as the basic unit of measure for offensive players; it already has for many of us. A player can have a good batting average but be a lousy hitter, but a guy with a good on-base percentage is by definition a good hitter. The reason: the player with the good OBP knows the strike zone and knows how to put himself into position to score a run or drive one in.

What's considered a good OBP? The league average is usually around .330, and the league leader is usually around .420; good is about .370 or so. TED WILLIAMS, who had the best batting eye in history, is the lifetime OBP leader, and until 2002, he also had the highest single-season OBP.

In 2002, BARRY BONDS eclipsed Williams's single-season mark thanks to 198 walks from frightened pitchers and managers, recording an absolutely astounding OBP of .582. And two years later, he raised the bar even higher with an OBP of .609. What that means is that Bonds got on base via hits (135) and walks (232) more than 60 percent of the time in 2004—possibly the most dominating offensive season of all time.

In the 2000s, OBP finally started to receive its due recognition. You're seeing OBP listed in the newspaper and on-screen during baseball broadcasts. And many general managers, led initially by Oakland's BILLY BEANE but now throughout baseball, base their personnel decisions on OBP. It's about time.

Through my homerunweb.com website, I've received questions from readers about why other things aren't included in on-base percentage, such as reaching base on a fielder's choice or error. There are two answers:

First, it's impossible to calculate that data after the fact. There's no standardized historical record of reaching on error or fielder's choice (although the RETROSHEET guys are probably on the case), so it would be impossible to assign those numbers to old-time players.

Second, and more importantly, on-base percentage is supposed to measure a player's skill at getting on base. Reaching on a fielder's choice indicates that you just created an out, but by chance there was someone else on base. Did you help your team? No. Your team is in worse shape than it was one batter ago. Reaching via error is also just a matter of luck. You should have been out, but the fielder screwed up. OBP makes the distinction between getting on base because of your ability and getting on base because of just plain luck.

That's why, as I stated at the beginning of this entry, OBP is possibly the truest measure of a hitter.

OPS (on base + slugging percentage)

This is a fairly new statistic that's starting to gain prominence among baseball fans and reporters. OPS* (called "Production" in some record books, such as *Total Baseball*) is a simple number that aims to measure the majority of a player's offensive contributions. The rationale is simple: On-base percentage measures only the ability to get on base; slugging percentage measures power. Combining the two gives you a well-rounded view of a hitter. The only contribution it doesn't measure is stolen bases.

The big flaw with OBP is that the number isn't very meaningful if you simply see it written. Baseball fans possess a kind of shorthand when it comes to statistically evaluating a player's excellence: .300 batting average, .400 on-base percentage, .500 slugging percentage, 30 home runs, 100 RBIs, and so on. But what's a good OPS? I'll tell you: Anything over .900 is excellent. Until the 1990s, over 1.000 used to lead the league; now you have to get about 1.100 to top your circuit. The league average is around .700 or so.

*Is it pronounced "O-P-S" or "ops"? I've heard it both ways, but I prefer "O-P-S." "Ops" just sounds weird.

RBI

Abbreviation for run batted in, an official league statistic since 1920. A batter gets an RBI when he brings a runner home via a hit, walk, hit batsman, sacrifice bunt or fly, fielder's choice, or sometimes on an error if the official scorer believes the runner would have scored even without the error. A batter doesn't get an RBI when he drives a runner home on a ground ball double play.

There's a (very) minor controversy going on today about how to pluralize the term RBI. Some people believe that since RBI stands for run batted in, and since the plural of run batted in is "runs batted in," then the plural of RBI is still RBI, as in "Longoria notched 4 RBI last night." But I and many others think that's wrong. We pluralize RBI separately from runs batted in, as in "Hack Wilson had 190 RBIs in 1930." I think RBI has gained its own stature as a baseball term and deserves its own plural—just like the Oakland Athletics are usually known as the "A's," not the "A."

Rolaids Relief Man

The award given each year to each league's top relief pitcher, sponsored, of course, by the famous antacid company. It's a simple statistical assessment that considers all the pertinent information about relief pitchers:

$$(3 \times \text{Saves}) + (2 \times \text{Wins}) - (2 \times \text{Losses}) - (2 \times \text{Blown Saves})$$

Rookie of the Year Award

The yearly honor awarded to each league's top rookie, as selected in a vote by the BASEBALL WRITERS ASSOCIATION OF AMERICA (BBWAA). To be eligible for the award, a player may not have totaled more than 130 at bats, 50 innings, or 45 days on a roster in any previous season(s). In 1987, commissioner PETER UEBERROTH changed the name of the award to the JACKIE ROBINSON Award, paying homage to the award's first recognized winner in 1947. Even though Robinson is considered the first winner of the BBWAA's version of the award, the Chicago chapter of the BBWAA made separate selections beginning in 1940. *THE SPORTING NEWS* got into the act in 1946, and the overall BBWAA finally woke up a year later.

The Rookie of the Year is a fun award but it doesn't always portend greatness for a player. Sam Jethroe (1950), Harry Byrd (1952), and Pat Listach (1992) are three players who disappeared from baseball soon after copping the award, and a number of others never lived up to the expectations. On the other hand, dozens of great players—many of whom are in or headed for the Hall of Fame—have captured the ROY, including WILLIE MAYS (1951), FRANK ROBINSON (1956), LUIS APARICIO (1956), WILLIE MCCOVEY (1959), TOM SEAVER (1967), among others.

Runs Created

A statistic invented by BILL JAMES to measure the value of an offensive performer. Unlike statistics that measure only part of a batter/baserunner's skills, Runs Created attempts to answer a simple question: How many runs did a hitter create for his team? Its simplest form is:

$$[(\text{Hits} + \text{Walks}) \, (\text{Total Bases})] \, / \\ (\text{At Bats} + \text{Walks})$$

The stolen base version assigns a value of approximately one-half of a base for each stolen base but also subtracts one base for every caught stealing; James's statistical models indicate that stolen bases add little to a team's offense:

[(Hits + Walks - Caught Stealing) (Total Bases + .55 x Stolen Bases)] / (At Bats + Walks)

There are a few more technical versions that incorporate other events, such as hit by pitch, grounded into double plays, sacrifices, and so on. How do we know this is an accurate statistic? All you have to do is run the formula for an entire team or league: The total for Runs Created will come very close to the actual number of runs scored by a team. For more on the subject, read James's NEW HISTORICAL BASEBALL ABSTRACT.

sabermetrics, sabermetrician

Sabermetrics is study of baseball using advanced statistics to analyze the game. The name "sabermetrics" was devised by BILL JAMES in the 1970s to honor the sport's foremost research organization, the SOCIETY FOR AMERICAN BASEBALL RESEARCH (SABR).

Many people possess a fundamental misunderstanding of sabermetrics and how it works. They think it means using numbers to slice the game into little pieces and take all the humanity out of it. They think it means inventing crazy new statistics to make players seem better or worse than they are. They think it means discovering that Zack Greinke is undefeated on Wednesday nights in June after his team has lost the previous three games, and using that data to draw some large conclusion about Zack Greinke.

Sabermetrics is none of that. In fact, that last item is exactly the *opposite* of what sabermetrics is all about, because as any good sabermetrician (or statistician) knows, you can't draw any conclusions if you don't have a large data set to work with—in other words, a large sample size.

What sabermetrics is really about, to me at least, is using statistics to gain a greater understanding of how baseball games are won and lost. For example, for a hundred years, fans focused on BATTING AVERAGE as the best indicator of batting skill. But thanks to sabermetrics, we know that winning games is more highly correlated to ON-BASE PERCENTAGE (OBP) than to batting average, more highly correlated to ON-BASE PLUS SLUGGING (OPS) than OBP, and even more highly correlated to RUNS CREATED than OPS. So if you had to choose a single number upon which to base your evaluation of a player's offensive skills, would you choose batting average—which measures only hits—or would you choose Runs Created—which measures hits and extra-base hits and walks and stolen bases and more?

And when I say "evaluate a player's skills," I'm not just thinking about what he did in the past. As a fan, I also want to know what he is going to do in the future. Should my team trade for him or sign him as a free agent? Would it be better off choosing player A or player B? We don't base those judgments on how a hitter *looks* at the plate. We base the judgments on what a player *did* at the plate. And so sabermetrics is concerned with the question: What is the best way to predict how a player is going to do next time? Some people—fewer now than in the past—look at RBIs as the main judge of a hitter's worth. "He's a run producer," they'll say about a guy who gets a lot of RBIs. But why stop at RBIs? Why not find out how many runners were on base in front of him and calculate the percentage of runners he drove in? Was that higher or lower than the league average for a hitter like him? Sabermetrics asks those questions and finds out the answers.

If you believe in sabermetrics, does that mean you ignore the classic stats, such as batting average and RBIs and ERA? Of course not. Those are part of the fabric of baseball, and everybody knows what they are and what they mean. Mike Trout comes to the plate, and even the most die-hard sabermetrician isn't going to say, "He's on a tear with 13 RCs in his last 10 games." No, the sabermetrician is going to be just like any other fan and say, "Wow, a .407 average in his last 10 games. He's on fire." However, the sabermetrician is going to have a deep understanding of the nature of hot streaks and know that you can't make an informed prediction about what might happen next based on only 10 games worth of data.

In today's baseball, there seems to be a conflict between traditional fans who've rejected sabermetrics and analysis-oriented fans who enjoy advanced statistics: the old-school crowd vs. the stathead crowd. *San Francisco Chronicle* columnist Bruce Jenkins exemplified the old-school aversion to advanced statistics when he angrily wrote, "For more than a century, .220 meant something. So did .278, .301, .350, an 18-4 record, or 118 RBIs. Now it all means nothing because a bunch of nonathletes are trying to reinvent the game?" (Bruce, FYI, nonathletes like HENRY CHADWICK and ERNEST J. LANIGAN invented the batting average, RBI, and won-loss record.)

But there is no reason for any conflict to exist. Sportswriter JOE POSNANSKI has written a lot about this topic, and his point—which I heartily agree with—is that there are many different ways to enjoy baseball, and they don't have to conflict with each other. Somebody loves stats and wants to dissect the game to an inch of its life? Go ahead! Another guy doesn't want numbers to get in the way? Great! Baseball is not a zero-sum game. One fan's type of love doesn't encroach on another fan's.

I believe sabermetrics is a doorway that leads to a greater enjoyment of baseball. Not everybody agrees, and that's fine, too.

Silver Slugger Award

An award given each season to the best hitters at each position, judged by a panel of sportswriters, sponsored by the Hillerich & Bradsby company (makers of the LOUISVILLE SLUGGER) and judged by a panel of sportswriters. Not many baseball fans pay much attention to the Silver Slugger Award, but you can see a list of winners at MLB.com.

slugging percentage, slugging average

A statistical measure of power hitting, determined by dividing the number of total bases into a players total at bats:

$$\text{(Singles} + [2 \times \text{Doubles}] + [3 \times \text{Triples}] + [4 \times \text{Home Runs}]) / \text{At Bats}$$

The numerator of that formula is known as total bases, and there's an easier way to calculate it without duplicating your efforts by subtracting extra base hits from total hits. Here's the simpler formula that produces the same result:

$$\text{(Total Hits} + \text{Doubles} + [2 \times \text{Triples}] + [3 \times \text{Home Runs}]) / \text{At Bats}$$

Real power hitters have slugging percentages above .500, higher than .600 often leads the league, more than .700 is TED WILLIAMS territory, and above .800 is positively Ruthian (or Bondsian, if you don't mind the taint of steroids).

Triple Crown, Hitter's

A mythical crown awarded to a hitter who leads the league in batting average, home runs, and RBIs. Because it takes a ballplayer with a truly unique blend of skills, only 18 players have won a Triple Crown including Miguel Cabrera in 2012:

Player	Team	Year	HR/RBI/AVG
Paul Hines	Providence	1878	4/50/.358
Tip O'Neill	St. Louis (AA)	1887	14/123/.435
Hugh Duffy	Boston (NL)	1894	18/145/.440*
NAP LAJOIE	Philadelphia (AL)	1901	14/125/.426
TY COBB	Detroit	1909	9/115/.377
Heinie Zimmerman	Chicago	1912	14/99/.372**
ROGERS HORNSBY	St. Louis (NL)	1922	42/152/.401
Rogers Hornsby	St. Louis (NL)	1925	39/143/.403
JIMMIE FOXX	Philadelphia (AL)	1933	48/163/.356
Chuck Klein	Philadelphia (NL)	1933	28/120/.368
LOU GEHRIG	New York (AL)	1934	49/165/:363
Joe Medwick	St. Louis (NL)	1937	31/154/.374
TED WILLIAMS	Boston (AL)	1942	36/137/.356
Ted Williams	Boston (AL)	1947	32/114/.343
MICKEY MANTLE	New York (AL)	1956	52/130/.353
FRANK ROBINSON	Baltimore	1966	49/122/.316
CARL YASTRZEMSKI	Boston	1967	44/121/.326
Miguel Cabrera	Detroit	2012	44/139/.330

*Some record books list Duffy as the RBI leader that year, but others list Sam Thompson as the leader. I'm going to leave in Duffy as the Triple Crown winner.

**Heinie Zimmerman gets an asterisk because, while he was originally credited with 103 RBIs, researchers who checked the records discovered some anomalies and determined that he really only had 99 RBIs, which retroactively gives the RBI title to HONUS WAGNER.

Not long ago, a writer in *Baseball Digest* magazine put forth the argument that the Triple Crown should be changed. Jerry Coen wrote that he believes no one will ever win another Triple Crown because the three Triple Crown stats are "remarkably incomplete measures" of a ballplayer's offensive abilities. Coen argues in favor of a modified Triple Crown: on-base percentage, slugging average, and runs produced (the combined total of runs and RBIs minus home runs, to avoid duplication). As we now know, his prediction suggesting no one would ever win was wrong, proving the old adage, "Predictions are hard, especially about the future." Even so, I don't buy the notion that we should change the Triple Crown. First of all, the title itself is mythical, so it's not as if there's a crown in a basement somewhere waiting to be awarded. Second, the traditional Triple Crown comprises stats that are basic and obvious to even the most casual fan. Third, I like the fact that it's such an exclusive title. Every year, one or two players make a run at the Triple Crown, and it's always a great story when somebody comes close in all three categories. Baseball has changed so much, there should be some things that stay the same.

Triple Crown, Pitcher's

This is a relatively new mythical award that goes to a pitcher who leads the league in wins, strikeouts, and ERA. It isn't quite as exclusive as the hitter's Triple Crown, but it does signify a truly dominant performance. Here are the winners since 1876 (as of 2014):

Pitcher	Team	Year	Wins/Ks/ERA
Tommy Bond	Boston (NL)	1877	40/170/2.11
CHARLES RADBOURN	Providence (NL)	1884	59/441/1.38
Tim Keefe	New York (NL)	1888	35/333/1.74
John Clarkson	Boston (NL)	1889	49/284/2.73
AMOS RUSIE	New York (NL)	1894	36/195/2.78
CY YOUNG	Boston (AL)	1901	33/158/1.62
RUBE WADDELL	Philadelphia (AL)	1905	26/287/1.48
CHRISTY MATHEWSON	New York (NL)	1905	31/206/1.27
Christy Mathewson	New York (NL)	1908	37/259/1.43
WALTER JOHNSON	Washington	1913	36/303/1.09
GROVER ALEXANDER	Philadelphia (NL)	1915	31/241/1.22
Grover Alexander	Philadelphia (NL)	1916	33/167/1.55
Grover Alexander	Philadelphia (NL)	1917	30/201/1.86
Walter Johnson	Washington	1918	23/162/1.27
Hippo Vaughn	Chicago (NL)	1918	22/148/1.74
Grover Alexander	Chicago (NL)	1920	27/173/1.91
Walter Johnson	Washington	1924	23/158/2.72

Dazzy Vance	Brooklyn	1924	28/262/2.16
LEFTY GROVE	Philadelphia (AL)	1930	28/209/2.54
Lefty Grove	Philadelphia (AL)	1931	31/175/2.06
Lefty Gomez	New York (AL)	1934	26/158/2.33
Lefty Gomez	New York (AL)	1937	21/194/2.33
Bucky Walters	Cincinnati	1939	27/137/2.29
BOB FELLER	Cleveland	1940	27/261/2.61
Hal Newhouser	Detroit	1945	25/212/1.81
SANDY KOUFAX	Los Angeles	1963	25/306/1.88
Sandy Koufax	Los Angeles	1965	26/382/2.04
Sandy Koufax	Los Angeles	1966	27/317/1.73
STEVE CARLTON	Philadelphia (NL)	1972	27/310/1.97
DWIGHT GOODEN	New York (NL)	1985	24/268/1.53
ROGER CLEMENS	Toronto	1997	21/292/2.05
Roger Clemens	Toronto	1998	20/271/2.65
PEDRO MARTINEZ	Boston	1999	23/313/2.07
RANDY JOHNSON	Arizona	2002	24/334/2.32
Johan Santana	Minnesota	2006	19/245/2.77
Jake Peavy	San Diego	2007	19/240/2.54
Clayton Kershaw	Los Angeles	2011	21/248/2.28
Justin Verlander	Detroit	2011	24/250/2.40

Any surprises on this list? There were several for me. The least impressive Pitcher's Triple Crown probably belongs to Bucky Walters, whose 137 strikeouts would barely register today. I was also surprised to see how dominant Lefty Gomez was for those two years. He was able to squeeze in those two ERA titles in the midst of Lefty Grove's amazing nine titles.

Wins Above Replacement (WAR)

A fairly new SABERMETRIC statistic that aims to quantify a player's contribution to his team in the field, at the plate, and on the bases compared to that of a generic "replacement player"—meaning a typical player readily available from the minor leagues (which is not the same as an average major leaguer). Like WIN SHARES, WAR is complicated to calculate, and even among those websites that do make the effort—including Fangraphs.com, BASEBALL-REFERENCE.COM, and

BASEBALL PROSPECTUS—they each make slightly different calculations, so the numbers for any given player don't exactly match up.

One thing to realize with WAR is that the calculation literally translates to the number of wins a player is responsible for above and beyond the contribution of a replacement player. For example, in 2014, Mike Trout registered a WAR of 8.0 (according to Fangraphs), the highest in baseball. That means his bat, glove, and legs personally delivered 8.0 wins to the Angels more than an average Triple-A minor league outfielder.

Does that seem low to you? At first glance, it does to me. I mean, Trout was one of the best players in the league that year, and he was only responsible for 8.0 wins? At second glance, however, it starts to make sense. Because of the nature of baseball, a team filled with Triple-A replacement players would probably win at least 40 games. A team filled with Mike Trouts would probably lose at least 40 games. The 82 games in between are what separate major league–quality teams from minor league–quality teams. In the case of the Angels, they won 98 games in 2014, which means there were about 58 marginal wins to divide between the 25 players on the Angels roster who all contributed to the club in one way or another. In that context—25 players diving up 58 wins, or an average of 2.32 per player—Trout's 8.0 makes more sense. WAR suggests that he was between three and four times as good as the average player on his team, and that seems about right.

It's possible to register a negative WAR, but in practice, players who do usually don't last long in the majors because teams will be quick to replace them with a cheaper, younger alternative from the minors. (However, some veterans do keep their jobs despite scoring poorly; Jay Bruce, Ryan Howard, and Billy Butler all scored negative WARs in 2014, but still have major league jobs because teams are hoping against hope that they'll return to their former glory.)

WAR is an exciting new statistic that is accepted in the sabermetric world but has a long way to go before casual fans can believe in it. But it'll get there.

Win Shares

Win Shares is BILL JAMES'S groundbreaking SABERMETRIC effort to take the sum of a ballplayer's contributions to his team—both offense and defense—and derive a single number that describes that player's total worth. (It's kinda like WINS ABOVE REPLACEMENT only it doesn't compare the player to anyone else.) The formulas are extremely complicated and require a careful reading of James's book *Win Shares* to fully understand. In a nutshell, here's what Win Shares takes into account:

- Batting
- Fielding, broken down by position
- Pitching, both relief and starting
- Ballpark effects
- Different eras of baseball

What is a Win Share? It's one-third of a victory. So if a team has 100 victories, then it has 300 Win Shares to pass around to all the players on the club.

How does it work? It takes James about 120 pages of his book to explain that, and there's no way I could do it justice here. But I will give you a quick overview. For offense, James uses his RUNS CREATED, which is a proven statistic, and puts it into the context of how many runs it typically takes to achieve a win for a team. For defense, it's much more complicated. He has devised formulas for each position in the field that take into account not only what an individual player accomplished (putouts, assists, double plays, etc.) but also what his teammates accomplished. For example, if a second baseman has achieved an extraordinary amount of putouts, is it because he's a tremendous fielder or because he takes chances away from his teammates (such as always taking catcher throws on steal attempts)? His system accounts for that and about a thousand other variables to come up with a number that corresponds to a player's defensive contribution to a victory. The pitching component is determined similarly: a bunch of pitching variables captured in a series of formulas to come up with a single number for a pitcher's contributions.

The beauty of Win Shares is that it expresses each player's worth in a single number, regardless of the player's position. So it's possible to make apples-to-apples comparisons of pitchers and hitters, starters and relievers, middle infielders and corner outfielders, players in COORS FIELD and players in Safeco Field, DEAD BALL ERA pitchers and LIVELY BALL ERA hitters.

The stat has been around for only a decade, but already it's being hailed as the most complete single method of evaluating players ever devised. And it has been accepted by the vanguard of baseball writers and analysts.

If you want to start looking at baseball games, statistics, history, and players in a whole new light, pick up a copy of *Win Shares* and start reading. It may take several reads to really grasp the implications of the system, but once you do, an exciting new world will open up for you.

8
RULES, GAME TERMS & BASEBALL BUSINESS

60 feet, 6 inches

The distance between the pitching rubber and home plate since 1893. In years prior, the distance was 45 or 50 feet, but as pitchers got stronger and learned trick pitches such as curveballs and spitballs, they became nearly unhittable. AMOS RUSIE, whose nickname, "The Hoosier Thunderbolt," provides an idea of how great his fastball was, is acknowledged to have been most responsible for the rule change.

90 feet

The distance between the bases on a baseball diamond. Sportswriter RED SMITH once wrote, "Ninety feet between bases is the nearest to perfection that man has yet achieved."

ace

A team's best pitcher. Obviously the term comes from the gambling world, where the ace is the best card a player can have. "Ace" was also the word for "run," used back in the mid–19th century. Item number 8 of the KNICKERBOCKER RULES said, "The game to consist of twenty-one counts, or aces." Yes, that means the first team to 21 runs—which is probably the most significant change from the Knickerbocker Rules compared to today.

agent

The person or team of people—usually lawyers but often relatives or close friends—hired by a player to represent him in salary negotiations with owners and in endorsement deals with such companies as glove, shoe, and baseball card manufacturers. Agents generally take a cut, usually between 4 and 15 percent, of all contracts negotiated. Owners forced players to negotiate for themselves until 1970, although BABE RUTH, baseball's preeminent revolutionary, was the first to hire an agent to handle his off-field activities and publicity. Baseball's first really powerful agent was Jerry Kapstein, a Harvard lawyer who worked for a while as the color commentator for Washington Bullets basketball games. He made his name in baseball handling salary ARBITRATION cases in the early 1970s, when he beat CHARLIE FINLEY in a number of high-profile cases. By the advent of free agency in 1976, Kapstein represented more than sixty players, including some of baseball's biggest stars: Steve Garvey, ROLLIE FINGERS, Tony Perez, and others. Today's most hated agent (from an owners' perspective) is SCOTT BORAS.

alley

The parts of the outfield between the center fielder and the left and right fielders. Also called the power alley or the gap. The deepest alley in today's baseball is in COORS FIELD, where part of right-center is 424 feet from home plate. Historically, YANKEE STADIUM had probably the deepest alley: from 1924 to 1937, the deepest part of left-center stood 490 feet from home. Even after remodeling in 1937, it was 457 feet, which probably cost JOE DiMAGGIO countless home runs.

aluminum bat

A bat made of aluminum or other metal alloy, used currently by most Little League, high school, and college baseball players as well as softball players. It's illegal in professional baseball, and in fact, amateur leagues are considering banning aluminum, too, or at least switching to new bat materials that are more like wood. The primary functional difference between wood and aluminum bats, aside from the sound each produces when striking a ball ("knock" vs. "ping"), is the size of the ideal hitting area, or sweet spot: It's larger on aluminum bats, which means a hitter can be fooled by a pitch and still make good contact. For this reason, the aluminum bat will never be used in the major leagues. Many believe that a pitcher could get killed by a batted ball.

amateur draft

Instituted in 1965 to make player selection more fair for teams that didn't have the money to award big bonuses, the amateur draft, also called the first-year player draft, is held every summer by conference call among the 30 major league clubs. The rules for determining eligibility are detailed, but basically draft eligibility is limited to the following types of players: high school players, if they have graduated from high school and have not yet attended college or junior college; college players from four-year universities who have either completed their junior or senior years or are at least 21 years old; junior college players, regardless of how many years of school they have completed; and 21-year-old players. Generally this applies only to players in the United States, Canada, and U.S. territories such as Puerto Rico. It doesn't include players from other countries and regions, such as Latin America or Asia—although occasionally there's talk of expanding the draft to include them. Like drafts from other pro sports, teams draft in reverse order of the previous year's finish. Unlike most other drafts, baseball teams to select players for 50 or more rounds.

appeal play

A fielding play that occurs when the defensive team contends that a runner missed a base or left a base early on a fly ball. Unlike most sports, baseball requires that the fielders appeal to the umpire to make the call. It's like a football linebacker having to ask the referee to call a holding penalty.

arbitration

A concession won by the players in 1973 Basic Agreement, arbitration is the method used to settle salary disputes between teams and players with between two and six years of major league experience. Under current rules, an independent arbitrator selects either the salary bid submitted by the player or the one by the owner; there is no compromise. To determine what the player deserves, the arbitrators use comparable players as reference points. For example, if power-hitting outfielder A makes $12 million and power-hitting outfielder B, with similar or better stats, is up for arbitration, B's agent will argue that B should get at least as much as A. Club representatives will usually present a case that highlights all of the player's faults—low clutch batting average, poor throwing skills, and so forth. It's up to the arbitrator to decide whose argument is most effective.

Owners would like to do away with arbitration because they say it artificially inflates salaries. In the above example, if player A didn't "deserve" (in the owners' minds) the $12 million, then the arbitrator is merely compounding one mistake if he rules in favor of player B. The MAJOR LEAGUE BASEBALL PLAYERS ASSOCIATION, however, believes that players operate in a system where a free market determines salaries. If a player is *getting* $12 million, then he is by definition *worth* $12 million, and there's nothing artificial about it. This chasm between the MLBPA and management over salary arbitration was one of the catalysts of the 1994 STRIKE and still causes consternation among owners.

around the horn

Baseball slang for a double play that goes third to second to first. It comes from the fact that until the opening of the Panama Canal, a ship could reach the Pacific Ocean from the Atlantic only by traveling around Cape Horn on the southern tip of South America. A strange source for a baseball term, if you ask me.

assist

A throw that puts out a runner. Every fielder makes assists, but middle infielders get the most. Rabbit Maranville holds the career (8,967) and Frankie Frisch the single-season (643) records for assists.

at bat, official at bat

A time at the plate by a batter in which he either gets a HIT, makes an OUT, or reaches base via ERROR or FIELDER'S CHOICE. A WALK, SACRIFICE, HIT BY PITCH, or CATCHER'S INTERFERENCE counts as a PLATE APPEARANCE but not an at bat.

bad-ball hitter

A hitter who is known for swinging at—and getting hits from— balls outside the strike zone. In recent times, Vladimir Guerrero is a great modern example of someone who employs this technique successfully; the minor leagues are filled with players who employ it unsuccessfully.

bad hop

A grounder that takes a strange bounce off the infield, usually causing a fielder to misplay the ball. One of the most famous bad hops occurred in Game 7 of the 1924 World Series. The Giants were leading the Senators 3-1 in the eighth inning when Washington's Bucky Harris hit a routine grounder to third that hit a pebble and took a bad hop over the third baseman's head. Two runs scored, and the Senators went on to win the game and series in extra innings.

balk

A pitcher's motion considered by the umpire to be deliberately deceptive toward a baserunner, like dropping the ball or faking a throw to first base while on the rubber. The penalty is that all baserunners advance one base. Few balks are as obvious as the examples just listed; most are nearly undetectable except by instant replay cameras and umpires, who seem to have an inexplicable sixth sense for balks.

Baltimore chop

A batted ball that hits the ground just in front of home plate, then bounces high enough that the hitter reaches first before he can be thrown out. The name refers to the old BALTIMORE ORIOLES of the 1890s, whose groundskeepers kept the area in front of home plate especially hard so its players could get hits by swinging down on the ball. Although the term is still used today, nobody ever really tries to hit a Baltimore chop like the old Orioles did. It's usually just accidental.

bandbox

A ballpark with small dimensions. Today, only WRIGLEY FIELD and FENWAY PARK qualify as bandboxes, although maybe Houston's ballpark is a contender. The term comes from the "boxes" that musicians stand in while playing their instruments.

bang-bang play

A play in which a runner and the ball reach the base at almost the same instant, creating a difficult call for umpires. However, instant replay has shown that umpires call a surprisingly high percentage of bang-bang plays correctly. How do they do it? Because they can't watch both the base and the ball at the same time, they're trained to keep their eyes on the base and listen for the sound of the ball hitting the fielder's glove.

barnstorming tour

An off-season tour in which teams play games against each other and against local players. In the first half of the century, major league and NEGRO LEAGUE teams would play in small towns and foreign countries that had no access to big league ball. The players would augment their salaries substantially, sometimes earning more on a barnstorming tour than from penny-pinching owners. Today, a team of major league all-stars "barnstorms" to Japan every year to play exhibition games against Japanese major leaguers; the U.S. team usually wins.

base

The white marker at each of the four corners of a baseball infield. Each base is 90 feet from the others and is marked by a 15-inch square bag, with the exception of home plate, which is a pentagon-shaped slab of rubber.

base on balls, walk

It's what occurs after a batter receives four pitches out of the strike zone during his time at the plate. The reward, of course, is a free trip to first base. For the first 30 or so years of the game's history, the number of balls it took to earn a walk fluctuated from as high as nine to four, which became the rule in 1889.

baseball

The hard, white, round ball used in a baseball game. Made of a small cork core followed by layers of rubber, yarn, and cowhide with 108 red stitches at the seams, the ball is between 9 and 9-1/4 inches in diameter and weighs between 5 and 5-1/4 ounces—dimensions that have ruled the manufacture of baseballs for more than 100 years. At various points in the game's history, when offensive totals would increase or decrease dramatically in one of the leagues, people would claim one league's ball was "juiced" while the other was deadened (*see* "RABBIT BALL"). In fact, the REACH COMPANY—owned by the SPALDING SPORTING GOODS COMPANY—manufactured all baseballs until 1976, even though American League balls carried the "Reach" label while National League balls said "Spalding." In 1977, the RAWLINGS COMPANY took over the contract to manufacture the balls, which is done now at a plant in Costa Rica.

baseball mud

The reddish-brown mud used by umpires to rub into new baseballs. The tradition began in the 1920s when, after the death of RAY CHAPMAN from an errant pitch, umpires were ordered to keep fresh new balls in play at all times. After pitchers complained of difficulty gripping the balls, league officials decided to institute a policy of "rubbing down" baseballs to remove the sheen from the leather. Today, umpires use Lena Blackburne's Baseball Rubbing Mud, named after the 1930s-era manager who discovered a secret location in the Delaware River that produced the exact consistency and color of mud to make a ball perfect.

basket catch

A method of catching a fly ball with your glove near your body at belt level. Generally accepted as a fundamentally poor way to field, it has nevertheless been used by many great fielders, including WILLIE MAYS and ROBERTO CLEMENTE (24 GOLD GLOVES between them). Rabbit Maranville, a shortstop in the early part of the 20th century, first popularized the basket catch.

bat speed

A measure of the time it takes for a hitter to move his bat from the "ready," upright position into the hitting zone. Scouts use a player's bat speed to judge his potential ability to connect with major league fastballs. You often hear broadcasters and managers refer to a player with a "quick bat"; this means, for one thing, that the hitter can misjudge a fastball and still make contact.

bat

The piece of sculpted pine used to hit the ball. They come in a variety of sizes, measured by both length and weight, and are manufactured in Kentucky, upstate New York, Japan, and other locales. One of the most famous bats in history is "SHOELESS" JOE JACKSON'S Black Betsy, a 36-inch, 40-ounce piece of lumber painted black.

batboy

The boy or girl who takes care of the bats, balls, and helmets during a game. The batboy picks up the bat and helmet after a hitter's at bat is finished and delivers new balls to the umpires between pitches.

batter's box

The boxes on each side of home plate, outlined by white chalk, where a hitter must stand when at bat. If a hitter makes contact with the ball while standing outside the box, he is supposed to be called out, although this rule is rarely enforced. If the pitcher has an excellent curveball, hitters will often stand in the front of the box to try to catch the curve before it breaks; if the pitcher has a good fastball, they'll stand at the back of the box. Next time you go to a game, watch the way the leadoff hitter rubs out the back line of the box to gain a few extra inches.

battery

Term for the pitcher and catcher in a game, which probably comes from military lexicon. "Battery" has been used in the baseball sense since at least 1868.

batting cage

(a) The big cage placed behind home plate during batting practice to help keep foul balls from rocketing into the stands and at bystanders. (b) An indoor cage with a pitching machine standing 60 feet from home plate where hitters can practice. A lot of new businesses have appeared during the last decade that sell time in a batting cage.

batting eye

Term for a player's ability to judge the strike zone. TED WILLIAMS possessed probably the sport's greatest batting eye, amassing the fourth-highest walk total in baseball history as well as the top on-base percentage.

batting glove

Soft leather glove worn by hitters, usually on their bottom hand (left for a right-hand hitter, right for a lefty), to help maintain a good grip on the bat and prevent blisters. Almost all players today use one or two batting gloves, but a few still like to feel the wood in their hands.

batting helmet

The hard plastic headgear batters wear to protect themselves from errant pitches. The 1941 Dodgers experimented with plastic liners inside their hats, but helmets weren't put into common use until the 1950s and weren't mandatory until the 1960s. Following the fatal beaning of RAY CHAPMAN in 1920, many writers called for the league to make players wear the helmets. But those calls were largely ignored, and although Chapman's was the only on-field death in major league history, countless careers would have been saved (MICKEY CO-CHRANE'S, to name one) if helmets had been instituted earlier.

batting order

The order of the players in a game LINEUP, from the first batter to number nine. Managers usually rely on conventional wisdom to help them decide whom to bat where. You may already be familiar with most of these guidelines, which seem to be passed down from generation to generation:

> #1, LEADOFF—speed, preferably a high on-base percentage
> #2—good bat control, preferably left-handed, able to hit to right or bunt to move a runner along if needed
> #3—best hitter on the team, high on-base percentage and power
> #4, cleanup—the team's best slugger
> #5—next-best slugger
> #6—best remaining hitter, hopefully with some power
> #7, #8—remaining batters in descending order of hitting prowess
> #9—in National League, the pitcher; in American League, preferably a batter with some speed to act as a second leadoff hitter

Of course, managers in the real world rarely can select the prototypical hitter in every spot in the lineup. Few teams have a RICKEY

HENDERSON or ICHIRO SUZUKI to plug into the leadoff spot; few teams can populate the numbers 3, 4, and 5 slots with power hitters who get on base a lot. So if you actually look at the lineup cards in today's game, you're not going to actually see this conventional wisdom in its totality manifest itself often.

Many fans obsess over whether a particular player is more suited to the number two slot or number six, whether the power hitter should bat number three or four, and other similar questions, believing that there exists some perfect batting order that's going to maximize the number of runs a team will score. In fact, for every nine selected players, there are over 350,000 possible lineups for a manager to choose from. And every study examining batting orders has shown that the difference between the best possible lineup and the worst possible lineup comes out to about 10 runs over the course of a season, hardly a reason to get worked up over a manager's choices.

batting practice

Pre-game hitting practice, usually two to three hours before game time. If you want to catch a foul ball or home run ball at a major league game, BP offers your best chance. The best batting practice show in baseball today is watching Ryan Howard launch ball after ball into the seats.

beanball

A pitch that hits a batter, often as retaliation for a previous offense against the pitcher's team. Beanball is usually used to describe a pitch that purposely hits the batter. It usually results in an ejection of the pitcher. *See also* HIT BY PITCH.

bench jockey

A player who screams insults at umpires and opposing players in an effort to break their concentration. Umpires have little tolerance for a bench jockey who directs his taunts at them. Sometimes, in an effort to quiet a particularly annoying bench jockey, the umpire will eject a random player who may or may not be the culprit. Often the ejectee is a player, such as the previous night's starter, who has little chance of getting into the game.

Here's a great bench jockey story: In September 1951, a DOUBLE-A player named Bill Sharman was called up to the Dodgers and was sitting on the bench for a game against the Braves. When the umpire made a call that went against the Dodgers, the whole Dodger dugout protested loudly, and the umpire responded by ejecting the entire bench, including Sharman. The young man never did get into a game that season, and he was released during the winter. He decided instead to try basketball. He played 11 seasons with the Boston Celtics and earned induction to the Basketball Hall of Fame in 1975.

big league, The Bigs, The Show

Synonym for major league. Possibly the greatest quote about the big leagues comes from the movie BULL DURHAM when Crash tells Nuke: "I was in The Show for 21 days once—the 21 greatest days of my life. You know, you never handle your luggage in The Show, somebody else carries your bags. It was great. You hit white balls for batting practice, the ballparks are like cathedrals, the hotels all have room service, and the women all have long legs and brains."

bleacher

Cheap, backless, uncomfortable, hard metal or wooden seats in the outfield sections of ballparks. They're also the home of the famous BLEACHER BUMS.

bloop, blooper

A weakly hit ball that barely clears the infield on the fly, resulting in a pretty cheap hit for the batter. Other terms include wounded duck, dying quail, and, most famously, TEXAS LEAGUER. Thought experiment: What's the most famous bloop hit of all time? I would nominate Luis Gonzalez's little blooper in the bottom of the ninth inning of Game 7 of the 2001 World Series. It came off MARIANO RIVERA, it won the series for the Diamondbacks, and it let TIM MCCARVER—who'd predicted it just moments earlier—preen a little for his prescience.

bonehead play, boner

A mistake, usually a mental error but sometimes a physical one. A player who commits a bonehead play that helps his team lose a game is called a goat, and baseball history boasts its share of famous goats:

FRED MERKLE and BILL BUCKNER are among the most ignoble. (And yes, Beavis, the word is "boner." Snicker away.)

The Book

Imaginary book of traditional "rules" that managers either follow or disdain (mostly disdain). Some of The Book's rules include calling for a sacrifice with the pitcher at bat and a runner on base, pinch-hitting a left-handed batter against a right-handed pitcher (and vice versa), and playing for the win on the road and the tie at home. The Book gives managers a built-in excuse when things go wrong. For example, one of The Book's rules is never to put the winning run on base intentionally. So let's say a team's best hitter is coming up with a one run lead and a runner on second base; The Book says you're not supposed to walk him to get to the next hitter. If a manager doesn't walk him and he hits a home run to win the game, the manager feels he shouldn't be second-guessed by the media because, after all, he was only following The Book. Of course, if he does walk him and the next guy hits a double that wins the game, he can be second-guessed to kingdom come because he disdained The Book and his team lost.

Not all managers act this way: "I never play by the book," said long-time manager Dick Williams, "because I never met the guy that wrote it." If you want to go deep on The Book, get *The Book: Playing the Percentages in Baseball* by Tom Tango, Mitchel Lichtman, and Andrew Dolphin.

box score

Daily statistical record of a baseball game, recording data such as at bats, runs, hits, RBIs, and complete pitching lines. Though HENRY CHADWICK, "the Father of Baseball," was the first to devise a box score that looks like the one in use today, the very first one—which looks nothing like today's—actually appeared in the New York Clipper on July 16, 1853, reporting a 21–12 victory by the KNICKERBOCKERS over the Gothams.

box seats

The seats closest to the field, down the foul lines or behind home plate, considered the best in the house. To gain more revenue, many clubs have installed box seats directly on the field, for which they can charge an arm, a leg, and a limb from your unborn child.

breaking ball

Any pitch that is meant to curve or break in some manner. The term can refer to a CURVEBALL, SLIDER, SCREWBALL, CHANGE-UP, or other breaking pitch, but broadcasters use breaking ball because sometimes it's hard to distinguish between them from the booth.

Bronx cheer

Also "raspberry," it's the sound made when you stick your tongue between your lips and blow hard. The term reputedly comes from a minor league outfielder named Doyle Raspberry, a player for the minor league Bronx Oilers in 1919, who responded to boos from the crowd by performing baseball's first Bronx cheer. *The Dickson Baseball Dictionary*, however, indicates that the first printed reference to Bronx cheer took place in 1931, so there is some dispute about the exact origin.

brushback

A pitch aimed at a hitter who's crowding the plate, intended to move him away. As Hall of Famer DON DRYSDALE once said, "You've got to keep the ball away from the sweet part of the bat. To do that the pitcher has to move the hitter off the plate." Brushbacks aren't meant to hit the batter, but they sometimes do.

bullpen

The place where pitchers warm up before they appear in a game. In some stadiums, the bullpen is located behind the outfield fence. In others, it's in foul territory along the left and right field lines. The origin of the term is unclear. Some say it's a reference to the Bull Durham tobacco signs that years ago adorned the outfield walls of hundreds of professional league ballparks, behind or under which pitchers often warmed up. CASEY STENGEL claimed the term came from the place where pitchers would sit and shoot the bull.

bunt

A batting play in which a hitter sticks his bat into the hitting zone just to make contact with a pitched ball. You can bunt for both a base hit (often a drag bunt) or to move a runner up a base (a sacrifice). Unlike a full-swing foul ball, a foul bunt with two strikes results in a strikeout. In modern times, baseball's best bunter is Omar Vizquel:

from 1997 through 1999, for example, he was successful on all 45 sacrifice bunt attempts, and in 1999, he posted a .679 batting average (19 for 28) when he tried to bunt for a base hit (which begs the question, why didn't he bunt every time up?).

bush, bush league

A derogatory term for an act or thing considered low class, crude, or amateurish. The term stems from the fact that the minor leagues are often called the bush leagues because they were once characterized by crude playing fields where bushes grew.

butcher

A poor fielder who "butchers" even the routine plays. Classic butchers have included Dick "Dr. Strangeglove" Stuart, Lonnie "Skates" Smith, and, when he tried to play the outfield, JOSE CANSECO.

catcher's interference

A play in which a catcher interferes with the batter, either inadvertently or on purpose, by touching the batter or his bat or some other way. The batter gets first base if it happens and is not charged with an official AT BAT.

change-up

A pitch that's thrown with the exact same arm motion of a fastball but hurtles toward the plate at a much slower speed than expected. Even though a change-up doesn't break like a curveball, it's effective because it keeps a hitter off-balance. WARREN SPAHN once said, "Hitting is timing. Pitching is upsetting timing."

check(ed) swing

An aborted swing by a batter, sometimes called a strike and sometimes not, based on how far around the hitter goes. Usually, if the hitter turns his wrists, it's a strike, but it's up to the umpire to decide. A hitter can also make contact on a check swing and, if he's lucky, beat out a ground ball for a hit or bloop it over the infield.

cleanup hitter

The number four hitter in a team's lineup. This hitter is usually the team's best slugger because it's his job to clean up the bases. A cleanup hitter should always lead his team in RBIs, or else he's just not doing his job very well.

closer

A term for a RELIEF PITCHER who finishes, or closes out, games to earn saves. FIRPO MARBERRY was major league baseball's first dedicated closer.

clutch

An important or pressure-packed situation, often in the late innings of a ball game when the score is close. REGGIE JACKSON is known as an impressive clutch performer based on his play in six World Series from 1972 through 1981. Although many baseball fans believe otherwise, there's very little statistical evidence to prove that some players are especially good in the clutch year after year. Players who hit well in the clutch one year will usually falter the next year, and vice versa. It's a question that baseball analysts will continue to study.

commissioner

The top official of major league baseball, elected and paid by the team owners. For the first 20 years of the two-league system, the game was ruled by the three-man National Commission, made up of the two league presidents and one team owner. After the 1919 BLACK SOX SCANDAL hit, however, owners feared an erosion in public confidence—i.e., profits—and created a powerful commissioner's office to oversee all operations and provide the appearance of total propriety. To fill the post, they hired former federal judge KENESAW MOUNTAIN LANDIS, who ruled baseball until his death in 1944. Owners quickly regretted handing Landis czarlike authority—which allowed no appeal and no recourse—and when he died, they decided to make some changes. They restricted the powers of the office and elected Kentucky Senator A.B. "HAPPY" CHANDLER, whose nickname should suggest what the owners expected: a goodwill ambassador. But what they got was a strong politician who believed that baseball belonged to America, not to a bunch of suits in a dozen major league cities. And in a set of circumstances that has typified the conflict between owners and the commissioner, Chandler was defeated for reelection when he term came up for renewal in 1951 because of his refusal to bow to all of ownership's demands.

Since then, owners have searched for a commissioner who could accomplish several seemingly irreconcilable goals: preserve the game's integrity, increase profits, and placate owners' requests. Following Chandler, seven men have held the full-time commissioner's post— FORD C. FRICK, Gen. William D. Eckert, BOWIE KUHN, PETER UEBERROTH, BART GIAMATTI, Fay Vincent, and today, BUD SELIG—each with varying degrees of success. Nearly all angered the owners in some way during their tenures, but none more than Vincent, who resigned in the middle of his term in 1992, claiming the owners had forced him out. Following Vincent's departure, baseball stood without a full-time commissioner for several years, as Milwaukee Brewers owner Selig served as acting commissioner (and got paid a quarter of a million dollars more than Vincent). In 1998, baseball officially named Selig commissioner, and he will probably serve in that capacity, like Landis, until he dies. What the owners seem to want is a person to act as both CEO and errand boy to 30 rich bosses, and Selig is apparently the only person willing to want that job.

corked bat

A bat that's been illegally tampered with to give the hitter a slight edge. The way it works is, you drill a deep hole into the barrel of the bat and fill it with cork (or shredded rubber balls), then plug it with glue and sawdust so it looks normal. The benefit a hitter gets is that the bat maintains the size of, say, a 36-ounce bat but the weight of a 33-ouncer. The result: a faster swing (although physicists doubt the effectiveness of the idea). Norm Cash is one of the most infamous corked bat users; he won the 1961 American League batting title with a bat he later admitted was doctored. Even a bat belonging to BABE RUTH that resides in the Hall of Fame appears to have been tampered. And every now and again, a hitter is accused of such chicanery and has his bat confiscated and X-rayed. I have no idea how an umpire or opposing manager can possibly tell—unless the bat breaks and the pieces of cork go flying, which happened to Astros outfielder Billy Hatcher back in the 1990s.

cup of coffee

Baseball slang for a short amount of time, usually used to refer to a minor leaguer who gets called up to the majors and sent back down just a few days or weeks later. He was only in the bigs long enough to have a cup of coffee.

curveball

A pitch thrown in such a way that it curves down and to the side on its way to the plate. Alternate terms for curveball include breaking ball, hook, deuce, bender, Uncle Charlie (or Lord Charles if it's a really good one), and others. The curveball has been the subject of perhaps more speculation and awe than any other single part of base-ball. First, there's some question over the pitch's true inventor; see CANDY CUMMINGS for more on that. Second, and most interestingly, a lot of baseball people throughout the years have claimed that the ball does not, in fact, really curve, that it's just an optical illusion. And many who believe that the ball does curve also think the ball travels along a straight line toward the plate, then breaks sharply at the last second.

Here's the real story, according to Dr. Robert K. Adair, a physicist at Yale University: The ball does curve, but it does so along a smooth, constant arc. In his book *The Physics of Baseball*, Dr. Adair provides a technical yet reasonable explanation for the action. Translated to Eng-lish, he says that when you increase the spin on the ball as you throw it, one side of it receives more air resistance than the other side. This difference in air resistance forces the ball to one side. He asserts that the curve itself is "nearly constant" during the ball's flight, but that most of the pitch's deviation from the original position occurs during the last half of the ball's flight. For example, after the first 30 feet of a pitch toward the plate, the ball may break only about three inches, but over the final 30 feet, it may break about 12 inches from its original vector—thus appearing to suddenly "fall off the table."

cycle

The term used when a player hits a single, double, triple, and home run in a single game. Bob Meusel and Babe Herman are the only players to do the trick three times. Although it seems like it shouldn't be that rare, hitting for the cycle actually occurs much less often than a no-hitter.

designated hitter

The player in the lineup who bats permanently for the pitcher. Since its inception in 1973 (*see* 1973: A DH IS BORN), the DH has been adopted by nearly every single baseball league in the world—major and minor, professional and amateur, high school, college, even youth leagues. Every league, that is, except the National League and Japan's Central League. The arguments in favor of the DH were that people like to see the extra offense the DH provides, that they don't want to watch a pitcher lamely attempt to hit, and that the DH allows popular aging sluggers to prolong their careers. I personally believe that none of those is reason enough to adulterate the game, but time has passed me by and I've long since given up.

In 1999, there was a sparkle of hope for guys like me when commissioner BUD SELIG floated the idea of eliminating the DH in the major leagues, and most owners seemed to support the plan. There was, however, a huge stumbling block: the players union. What the owners were offering in exchange for the removal of the DH was the addition of a 26th spot on major league rosters. But the union believed that eliminating the DH meant eliminating 14 high-paying jobs, and simply adding a roster spot, which would probably be filled with a low-paid rookie, doesn't make up for it. It's impossible to support the union on this one. But they hold veto power, so the DH is here to stay, and it's time for people like me to give up on changing it. (In fact, I've come around on the issue so far that it wouldn't bother me much if the National League just gave in and adopted the DH. At this point, I would just rather see one set of rules than two.)

diamond

The layout of a baseball field. Some people describe the infield as diamond-shaped but it is, of course, a perfect square.

disabled list

The list of players on a given team who are injured. There are now three lists: 7-day, 15-day, and 60-day. The 7-day DL is for players recovering from a concussion (it was implemented in 2011). The 15-day list is for players with an ankle sprain or pulled hamstring, injuries that require rest and rehabilitation. And the 60-day list is for players who undergo surgery and are expected to be out for all or most of a season. The number of days is a minimum. Sometimes a player gets hurt and the team isn't sure how bad the injury is, so the club waits a few days before deciding. If the club decides to place him on the 15-day list, the club will do it retroactive to the day after the last game he played.

double

A two-base hit. TRIS SPEAKER holds the career doubles record with 792 doubles from 1907 to 1926. Boston Red Sox outfielder Earl Webb, meanwhile, set the single-season record for doubles with 67 in 1931. Who is Earl Webb? He played only seven seasons in the majors and appeared in 140 games only twice, never hitting more than 30 doubles in any other season. But he lives on in the record books. Stories like Earl Webb's—and Chief Wilson's, who is the unlikely possessor of the record for TRIPLES—are part of baseball's unique charm.

doubleheader

A day in which teams play games back to back. Baseball used to schedule a number of doubleheaders every year, often on holidays or Sundays. Today, however, a doubleheader occurs only when a rainout necessitates a makeup game. For obvious reasons, owners would prefer us fans to buy two tickets rather than just one.

double play

A single defensive play that results in two outs made. It can be a ground ball that goes shortstop to second base to first, a line drive that doubles off a runner who has taken too big a lead, a strikeout/caught stealing on the same pitch, or even the strange play that happened to the Brooklyn Dodgers on August 15, 1926.

With Hank DeBerry at third, Dazzy Vance on second, Chick Fewster on first, and one out, Dodger outfielder Babe Herman turned on a fastball and sent it to the right field wall. DeBerry scored easily. Vance should have, too, but instead, he rounded third and retreated to the bag, unaware that Fewster was racing there as well. Herman, meanwhile, never looked up as he chugged around second base and headed for now-crowded third base. One can only imagine the scene as the Boston catcher tagged out every Dodger he could find, including probably the third base coach. Since only Vance was entitled to the base, umpires called Fewster and Herman out for perhaps the strangest double play in history. There's an old baseball myth saying that Babe Herman tripled into a triple play—impossible, since there was already one out. He merely doubled into a double play, which, as writer John Lardner pointed out, is "the next best thing." Years later, a story goes, a Brooklyn fan shouts out of his tenement asking for an update of a game. Somebody else shouts, "The Dodgers have three men on base." The first man replies, "Which base?"

double steal

When two baserunners attempt to steal on the same pitch at the same time. A *delayed* steal is a variation of the play, an attempt to catch the defense off guard. With runners at first and third, the man on first takes off on the pitch, hoping to draw a throw from the catcher. If the throw comes down, the guy on third can try for home to complete the delayed double steal. Sometimes, the catcher will fake the throw to second to prevent the runner on third from scoring, and sometimes he'll throw to third to try and catch the runner off base. It's always an exciting play.

double switch

A double substitution in which the manager replaces two players at the same time and swaps their respective positions in the batting order. It usually happens with a pitcher and a position player. Let's say the manager wants to remove the pitcher from the game while his team is still in the field, but the pitcher's spot in the batting order is scheduled to come up third the following inning. The manager doesn't want to waste a new pitcher by sticking him in the game and then pinch-hitting for him the very next inning. So he'll take out a position player who has just batted, say the shortstop, and place the new pitcher in that shortstop's spot in the batting order. A new shortstop enters the game and is placed in the pitcher's spot in the batting order. This is one of the maneuvers that an American League manager never has to do (because of the DESIGNATED HITTER) but that a National League manager always has to be thinking about.

dugout

The two enclosures along the first and third baselines where the teams sit during the game. Seats behind the dugout are premium seats in the house. When building the ASTRODOME, former Astros owner Roy Hofheinz made the dugouts extra long so that more seats could reside behind the dugouts and the team could charge more for them.

E

Scorecard and box score symbol for fielding ERROR. When the shortstop makes an errant throw, for example, a scorer writes "E-6" into his scorecard.

earned run/unearned run

A run that is deemed to be the pitcher's fault. That means a run that is scored without the help of an error, interference, passed ball, or other defensive miscue; those kinds of runs are called *unearned* runs.

There's a flaw to that guideline. Let's say the score is tied 0–0 and, with two outs, the batter lofts a weak fly ball to right that gets muffed by the outfielder. The batter ends up at second base. Rattled, the pitcher allows a hit, then walks a guy, then surrenders back-to-back home runs. Now it's 5–0 and the pitcher is pulled from the game. His team is losing big now, but none of those runs count against that pitcher since none of those runs are "earned." Why? Because the scoring guidelines say the inning should have been over, so the subsequent runs shouldn't have scored. Sure, that original guy on second wasn't the pitcher's responsibility, but what about everybody else? It's the pitcher's job to keep his team in the game, and since errors are an inevitable part of baseball, a good pitcher should be able to overcome them and pitch out of it without any more damage done. A pitcher who allows a lot of unearned runs might be saddled with a poor defense, but at the same time, he isn't helping his team much.

error

A defensive misplay, muff, fumble, or wild throw that either prolongs a batter's time at bat, helps a runner advance, or puts a runner on base. In the early days of baseball, when fielders used their bare hands, error totals in the double-digits per game were common. As glove technology advanced, fielding got much better and error totals went way down. HONUS WAGNER, for example, was a great shortstop, probably the best of his era, but he never made fewer than 35 errors for a full season. OZZIE SMITH, meanwhile, was the best of the last 50 years, and he averaged just 16 errors per year.

expansion team

Generic term for one of the 14 teams added to major league baseball since its first expansion in 1961. For the first 60 years of the 20th century, baseball had survived with just 16 teams in mostly eastern cities. But as the nation's population exploded, owners saw few reasons not to expand into other cities. And although many believe expansion hurts the quality of play, owners are more eager than ever to add major league franchises. A list of expansion teams reads like this: in the AL (in order of appearance), the Angels, Rangers (first as the Washington Senators), Royals, Mariners, Blue Jays, and Rays; in the NL, the Mets, Astros (as the Colt .45s), Brewers (as the Seattle Pilots), Expos, Padres, Marlins, Rockies, and Diamondbacks.

In the midst of the 1994 LABOR DISPUTE, the owners pulled a public relations boner: They announced that, even though their labor battle was based on claims of poverty, they were going to allow two new expansion franchises to enter baseball in 1998. They never adequately explained how an industry that was supposed to be in bad financial shape could seriously consider expanding. But they did, and baseball will probably expand again someday to make 32 teams.

farm system

The system of minor league teams that affiliate themselves with major league clubs to supply players. BRANCH RICKEY is responsible for creating the farm system for the St. Louis Cardinals, an invention so useful that other teams copied it almost immediately. At its peak, the St. Louis farm system featured dozens of teams and hundreds of players throughout the nation; the cream of the human crop would go to St. Louis while the rest would either languish in Class D leagues or get sold to other clubs. Minor league baseball as a whole reached its peak in 1949, when 59 leagues included over 450 teams. Today, farm systems have diminished enough that every big league team owns or affiliates itself with just a half-dozen lower league clubs, and the number of affiliated minor leagues is less than 20.

fastball

A pitch that's thrown at top speed. Who had baseball history's fastest fastball? NOLAN RYAN was measured at 101 miles per hour, but the young phenom Aroldis Chapman has been clocked at 104. Other contenders for the title are Smokey Joe Wood, SMOKEY JOE WILLIAMS, WALTER JOHNSON, LEFTY GROVE, BOB FELLER, GOOSE GOSSAGE, and J. R. Richard. Sometimes, fastballs are thrown with such speed that they seem to "hop" or "rise" before they reach the catcher's mitt. In fact, the rising fastball travels on a continuous, smooth arc slightly upward as it reaches the plate; it's the same principle as the CURVEBALL.

fielder's choice

A fielder's choice is a play that usually results a baserunner getting thrown out at a base while the batter reaches safely. For example: Runner on first, ground ball hit to shortstop. The fielder has a choice to make: get the lead runner at second or throw to first and retire the batter. Usually, he'll choose to get the lead runner and let the batter reach base, but he could have thrown out the batter if he'd wanted to. For statistical purposes, it counts as an AT BAT and an OUT for the batter.

foul pole

The big yellow poles sticking up along the outfield lines that help the umpire decide whether a ball hit into the stands is foul or a home run. Nonsensically, a ball that hits the foul pole is ruled a fair ball.

free agent/free agency

A free agent is a player who is not under contract with any team and is free to negotiate with whoever wants to pay the right money. In today's baseball, free agency is available to any player with an expired contract who has played six or more years in the majors. The MAJOR LEAGUE BASEBALL PLAYERS ASSOCIATION, led by MARVIN MILLER, won the right of free agency with the ANDY MESSERSMITH–DAVE MCNALLY ruling in 1975. Before that, the RESERVE CLAUSE in every player's standard contract bound a player to his team for as long as the club wanted him. During salary negotiations, players had absolutely no rights and had to accept whatever offer the team made or else not play baseball at all. Some might argue that players now have too much power, but why should the clubs have all the authority over a player's livelihood?

general manager

The person who's responsible for making or approving all the personnel decisions for a club, including trades, ROSTER moves, the AMATEUR DRAFT, minor league call-ups, FREE AGENT signings, and more. The buck stops with the general manager, who reports to a team president or owner.

In the old days of baseball, the field manager was often responsible for scouting and signing new players. JOHN MCGRAW, CONNIE MACK, and many others—including BRANCH RICKEY in his early years—did double- and triple-duty for many years. When the Yankees hired ED BARROW from the Red Sox, he may have been the first to serve as a modern-style general manager.

glove

The leather equipment worn to protect the hand and make it easier to catch a ball. All fielders use gloves except the first baseman and catcher; they use mitts, which have more padding. The first gloves were the tight-fitting kind, worn on both hands, with the fingers cut off the player's throwing hand. Gloves were introduced around the early 1870s, and the few players who wore them were ridiculed. When the great ALBERT SPALDING donned gloves in 1877, the jeering stopped.

Gloves have gone through an amazing evolution in the past 100 years, the trend being toward larger, more comfortable gloves. Hall of Famer BUCK EWING used the first heavily padded catcher's mitt in the mid-1880s, and padded, oversized fielder's gloves came into general use soon after. In 1912, the RAWLINGS COMPANY introduced the "Sure Catch" glove, the first one of its kind with sewn-in finger channels. The next significant advancement came nearly a decade later, when pitcher Bill Doak approached Rawlings with an idea: a piece of leather stitched between the thumb and forefinger to act as webbing. That's the kind of glove we see today, though the company has improved upon that development over the years, adding a "Deep Well" pocket, "Basket Web," "Edge-U-Cated Heel"—all terms that are very familiar to people who have owned Rawlings gloves. Rawlings is rightly seen as the world's premier glove manufacturer, and the majority of all major league players use the company's gloves and mitts.

grand slam

A home run with the bases loaded. I know people who get angry when a broadcaster says a player has just hit "a grand slam home run," claiming the phrase is redundant. The term comes from the game of bridge, where it indicates the taking of all 13 tricks, and was first applied to baseball around 1940. The lifetime record for grand slams is 23 by LOU GEHRIG and ALEX RODRIGUEZ.

green light

The manager's metaphorical sign allowing a baserunner to steal whenever he wants or giving a hitter the right to swing on a 3–0 count. The great base stealers have a permanent green light, unless a slugger is at the plate.

hanging curve

A CURVEBALL that doesn't break as much as it's supposed to—or not at all—giving the hitter an inviting target that usually ends up in the seats.

heat

A term for an extremely fast FASTBALL. Other descriptions include high heat, heater, smoke, high cheese, hummer, the high hard one, a pitch with a lot of mustard, and gas. Another term is "dead red," and when a broadcaster says a hitter was "sitting dead red," it means he was waiting for the heater.

hit

A ball struck so that the batter reaches base safely without benefit of an ERROR or FIELDER'S CHOICE. Hit in the generic sense refers to all kinds of hits, including extra-base hits, but it also can refer to a single, depending on the context.

hit by pitch, hit batsman

A pitch that hits a batter. These days, a hit batsman—whether accidental or not—often results in a big fight that starts between hitter and pitcher and ends after both benches have emptied. WALTER JOHNSON is baseball's all-time leader in hit batsmen with 205, even though Johnson was a nice, beloved guy who was famously afraid of hitting batters for fear of killing or injuring them.

hit and run

An offensive play involving a baserunner and the batter. During the pitcher's windup, the runner takes off for second base, and the batter is obligated to make contact with the pitch, in the hope of sending the ball into the outfield so that the baserunner can take an extra base. A variation is the run-and-hit, where the runner attempts a steal but the batter doesn't have to swing. The hit-and-run is a good play when the manager wants to stay out of a ground ball double play. Hitters who have good bat control are the best at executing the hit-and-run.

JOHN MCGRAW liked to claim that his old Baltimore Orioles of the 1890s invented this strategy, but it's likely that the play was around much earlier. BILL JAMES, in his *HISTORICAL BASEBALL ABSTRACT*, quotes JOHN MONTGOMERY WARD describing the play in 1893, which was McGraw's first full season in the majors—and it's hard to believe that a near-rookie would be able to introduce such a new strategy. Ward actually credits Hall of Famer Tommy McCarthy, an innovative player and manager who also developed on-field signs, as the hit-and-run's real inventor.

home run
A fair ball that either goes over the outfield fence or eludes the fielder long enough so that the hitter can run all the way around the bases, which is called an inside-the-park home run. Other terms for home run include homer, dinger, downtown, long ball, four bagger, round-tripper, and tater; in Spanish, the word is either *honron* or *cuadrangular*. The pitch is often called a gopher ball.

Until the late 1990s, BABE RUTH was the greatest home run hitter the game had ever seen, having slammed 714 in 8399 at bats for a ratio of one home run every 11.8 at bats. In the 1990s, however, MARK MCGWIRE has stormed past Ruth to take the number one spot. His total: an other-worldly one home run for every 10.8 at bats. During his amazing 1998 SEASON, McGwire averaged a homer every 7.27 at bats—basically one every two games. But then in the 2001 SEASON, BARRY BONDS one-upped McGwire with an even more in-credible homer every 6.52 at bats. With the steroid era mostly behind us, it seems unlikely we'll see that record broken for a while.

hot dog
In addition to the fat-laden sausage invented by HARRY STEVENS that people love to eat at ball games, "hot dog" also refers to a showoff, a player who likes to draw attention to his own actions. PETE ROSE, WILLIE MAYS, BARRY BONDS, and RICKEY HENDERSON are all well known for their hot doggery, but the hottest of all dogs has to be REGGIE JACKSON. If he didn't invent the practice of admiring deep

home run balls, he sure made it an art form. As onetime teammate Darold Knowles said, "There isn't enough mustard in the world to cover Reggie Jackson."

infield fly rule

Whenever people want to make a joke about how complicated baseball rules are, they always use the infield fly rule as exhibit A. But it really isn't complex, it just sounds like it. The infield fly rule is invoked when: (a) a batter hits a fair fly ball that can be caught with ordinary effort by an infielder; and (b) first and second or first, second, and third are occupied; and (c) there are less then two outs. The batter is automatically out, regardless of whether the infielder actually catches the ball.

It's important to understand why the rule was enacted: to prevent the defense from benefiting from its own deception. Imagine this situation: Bases loaded, one out. The batter hits a high pop fly in the infield, so the runners retreat to their bases. But instead of catching the ball, the third baseman lets the ball drop at his feet. Stunned, the runners try to advance, but the third baseman tags third for one out and guns it to the second baseman for a double play. The inning is over, and the defense has stolen two outs. The infield fly rule was enacted in the 1890s to prevent such underhanded play. When the umpire waves his arms and shouts "Infield fly!" the play is basically over; the runners may advance if they want, but they'll almost certainly be tagged out. It's a great rule, part of what makes baseball baseball.

inning

The units that divide a baseball game. There are nine innings in a regulation game, less if the contest gets shortened by rain and more if the teams are tied after nine. Some writers who love their thesaurus like to use the word "stanza" as a synonym for inning.

intentional walk

The strategy of intentionally putting the batter on base rather than pitching to him. This is a bad play for fans on at least two levels: first, because they paid to see the hitter hit, not get the bat taken out of his hands; and second, because the play is dull, dull, dull. In fact, I can think of only two instances when this play has generated any excitement. One came in the 1972 World Series. Cincinnati's JOHNNY

BENCH was the batter, and the A's pitcher reached a 3–2 count. The A's ostensibly decided to intentionally walk Bench as catcher Gene Tenace stood up with his right hand outstretched, as if to signal that the next pitch should be intentionally thrown outside. Bench relaxed, expecting the base on balls, but at the last second, Tenace got back down in his crouch and the pitcher whizzed a fastball past the startled Bench for a called strike three.

The next time we saw an exciting intentional walk was in the 1998 season, as the Diamondbacks played the Giants in San Francisco. It was the bottom of the ninth, two outs, and Arizona was protecting a two-run lead with the bases loaded and BARRY BONDS at the plate. To the utter disbelief of every player, coach, manager, broadcaster, and fan in attendance or watching on TV (as I was), Diamondbacks manager Buck Showalter ordered Bonds intentionally walked to bring in a run! Arizona now had a one run lead, and the bases were still loaded. But the next batter, Brent Mayne, made out, and Showalter's gamble paid off. Baseball researches quickly determined that nobody had attempted a bases-loaded intentional walk since it happened to batter Bill Nicholson in the 1940s.

junk

A term for an assortment of pitches that includes only non-fastballs such as slow CURVEBALLS, KNUCKLEBALLS, off-speed pitches, and the like. A pitcher who survives on such pitches is called a junkballer.

K

The scorecard symbol for strikeout; if it's a called strikeout, many people turn the K backwards. The symbol was originated either by New York Herald sportswriter M. J. Kelly or by "Father of Baseball" HENRY CHADWICK in the 1860s—chosen because an "S" would confuse it with single or sacrifice and because "K" is the last letter of the word "struck."

knuckleball

A pitch that's held by the tips of the fingers and thrown with little or no spin so that the ball moves erratically on the way to the plate. Some famous knuckleballers include PHIL NIEKRO, Hoyt Wilhelm, and Tim Wakefield, each of whom has had an extremely long career because the knuckler exacts very little toll on a pitcher's arm. The perfect knuckleball makes exactly one revolution on the way to the plate. Air currents strike the stitches on the ball wildly and the ball dances and weaves through the air, making it difficult to hit, catch, or umpire. Today, few pitchers take the time to master the art of the knuckler. And catchers don't mind. Bob Uecker once said, "The easiest way to catch a knuckleball is to wait until it stops rolling and then pick it up."

leadoff hitter

The hitter who bats in the number one spot in the batting order. The test of a good leadoff man is whether he regularly scores 100 runs for your team. To be able to achieve that milestone, he generally has to get on base around 40 percent of the time and be smart on the bases. RICKEY HENDERSON is acknowledged as baseball's greatest lead-off hitter because of his deadly combination of speed and strike zone judgment—in addition to his excellent power.

After Henderson, it's a tough call as to who would be history's second-greatest leadoff hitter. In the first part of the century, batters such as HONUS WAGNER, TY COBB, and TRIS SPEAKER—who, like Henderson, could hit well and steal bases—batted third or fourth. From 1920 through the 1950s, few players stole many bases. LUIS APARICIO led the league in steals for many years, but his career on-base percentage was .313, so he didn't get on base enough to really help his team; Maury Wills had the same problem. During that era, Richie Ashburn, who didn't steal that much, probably dominated the leadoff men.

By the 1970s, Lou Brock had helped introduce the all-around player to the leadoff position; Brock could steal bases, draw a few walks (though not enough to bring his on-base percentage up to .400), and hit for power. Since the 1980s, we've witnessed the golden age of leadoff hitters: Henderson, Tim Raines, Kenny Lofton, Len Dykstra, CRAIG BIGGIO, Jose Reyes, Jimmy Rollins, and ICHIRO SUZUKI among others. Alas, MVP voters usually overlook the number one hitters when filling out their ballots: Of all the lead-off men in recent times, only Henderson, Suzuki, and Rollins have captured an award (Dustin Pedroia was mostly a number two hitter when he won his MVP).

line drive

A batted ball that travels fast and straight and fairly low to the ground. Also called a frozen rope, bullet, or clothesline. Although every player hits line drives, some batters are known as line-drive specialists. ROBERTO CLEMENTE, George Brett, and Al Oliver are a few famous recent ones.

lineup

The nine (or 10 with the designated hitter) players who start a given game. Before first pitch, managers are required to turn in their lineup cards, which include the BATTING ORDER and defensive alignment. Some by-the-book managers examine lineup cards intently for any mistakes, hoping to catch the opposition in a costly error.

luxury tax

The "tax" levied on teams with high payrolls and given to clubs with lower revenues, known officially as the "Competitive Balance Tax." The luxury tax was first enacted as part of the collective bargaining agreement negotiated following the 1994 STRIKE and tweaked in every agreement since then. Before the strike, owners seemed adamant about instituting a salary cap, but the players didn't go for it. Players wanted owners to share their revenues; under such a plan, teams would split a pool of money earned from local TV contracts, licensing deals, and ticket sales, much like in the National Football League. But high-revenue clubs such as the Yankees, who at that point earned about $60 million per year in local TV money, didn't want to share that cash. So instead, the owners settled on a luxury tax, which is Revenue Sharing Lite.

Under the plan in effect in 2011, the luxury tax salary threshold is $178 million. Teams with payrolls above the threshold pay a "tax" of 22.5 percent for first-time taxpayers, 30 percent for second-time offenders, and 40 percent for repeat offenders. In practice, the luxury tax amounts to a Yankees tax, because they're the team that pays the vast majority of it; the Red Sox are the second biggest payer. So every time the Yankees sign a player to a $20 million deal, just realize that they're actually paying that guy $28 million: the $20 million base plus $8 million, or 40 percent, in luxury tax payments.

Is the luxury tax working? Well, it hasn't seemed to help the Royals or Pirates win any more games, and it hasn't slowed down the Yankees'

or Red Sox's spending. What seems to be happening is that teams receiving luxury tax revenue aren't necessarily reinvesting that money
into their teams; instead, they're keeping the money to increase profits. It's up to commissioner BUD SELIG to enforce the rules, and it's
not clear that he's making much of an effort.

Of course, if the goal is to stick it to the Yankees, then the luxury tax
has been a huge success.

magic number

The combined number of wins by a first-place team and losses by a
second-place team it would take for the top team to clinch the division title. Here's the formula:

[(Second place wins + games remaining) - First place team wins] +1

For example, if the Twins lead the Royals by five games with 10 remaining, then any combination of Twins wins plus Royals losses totaling six would hand the division to Minnesota. Every September,
newspapers and websites print magic numbers for all the leading
teams. And every April, some clever sportscaster announces that the
hometown team's magic number, after an Opening Day victory, is
161.

manager

The person who runs the team on the field, making the important
decisions like filling out the LINEUP card, changing pitchers, sending
in PINCH HITTERS, ordering steals, and sometimes calling pitches.
Other terms include skipper and field general. One of the cool things
about baseball, as opposed to other sports, is that the head guy is
called the manager, not the coach (European professional soccer is
another such example). One of the bad things about baseball is that
the manager wears the same uniform as his players, so fans are treated
to the sights of rumpled and bumpy old men in tight polyester knick-
ers. I think it would be great if a manager would wear a suit and tie in
the dugout like CONNIE MACK and Charlie Dressen did way back
when. Imagine if Phil Jackson coached a basketball game in shorts
and a tank top.

mascot

A costumed character who's supposed to bring good luck to a team. The San Diego Chicken is one of the most famous mascots, and today the Phillie Phanatic also entertains fans. Does anyone remember the Crazy Crab (Krazy Krab?) of the San Francisco Giants? Around 1984, the team polled its fans about what kind of mascot they'd like to see representing the Giants. By a nearly 2–1 margin, the fans asserted that they didn't want any mascot. Undaunted, the team introduced one anyway: the Crazy Crab, a purposely pathetic-looking orange thing whose job was to absorb whatever abuse the fans of a last-place team could muster. When he came out during the game, fans would boo, dump beer, throw trash, and otherwise abuse it any way they could. For about a year, the team used that crab as a marketing gimmick to get fans out to cold Candlestick. It didn't work, so they dumped it.

National Agreement

First signed in 1883, the National Agreement governs organized professional baseball. In the early years, the Agreement established the RESERVE CLAUSE and provided for a "gentlemen's agreement" that allowed clubs in the National League and American Association to blacklist any player who tried to jump his contract for more money. Later, the Agreement was revised to govern the dealings between major and minor league clubs. The Agreement has been tested in court on antitrust grounds, first by the FEDERAL LEAGUE and later in the 1973 FLOOD V. KUHN CASE. The major leagues ultimately won both cases.

night game

A game played at night under the lights. Major league baseball's first night game took place on May 24, 1935, at Crosley Field between the Reds and Phillies, won by Cincinnati 2–1. The reaction from the rest of baseball was decidedly negative: "There is no chance of night baseball ever becoming popular in the bigger cities. People there are educated to see the best. High-class baseball cannot be played under artificial light," said Senators owner Clark Griffith, typical of his era. Alas, night baseball proved immensely popular everywhere, and despite wails of complaint from traditionalists, bottom-line concerns forced the rest of major league baseball to adopt lights within a few years—all except the Chicago Cubs, who resisted modernization until 1988.

But the real history of night baseball actually begins not in 1935 but rather in 1880. That was when two department store teams played a 16–16 night game as a publicity stunt put on by the local electric company. Over the next 50 years, various entrepreneurs and inventors scheduled amateur and semipro games under the lights, many attempting to lure baseball owners to invest in their equipment. In 1930, three teams, including the KANSAS CITY MONARCHS of the NEGRO LEAGUES, successfully implemented quality lighting systems and attracted big crowds, leading most minor league clubs around the country to follow suit. LARRY MACPHAIL, just up from the minors, spearheaded the effort by the Reds to install lights.

no-hitter

A complete game in which a pitcher (or pitchers) does not allow the other team to get a hit; a PERFECT GAME is a stricter variation of the no-hitter. Joe Borden of Philadelphia's National Association club tossed major league baseball's first no-hitter in 1875. Since then, the majors have seen more than 220 no-hitters—seven by NOLAN RYAN for the all-time record. Johnny Vander Meer is the only pitcher to throw no-hitters in consecutive games (*see* 1938: THE DOUBLE NO-NO), and Bobo Holloman is one of three men to pitch a no-hitter in their first major league start.

official scorer

The man or woman whose job it is to keep the official score of a ball game. The scorer decides, among other things, whether a play should be ruled a hit or an error—a decision that often prompts bitter disagreement from the fans or even the players. Back in the 1990s, New York Mets third baseman Bobby Bonilla, for example, was once accused of telephoning the official scorer between innings after he'd been charged with an error on a play; he wanted the scorer to change the ruling, apparently to help his fielding stats.

on deck

A circle between home and the dugout where a hitter stands while awaiting his turn at bat. The phrase comes from the nautical lexicon, where to be "on deck" means to be on the main deck of a ship, presumably awaiting orders.

option

This is a very complicated and little-understood rule that covers a team's ability to move players between the majors and minors. For a player with at least three years of professional experience who is also part of a team's 40-man roster, the team holds "options" on that player for the next three years. (If he's not part of the 40-man roster, he's eligible for the Rule 5 Draft; *see* ROSTER for more.) That means that for the next three years, the player can be sent up and down between the majors and minors as many times as the club wants. After those three years, the player is considered "out of options," and before he can be sent down again, he has to clear WAIVERS. General managers have to keep close tabs on which players are still option-eligible when making personnel decisions. (Thanks to ROB NEYER for providing a "transactions primer" on his old website at ESPN.com)

out

You know what this means, don't make me explain it. There are three per half-inning, 27 per nine-inning game.

out pitch

A pitcher's best pitch, the one he uses most often when he wants an out.

pennant

The symbolic flag awarded to the champion of each league. Prior to the 1969 season, the team with the best regular-season record won the league's pennant. But with the advent of divisional play, a team had to capture the league championship series. Then, beginning with the 1995 season, the pennant moved a step further from the regular season when the league instituted a preliminary round of playoffs involving WILD CARD teams. Although the leagues don't actually award a physical pennant to the champions, most teams have one made for them to fly in the stadium or hang in the team's offices.

pepper

A quick-moving bunting-and-fielding game that helps players improve their reflexes. In it, a hitter stands about 20 or 30 feet from a fielder or group of fielders. One of the fielders tosses a ball to the hitter, who bunts the ball back to the fielders. Whoever picks it up pitches it right back immediately, and play continues quickly in that manner. It's a fun game that should be a staple of youth league practices.

perfect game

A NO-HIT game in which a pitcher goes a step further: he prevents the other team from reaching base in any way—hit, walk, or error. In the early 1990s, major league baseball redefined the perfect game. Under the new rules, a pitcher gets credit for a perfect game only if he pitches a complete game that goes at least nine innings. That definition eliminated two perfect games with asterisks listed below, but I think they deserve mention, so I'm going to include them in this book. I'm also going to include the Armando Galarraga perfect-game-that-wasn't. Here's a list of all official (and select unofficial) perfect games in major league history:

June 12, 1880: Lee Richmond, Worcester vs. Cleveland (NL), 1–0

June 17, 1880: JOHN MONTGOMERY WARD, Providence vs. Buffalo (NL), 5–0

October 2, 1908: Addie Joss, Cleveland vs. White Sox, 1–0

June 23, 1917: Ernie Shore, Red Sox vs. Senators, 3–0*

April 30, 1922: Charlie Robertson, White Sox vs. Tigers, 2–0

October 8, 1956: Don Larsen, Yankees vs. Dodgers, 2–0

May 26, 1959: Harvey Haddix, Pirates vs. Braves, 0–1**

September 9, 1965: SANDY KOUFAX, Dodgers vs. Cubs, 1–0

May 8, 1968: Catfish Hunter, A's vs. Twins, 4–0

May 15, 1981: Len Barker, Indians vs. Blue Jays, 3–0

September 30, 1984: Mike Witt, Angels vs. Rangers, 1–0

September 16, 1988: Tom Browning, Reds vs. Dodgers, 1–0

July 28,1991: Dennis Martinez, Expos vs. Dodgers, 2–0

July 29, 1994: Kenny Rogers, Rangers vs. Angels, 4–0

May 17, 1998: David Wells, Yankees vs. Twins, 4–0

July 18, 1999: David Cone, Yankees vs. Expos, 6–0

May 18, 2004: RANDY JOHNSON, Diamondbacks vs. Braves, 2–0

July 23, 2009: Mark Buehrle, Whites Sox vs. Rays, 5–0

May 9, 2010: Dallas Braden, A's vs. Rays, 4–0

May 29, 2010: Roy Halladay, Phillies vs. Marlins, 1–0

June 2, 2010: Armando Galarraga, Tigers vs. Indians, 3–0***

April 21, 2012: Philip Humber, White Sox vs. Mariners, 4–0
June 13, 2012: Matt Cain, Giants vs. Astros, 10–0
August 15, 2012: Felix Hernandez, Mariners vs. Rays, 1–0

*Starting pitcher BABE RUTH walked the first batter and then protested the calls to the umpire so badly that he was tossed from the game. Ernie Shore entered in relief, the runner was caught stealing, and Shore retired the next 26 batters.

**Perhaps the greatest game ever pitched, which resulted in a loss for starter Harvey Haddix. Haddix had pitched a perfect game through 12 innings—recording 36 consecutive outs—against a powerful and hard-hitting Braves team that, according to a recent admission by Braves catcher Del Crandall, had been stealing Haddix's signs all game long! Even still, Haddix was masterful, mowing down the Braves hitters with barely a difficult chance for his fielders. The end came in the 13th. Felix Mantilla led off the inning with a ground ball to Pirates third baseman Don Hoak, who made a throwing error to break up the perfect game. Eddie Mathews sacrificed Mantilla to second, and Haddix walked HANK AARON intentionally. The no-hitter was still intact, but not for long. First baseman Joe Adcock sent Haddix's second pitch over the right field fence for an apparent 3–0 victory. Mantilla crossed home, but in the misty evening, Aaron thought that the ball had landed short of the fence and that Mantilla's run ended the game. He trotted toward the clubhouse, and Adcock passed him on the bases. The umpires ruled Adcock out and only allowed one run, changing Adcock's home run into a game-winning RBI double and a 1–0 Braves victory—a peculiar end to a remarkable game.

***See 2010: PERFECTION TIMES TWO. AND ALMOST TIMES THREE.

pickoff

A throw by a pitcher or catcher to nail a runner off base. Some catchers like to show off their strong arms by attempting pickoff plays even when there's little chance of getting the runners. Of recent catchers, Ivan Rodriguez falls under that category.

pinch-hitter

A hitter who substitutes for another in the BATTING ORDER, usually for just one at bat. It's called that because such a hitter is mostly used "in a pinch," when the game is on the line. Pinch-hitting wasn't officially sanctioned by the National League until 1891, when the rules were changed to allow substitutions for reasons other than injuries. Longtime utility player Lenny Harris holds the career record for pinch-hits with 212, while Rockie John Vander Wal set the single-season record with 28 pinch-hits in 1995.

pinch-runner

Pinch runners are usually speedy runners who substitute for slow guys in the later stages of a game. Always-innovative CHARLIE FINLEY even went a step further in 1974 by signing world-class sprinter Herb Washington to be baseball's first ever—and still only—"designated runner." In his first season with the A's, Washington appeared in 92 games, attempted 45 steals, succeeded on 29 of them, and scored 29 runs. He came back in 1975 but lasted just 13 more games before the experiment mercifully ended.

pine tar

The black sticky substance derived from tree goo that hitters use to maintain a good grip on their bat. Owing to the infamous 1983 PINE TAR INCIDENT, pine tar has earned an ignominious place in baseball history.

pitcher's mound

The mound of dirt in the middle of the infield where the pitcher throws from. Pitchers didn't always throw off mounds. Until 1893, pitchers threw from a rectangular box 45, then 50 feet from the plate. The mound was added after the league moved the pitching RUBBER back to its current distance of 60 feet, six inches from home plate. The rules say the mound can be no more than 10 inches in height, but that rule has historically been loosely enforced. Dodger Stadium, for example, was known to feature a big, built-up mound in the 1960s, enabling SANDY KOUFAX and DON DRYSDALE to really bear down on opposing hitters (as if they really needed much help). Following the outrageous 1968 SEASON, in which pitchers dominated hitters to an extent not seen since the DEAD BALL ERA, the leagues cracked down on the big mounds and brought the game back to normal. In the late 1990s and early 2000s, probably owing to steroid use, just the opposite happened and batters went wild. To put a damper on skyrocketing offensive totals, baseball observers began tossing around the idea of *raising* the mound. I have serious doubts about whether such a move would accomplish anything other than increase strikeout totals. And now that the steroid era is effectively over, offensive totals are returning to a more normal 1969–1993 level.

pitchout

In an attempt to catch a baserunner trying to steal, a pitcher can intentionally throw the ball way outside the strike zone so that the catcher can get a better throw to the base. That's called a pitchout. Basically, the defense is trying to outsmart the offense by guessing when the offense is going to attempt a steal. The best counts on which to call a pitchout are 0–2 and 1–2 because the pitcher can afford to waste a ball. That being the case, however, the opposing team will rarely steal on those counts. Conversely, managers are reluctant to call pitchouts on two-ball counts since they don't want to put their pitchers in a hole. But a manager might make such a call to throw the other team off balance, especially if he has a pitcher with good control. Calling pitchouts is just one of the many mind games that occur during a game between opposing managers. It's part of what makes baseball fun to watch.

plate appearance

A trip to the plate by a hitter. For statistical purposes, a plate appearance (PA) differs from an AT BAT (AB) because AB refers only to a trip to the plate that results in a HIT, OUT, or ERROR, while a PA covers everything: hit, out, error, WALK, SACRIFICE, CATCHER'S INTERFERENCE, HIT BY PITCH, and so forth. A player's PA total, which is used in the calculation of ON-BASE PERCENTAGE and other stats, is virtually always higher than his AB total.

platoon

A system of alternating players at a position in order to take advantage of their batting strengths. Traditionally, platoons occur between right- and left-handed batters because conventional wisdom says right-handers hit better against left-handed pitchers and vice versa. CASEY STENGEL often gets the credit for popularizing platoons, but the practice long predates him. Stengel did it with the Yankees in the 1950s, but TRIS SPEAKER platooned his Indians extensively beginning in 1920, and prior to that, isolated cases of platooning existed. From about 1930 until Stengel came to New York, few managers platooned. Stengel's success returned the practice to favor, and, later, managers like EARL WEAVER took it to new heights.

play-by-play

The verbal descriptions of a ballgame by a radio or television broadcaster. Play-by-play can also refer to any kind of verbal or written account of each play of the game. One of baseball's great stories is the one about Potter Stewart, the Supreme Court justice and baseball fan, who was in the courthouse listening to oral arguments during a 1973 playoff game between the Mets and Reds. Justice Stewart had asked one of his clerks to keep him apprised of the game through notes describing each play. It was a tumultuous time in American politics, as one illuminating note revealed: "Kranepool flies to right. Agnew resigns."

player-manager

A team member who doubles as the team's manager, calling plays and changing pitchers from his position on the field. Teams don't employ player-managers these days; the last one was PETE ROSE in the mid-1980s. Historically, however, some of baseball's best players also player-managed for part of their careers, including EDDIE COLLINS, TY COBB, Lou Boudreau (who was only 24 when the Indians named him player-manager), FRANK ROBINSON, and many others. I don't know why teams don't hire player-managers more often anymore, since it would seem like a good cost-cutting move. My guess would be that teams don't believe that players would have enough experience to do both jobs. But if a player has a smart baseball mind, is recognized as a team leader, and is popular with the fans, it would seem to make smart business sense to promote the guy.

protest

When a manager believes the umpire has made a call that contradicts the rule book—not a judgment call such as a ball/strike or out/safe call—the manager can file an official protest with the league office to have the results of the game overturned. He must announce to the umpire that he's playing the game under protest immediately, before the next play begins. If the protesting team wins the game, the protest is immediately dropped. But if it loses, the league office investigates and makes a ruling. Some grounds for protest include ending a game too quickly during a rain delay, incorrect interpretation of the interference rule, and use of an ineligible player; there are many others. League offices rarely rule in favor of the protesting teams, but one infamous protest that was upheld was the PINE TAR INCIDENT.

purpose pitch

A pitch that has a purpose: to move the hitter away from the plate. After his retirement, Hall of Famer Early Wynn was quoted in Roger Kahn's *A Season in the Sun* as saying, "I've got a right to knock down anybody holding a bat." Wynn had just knocked down his son in a father-son game.

radar gun

The high-tech gadget used by cops to nail motorists for speeding and by baseball scouts to measure the speed of pitches. According to *The Dickson Baseball Dictionary*, there are two types of radar guns: a "fast" gun and a "slow" gun. The fast gun, known as the Jugs gun (manufactured by the Jugs Co.), measures the speed of the ball as it leaves the pitcher's hand. The slow gun, called the Ra-Gun, measures the speed as the ball crosses home plate.

regular season

The 162-game season that determines the leagues' playoff participants. Before the 1969 SEASON, the team in each league with the best regular-season record would meet in the World Series. In 1969, baseball added a round of playoffs, then beginning in 1995, they added a second round.

release

To cut a player from the ROSTER. When a player is released, he's free to sign with any other team, but the original team is still obligated to pay him if he has a guaranteed contract. In 1994, for example, the Dodgers released Darryl Strawberry because of the outfielder's drug and alcohol problems. They bought out the remaining two years of his contract for about $4 million. Two months later, Strawberry signed with the Giants for the major league minimum salary, and so even though he was performing for Los Angeles's hated rivals, the Dodgers were still paying the bulk of his salary. It's rare that a released player will return to post big numbers in the majors, but when it happens, you can bet the team that released him will hear about it.

relief pitcher

Generic term for a pitcher who doesn't start the game. Relief pitching breaks down into six indistinct roles, perhaps more:

Long reliever: Enters the game in the early innings, usually after the starter has been shelled or injured; long reliever is expected to pitch four or five innings.

Middle reliever: Pitches the middle innings, often in relief of a battered or tired starter when the score is close.

Mop-up man: Pitches anytime the game is way out of hand.

Set-up man: Keeps the game close in the seventh and eighth innings, setting up the CLOSER.

Left-handed specialist: A left-handed pitcher whose job is to get out one or two tough left-handed hitters. Lefties such as Jesse Orosco can have long, lucrative careers in this role.

Closer: Pitches the final one or two innings of a close game, often garnering a save if he shuts down the opposition.

The history of relief pitching could fill its own book, or at the least an entire chapter. Over 150 years of evolution, baseball has gradually shifted from a system demanding that a pitcher complete all of his starts to today's system of five-man starting rotations who complete less than five percent of their starts. Teams started adopting late-inning relief specialists in the 1920s, when FIRPO MARBERRY became the first good pitcher who spent most of his time in the bullpen. Before him, a team's relief corps was generally made up of failed starters. The concept caught on after a while, so by the 1950s, most teams had a designated closer who was every bit as important as the starters; Jim Konstanty even won the 1950 National League MVP Award. Since then, relief pitching seems to undergo decade-by-decade transformations: It wasn't the same in 1970 as 1960, nor in 1990 as 1980. The trend is toward fewer games and fewer innings pitched, using the top closer only in actual SAVE situations: when the team is leading by three or fewer runs in the ninth inning.

As of 2015, there are only five relief specialists in the Hall of Fame: ROLLIE FINGERS, Hoyt Wilhelm, DENNIS ECKERSLEY, GOOSE GOS-

SAGE, and Bruce Sutter. Next up will be Trevor Hoffman (maybe) and MARIANO RIVERA (definitely), and beyond that, I have no idea.

I do know that relief pitching is not a position that's ever going to get much recognition in the shrine. Why? Mainly because few good relievers are able to sustain a high level of performance for more than a few years. The list of relief burnout cases is long and distinguished and includes such names as Bobby Thigpen, Sparky Lyle, Mike Marshall, Elroy Face, and Dick Radatz. Eventually, baseball may discover a way to keep top relievers healthy and effective longer.

reserve clause

The part of a player's contract that, until 1975, kept him bound to his club forever. In the 1880s, Chicago White Stockings owner ALBERT SPALDING helped institute the clause as a way to help owners control costs and keep player salaries down.

For many years, the baseball establishment considered the reserve clause to be the backbone of baseball. What they really meant was that it was the backbone of their financial security—for the reserve clause, more than anything else, kept player salaries artificially low. With the reserve clause in place, a player had absolutely no rights. If he thought he was being underpaid, if he objected to his treatment by the owners, if he was stuck in the minor leagues because the big club had a better player at his position, he had absolutely no recourse except to quit baseball entirely. CURT FLOOD challenged the reserve clause in court—but lost (*see* 1972: LABOR UNREST AND FLOOD V. KUHN).

Owners claimed that without a reserve system, the richest teams would dominate baseball because only they could afford the high prices free agents would charge. That was the argument that many players, media members, and fans believed. But for the first 20 years of free agency, it proved totally wrong. And it was wrong even at that time. Which team dominated baseball for the 50 years *prior* to the destruction of the reserve clause? It was the richest team in baseball: the Yankees, who could afford to have the best scouting system and pay out the best bonuses to young players. The end of the reserve system and the advent of FREE AGENCY—because of the MESSERSMITH–MCNALLY arbitration decision—has allowed more teams to compete, not fewer.

rookie

A first-year player. "Rookie" probably derives from the Army word "recruit" and was first applied to ballplayers around 1908. Before that, such players were usually called "yannigans"—a quaint and distinctly 19th-century word.

There's a great legend (recounted in THE BILL JAMES HISTORICAL BASEBALL ABSTRACT) about a player who wanted badly to become a rookie. It was 1916, when a young pitcher sent a letter to TY COBB'S manager claiming he had such good stuff he could strike out Cobb on three pitches; all it would cost the Tigers was a train ticket. The manager figured he had nothing to lose, so he brought the kid into Detroit to pitch to Cobb. After a few warm-up tosses, Cobb stepped into the batters box. The first pitch came in and, bang, Cobb slammed it off the right-field wall. Next pitch, *over* the right field wall. Third pitch, over the *center* field wall. The manager came out and asked the kid what he had to say for himself. "You know," the kid replied, "I don't think that's really Ty Cobb up there."

roster

The list of all players under contract with a given club. The major league roster consists of 25 players, usually 14 or 15 position players and 10 or 11 pitchers. Clubs also manage a larger, 40-man roster consisting of both major leaguers and minor leaguers. The 40-man roster is critical for a number of reasons; one of them is to protect minor leaguers from what's called the Rule 5 Draft. Under that rule, players with more than three years of professional experience (at any level) who are not on a 40-man roster are eligible to be drafted by any other club. (There are some minor wrinkles to the eligibility rules.) The drafting club must keep that player on its major league roster for the entire season following the draft, or else the original club can snatch that player back. At the end of each season, clubs re-work their 40-man roster to make sure they protect their quality minor leaguers. The Rule 5 Draft was instituted to keep teams from stockpiling minor league players. *See also* OPTIONS, WAIVERS.

rubber

The 6-by-24-inch rubber slab on top of the PITCHER'S MOUND. A pitcher must start his motion with his foot touching the rubber. In the early days of baseball, there was no mound or rubber, just a box. A pitcher would stand at the back of the box and take a running start, releasing the ball from the front line, then 45 feet from home. The rubber was added in 1890.

run

Baseball's scoring unit, which occurs when a player has safely made it around all the bases and touched home plate. Though the term comes from cricket, the KNICKERBOCKER RULES called them "counts, or aces," so the word "run" came into use sometime between 1845 and 1854, which is when the first known printed reference to "runs" appeared.

sacrifice bunt

A bunt in which the bunter's job is to advance the runner at the expense of himself. Sacrifices always come with less than two outs and usually are attempted by the team's weakest hitters. Sacrificing was big in the DEAD BALL ERA, when runs were hard to come by. But as home runs became more frequent, sacrifices became less useful. Many players never even bothered to learn how to do it. Slugger Harmon Killebrew, for example, never in his entire career executed a successful sacrifice bunt. Today, few managers order sacrifices with much frequency; the last guy who really used it a lot was Gene Mauch. EARL WEAVER hated one-run strategies like the sac bunt, but even he used it in the late innings of close ball games.

sacrifice fly

A fly ball hit deep enough to score a runner from third base, giving the hitter credit for an RBI. It can be an exciting play on medium-deep fly balls when the outfielder has a good arm, but if the ball is too deep, the outfielder doesn't even risk the throw home.

save

Statistical credit—invented by sportswriter Jerome Holtzman—given to the relief pitcher who locks down a team's victory in a close game. There are several rules governing the awarding of a save to a reliever. Most importantly, he must finish the game on the winning team and not get credit for the victory. Aside from that, his appearance must come under one of the following game conditions:

- He enters the game with his team leading by three or fewer runs.
- He enters the game with the tying run on base, at bat, or on deck.
- He pitches three effective innings regardless of the score.

Francisco Rodriguez holds the single-season record for saves with 62 in 2008 (*see* 62); the next highest is Bobby Thigpen, who notched 57 in 1990. The save didn't become an official league statistic until 1969, but researchers have recalculated save totals for all pitchers back through the 1870s. To illustrate the changing role of relief pitching, here's a list of the major league leaders in saves at 10-year intervals:

Year	Player	Team	Saves
1880	Lee Richmond	Worcester	3
1890	Kid Gleason	Philadelphia	2
1900	Frank Kitson	Brooklyn	4
1910	"Three-Finger" Brown	Chicago (NL)	7
1920	Bill Sherdel	St. Louis (NL)	6
1930	LEFTY GROVE	Philadelphia (AL)	9
1940	Al Benton	Detroit	17
1950	Jim Konstanty	Philadelphia (NL)	22
1960	Lindy McDaniel	St. Louis	26
1970	Wayne Granger	Cincinnati	35
1980	Dan Quisenberry	Kansas City	33
1990	Bobby Thigpen	Chicago (AL)	57
2000	Antonio Alfonseca	Florida	45
2010	Brian Wilson	San Francisco	48

What's interesting is that two of those pitchers—"Three-Finger" Brown and Lefty Grove—were also fantastic starting pitchers whose managers realized the importance of a fresh, quality arm late in the game. Any discussion of relief pitching isn't complete, however, without a mention of the first really good relief specialist: FRED "FIRPO" MARBERRY, who saved 101 games and won 148 others, mostly for the Senators, from 1923 to 1936.

scorecard

The graphical representation of a baseball game. Using a scorecard, you can track a game play by play. The scoring system assigns numbers and letters to fielders and plays. For example, a ground ball out, shortstop to first, would be marked as G6–3, or just 6–3. A fly out to right would be F9. A dropped third strike that gets thrown to first base for the putout would be K2–3. An around the horn double play would be 5–4–3 DP. Keeping score is the best way to really follow a baseball game, either on the radio, on TV, or especially at the ballpark.

scoring position

A runner on second or third base is said to be in scoring position because almost any hit to the outfield will bring him home. By the same token, some prolific home run hitters are said to be in scoring position when they're at the plate.

scout

A person whose job is to evaluate talent, usually for a major league team or for the Major League Scouting Bureau. Scouts scour high school, college, and minor leagues to look for players in anticipation of the yearly amateur draft and possible trades. The job of an advance scout, meanwhile, is to watch other major league teams, noting players' strengths and weaknesses in preparation of a future series between those teams and the scout's employer. The classic book on scouting is *Dollar Sign on the Muscle* by Kevin Kerrane.

screwball

A BREAKING BALL that's thrown exactly the opposite of a CURVEBALL so that, for example, a left-hander's screwball curves away from a right-handed batter. Lefties are, in fact, the best known practitioners of scroogies because it gives them an advantage over right-handed hitters; CARL HUBBELL and Fernando Valenzuela are two lefties who rode the screwball to great success. The first popular use of a screwball, however, was by CHRISTY MATHEWSON, a right-hander who called the pitch a "fadeaway." Today few pitchers throw the screwball, choosing instead to perfect SPLIT-FINGER FASTBALLS and SINKERS.

seventh-inning stretch

The break in the action between the top and bottom of the seventh inning, known as the "stretch" because fans traditionally stand up to stretch their legs. Most ballparks play "TAKE ME OUT TO THE BALL

GAME" during the break, and in WRIGLEY FIELD, broadcaster HARRY CARAY used to lead the fans in singing baseball's anthem.

Legend has it that President William Howard Taft inaugurated the practice when he stood up in the middle of the seventh of a game in 1910. The fans thought he was leaving, and, ever respectful, they stood to honor him. Another oft-told story credits the students of Manhattan College with initiating the practice in 1882. Cincinnati Red Stocking HARRY WRIGHT, however, wrote a letter to a friend saying, "The spectators all arise between halves of the seventh inning, extend their legs and arms and sometimes walk about. In so doing they enjoy the relief afforded by relaxation from a long posture upon hard benches." That was in 1869.

shift

A change in the position of the fielders to defend against a particular hitter's strength. TED WILLIAMS was the victim of the famous "Williams shift" that positioned every infielder on the right side of the diamond to protect against the deadly left-handed pull hitter. People were angry that Williams stubbornly refused to drop in hits to left field, but Williams knew that he was paid to hit home runs, not singles. Even so, he won six batting titles. Today, the shift is employed rarely and only against the toughest—mostly left-handed—sluggers; BARRY BONDS, for example, got shifted against aggressively

shutout

A complete game in which a pitcher holds the opposition scoreless. The single-season record for shutouts is 16 by GROVER CLEVELAND ALEXANDER; career, WALTER JOHNSON with 110. Today, since few pitchers complete their games, shutouts are much more rare. The highest single-season total since 1969 is 10, achieved by John Tudor in 1985, but since 2000, the highest single-season total has been six by Cliff Lee.

sign

Developed by Hall of Famer Tommy McCarthy in the 1880s, signs are secret, on-field signals that give instructions to the players. The catcher gives signs to the pitcher to determine the next pitch. The third base coach signals the batter whether to hit, take, bunt, hit and run, and so forth; he also signals the baserunner whether to steal. A shortstop might signal the second baseman about who should cover the base on a steal attempt. Fans are accustomed to seeing the third base coach go through an array of signs: he touches his nose, chest, ears, elbow, knee, nose again, back of the head, cap, sleeve, ears again, and so on. Usually, only one of those touches means something, and the rest are there to confuse the other team.

single

A hit that allows the batter to reach first base safely; a one-base hit. Singles come in a variety of shapes and sizes: a dribbler that barely scoots past the pitcher, a ground ball deep in the hole at shortstop, a blooper that falls just behind the first baseman, a line drive that falls in front of the outfielder, a booming smash that caroms off the outfield wall so hard that it bounces back to the infield before the batter can make it to second base, and a hundred other possibilities. But, as the cliché goes, they all look the same in the scorebook.

sinker

A low pitch thrown so that it curves slightly downward, usually resulting in a ground ball. To be successful, sinkerball pitchers must have a good infield defense behind them to turn those grounders into outs.

slider

A type of CURVEBALL that's thrown faster and curves less; it's really a hybrid fastball-curveball. STEVE CARLTON made the Hall of Fame on the strength of his deadly slider, universally called the best in baseball history. The pitch first came into popular use in the 1930s, featured prominently by George Uhle, who won 200 games in his 17-year career, and George Blaeholder, who posted a 104–125 record mostly with the Browns.

slugger

A player who specializes in slamming home runs—to the exclusion of other offensive weapons. Today, Ryan Howard ranks as a quintessential slugger.

softball

The baseball-like recreational sport played throughout the country. Although the basic rules are the same as baseball, there are a number of fundamental differences:

- The ball is larger and lighter, so it doesn't travel as far when hit.
- The bases are 60 feet apart instead of baseball's 90.
- The pitcher throws from 46 feet instead of 60.
- The ball is pitched underhand. In slow-pitch softball, the ball travels in a high, slow arc toward the plate. In fast-pitch, the ball can come as fast as 70 mph.
- Some leagues allow the use of a roving 10th fielder, the buckshort.
- The bat has a thinner barrel.

Slow-pitch games are much higher-scoring contests compared to baseball, while fast-pitch games are usually pitcher's duels, won with bunts and sacrifices.

southpaw

A left-handed pitcher. The term comes from the early baseball practice of positioning home plate on a field so that the batter wouldn't have to look into the setting afternoon sun. Since the batter is facing east, a left-handed pitcher's arm is on the southern side. Like many other sports-related words, this is an example of a term that originated with baseball and has been applied to other sports. Left-handed boxers, quarterbacks, golfers, and people in general are called southpaws.

spitball

A pitched ball that has been moistened—by spit, sweat, petroleum jelly, or another method—causing it to behave erratically as it travels toward the plate. To understand how it works, try applying a spot of glue to a Ping-Pong ball and roll it across the table. It will roll asymmetrically and oddly. That's what happens when a doctored baseball flies through the air at 90 miles per hour. The first pitcher to throw the spitball with frequency in the majors was Elmer "Spitball" Stricklett, who lasted just four years. Stricklett taught the pitch to Ed Walsh, who fashioned a Hall of Fame career with it.

Spitballs have been illegal in major league baseball since 1919, when the leagues cracked down in the fear that a spitball might get away from the pitcher and hurt somebody. They did install a grandfather clause that allowed 17 pitchers to continue using the pitch, and Burleigh Grimes, a Hall of Famer, used the doctored pitch until 1934.

Throughout the years, a number of pitchers have been accused of throwing spitters. GAYLORD PERRY practically made a career out of denying he ever threw a spitball even though the whole world knew what he was doing. Perry was caught just once, earning a 10-day suspension. Then he went on the television show "Lie Detector" and passed six different tests. In his book *Me and the Spitter*, however, he wrote that he always kept his stash of grease in at least two places, "in case the umpires would ask me to wipe off one. I never wanted to be caught out there without anything. It wouldn't be professional."

split-fingered fastball

A FASTBALL variation that sinks as it reaches the plate. It's very similar to a forkball in that the ball is held tightly between the forefinger and middle finger, but the split-finger is thrown a little harder. It caused a sensation and was called the "pitch of the 1980s" when it was featured by Jack Morris, Mike Scott, Bruce Sutter, and a number of other pitchers who came in contact with split-finger guru Roger Craig.

squeeze play

A squeeze sometimes comes when there's a runner on third and less than two outs. As the pitcher begins his windup, the runner on third breaks for home. The batter's job is to bunt the ball far enough from home plate that the runner can score the run. That's a suicide squeeze—"suicide" because if the batter doesn't make contact, the runner is dead. A variation is the "safety squeeze," where the base runner waits to see if the ball has been bunted effectively before charging down the line. The best defense against a successful squeeze is the PITCHOUT.

starting rotation

A team's rotating group of starting pitchers. Today's five-man rotation means starters will only get about 34 starts per season—all but ruling out the possibility that a pitcher will ever again notch 30 victories in a season. When the Phillies signed Cliff Lee for the 2011 season, they created possibly the greatest rotation in modern times—on paper—with Lee, Roy Halladay, Roy Oswalt, and Cole Hamels as the top four (although Oswalt didn't really pan out). Probably only the 1990s Braves—with GREG MADDUX, Tom Glavine, John Smoltz, and Denny Neagle—and the 1970s Orioles—with Jim Palmer, DAVE MCNALLY, Mike Cuellar, and Pat Dobson—could match up against the Phillies statistically.

stolen base

A legal maneuver where a runner advances, or "steals," a base while the pitcher is in his motion. Hall of Fame left fielder RICKEY HENDERSON, the king of the stolen base, possesses both the single-season (130) and career (1,406) records for steals. In the early days of baseball, players were credited with a steal when they advanced an extra base on a hit; for example, a runner who went from first to third on a single would get a steal. That's how Harry Stovey was able to "steal" 156 bases in 1888; today's researchers have lowered that total to 87. In 1898, those rules changed to reflect a stolen base as we know it today.

stopper

"Stopper" is a 60-plus-year-old baseball term that has a couple of different meanings. It's a starting pitcher, usually the ACE of the staff, who is often counted on to put a stop to a team's losing streak. And it's also a synonym for CLOSER. Since we already have a word for closer, baseball writer ROB NEYER once wrote a column encouraging fans to use it only as the first meaning.

strike zone

According to the rule book, the strike zone is the rectangular area from the top of the knees to the letters on a batter's shirt and the width of home plate. In actual practice, it varies from umpire to umpire and usually goes from the bottom of the knees to the belt buckle. "The ever-shrinking strike zone" is what broadcasters, writers, fans, and pitchers called it throughout the 1990s—and it has gotten the blame for the explosion of home runs in the last 20 years as well as the increasing length of ballgames. There's really no explanation for the shrinking strike zone, and every year, people complain that something has to be done about it. In the late 1990s, in fact, the commissioner's office actually shrank the rule book's strike zone (changing the top level from the armpits to the letters), hoping that the redefinition would cause umpires to start calling the high strike. That hasn't really worked. Just about every year, in fact, the commissioner's office orders the umpires to adhere to the strike zone, usually to no avail. The question is, why? The answer is, probably because umpires are too stubborn to change.

My favorite strike zone story was told by Marty Springstead, an umpire who first joined the American League in 1965. During one of his first games, he was behind the plate when big Frank Howard, one of the most intimidating players in the majors, stepped up to hit. The first pitch came in, and it was over the plate at the knees. Springstead called it strike one. Howard turned his massive body around and yelled, "Get something straight, pal. I don't know where you came from or what you're doing in the major leagues, but they don't call a strike on me with that pitch. Understand?" The next pitch came in and hit the same spot. Springstead yelled, "Two!" Howard immediately turned back and shouted, "Two what!" And Springstead replied, "Too low, Frank. It was much too low."

strike

A pitch that either (a) is swung on and missed, (b) is hit foul, or (c) crosses the plate in the strike zone. A foul ball can be called a strike only for the first two strikes; after that, it's nothing, unless the ball is foul tipped into the catcher's glove and he holds onto it.

Foul balls weren't even called strikes at all until around 1900, which is one reason modern baseball researchers draw a line at 1900 when discussing "modern" baseball. Before that, it was just that much easier to get a hit because you could foul off pitch after pitch without any consequences.

strikeout

The result of a batter getting three strikes. REGGIE JACKSON is the all-time leader in strikeouts by a batter with 2,687 for his career, with Jim Thome not too far behind. In terms of single-season strikeout kings among batters, nobody can touch Mark Reynolds, who holds three of the top six slots with 204, 223, and 211 Ks from 2008 through 2010. Other top free swingers include Adam Dunn (222 Ks in 2012), Chris Carter (212 in 2013), and Drew Stubbs (205 in

2011). As far as the best strikeout pitchers, who else? NOLAN RYAN holds both the career and single-season records (*see* 5,714 and 383). On a per-game basis, the major league record for strikeouts in a nine-inning game is 20, by ROGER CLEMENS in 1986 and 1996, Kerry Wood in 1998, and RANDY JOHNSON in 2001.*

Unlike the BASE ON BALLS, whose criteria fluctuated during baseball's early years from nine balls to the present-day four, three strikes have always been enough for a strikeout. It's even written into the KNICK-ERBOCKER RULES: "Three balls struck at and missed and the last one caught, is a hand out; if not caught is considered fair, and the striker bound to run." That's one of the unique rules in baseball: If the catcher drops the third strike with first base open or two outs, the batter can try to make it to first before a throw or tag. It's like giving a wide receiver a second chance to catch an incomplete pass.

*Johnson struck out 20 in the first nine innings of an extra-inning game. The record for strikeouts in an extra-inning game is 21 by Tom Cheney in 1962.

sweet spot

The best part of a bat to hit the ball, a few inches from the thick end. When you're hitting, you can't see the ball hit the sweet spot, but you can sure feel it. There's no feeling like it.

switch-hitter

A hitter who can bat from both sides of the plate. Such a player gains the PLATOON advantage of not having to face a pitcher whose curveball breaks away from him. Right-handed batters have a tougher time against right-handed throwers than against lefties, and, of course, left-handed batters hit better against righties. That's why platooning exists. A switch-hitter who bats equally well from both sides never has to worry about being benched against a particular group of pitchers—which is why MICKEY MANTLE'S father taught his son to switch-hit at a very early age. Baseball's first switch-hitter was Bob Ferguson, who played from 1871 through 1884 and compiled a not-so-spectacular .265 batting average.

take

To let a pitch go by without swinging at it. On 3–0 or 3–1 counts, managers often order their mediocre hitters to take the next pitch, no matter how enticing, to force the pitcher to throw a strike.

Texas Leaguer

A looping fly ball that lands for a single in the unoccupied space between the infielders and outfielders. The term is over a century old, with a variety of possible origins. Did it come from a famed Texas League team that featured a number of players who specialized in such hits? From Texas League veteran Arthur Sunday, who used many looping hits to bat .398 with Toledo in 1889? From the major league debut of former Texas Leaguer Ollie Pickering, whose first seven hits were supposedly bloopers (which is Wikipedia's choice)? From the fact that Texas League ballparks were very large, forcing outfielders to play deep and leave a lot of space between them and the infielders? Or from the strong Gulf Stream winds that affected fly balls in most Texas League cities, forcing a seemingly catchable ball to land in front of outfielders? Take your pick.

trade

An exchange of players between two (or more) teams. Sometimes, a team will make a trade for the ubiquitous "player to be named later."* Twice in baseball history, it resulted in that player being traded for himself—the ultimate fair trade. In 1962, Harry Chiti batted .195 in 15 games for the lowly Mets after coming to New York in a deal with the Indians for a player to be named. Chiti's performance stunk so badly—even on that awful team—that the Mets named him as that player and sent him back to Cleveland. In 1987, the Cubs "traded" Dickie Noles to Detroit for the month of September, then got him back when the clubs couldn't agree on a fair deal.

Players aren't the only people who can be involved in trades. Teams have traded managers for players 13 times, and in 1960, Detroit and Cleveland swapped their managers straight up, Jimmy Dykes for Joe Gordon. I doubt we'll ever see that again. *See also* WAIVERS.

*Bonus explanation: *Why* do teams trade "players to be named later"? Usually because at the time of the deal, they can't decide on who they want to include, so they just table it for later.

triple

A three-base hit. Triples are the most exciting single play in baseball, usually resulting in a long relay from the outfield to third base and culminating in a slide, a tag, and a cloud of dust. The all-time single-season leader in triples is Owen "Chief" Wilson, which makes this one of baseball's oddest, least-challenged records: Odd because Wilson never totaled more than 14 triples in any other season, least-challenged because nobody in the past 100 years has come within 10 of breaking the mark.

In terms of career numbers, the triples champ is Sam Crawford, who banged 312 in his 19-year career. That's an average of 16 per season, which is about what today's league leaders hit. In fact, the top 18 players on the all-time triples list played before World War II, and many played in the DEAD BALL ERA. The reason is probably because the hits that used to be triples in the dead ball days now go for home runs. For the past 50 years, the number of triples hit per team has been fairly stable at about 35 to 40 per season.

triple play

A single defensive play that results in three outs recorded. TPs only happen a couple times a year, and the unassisted triple play—when the same fielder makes all three outs—ranks as one of baseball's rarest occurrences: UTPs have happened only 14 times during the regular season in major league history, plus once in the World Series, making them less frequent than a PERFECT GAME (21) but much more frequent than a Chicago Cubs world championship (two). Second baseman Eric Bruntlett of the Phillies last did the trick in 2009, against the Mets. With no outs in the top of the ninth and the Phillies holding a 9–7 lead, the Mets put runners on first and second for Jeff Francoeur. He lined a shot to Bruntlett, who caught the ball, then stepped on second to double off Luis Castillo, then tagged the unsuspecting runner from first, Daniel Murphy, for the third out of the inning and the final out of the game, preserving the win for the Phillies.

Strangely, of the 15 UTPs in major league history, five occurred during the 2000s and six occurred during the 1920s—including two on consecutive days: the Cubs' Jimmy Cooney on May 30, 1927, and Detroit's Johnny Neun a day later.

umpire

The person on the field who calls balls, strikes, and outs and interprets the rule book for other plays. Today, four umpires call the plays for regular season major league games: a home plate umpire and one at each base. For postseason and All-Star Games, extra umpires man the outfield foul lines. In the early days of the sport, only one or two umpires called a game.* And they had a really tough time of it. They often volunteered for the job, until the National League decided to pay them five dollars per game. The American Association was the first league to pay umpires fixed salaries, and the American League was the first to give its umpires full and unwavering support.

In the 1970s, as baseball players fought for labor equity, the umpires' union rose to powerful heights. They struck at the beginning of the 1979, demanding better pay and better working conditions. The leagues called up replacement umpires from the minor leagues, but many games proved farcical when the rookie umps couldn't keep control of the games; the leagues then settled the dispute.

In 1999, however, the umpire's union miscalculated its power. Its contract with baseball was expiring at the end of the year, and so to force renegotiations, umpires decided to resign from their jobs en masse. It was a terrible miscalculation. Half the umpires quickly rescinded their resignations, but baseball decided to accept 26 resignations and called up rookie umpires from the minors. The disaster cost the union president, Richie Phillips, his job when the union disbanded, and a new union was organized to take its place. There's been labor peace ever since.

Today's major league umpires earn between $84,000 and $300,000 plus vacation time in the middle of the season. But they also have to pay their dues. Like ballplayers, umpires have to work their way up the minor league ladder, and most never make it to the big leagues. And the pay in the minors isn't much: about $1,800 per month.

Pam Postema nearly became the first woman to umpire in the major leagues, but she never received the call and was released from Triple-A after 13 years. She had more experience than many of her colleagues who made it to the majors, and, having endured the constant taunting and sexist remarks by obnoxious fans and players throughout her career, she had to have more guts. The fact that the American League refused to hire her showed that they had less guts than Postema.

*In most minor and youth leagues, two umpires call the action.

uniforms

What players wear on the field. Major league teams wear different uniforms at home and on the road. In the past, the home uniform was usually white and the road one was gray or light blue. But today, teams have introduced all sorts of variations, including black jerseys for teams whose primary colors have no black. The goal is to get fans to buy as many of the new replica uniforms as possible. The evolution of baseball uniforms—from dull flannels to today's colorful, double-knit polyesters—is a fascinating subject worthy of its own book. The best one on the market is Marc Okkonen's *Baseball Uniforms of the Twentieth Century*, which includes full-color drawings of every uniform ever worn at the major league level.

utility player

A versatile player who can man more than one position. PETE ROSE was the ultimate utility player because he could play first, second, third, and any outfield spot while also performing well offensively. More recently, one of the better utility men was Tony Phillips, who could play any position and hit for average and power. Neither of them, however, typify the utility player. Most utility players aren't good enough to be regulars, either at the plate or in the field, so they fill in for injured starters. Some utility players can make a decent career out of it. Jerry Royster, for just one example, played 634 games at third, 416 at second, 187 at short, and 153 games in the outfield over 16 years in the majors.

waivers

A waiver is a permission granted to a team that wants to assign or RELEASE one of its veteran players who has been on a team's 40-man ROSTER for at least three years. Basically, there are two types of waivers: waivers for the demotion of a player to the minor leagues and waivers for the unconditional release of a player. In both cases, waivers are granted only after all the other teams have had the chance to claim the player but none has done so. After receiving unconditional release waivers, a player becomes a FREE AGENT.

This is also the system by which players can be claimed in trades during the period from August 1 the end of the season. Team A wants to trade a player to Team B because Team B is in a pennant race with Team C. It's after July 31 (the trading deadline), so Team A first places the player on waivers, making him available to any team in reverse order of the standings. The way it's supposed to work is, all the teams except Team B are supposed to "waive" their right to that player. Team B claims the player, usually in exchange for a "player to be named later," and the deal is done. If another team makes a claim for the player, Team A can decide instead to keep the player. If Team C's record is worse than Team B's, Team C can block the deal. Usually waiver claims are kept secret until a deal is consummated, but every now and then, word leaks out that, say, Team A's star outfielder was on the trading block until Team C put a stop to it. *See also* OPTION.

walk-off home run
Only coined in the 1990s, probably by DENNIS ECKERSLEY, walk-off describes an offensive play that wins a game for the home team in the bottom of the last inning. Usually the term refers to a home run, say, a two-run shot in the bottom of the ninth to win the game 4–3. But sometimes it gets abused. I've even seen the term "walk-off balk" used. Ugh.

warning track
The strip of dirt in front of the outfield fences, designed to warn outfielders of their proximity to the walls. PETE REISER, the Dodgers phenom whose career was ruined by his numerous run-ins with hard outfield walls, is partially responsible for warning tracks.

waste pitch
A pitch deliberately thrown outside the strike zone in an attempt to set up the next pitch or to get the batter to chase the bad ball. Waste pitches often come on 0–2 or 1–2 counts. A pitcher who gives up a home run on one of those counts probably didn't waste the pitch far enough from the plate.

wild card
The playoff team in each league with the best record of any team that didn't win a division. The wild card team plays the division winner with the best record in what's called the Division Series. This system was introduced in 1994 but not implemented until 1995 owing to

the 1994 STRIKE. It took only two years for a wild card team to win a World Series, when the Marlins did the trick against the Indians. In 2011, baseball and union officials agreed to add a second wild card team in each league and force the two teams to play a one-game play-in to make it to the next round. Although the new system offended purists, it kicked off in 2012 and is probably with us to stay.

wild pitch

A pitched ball that's thrown wildly enough to get past the catcher. If the catcher is at fault, it's a passed ball. A wild pitch only gets charged to the pitcher—and a passed ball to the catcher—when a runner advances a base or on a third strike if the batter reaches base safely.

There have been two very famous, very devastating wild pitches in major league history:

Jack Chesbro, New York (AL) vs. Boston, October 10, 1904

In the ninth inning of a must-win game on the final day of the season, Chesbro, a 41-game winner that season, sailed a pitch over the catcher's head to allow the go-ahead run to score and enable Boston to win the pennant. It was pretty much the last time Boston got the better of New York for the next 100 years.

Bob Stanley, Red Sox vs. Mets, October 25, 1986

It was Stanley's wild pitch in the famous 1986 WORLD SERIES GAME 6 that allowed the Mets to tie the score in the bottom of the 10th. Once that happened, it was basically over for the Sox.

winter league

A baseball league that plays in Florida, Arizona, or Latin America during the winter months. Many players in winter leagues are assigned by their teams to improve their skills or learn a new position, and many Latin American ballplayers return to their homes to play for their local teams. After batting .203 in DOUBLE-A in 1994, Michael Jordan played in a winter league, but it didn't help much.

winter meetings

The conferences held every year in November or December among all the big league clubs to discuss trades and other business matters. These days, it's rare that any real trading action springs out of the winter meetings. Mainly, teams announce free-agent signings and minor deals.

SOURCES

Much of the information on these pages comes from a lifetime of reading hundreds of baseball books. But I want to highlight a few of the books and other resources that I used most, several of which are profiled in this book.

Publications

Dickson, Paul. *The New Dickson Baseball Dictionary: A Cyclopedic Reference to More than 7,000 Words, Names, Phrases, and Slang Expressions That Define the Game, Its Heritage, Culture, and Variations.* Houghton Mifflin Harcourt, 1999.

James, Bill. *The New Bill James Historical Baseball Abstract.* Free Press, 2001.

Thorn, John, Pete Palmer, Michael Gershman, and David Pietrusza. *Total Baseball: The Official Encyclopedia of Major League Baseball.* Total Sports, 1999.

Various writers. *The Baseball Research Journal.* Society for American Baseball Research. Series.

Various writers. *The National Pastime.* Society for American Baseball Research. Series.

Websites

SABR Bio Project: http://bioproj.sabr.org

Baseball-Reference.com: http://www.baseball-reference.com

Baseball Almanac: http://www.baseball-almanac.com

Retrosheet: http://www.retrosheet.org

Fangraphs: http://www.fangraphs.com

MLB.com: http://www.mlb.com

ABOUT THE AUTHOR

In addition to writing *The Book of Baseball Literacy* and ebooks about baseball history and statistics, David Martinez has worked as a news reporter, college sports broadcaster, and advertising copywriter, but his biggest love has always been baseball. A member of the Society for American Baseball Research, he reads extensively on the sport and owns an expansive baseball library.

A California native, he received his bachelor's degree in English from the University of California, Berkeley, and he now makes his home in San Jose with his wife and two young children.

Visit him on the web at www.homerunweb.com.

Send email to david@homerunweb.com.

45439325R00236

Made in the USA
Lexington, KY
28 September 2015